THE NEO-CATHOLICS

THE NEO-CATHOLICS
IMPLEMENTING CHRISTIAN
NATIONALISM IN AMERICA

BY

BETTY CLERMONT

CLARITY PRESS, INC.

© 2009 Betty Clermont
ISBN: 0-932863-63-9
       978-0-9328-63-8

In-house editor: Diana G. Collier
Cover: R. Jordan P. Santos

Library of Congress Cataloging-in-Publication Data

Clermont, Betty.
  The neo-Catholics : implementing Christian nationalism in America /
Betty Clermont.
      p. cm.
  Includes bibliographical references (p.   ) and index.
  ISBN-13: 978-0-932863-63-8
  ISBN-10: 0-932863-63-9
  1. Conservatism--Religious aspects--Catholic Church. 2. Conservatism-
-United States. 3. Catholic Church--United States. 4. United States--
Church history. I. Title.
  BX1407.C76C58 2009
  282'.7309045--dc22
                                      2009039916

Clarity Press, Inc.
Ste. 469, 3277 Roswell Rd. NE
Atlanta, GA. 30305, USA
http://www.claritypress.com

Dedication

Words cannot express my love and indebtedness to
my mother, Frances Marie Vitolo Espino, and my late
father, Carlos Jesus Espino Gomez, for their confidence,
encouragement and deep Catholic faith.

ACKNOWLEDGMENTS

If this book has any success, it will be due first, to my editor, Diana Collier, for her advice, suggestions, much needed deletions and patience. Credit is also due to my internet friends, a group of Catholic scholars, for their teaching and correction, especially those who contribute worthwhile articles and news items which keep us informed. This book was greatly improved by my daughters' counsel and technical expertise. My greatest debt, however, is to my parents' confidence, encouragement and deep Catholic faith with a healthy cynicism toward its leaders. And there would be no books, in fact no civilization, without teachers.

Any failure is due to my stubborness in not learning all I could from those mentioned above.

TABLE OF CONTENTS

CHAPTER 1

NEOCONSERVATISM BEGINS

The 1960s were a tempestuous time in the United States. America's flagging prospects in Vietnam, civil rights unrest at home, and the assassination of three of its leaders (John F. Kennedy, Robert F. Kennedy, and Dr. Martin Luther King Jr.) deepened divisions between young and old, black and white, intellectual elites and business moguls. While US and South Vietnamese forces ultimately won a military victory in the January 1968 Tet Offensive, shock over the Viet Cong's initial success led many Americans to question for the first time not only their military involvement in Southeast Asia but also their government's credibility since they had been repeatedly assured the US was winning the war. The engagement of US troops, begun as a limited effort to support the South Vietnamese army, had become an American-led offensive against the North Vietnamese justified by what was already recognized by many as a fabricated pretext, the 1964 Gulf of Tonkin incident. The number of US troops "in country" had climbed from fewer than 1000 in 1961 to 537,000 in 1968.[1] Between 1964 and 1968, the United States dropped more than a million tons of missiles, rockets and bombs on North Vietnam. President Lyndon Johnson's refusal to send additional troops in 1968 seemed to be an admission the war was lost and by the time he left office, 30,000 Americans had already lost their lives.[2]

At the same time, substantial profits from Defense Department contracts were expanding the "military-industrial complex" which President Dwight Eisenhower had warned against.

In fiscal 1968, the Defense Department contracted for $38.8 billion in goods and services, plus $6.5 billion for research and development, amounting to 5.3 percent of the 1968 GNP. These funds went to many thousands of prime contractors and subcontractors. Generally, the effect of the military-industrial complex is to foster heavy defense spending and impede cutbacks, even in an inflationary period. Not at all by coincidence, the legislators who have the most to say about military spending—the chairmen of the Senate and House Armed Services and Appropriations Committees—have been blessed over the years with substantial military business in their states and districts.[3]

That same year, the Defense Department paid almost $4 million for approximately 340 people to lobby members of Congress, and Senator William Proxmire (D-Wisc.) noted that 2,072 retired military officers were employed by the top 100 defense contractors.[4]

On October 31, 1968, President Johnson ordered a halt to the bombing of North Vietnam to energize the stalled peace talks begun with the Ho Chi Minh government the previous May. Fearing that news of a negotiated settlement might throw the election to Hubert Humphrey, the Democratic candidate, Richard Nixon sent his friend, Anna Chenault, to meet with South Vietnamese president, Nguyen Van Thieu. Chenault, widow of the famed "Flying Tigers" General Claire Lee Chenault, was leader of the "China Lobby" which had supported US involvement in both Korea and Vietnam as a means of containing Red China. Sacrificing American lives for a Republican victory, Chenault convinced Thieu to put off joining the talks until Nixon was elected by promising Thieu a better deal from the Republicans if he waited.[5]

Nixon was elected president on November 5, 1968, with 43.4 percent of the popular vote, defeating Humphrey who had 42.7 percent. The third party candidate, Alabama Governor George Wallace, captured the Deep South with 13.5 percent of the popular vote which represented the defection of white Southerners from the Democratic Party due to Presidents Kennedy's and Johnson's support for civil rights. Patrick Buchanan, an orthodox Catholic who joined the Nixon campaign in 1966, explained the Republicans' winning strategy:

> From Day One, Nixon and I talked about creating a new majority....What we talked about, basically, was shearing off huge segments of FDR's New Deal coalition, which LBJ had held together: Northern Catholic ethnics and Southern Protestant conservatives—what we called the Daley-Rizzo Democrats in the North and, frankly, the Wallace Democrats in the South.[6]

It marked the beginning of the strategy for Republican national electoral dominance. What it needed was a glue to hold the disparate parts together, an ideology to weld "the silent majority" together by more than just their purported silence.

The phrase—the silent majority—coined by Nixon during a November 3, 1969, television broadcast, included Americans who, by the end of the 1960s, were apprehensive about the US failure to keep communism in check. While every military means short of nuclear weapons had failed to bring victory in Vietnam, Soviet tanks had crushed the "Prague Spring" in August 1968 without intervention from the Free World, and communism had a foothold just ninety miles off the US coast in Cuba.

The silent majority also described those who had pulled together through the Great Depression and World War II and disapproved of anyone who questioned or opposed the government in time of war. They were shaken by the widespread civil disorder of anti-war demonstrations and by race riots which spread across the country in the wake of King's assassination, yet also unnerved by the police brutality at the 1968 Democratic National Convention in Chicago.

The Northern white working class was as bitter about leaving their comfortable neighborhoods to avoid court-ordered bussing as Southern whites were afraid of African American equality. Their traditional morality was under assault by the sexual revolution and their culture by the new feminism. The 1968 King and Kennedy assassinations added to their angst that the well-ordered post-war society was coming apart at the seams. Fear, doubt and insecurity create fertile ground for a movement promising restoration of a lost, idealized order.

A group of intellectuals seized upon the discontent and alarm created by the upheavals of the 1960s to formulate an ideology which would win majority approval and a road to power. Irving Kristol, "godfather" of the neoconservatives; Allan Bloom, the best known proponent of the philosophies of Leo Strauss; and Francis Fukuyama, a student of Bloom, demonized the demonstrations as well as equal rights for African-Americans and women as the "root of all evil," equating liberty with licentiousness.

> Licentiousness is a harbinger of social decay—divorce, delinquency, crime, and creature comforts. For Kristol, the solution was to use democracy to defeat liberty. Convince the people that liberty undermines piety, leads to crime, drugs, rampant homosexuality, children out of wedlock, and family breakdown. And worst of all, liberalism is soft on communism or terrorism—whatever happens to be the enemy of the moment. And if you can convince the people that liberty undermines their security, then, you will not have to take away their liberty; they will gladly renounce it.[7]

What differentiated this movement from traditional conservatism was their emphasis on "social issues"—or what would become known as "family values"—in the popular media and direct mailings, while maintaining support of traditional conservative economics favoring the wealthy in their more serious journals. Whereas conservatives were willing and able to argue for their positions on a scholarly basis using accurate data, neoconservatives would persuade by pandering to fears, prejudices and lack of intellectual curiosity through lies.

Kristol was a graduate of the City College of New York and his original associates were fellow Jews of Eastern European descent who considered themselves socialists and Trotskyites. Leon Trotsky, son of a Jewish farmer, had been second-in-command to Lenin in the early Bolshevik Party. When Lenin died in 1922, Stalin became increasingly anti-Semitic, the Jewish Trotskyites were persecuted and Trotsky was killed by one of Stalin's followers in 1940. A worldwide movement, the Trotskyites remained influential in leftist groups in the West, but their days of wielding exceptional powers—the power of government—seemed to have swiftly come to a close.

After World War II, when the USSR sided with the Arabs against Israel, the American Trotskyites became vehemently anti-communist and hostile to any US politician who warned against exaggerating the Soviet threat during the Cold War. The neoconservatives' initial primary, though not exclusive, goal was to protect Israel and they promoted American military supremacy as the means.

> [Neoconservative *National Review* editor] Jonah Goldberg put their view at its most blunt when he said: 'Every ten years or so, the United States needs to pick up some small crappy little country and throw it against the wall, just to show we mean business.'"[8]

The neoconservatives were initially able to promulgate their views through the publications Kristol founded and/or edited. From 1947-1953, Kristol was editor of *Commentary*, founded by the American Jewish Committee in 1945.[9] Kristol left *Commentary* to co-found *Encounter*, a literary magazine, along with poet Stephen Spender, which Kristol edited until 1958. Although published in the UK, it was funded by the CIA.[10]

During the 1960s, Kristol and his followers were joined by other hawks especially those profiting from maintaining the US in a constant state of war, corporate interests wanting a Third World available for unfettered exploitation and Zionists advocating for the defense of Israel. These "hardliners" demanded a bellicose stance not only against communism but also against any leader or country not actively engaged in supporting American domination.

Kristol et al adhered to the philosophy of University of Chicago professor, Leo Strauss, an émigré from Nazi Germany.

> [Strauss] was widely known for his argument that the works of ancient philosophers contain deliberately concealed esoteric meanings whose truths can be comprehended only by a very few, and would be misunderstood by the masses.

This has come to be known as the "hidden meaning" thesis, Seymour M. Hersh wrote May 12, 2003, in *The New Yorker*.

Other elements of the philosophy of Strauss are controversial with ideals that seem to go contrary to democracy. According to a 2003 analysis by Jim Lobe for the Inter Press Service, Strauss believed the world to be a place where policy advisers may have to deceive their own publics and even their rulers in order to protect their countries. Shadia B. Drury of the University of Calgary, author of 1999's *Leo Strauss and the American Right*, says "Strauss was neither a liberal nor a democrat... Perpetual deception of the citizens by those in power is critical (in Strauss's view) because they need to be led, and they need strong rulers to tell them what's good for them."

According to Drury, Strauss like Plato taught that within societies, "some are fit to lead, and others to be led." But, unlike Plato, who believed that leaders had to be people with such high moral standards that they could resist the temptations of power, Strauss thought that "those who are fit to rule are those who realize there is no morality and that there is only one natural right, the right of the superior to rule over the inferior."[11]

Stephen Eric Bronner, professor of Political Science at Rutgers University, wrote:

> The influence of conservative political philosophy on the neoconservative mandarins is overrated. Those preoccupied with it, indeed, only lend an air of intellectualism to what is little more than a brutal reliance on power and propaganda. They are counter-revolutionaries intent on undoing the progressive political achievements of the twentieth century. As important as the idea of elite conservatives is the belief that truth matters little and morality—other than the morality of unquestioning allegiance to the given political project—matters less and that power comes only from the barrel of a gun.[12]

Strauss considered religion necessary to pacify the populace, a political tool used by rulers to control the masses.[13] According to Drury, "any religion so long as it was monotheistic, patriarchal, hierarchical, and authoritarian," would serve the purpose.[14]

Other autocrats throughout history had reached the same conclusion. Egyptian and Roman leaders declared themselves to be gods. Confucianism was considered essential to an orderly society. Napoleon wrote of the First Estate:

What is it that makes the poor man take it for granted that ten chimneys smoke in my palace while he dies of cold, that I have ten changes of raiment in my wardrobe while he is naked, that on my table at each meal there is enough to sustain a family for a week? It is religion which says to him that in another life I shall be his equal, indeed that he has a better chance of being happy there than I have.[15]

The histories of Europe and Latin America witness this truth. In exchange for Catholic clerics' exhortations to the faithful to be docile to secular leaders—preached as the virtues of obedience and humility—the rulers supported the Church's preeminent position in society and paid the tribute demanded. Sometimes the power of the prelates superseded that of the state—it was the pope or his representative who crowned the emperor, not vice-versa.

Writing about Ireland, one author observed:

The Roman Catholic Church organized a total community without as little as a flicker of rebellion [through a] set of religious values which dominated every shade and aspect of Irish life....that is, as a unity of social arrangements in which the Church tied the political party system, the Irish media, and the legal and constitutional establishment to her exclusive universal ambitions.[16]

If Straussians were looking for "any religion so long as it was monotheistic, patriarchal, hierarchical, and authoritarian," the all-male, monarchical and dictatorial structure of Roman Catholicism's government not only fit that description better than any other but the same religion is also the largest religious denomination in the US. In the 1960s, Catholics were 23 percent of the population; however, almost 30 percent of voters in national elections were Catholic. Even in the year 2000, Catholics numbered more than the next twelve largest denominations combined. Moreover, Catholics are concentrated in the states with the most electoral votes—California, New York, Pennsylvania, New Jersey, Massachusetts, Ohio, Illinois and Michigan.

Since the Soviets and Red Chinese had persecuted Roman Catholics, many Catholic refugees from Korea, Vietnam, Cuba and Eastern Europe were fervent anti-communist hawks favoring the Republican Party. The progeny of earlier Irish, Italian and Polish immigrants, often obtaining college degrees under the GI Bill, were shifting to the GOP as their incomes rose. Catholic blue-collar ethnics were fighting segregation in their Northern neighborhoods. They were a natural fit with what would become the tenets of "family values."

Some wealthy Eastern-Establishment Catholics—Straussian elites—already belonged to a powerful international commercial complex based not only on their financial interests but also connected through the Vatican to a global network of anti-communists. (Communism was anti-capitalistic *and* atheistic.) With monetary and political backing from their American confreres, right-wing Catholics had already defeated the "Red" parties in Western Europe, contained Red China, and supported Latin American military dictatorships established to eliminate "leftist" rebels.

For those inside and connected to the Vatican still seeking a traditional alliance with a secular state which would uphold the Church's cultural domination as it had in centuries past, America's power and wealth in 1968 was unsurpassed making it the most attractive partner. Unfortunately for those on both sides of the Atlantic who would benefit from the alliance, the two pontiffs who ruled during the 1960s—Popes John XXIII and Paul VI—were uninterested in power politics. As the Church is a monarchy, only a cooperative pope could direct his institution to champion US neoconservatism.

CHAPTER 2

CATHOLICISM: THE NEOCONSERVATIVE RELIGION OF CHOICE

Those in charge of the Vatican are the self-proclaimed guardians of the "deposit of faith," but some are more concerned with temporal intrigue, even murder, as factions have vied in each era to have "their man" placed on the Throne of St. Peter. These crimes and maneuvers are connected to the capacity of the Roman Catholic Church to place and keep civil governments in power.

By the twentieth century, the ordained were generally no longer permitted to hold government positions, but there were two groups of powerful laymen—the Knights of Malta and Opus Dei—whose ambitions were intertwined with powerful churchmen, all willing and able to promote Roman Catholic interests in the secular sphere. Both groups were enabled by access to a secret financial institution beyond the reach of any national regulation or international scrutiny—the Vatican Bank.

It is their historical networks, global reach, financial proficiency—and expertise in wielding power—which would make Catholicism the religion of choice to forward the neoconservative agenda in America.

The Knights of Malta

After the French Revolution, Catholic aristocrats took up the cause of keeping church and state united. Losing their ancestral rights and privileges during the democratic and nation-building movements sweeping across Europe in the nineteenth century, the nobles struggled to reverse history. While the Sovereign Military Order of Malta (SMOM *aka* Knights of Malta) traces its history back to the Crusades, the modern Knights were aristocrats who banded together for mutual protection during this period. They fought for a return to the "divine right of kings" type of monarchy in their various countries, as did the Vatican. Together, the Knights and the Catholic Church opposed democratization as an assault on the power of both the nobility and the hierarchy.

By the end of World War I, it was clear the old order had permanently passed away, but the growing menace of communism, which eliminated not only the aristocracy but also private wealth and religion, was even worse than democracy. Fascism was viewed by these nobles and the Roman Curia (the Vatican bureaucracy) as the best line of a defense against the spread of Bolshevism.

The growing prominence of the American *nouveau riche* in international commerce and finance, and their wealth at a time when European aristocrats were losing theirs, made them extremely attractive recruits for membership in the Knights. The requirement of a royal bloodline was abolished and a US branch was founded in 1927 in New York. John J. Raskob, chairman of the board of General Motors and leader of a fascist plot to overthrow President Franklin D. Roosevelt, was the first member.[1] John Farrell, president of US Steel; George MacDonald who made a fortune in oil and utilities; Joseph Kennedy, a Boston entrepreneur and father of President John F. Kennedy; and Joseph P. Grace, of W.R. Grace & Co., were early invitees.[2] Worldwide, the Knights went from 1,363 members in 1880 to 7,557 in 1961. In 1999, there were 3,100 American members.[3]

The SMOM calls itself "a lay, religious order of the Catholic Church" whose only official function is charitable works but, like other organizations of its ilk, it was an internationally elite "good-old-boys" club. Members were from the highest echelons of business and government, including heads of state. Right-wing North and Latin Americans who considered themselves part of the class set apart and destined to rule were welcome. What differentiated the Knights of Malta from similar anti-communist groups was its ties to the Vatican and the deep collective memory of both organizations of centuries of intrigue and Machiavellian political maneuvers.

The Knights of Malta became one of the most reactionary and powerful groups in the world. The World War II-era members were allied with the Falangist groups in Spain, the Catholic integralist-Vichy French, Italian fascists and the German-Austrian supporters of Adolf Hitler. During the war, many Knights—even citizens of Allied or non-aligned countries—continued doing business with their trading partners in the Third Reich. William "Wild Bill" Donovan, a Catholic Wall Street attorney and head of the wartime OSS, predecessor of the CIA, used his connections with the SMOM and the Vatican to gather intelligence. The first director of the CIA, Allen Dulles, while not a Catholic, also collaborated with international Catholic power-brokers to fight the Soviets and Red Chinese. Three later CIA directors—John McCone, William Colby and William J. Casey—were themselves Knights of Malta. Their covert operations conducted in South Vietnam, Eastern Europe and Latin America required operatives familiar with the local power structures which included the Catholic Church.

The Italian government granted sovereign status to the Palazzo Malta, the SMOM headquarters in Rome, in 1951. Like the Vatican, the Knights are able to issue their own stamps, currency and passports. They have diplomatic relations with over 100 countries as well as permanent observer status with the UN. The Grand Master holds a rank in the Roman Catholic Church equivalent to a cardinal.

The Knights of Malta were especially influential during the Nixon administration. Nixon's confidant, aerosol magnate Robert Abplanalp, was a Knight and the president appointed two Secretaries of the Treasury with SMOM connections. David M. Kennedy, although a Mormon, became chairman of Chicago's Continental Illinois National Bank and Trust Company after he left Nixon's cabinet. This institution handled the bulk of the Vatican's US investments and was also the conduit for moneys flowing back to the Vatican for anti-communist causes, especially in Eastern Europe.[4] When the Vatican Bank's Italian partner, the Banco Ambrosiano, collapsed in 1984 so did the Continental, replacing another financial institution, Long Island's Franklin National Bank, owned by Knight of Malta Michele Sindona, as the largest US bank failure up to its time. Both banks received massive amounts of US tax dollars to bail them out. Shortly before resigning from office, Nixon appointed Knight of Malta William E. Simon as Secretary of the Treasury. Simon would play a crucial role in funding the neoconservative propaganda machine.

In 1969, National Security Advisor Henry Kissinger issued orders through his military assistant, Knight of Malta General Alexander Haig, to work with right-wing Italians to defeat a resurgent Italian Communist Party.[5] A "black-ops" campaign, known as the "strategy of tension," was begun with American backing. Nixon's US Ambassador to Italy, Graham Martin, handled some of the funding.[6] Terrorist attacks on Italian civilians were executed in such a way so that the Communists would be blamed for the carnage.

In 1975, when Pope Paul VI favored an Italian coalition government to include both the Italian Communist Party and the Christian Democrats, Dame of Malta Clare Booth Luce was named to a panel which included fellow Knight, CIA Director William Colby, and CIA official Ray Cline to respond to this threat.

> They made sure [Pope Paul VI] knew the US would never tolerate Marxist participation in the Italian government....
>
> When the pope criticized colonial repression and recommended more equitable economic and social systems, an international group of businessmen headed by George C. Moore, chairman of Citibank, asked the pope to "clarify" his position. The pontiff issued a follow-up statement that he was not against private enterprise.[7]

As the Eastern-Establishment patricians were replaced in leadership positions in the US Republican Party by the more aggressive, no-holds-barred neoconservatives, so power in the Catholic Church shifted under the patronage of Pope John Paul II from the Knights of Malta to Opus Dei.

Opus Dei

The Spanish cleric, Josemaria Escrivá, might well be regarded as the neo-Catholic version of the neoconservatives' foundational ideologue, Leo Strauss. Opus Dei, Latin for "God's Work," was founded in Spain by the venal and arrogant priest in 1928. (For decades he altered or added to his name to give the appearance of a more aristocratic lineage: changing his last name from Escriba to Escrivá and adding "de Balaguer"; changing his first name from the common Jose Maria to Josemaria; using the unearned title "Doctor" and later requesting the title "Marquis."[8])

Escrivá's organization, like the Knights, would be composed of only laymen—the best and the brightest of Spain's middle class of doctors, lawyers, professors, politicians, financiers and military officers. Ineligible for membership in the Knights of Malta for lack of noble pedigree, these professionals and militarists formed an aristocracy of ambition and ability if not actual lineage. They rallied to the cause of Fr. Jose Maria Escriba in the 1930s. The most orthodox form of Catholicism was embraced, the better to attract adherents who cherished obedience and conformity in their followers. Like Straussians, Opus Dei leaders brandish religion as a weapon of condemnation against dissent and intellectual independence. Opus Dei also made it a point to recruit educators for their schools and universities. The first Opus Dei center was opened in 1933 in a Madrid academy specializing in the study of law.

Weekly confession is standard in orthodox Catholicism, so in the beginning of his organization, details of Opus Dei's internal operations and methods of coercion were being disclosed to outsider priests. Therefore, Escrivá added an order of clergy to his organization, the Priestly Society of the Holy Cross, and in 1944 the archbishop of Madrid ordained three men into the Society. Members were now required to confess to, and receive spiritual guidance, solely from Opus Dei priests.

The Spanish journal, *Tempo,* outlined the steps taken by "The Work" to achieve a "national catholicism" in Spain, a unity of church and state to be ruled by Opus Dei. The pattern should be familiar to most Americans:

- Escrivá blamed liberals for the growing secularization of Spain, which he portrayed as damaging to the morals of the nation.

- Following the Spanish Civil War, Opus Dei university professors controlled newly created research institutes, such as the Consejo Superior de Investigaciones Científicas (CSIC).

- Escrivá founded Ediciones Rialp, a publishing house. Escrivá placed special emphasis on Opus Dei's journalistic endeavors. "We must wrap the world in printed paper," he wrote.

- Members of "The Way" were appointed to the cultural arm of the Franco administration, starting with the Ministry of Propaganda.

- During the 1950s and 1960s, Franco entrusted Opus Dei members with reversing the faltering Spanish economy. They discarded the model of national self-sufficiency in favor of an economy dependent on international financial interests.

- Opus Dei created its own primary and secondary schools as well as universities, separate from the state-funded but basically Catholic educational system.[9]

From the beginning, Escrivá envisioned a worldwide organization. His initial plans were delayed by the Spanish Civil War. He joined with the Catholic hierarchy in backing the fascist General Francisco Franco and by 1939, Opus Dei was established in several major Spanish cities.

"There's no doubt about it: he [Escrivá] saw himself as the twentieth-century reincarnation of the word, 'God.' A messiah....The thing that most stuck in my mind was a remark he made about Adolf Hitler....The founder said to me: Vlad, Hitler couldn't have been such a bad person. He couldn't have killed six million. It couldn't have been more than four million,'" reported Msgr. Vladimir Felzmann. Explaining the Opus Dei commitment to founding schools, Felzmann added, "When I was a member, Opus Dei would take teenagers as young as fourteen, and they had to make a lifelong commitment to the movement. Minors are still instructed not to tell their parents about Opus Dei because they 'wouldn't understand'. Felzmann described Opus Dei as "a culture built on a foundation of fear, deceit, and paranoia."[10]

Eventually, Escrivá was able to expand his influence throughout Spain. After the civil war ended and an additional 50,000 Spaniards had subsequently been assassinated by the Franco regime, ten out of 19 cabinet officers belonged to or were closely allied with Opus Dei.[11] Escriva's plans for further expansion were again put on hold with the outbreak of World War II.

Opus Dei members helped draft Franco's 1953 concordat with the Vatican giving special benefits to the Church and supporting the restoration of the Spanish monarchy. In 1976, Knight of Malta King Juan Carlos chose Adolfo Suarez, a member of Opus Dei, as new chief of government following the death of Franco.[12]

By 2002, Spanish defense, law and order, and the judiciary were controlled by members of Opus Dei. They held high positions in government, finance, education and the media. Worldwide, they operate about 500 colleges and universities, 52 radio stations, 12 television and movie studios, 12 newspapers, 604 magazines and periodicals, and 38 news agencies.[13]

Most members are "supernumeraries" who marry and are encouraged to produce children. They are pressured to send their children to expensive Opus Dei schools. The larger source of income is provided by the "numeraries," members who vow not to marry, live in communal settings and turn over all their earnings to the organization keeping only a small amount for personal use. Since Opus Dei recruits from the professional and well-to-do classes, numeraries provide a steady stream of substantial income.

Most of what is known about life inside Opus Dei comes from former members. According to John Roche, a professor at Oxford University in England who broke his oath of secrecy after leaving, self-flagellation with whips and spiked chains is a normal part of the rigid spiritual discipline that Opus Dei imposes on its full-time members, including college-age recruits of both genders. "Personal identity suffers a severe battering: some are reduced to shadows of their former selves, others become severely disturbed," wrote Roche in a paper titled "The Inner World of Opus Dei." "Internally, it is totalitarian and imbued with fascist ideas turned to religious purposes, ideas which were surely drawn from the Spain of its early years. It is virtually a sect or cult in spirit, a law unto itself, totally self-centered, grudgingly accepting Roman authority because it still considers Rome orthodox, and because of the vast pool of recruits accessible to it as a respected Catholic organization."

Opus Dei in America

The first American branch was established by a Spanish priest in 1949 and located near the University of Chicago where Strauss was a professor and Dr. Milton Friedman led the School of Economics. Friedman was the leading proponent of a free-market economy unrestricted by government regulation. Graduates and followers of his "Chicago School" would have influential government, academic, and institutional positions all over the world. Friedman's students were targeted for recruitment into Opus Dei and numeraries were enrolled in his classes.[14]

Opus Dei's US headquarter is now located in Manhattan close to the UN with another center on Washington DC's K Street. Opus Dei centers and schools do not have Catholic or even Christian names in order to mask their sponsorship. To give some idea of their growth and strength in the US, the following are Opus Dei institutions located in the Chicago area alone:

- The Alliance for Character in Education operates the Willows Academy and the Northridge Preparatory School, both grades 6 to 12. (Northridge for males, Willows for females.)

- The Association for Educational Development establishes facilities to carry out Opus Dei activities such as philosophy and theology courses, care of chapels, youth camps and clubs, sports activities and classes in ascetical and ethical formation of men.

- The Castlewood Foundation supports activities for men: spiritual guidance, retreats, theology classes, direction of recruitment activities, distribution of religious literature

- The Corporation for Social and Educational Development operates various activities for teenage girls and women including spiritual retreats, study classes, grammar school clubs, day camps, leadership programs for high school, college and professional women and housing of students.

- The Euclid Foundation is an Opus Dei center for men. It runs the Midtown and Metro Centers which provide after-school programs for African-American and Hispanic youth in inner-city Chicago. (Midtown is for males, Metro for females)

- Kingswood Academy is a pre-K through Grade 8 grammar school.

- Lincoln Green Foundation is the Opus Dei center for men near the University of Illinois.

- The Midwest Theological Forum publishes and distributes religious books and sponsors conferences, workshops and retreats for priests.

- The Northview University Center is a residence for male numeraries.

Opus Dei's Lexington College in Chicago is the only school for "hospitality management" in the US which is women-only because the chief responsibility for Opus Dei women is domestic work. The associated Lexington Center provides domestics for Opus Dei institutions, particularly those for celibate males, the same way certain religious orders provide nuns to do the domestic chores in the Vatican and other hierarchical residences.

From the beginning, an Opus Dei presence in the US received support from American SMOM members such as Francis X. Stankard (Chief Executive Officer, International Division, Chase Manhattan Bank), William Simon (financier and Nixon Secretary of the Treasury) and Frank Shakespeare (RKO General and Reagan Ambassador to the Vatican), all active in right-wing and neoconservative causes.[15]

In the post-war era, Opus Dei "enjoyed CIA backing which marked the beginning of a working relationship between Opus Dei and the CIA."[16] On an international scale, Opus Dei participated in "dirty tricks" in Northern Ireland and they controlled Chile's Institute for General Studies, financed by the CIA, where General Pinochet's 1973 coup against President Salvador Allende was planned.[17] "Opus Dei's global influence makes the Orange Order and the Freemasons look like a bunch of Boy Scouts," Henry McDonald wrote in *The Guardian*. Robert A. Hutchinson, a Canadian reporter, first became acquainted with Opus Dei while living in Switzerland and learned they were major players in the Eurodollar market. His book, *Their Kingdom Come: Inside The Secret World Of Opus Dei*, first published in London in 1997, describes their manipulation of political power through intrigue, murder, money laundering, drug peddling, arms trafficking, manipulation of financial markets and other illegalities.[18]

The Vatican Bank

In 1870, the Catholic Church lost the Papal States, a wide swath of land across central Italy, during political unification of the country. This was the last remaining territory the pope ruled directly and its loss deprived the Church of important revenues (the other source being donations). By 1929, the Vatican was bankrupt. Italian Prime Minister Benito Mussolini, needing political support from the Church for his fascist government, agreed to compensate the Holy See—the name of the government of the worldwide Roman Catholic Church—for the confiscated territory. Bernardino Nogara, an internationally-connected financier, was given sole control over the entire fortune of $92.1 million which the Vatican received from the Italian government—the seed money for all future Vatican finances.

Known as the Lateran Treaty, its terms were negotiated by Cardinal Eugenio Pacelli, the future Pope Pius XII. Italy forfeited any claims to authority over Vatican City, the small enclave situated within the City of Rome. The Holy See was recognized as an independent legal entity, making the Catholic Church the only religion with its own civil government which receives and dispatches ambassadors, is seated at multiple international organizations as a sovereign nation and, most importantly, has an unregulated and privately held bank. It also meant the Vatican would remain beyond the reach of all outside law enforcement agencies and that any perpetrator, suspect or material witness living in the Vatican City State was immune from arrest, prosecution or being forced to give testimony.

Another treaty negotiated by Cardinal Pacelli was a concordat signed with Germany in 1933 providing prestige and legitimacy to Hitler's government. Pacelli signed the agreement with Knight of Malta, monarchist and nobleman, Franz von Papen, Hitlers' vice chancellor and member of the Catholic Center Party. Earlier in 1933, the party had made a deal with Hitler whereby their votes in the Reichstag helped pass the Enabling Act giving Hitler legislative powers. The treaty with the Catholic Church was signed four months later.

The concordat granted the Church freedom to continue its pastoral activities unrestricted by the government. Hitler also agreed to protect Church assets and turn over monies collected from Catholics via an income tax known as the *kirchensteuer*, thus creating a steady stream of income to the Vatican. ("By 1939 the *kirchensteuer* was producing $100 million a year for the Holy See."[19]) In return, members of the Catholic Center Party agreed to vote in favor of the Enabling Act which granted Hitler's cabinet legislative powers. The Catholic Center Party was the third largest party in the Reichstag and added to the necessary two-thirds majority for the Act to pass.

Pacelli, now Pope Pius XII, reorganized the Vatican's financial structure and renamed his bank the Istituto per le Opere di Religione, or IOR, in 1942. As John F. Pollard noted in his book, *Money and the Rise of the Modern Papacy: Financing the Vatican 1850-1950*, money made the modern papacy possible.[20]

Deploying the initial funding from the fascists, Nogara built up the gold reserves and invested in a full range of Italian business enterprises—banks, insurance, metals, manufacturing, food processing, utilities—including a controlling interest in Italgas, the principle supplier to major cities. Francesco Pacelli, the pope's brother, was on the Italgas board. Francesco's three sons—Princes Carlo, Marcantonia and Giulio Pacelli—became members of an inner elite whose names appeared as directors on a long list of Vatican-controlled companies. When the Holy See bought shares in the construction and real estate giant, Immobiliare, the Church became one of Italy's principle landlords. Italian "Catholic banks" located throughout the nation and established to handle the accounts of the clergy, religious orders and their charities were also reorganized by Nogara.[21]

Nogara formed partnerships with other banking giants: Credit Suisse, Hambros Bank in London, Banque de Paris et des Pays-Bas (Paribas), Bankers Trust of New York, J. P. Morgan Bank, Chase, Continental Illinois National Bank and Trust Company of Chicago, and the Rothschilds of London and Paris who had been doing business with the Vatican since the early 1800s. When Europe was threatened by a second World War, Nogara invested in South American and US companies—General Motors, Gulf Oil, General Electric, Bethlehem Steel, TWA and IBM.[22]

Nogara had been Italy's representative on the Ottoman Debt Council, established to collect debt that the Ottoman Empire owed to countries in Europe after World War I. He was head of a Masonic temple in Istanbul, part of the faction supporting the coup of the "Young Turks." When he returned to Italy, Nogara joined a Masonic lodge in Rome and helped create a similarly useful secret organization, eventually known as P2 (Propaganda Due), for political plots as well as business deals. After World War II, the British, lacking the intelligence ties to the Vatican the Americans had fostered, used P2 for anti-communist clandestine activities.[23] P2 became one of several groups composing the Anti-Bolshevik Bloc of Nations which was not actually a coalition of countries but consisted primarily of former Nazi collaborators who led anti-Soviet conspiracies. The ABBN became the European branch of the World Anti-Communist League (WACL), founded by Taiwanese businessmen to combat the Red Chinese. The WACL, always a clandestine organization, was eventually an umbrella for the internationally mega-wealthy for funding right-wing terrorism not only in Asia, but also Europe and Latin America. P2, with its ties to the Vatican Bank, emerged as one of its most powerful factions.[24]

Nogara ran the Vatican Bank (the IOR) with a group of financial advisors known as "Uomini Di Fiducia" or "men of trust." In the early 1960s, Licio Gelli was sponsored by a fellow Knight of Malta and member of P2 to become a "man of trust."

Gelli had volunteered in the fascist Black Shirts Battalion in order to fight in the Spanish civil war. During World War II, he was liaison between the Italian Black Shirts and the German Gestapo and was charged by the Italian partisans after the war with collaborating with the Nazis.

Gelli made his most profitable contacts while working on Catholic "ratlines," diplomatic channels arranged to smuggle Axis officials out of Europe to avoid prosecution as war criminals. A defeated Germany could no longer produce much revenue from the *kirchensteuer*, but the fleeing leaders of the Third Reich who had stolen most of their country's wealth and the assets of their victims would pay handsomely for their freedom.[25] The men whom Gelli helped escape to South America guided his business investments on that continent and he became a wealthy man.

In the post-war period, Gelli sold his services as an informant to Italian, British, and American intelligence and the KGB. Gelli was an operative in NATO's Operation Gladio/"stay-behind" secret militia designed to be the first line of defense against Soviet aggression in Western Europe, sealing the connections with his CIA, Mafia and Vatican contacts. By 1969, Gelli had blackmailed his way to the top of P2 and was Haig's contact in engineering the "strategy of tension." Connected to worldwide Freemasonry in name only, P2 was a shadow government where the real decisions directing Italian politics and commerce were made. At the height of its power, membership in P2 included over a thousand leading political, financial, government, military, intelligence, media and ecclesial officials.

Another of Nogara's "men of trust" was Michele Sindona. Sindona, a poor Sicilian, made his initial business contacts with the Mafia through Vito Genovese, the American military's contact for assistance in the invasion of Sicily. Sindona studied law and in 1946 moved to Milan with a letter of introduction from the Archbishop of Messina addressed to Giovanni Battista Montini, who would become Archbishop of Milan in 1954 and Pope Paul VI in 1963. Montini worked in the Vatican's intelligence network and was part of the US/Vatican collaboration established by William "Wild Bill" Donovan. He maintained important political contacts in the post-war era. "Every CIA station chief in Italy made a point of getting to know [Montini], and CIA 'project money' was donated to various orphanages and charities whose principal benefactor was the Archbishop of Milan."[26]

Sindona became a "man of trust" and through his association with the IOR made a series of international inter-locking investments to launder mob money more efficiently. In all his endeavors, Sindona's deals were legitimized through his association with the Vatican Bank.[27] Through his CIA connections, Sindona partially funded the 1967 Greek military coup.[28]

The Vatican Bank was exempt from paying taxes on stock dividends, making it an "offshore" tax haven in the middle of Rome. In 1968, the Italian government stated it would withdraw the Vatican's tax exemption on income from domestic investments. The Holy See's financial experts threatened to divest the Vatican Bank of all its Italian stocks at once and throw the financial markets into chaos, but the "men of trust" could not risk disclosure of the enormity of Vatican holdings or any subsequent inquiries which might lead to disclosure that the IOR was a shelter for organized crime, right-wing terrorists and the intelligence agencies backing them. They made plans to move part of the IOR portfolio into foreign holdings as quickly as possible and needed another bank as cover for the project.[29]

Sindona was acquainted with banker Roberto Calvi who began working for the Banco Ambrosiano in 1947. The bank, named after Ambrose, patron saint of Milan, was founded in 1896. Banco Ambrosiano "had very specific Catholic connections....Catholics were encouraged to invest in it by the Catholic Church."[30] By 1965, Calvi was a manager but had reached a dead-end in his career. In exchange for arranging his promotion to chairman of the Banco Ambrosiano, Calvi agreed to cooperate with the "men of trust" and was provided with membership in the Knights of Malta and P2. Calvi first formed a Luxemborg holding company, Banco Ambrosiano Holding. With a foreign subsidiary, he then used the Luxemborg company to set up banks in Switzerland, the Bahamas, Peru and Nicaragua. When Sindona's financial empire collapsed after the 1974 failure of the Franklin National Bank, Calvi replaced Sindona as the Mafia's chief money launderer. He became known as "God's Banker" as he assumed Sindona's role as the Vatican's most visible lay partner.

Pope Paul VI has often been quoted as stating, "The smoke of Satan has entered the Vatican." If so, it occurred when he put Bishop Paul Marcinkus, an American from Chicago who had been a member of the pontiffs' personal staff, in charge of the Vatican Bank. Nixon's second ambassador to Italy, Knight of Malta John Volpe, stated Marcinkus was "his most trusted advisor on Italian political matters."[31] (Volpe presented Sindona with a citation as "Man of the Year of 1973." The next year Sindona fled to Switzerland to avoid being arrested.[32]) Marcinkus collaborated with Gelli, Sindona and Calvi in masterminding what would later become known as "The Vatican Bank Scandal." Through a series of dummy corporations, including those set up throughout Latin America and the Caribbean with the Banco Ambrosiano, $1.4 billion of depositors' money disappeared into a black hole of fraudulent investments.

The Institution of the Papacy: "A Perfect Vehicle"

The pope remains a great influence in the world for good or ill in matters that extend far beyond religion. He maintains control of his global institution by having sole power to appoint prelates (those with the rank of bishop and higher). Pope Pius XII, referred to as the "Chaplain of NATO,"[33] died in 1958 and was replaced by Cardinal Angelo Roncalli, one of the few prelates who had openly opposed the Nazis. As Pope John XXIII, Roncalli called for a Second Vatican Council (1962-65) to "open" the Church to the modern world resulting in sweeping changes to world Catholicism including enabling the laity to participate in Mass and in their own language. Anti-Semitism was renounced and the Church rejected state-imposed religion.

In May 1963, Knight of Malta/CIA director, John McCone, received a memorandum from James Spain in the agency's Office of National Estimates. "There is no doubt that vigorous new currents are flowing in virtually every phase of the Church's thinking and activities," Spain wrote. Pope John XXIII had instructed his bishops and clergy to maintain neutrality in politics and the US-backed Christian Democrats had lost their first Italian election. Spain reported that conservative members of the Curia, especially members of the nobility, were upset about the privileges they lost when Pius XII died. McCone instructed the station chief in Rome to increase Vatican espionage.[34]

The CIA was still very much interested in maintaining its own direct contacts with the Vatican. It has been said the Catholic Church has the best spy network in the world, especially in localities with a Catholic-majority. There is not much that goes on within a parish that the local priest doesn't know about and communications between clerics, prelates and Rome are often considered "privileged." Many countries maintain ambassadors or delegates to the Holy See just to have representatives in Rome privy to the diplomatic chatter.

When John XXIII died of inoperable carcinoma in June 1963, the CIA promoted the candidacy of the pro-American Cardinal Siri during the interregnum. The CIA was so concerned that they bugged the conclave through a hidden transmitter brought into the Sistine Chapel by a US cardinal and the agency knew the identity of the new pope, Giovanni Battista Montini/ Paul VI, before the official announcement was made.[35]

As Paul VI grew older, there was great concern within intelligence circles over who would succeed him. "Agency analysts drew up profiles on leading papal candidates, identifying those who were likely to be sympathetic to American interests... The [CIA] courting of John Paul II began when he was still the archbishop of Krakow." At the time, the CIA was collaborating with right-wing Catholic groups to counter the actions of progressive clergy and religious (the collective term for nuns and brothers) in Latin America. The agency supported the factions who would be "instrumental in promoting and electing John Paul II... a perfect vehicle for US foreign policy."[36]

Karol Wojtyla, the son of a Polish patriot and military officer, was unknown outside his own country, undistinguished from thousands of other bishops throughout the world. During World War II and the Soviet occupation, Wojtyla lived in relative comfort, safety and obscurity. His only resistance to the Nazis was performing as an actor in underground patriotic productions. After his ordination in 1946, Wojtyla was sent to Rome to study. Failing to receive a doctorate, he returned to Poland to secure it.[37] His only defiance of the Communists was to insist that a parish church be built in the newly constructed "workers' paradise" of Nowa Huta. His ecclesial career was marked by a "go along to get along" cooperation with the government.

The Polish Communist Party had veto power over selection of Catholic hierarchs. When the archbishop of Krakow died in 1964, Zenon Kiszko, chief ideologist of the Party, said he would keep declining candidates put forward by the Church until he got the name he wanted—choosing Wojtyla because as bishop he had shown little interest in politics.[38] From the Party's viewpoint, Bishop Wojtyla was a preferable candidate to others such as Bishop Jerzy Stroba, who was "a decided opponent of all state cooperation."[39] Jonathan Kwitny, in his book, *Man of the Century*, confirmed Kiszko thought Wojtyla the "least political" and "least likely to get into political fights with the Party....Prominently noted in Wojtyla's files was his voluntary, friendly approach to the Party's first secretary in 1959, to negotiate a common-sense compromise in a silly dispute over dormitory space. Such cooperation was unprecedented in high churchmen."[40] After refusing the first seven names put forward by the Church, Kiszko approved Wojtyla as archbishop. "His appointment was welcomed by the [Polish] government. Wojtyla was considered 'tough but flexible' and a moderate reformer, and an improvement on the old-school hardliners who were unalterably opposed to communism and communists."[41]

At the extremely young age of 47, Wojtyla was elevated to cardinal by Pope Paul VI in 1967 at the urging of Msgr. (later Cardinal) Agostino Casaroli, a member of P2 who worked in the Vatican Secretariat of State at the time.[42]

In 1968, the Polish government commenced a new and terrible anti-Semitic purge. More than 34,000 Jews left the country. The Polish Church did not speak out then, just as it had not protested the genocide of Polish Jews during World War II, nor the persecution of the remnant Jews who returned after the war. Having never spoken in public to condemn the atrocities wrought against the Jews or the anti-Semitism for which his fellow churchmen were noted, on February 28, 1969, Wojtyla visited a synagogue in Krakow.[43] This was followed by a trip to the US and Canada. Wojtyla went to New York, Philadelphia, Boston, Washington DC, Baltimore and St. Louis.

In 1970, when the Gomulka government fell after the outbreak of bloody riots and strikes due to rising food prices, Wojtyla was nonetheless able to tour throughout Europe.[44] In 1973 Wojtyla attended the Eucharistic Congress in Australia, with stopovers in New Zealand, the Philippines and Papúa, New Guinea. When Poland experienced another year of food shortages in 1976, Wojtyla was again absent for three months, including another trip to the US. This time, Wojtyla's itinerary included all the cities in his prior trip plus San Francisco and Los Angeles (to meet with Reagan supporters?). To increase his visibility even further, he was invited to lecture at Harvard, where he was introduced as "the next Pope,"[45] and at the Catholic University of America in Washington, DC.

It is reasonable to question how an obscure but "flexible" prelate from an impoverished country who had never traveled any distance further than Krakow to Rome, suddenly developed the resources and connections to become a globetrotter. A Spanish author stated it was Opus Dei who selected and funded Wojtyla to be the next pope.[46] In 1977, New York Cardinal Terence Cooke, Grand Protector of the American Knights of Malta, flew to Krakow to discuss with Wojtyla his candidacy to succeed Pope Paul VI.[47] David Yallop concluded in his seminal book about the Vatican Bank Scandal, *In God's Name*, the "men of trust" would support a "cooperative" pope who would not disturb their financial empire. Martin A. Lee, author of "Their Will Be Done" published in *Mother Jones,* asserted there were several right-wing groups backed by the CIA which were "instrumental in promoting and electing John Paul II."

CHAPTER 3

HAWKS AND NEOCONS ALIGN

Ronald Reagan Materialized Out of Nowhere

Lyn Nofziger, White House advisor in the Nixon and Reagan administrations, referring to the 1966 California gubernatorial election, noted, "Ronald Reagan materialized out of thin air with no political background, no political cronies, and no political machine....He didn't even run his own campaign."[1]

In 1954, Reagan began an eight-year relationship with General Electric acting as host, occasionally as producer and eventually part-owner of their television anthology. The company provided Reagan with a platform as company spokesman to make numerous personal appearances, including visits to various plants to convince their employees not to unionize. Reagan, now remembered as "The Great Communicator," used the opportunity to hone his talents as a public speaker.

Reagan and GE were a good match. The corporation, epitomizing the worst of the "military-industrial complex," was given a "Special Lifetime Achievement Award" in 2002 by the watchdog group, United for a Fair Economy, for scoring the highest average rank among all US companies in the combined areas of violations of securities laws, tax ripoffs, labor relations complaints, employment discrimination, environment and product safety abuses, pollution, abuses against human rights, anti-competitive and anti-consumer practices, and unlawful debt collection.[2] And even though it also led the field in defense contract fraud, General Electric was awarded defense contracts totaling $1,483,886,179 for just the period November 2006 through July 2008.[3]

The *General Electric Theater* went off the air in 1962 amid publicity surrounding the Justice Department's anti-trust investigation of Reagan's MCA/SAG deal. While president of the Screen Actors Guild, Reagan signed a permanent waiver exempting the Music Corporation of America from SAG rules in 1952. A Justice Department memorandum indicated that the waiver became "the central fact of MCA's whole rise to power" in the entertainment industry.[4] In return, Reagan had become part owner of MCA.[5] The disclosure that Reagan not only signed the waivers but also benefited from the deal lessened his value as TV-host and company spokesman. "The suggestion of impropriety fueled Reagan's increasingly anti-government demeanor on tour, and his insistence upon producing and starring in episodes combating communist subversion in the final season of *General Electric Theater*."[6]

Reagan remained on the speakers' circuit for Republican and conservative causes. His political career began when a group of powerful businessmen heard him deliver a Republican fundraising speech at the Coconut Grove nightclub in 1964. They asked Reagan if he would give the same speech on national television as part of Barry Goldwater's campaign if they paid for the airtime. The result was his famous "A Time for Choosing" exhortation where Reagan railed against high taxes and government regulation. His performance impressed the conservative back-room movers and shakers. Soon after Lyndon Johnson's landslide victory, a delegation including Henry Salvatori, an Italian immigrant and self-made billionaire, met with Reagan to ask him to run for governor.[7] The group, which organized themselves as the "Friends of Ronald Reagan" committee, promised Reagan all the funding he would need.[8]

Salvatori was a Knight of Malta and one of the founders of *National Review*. In 1960, he sold his company, Western Geophysical, a global industry leader in offshore oil exploration, to devote himself full-time to right-wing causes, including funding the Heritage Foundation and college-level orthodox Catholic studies. It was Salvatori who had persuaded Goldwater to allow Reagan to give his televised speech on his behalf. Salvatori later served as state finance chairman for Reagan's 1966 campaign for governor.

Another member of Reagan's inner circle was Knight of Malta, Patrick J. Frawley Jr., who owned Paper Mate, Schick Safety Razor Co. and Technicolor, Inc. He also owned the *National Catholic Register*, a reactionary weekly promoting Roman Catholic hegemony in the US and Europe. Frawley was a member of the American Security Council, as was Salvatori. The ASC was founded in 1955 and embodied the principles of the military-industrial complex. The ASC maintained close ties to the World Anti-Communist League and other right-wing groups. Its board of directors consistently includes retired senior military officers, executives of the world's largest multi-national corporations and defense contractors.

William A. Wilson, married to a Pennzoil heiress, was another close advisor. Wilson, a convert to Catholicism, made his own fortune in California real estate, oil and cattle and had deep business connections in Latin America. Reagan would name Wilson as his envoy to the Vatican after his election as president.

After Reagan won the 1966 Republican gubernatorial primary, Leonard Firestone, Taft Schreiber of MCA, A.C. Rubel of Union Oil, and other California businessmen joined the campaign. Later known as the "Businessman's Taskforce," they not only provided advice and deep pockets for whatever the campaign needed, but also their connections to the international cabal of pro-Israel, anti-communist "masters of the universe."

Reagan's 1966 gubernatorial campaign was run by these businessmen. They hired marketing and consulting firms. The consulting firm subcontracted behavioral psychologists to tutor Reagan and shape his public image. Others were hired to give Reagan a crash course on California issues, prepare position papers and provide him with constant feedback and analysis. After his election, many in this group continued as members of Reagan's kitchen cabinet who chose the top staff members for both his gubernatorial and presidential administrations."[9]

The Nixon/Ford Administration

The 1972 presidential campaign helped further the cause of the neoconservatives—the term having first been used by liberals to describe their associates who were abandoning their domestic policy positions to assume a hard-line posture in foreign affairs. Irving Kristol's endorsement of Richard Nixon's re-election severed many of the remaining ties. Traditional conservatives supported détente and containment; the neoconservatives pushed for direct confrontation and the use of military force.[10] Ardent pro-Israel staffers of Senator Henry "Scoop" Jackson (D-Wash.), including Paul Wolfowitz and Richard Perle, bolted to the far right of the Republican Party in opposition to the Democratic Party's pro-peace nominee, George McGovern. Angered by what they viewed as a liberal tendency to be soft on communism and by the rise of the counterculture and anti-war movement in the 1960s, the Jackson Democrats embraced an aggressive foreign policy, part of the glue which would continue to hold the neoconservatives together.[11]

Nixon aides Patrick Buchanan and Charles Colson invited Kristol to dinner with the president in 1970. According to records kept by H. R. Haldeman, Nixon's chief of staff, "In Oval Room [Office] after dinner the talk heated up, about whole subject of condition of the country, focused on radicalization of large number of college students, strength of nihilistic groups (in influence, not numbers), and how to deal with it all ... Must say, Kristol didn't add much."[12]

Kristol, however, had far more success in the West Wing during the Ford administration.

According to the book *Intellectuals and the American Presidency* by Tevi Troy, during the early 1970s both Donald Rumsfeld and Richard Cheney came under the sway of leading Strauss protégé and Ph.D. student later professor, Robert Goldwin. Goldwin became director of the Public Affairs Conference Center in Chicago, a Straussian institution. Rumsfeld attended a seminar there. In 1973, Goldwin became Rumsfeld's deputy when the congressman accepted Richard Nixon's appointment as US Ambassador to NATO. When Gerald Ford became president, Rumsfeld, and his protégé, Dick Cheney, came to the White House as chief of staff and deputy. [Rumsfeld was replacing Alexander Haig, Nixon's last chief of staff. Haig became Supreme Allied Commander of NATO. Cheney had also been Rumsfeld's assistant when Rumsfeld served as counselor to Nixon.] Goldwin also came to the White House as special consultant to the president. Goldwin's first assignment was to organize a small White House seminar for Ford and senior staff. The guest scholar for the kickoff seminar was Irving Kristol.[13]

[Kristol] soon began recommending neo-conservatives to positions on the National Endowment for the Humanities and Library of Congress, intellectual cadres who would act as a vanguard to guide the masses of Nixon's "Silent Majority" against the class enemy....

According to documents in the archives of the Gerald R. Ford Presidential Library, Cheney wrote Goldwin on Jan. 25, 1975, "I greatly appreciate receiving the stuff you've been sending me... Anything like that that comes in from Kristol or others, I'd love to see."[14]

Kristol followed up by urging "the political necessity of fostering a conservative Counter-Establishment" funded by, among others, the Smith Richardson Foundation (Vicks Vaporub), the Earhart Foundation (oil) and the Scaife Family Trust (the Mellon industrial, oil, uranium and banking fortune). At Kristol's suggestion, Goldwin held seminars for administration officials headed by neoconservative speakers.

In order to move Ford towards a more bellicose foreign policy,[15]

Cheney and Rumsfeld pushed for the creation of a parallel commission dubbed the Team B to second-guess the CIA on Soviet military capability. The Team B's report projecting a rapidly expanding Soviet threat turned out to contain faulty data. Then-CIA director George H. W. Bush, who had acceded to Team B's creation, later condemned it as having set "in motion a process that lends itself to manipulation for purposes other than estimative accuracy." Nonetheless, Team B served as an important milestone in legitimating neoconservatism within the Republican Party.[16]

The neoconservatives were attracting non-patrician but orthodox Catholics like Buchanan, who were vehemently opposed to civil rights, women's rights, abortion rights and gay rights. As it is a secret society, it is unknown how many were members of Opus Dei, but they supported the Opus Dei/Strauss philosophy that they were an intellectual rather than a hereditary elite destined to control and direct the masses. "They employed many of Strauss's terms such as 'nihilism' and 'moral relativism' while impugning modernity."[17] Though traditionally anti-Semitic, they accepted the notion that Israeli militarism needed to be preserved and enhanced for the sake of US interests in the Middle East.

The Heritage Foundation

Beer magnate, Joseph Coors, had been a supporter of Ronald Reagan since the 1968 Republican National Convention.[18] According to an article attributed to Paul Weyrich, the Colorado-based Coors was looking for ways to apply his fortune to advancing the conservative cause. The news director of a Denver radio station introduced Coors to Weyrich, then an aide to Senator Gordon Allott (R - Colo.) Along with others, Weyrich had been working on plans for an "outside operation that could provide timely information to Members of Congress from a principled perspective. Such an organization could supply witnesses for hearings and experts to privately brief senators and congressmen."

The initial operation was a subsidiary of the Coors Corporation and was called The Analysis and Research Association. When they learned about tax-exempt 501(c)(3) organizations (named for the applicable tax code), Weyrich recruited fellow-Catholic, Edwin J. Feulner Jr., then chief of staff to Representative Phil Crane (R - Ill.) to join the new entity.[19]

The Heritage Foundation, established in 1973, was funded initially by Coors and later by Richard Mellon Scaife (publishing and principal heir to the Mellon fortune). Coors and Weyrich set up the Foundation as an educational research entity. The prospectus mentioned several areas that would receive "particular emphasis," including international trade, energy, federal spending, public campaign financing, tax reform, environmental issues, legal services, education, and Social Security. The Foundation also committed to outreach to college and university students and to disseminate information to the press and news media.[20] Prototype for the neoconservative think tank, the Heritage Foundation is still among the most influential.

Weyrich served as president of Heritage Foundation until 1974 when he founded the Committee for the Survival of a Free Congress, which became the Free Congress Foundation, the political arm of the Heritage Foundation. Weyrich was one of the earliest neoconservatives to promulgate the idea the US was immersed in a cultural civil war requiring the same spirit and dedication as needed to wage a shooting war.[21] His Free Congress hosted a radio program, "America's Voice."

> Each week, hosts Bill Lind and Brad Keena say what people are thinking but are often afraid to say.... that "multicultural" nations break apart in civil war, and that uncontrolled immigration and rising crime are turning America into a Third World nation. They ask the "forbidden" questions: is real reform still possible, or will a new Revolution be necessary to restore America's traditional— and very successful—culture? Is the United States Government still a legitimate government? Is "racism" the real problem or do cries of racism arise as a result of bad behavior by minority groups?[22]

Weyrich and Coors arranged for Laszlo Pasztor, a convicted Nazi-collaborator, to run the Coalition of the Americas, a subsidiary of the Free Congress Foundation. Pasztor was instrumental in establishing the ethnic-outreach arm of the Republican National Committee and was referred to as "Weyrich's right-hand man" by Martin E. Lee in his book, *The Beast Reawakens*. In 1988, Pasztor was one of six leaders in the George H. W. Bush presidential campaign forced to resign when the press reported the presence of émigré Nazis and anti-Semites in Bush's inner-circle.[23]

Eugenicist and white supremacist Roger Pearson, organizer of the Nazi Northern League of Europe and writer for the racist journal *Mankind Quarterly*, joined the editorial board of *Policy Review*, the monthly Heritage publication, in 1977 and chaired the American branch of the World Anti-Communist League in 1978-79. Pearson left Heritage after a *Washington Post* exposé of the racist/fascist orientation of the World Anti-Communist League.[24]

The 1975 congressional investigation of the Korean Central Intelligence Agency (KCIA) noted the connection between Heritage president Ed Feulner and Sun Myung Moon's Unification Church. The Freedom Leadership Foundation, a political organization established by members of the Unification Church in the US and described as "an organization to be used to achieve KCIA objectives" by the congressional report, was also linked to the World Anti-Communist League. There is also a substantial body of evidence linking Moon to Asian and South American drug cartels.[25]

In the early 1980s, Heritage received large donations from Taiwan and South Korea to fund its Asian Studies Center which, *The Nation* magazine stated, "quartered apologists for [South Korean Prime Minister] Chun's regime." The *Wall Street Journal* reported the Heritage Foundation promoted and actually wrote pro-Korean legislation.[26] The Heritage Foundation also co-sponsored a forum with the Anti-Bolshevik Bloc of Nations.[27]

A 1995 *Wall Street Journal* article noted the formidable influence of the Heritage Foundation on government policies since the Reagan era:

> Over the first 100 days of the current GOP Congress, Heritage scholars testified before lawmakers 40 times—more than any other organization, Hill staffers say....
>
> "They talk to me sometimes 12 times a week," said Heritage budget analyst Scott Hodge earlier this year, explaining his ties to the staff of the House Budget Committee. "We—I mean House members—are putting together a final list of [budget] cuts."[28]

Following the steps laid out by Opus Dei, additional neoconservative "think tanks" were instituted to develop the apologetics for the New Right.

Bob Burton of the Center for Media and Democracy described the Heritage Foundation and similar institutions as

> ...the intellectual equivalent of battle tanks, which rely on a combination of speed, defensive armor and offensive firepower to overwhelm opposition forces. The goal of conservative think tanks, in combination with air cover provided by conservative commentators, is to clear the way for supporting politicians and officials to implement policies once deemed too toxic for even conservatives to touch. In 1993, the former senior vice president of the Heritage Foundation, Burton Yale Pines, himself adopted the military analogy, describing think tanks as "the shock troops of the conservative revolution."
>
> The enthusiasm of corporations and conservative philanthropists for funding think tanks is based on what is known in the PR trade as the third-party technique—finding a more credible organization to articulate what might otherwise be seen as a self-interested policy....
>
> To be effective, think tanks don't need to appear in peer-reviewed academic publications. Indeed, much of their effectiveness comes from their willingness to eschew the cautiousness and caveats of traditional academic work. Instead of balancing pro and cons and recommending further research like an academic enterprise, a think tanker will deliver a snappy policy prescription.
>
> For politicians, think tanks provide access to a pool of researchers capable of reducing a complex policy area to a set of conservative proposals and a sound-bite. For the media, the allure of think tankers is their accessibility, sound-bite savvy and a level of specialist knowledge greater than that of the reporter. So much the better if they were a former administration official or have an expansive publications list enabling them to be packaged as "experts."
>
> In short, think tanks are a way in which media outlets and politicians can outsource the time consuming business of research and independent thinking.[29]

CHAPTER 4

FORMATION OF THE RELIGIOUS RIGHT

In 1976, Nixon's former treasury secretary, Knight of Malta and Opus Dei supporter, William Simon, was appointed head of the John M. Olin Foundation (chemicals and munitions). Along with the Sarah Scaife, Smith Richardson and J.M. foundations, the Olin Foundation established "clearinghouses" for corporate donations.

> [The] plan was straightforward and simple. Wealthy conservatives would support foundations that would in turn cultivate conservative voices in universities, in the media and of course, in religious politics. The goal was to change not only the message, but the entire political landscape by disguising the message to make it appear more centrist than it actually is. A unified message on any given subject would descend intact from the think tank, complete with talking points, directly to the pundit whose job is to get that message into the daily discourse and finally to the political candidate who campaigns on it as an issue. Repetition and unity has become the hallmark of their success even if the facts are incorrect.[1]

In order to foment a populist backlash against progressive economic policies such as equal pay for equal work, protection of workers and consumers, and the social securities of the New Deal, "their weapon of choice was and still is to broad-brush it all as immoral and ungodly."[2]

Think tanks would produce secular propaganda, but only a national religion similar to Spain's could convince enough Americans that the redistribution of wealth from the poor and middle class to the very wealthy was not only in their best interest but was "God's will." In his paper, "Metaphor, Morality and Politics,"[3] George Lakoff explained how this was possible. He concluded that political conservatives understood the world through a "strict-father" metaphor. "In the Strict Father model of the family, the mother is subordinated to running the day-to-day affairs of the home and raising the children according to the father's direction. It is the father that bears the major responsibility and makes the major decisions." Not only does "the protection function of the strict father lead to conservative support for a strong military and criminal justice system" but in a male-dominated universe, an anti-feminist and homophobic bias is as common in their dependent women as in the men themselves.

According to Lakoff, the most valued trait in the conservative worldview is obedience: "Just as the good child obeys his parents, a moral person obeys a moral authority, which can be a text (like the Bible or the Koran), an institution, or a leader." The creation of "moral authorities" espousing the desired political ideology and acquiescence of the populace to these leaders formed the ideational framework for the religious right. The neoconservatives could prey on people's insecurities by promising not only a strong military and police force but also religious certainty and rectitude. Moral values based on "thou shalt not" rather than "love thy neighbor" were incorporated into the political platform for the Republican Party.

The foundation donors who paid for think-tank staffers, publications and media access were also happy to pay for Christian leaders preaching fealty to the GOP. In many ways religion produced more "bang for the buck" than the secular media since clergy have advantages over political pundits. They operate with certain immunities, deference and privileges. They are free to rail against any civic policy or public official as an exercise of religious freedom and with tax-free revenues as long as they support "positions" and not individuals. Any opposition to a religious leader's position can be portrayed as religious persecution by the "liberal establishment."

While Cardinal Karol Wojtyla was being prepped as leader of the largest US denomination, other conservative Christians were needed to form a voting majority. Fundamentalists and evangelicals were not known for their civic engagement and required prodding to increase their political participation. Weyrich stated his intention to unite right-wing Catholics and Protestants into a political bloc by emphasizing emotion-charged "family values."[4] Fundamentalist and evangelical pastors were recruited with promises of funding and access to national media, but Catholic power-brokers, already familiar with a politically proficient and authoritarian religious institution and connected to international financial and right-wing networks, remained firmly in charge. They founded and directed the new "national Christianity"—a union of church and state made possible by a compliant and controlled electorate.

The Moral Majority

The first religious right organization, Christian Voice, was founded in 1978 nominally by Robert Grant. It was an "issues" advocacy group supported by the Rev. Sun Myung Moon's Unification network and operated out of the Heritage Foundation headquarters.[5] In a 1979 news conference, the disillusioned Grant claimed the organization was a "sham...controlled by three Catholics and a Jew"—Paul Weyrich, Terry Dolan, Richard Viguerie and Howard Phillips who had converted to evangelical Christianity.[6]

Weyrich, Dolan, Viguerie and Phillips abandoned Christian Voice and approached televangelist Jerry Falwell to establish the Moral Majority.[7] It was Weyrich who coined the phrase "Moral Majority"—evocative of Nixon's silent majority—and hand-picked Falwell.[8] Falwell announced the goal of his new group: "To defend the free enterprise system, the family, Bible morality, fundamental values."[9]

Moon helped fund the Moral Majority and when he was indicted in 1981 for fraud and criminal tax evasion, Falwell joined with other religious leaders to present an amicus curiae on behalf of Moon.[10] Moon returned the favor in 1995 by bailing out Falwell's Liberty University when debt threatened to shut it down for the second time.[11]

Falwell was an attractive candidate to lead the Moral Majority because of his firm belief that church and state should be inseparable, his past success in building the Thomas Road Baptist Church of Lynchburg, Virginia, into a community of over 20,000 members, and the popularity of his "The Old Time Gospel Hour" television show also broadcast by radio. His church's campus included the K-12 Lynchburg Christian Academy and Liberty University. In addition, Falwell already had experience in high finance. In 1972 the SEC had filed "charges of 'fraud and deceit' against Falwell's church for the issuance of $6.5 million in uninsured bonds." Falwell won the case in 1973, but Liberty University had to file for bankruptcy and reorganize, losing millions in church investors' money.[12]

Other televangelists were brought into the movement and Weyrich boasted, "A year or two ago nothing was happening. Now we're moving."[13] The Moral Majority, however, functioned primarily through direct mailings to an extensive list of individuals and groups. Richard Viguerie was the direct-mail fundraiser for Weyrich's Committee for the Survival of a Free Congress. During the 1970s, Viguerie grew his direct-mail company into a multi-million dollar business which used its considerable power to influence the election of right-wing candidates. Viguerie helped train political operatives, and established, staffed, and funded other neoconservative organizations. His autobiographical note reads:

> Since 1965, owner of direct marketing/advertising companies such as American Target Advertising, political/ campaign strategist, activist and conservative spokesman and writer. Pioneered political use of computerized direct mail. That technology was the Internet of its day: it enabled conservatives to get around liberals' dominance of the mass media; it allowed thousands of conservative candidates, organizations and causes to get their messages to grassroots Americans.[14]

Viguerie had perfected the art of not only personalizing mail so that recipients would open it rather than discarding it as "junk mail", but he was also able to shape the message to address his readers' fears and prejudices. Viguerie connected people to the Republican Party by manipulating their emotions and the donations poured in.

The National Conservative Political Action Committee

Terry Dolan, a closeted gay who railed against homosexuals "weakening our nation's moral fiber,"[15] instituted the National Conservative Political Action Committee (NCPAC) which emphasized propaganda rather than organizing campaign workers. Dolan's "Target 80" aimed to defeat five prominent Democratic senators: Frank Church of Idaho, Alan Cranston of California, George McGovern of South Dakota, John Culver of Iowa and Birch Bayh of Indiana. Dolan was on the advisory board for another of Moon's political organizations, Causa International, which funded another Dolan lobbying firm, Conservatives Against Liberal Legislation (CALL).[16]

Frank Church was a particularly attractive target for the neocons. He had sponsored bills prohibiting the use of ground troops in Laos and Thailand and limiting the power of the president during a war situation. Church had been actively engaged in efforts to end the Vietnam War. He chaired a subcommittee investigating the political influence of multi-national corporations. His Senate committee investigated abuses of power by the CIA and FBI, uncovering CIA plots to assassinate foreign leaders. On domestic issues, Church sponsored legislation benefiting Social Security recipients and preservation of the wilderness. Church had won re-election three times in a Republican state because of his honesty and principled positions.

An NCPAC affiliate in Idaho began TV and radio commercials in June [1979]....Church was accused of having "almost always opposed a strong national defense." A TV spot was taped in front of an empty ICBM silo....

In Idaho, where air time is cheap, NCPAC will talk about its view of Church's record over and over. One radio spot was aired 150 times a day throughout the state for five days. The cost was just $4,000. Predicts Dolan: "By 1980 there will be people voting against Church without remembering why."

While NCPAC wages war with words, others affiliated with the New Right are attempting to organize single-interest groups against Church. A new antiabortion group called Stop the Baby Killers...describes Church, Culver and Bayh as "men who apparently think it's perfectly okay to slaughter unborn infants." In fact, Church favors a constitutional amendment that would outlaw abortion in most circumstances.[17]

All the targeted senators lost the 1980 election except Cranston. Church was defeated by Congressman Steve Symms by less than 1 percent of the votes. In Reagan's first term, Moon's Freedom Leadership Foundation paid for Symms' staff members to go to Central America to meet with government officials in Honduras and Guatemala.[18] Symms, along with other right-wing candidates, received funding from the World Anti-Communist League and participated in WACL events as did other Republican lawmakers.[19]

The Conservative Caucus

Howard Philips, the only non-Catholic of the four architects of the religious right, established The Conservative Caucus (TCC) which concentrated on national issues and local organization rather than elections. By 1979, it claimed 300,000 dues-paying members, coordinators in 40 states and committees in 250 congressional districts.

The caucus produced "fact sheets" on controversial questions. "The summaries give both sides of the issue, but leave no doubt where virtue lies."

> An item on federal assistance to New York City is accompanied by a cartoon portraying the city as a prostitute. A piece on abortion in military hospitals shows a baby being put into a trash can with a bayonet. The caucus helped lead the fight against the Panama Canal treaties, and is now organizing opposition to SALT II with a Viguerie direct-mail campaign and a series of seminars around the country.[20]

TCC shared board members with the United States Council for World Freedom (USCWF), the official name of the American branch of the WACL. Another TCC board member was Richard Shoff, former Grand Kilgrapp of the Indiana Ku Klux Klan—apparently no longer a problem for a Jewish convert to Christianity.

> Officials of TCC were instrumental in the campaign to make death squads of Central America acceptable to the American public in the early 1980s and also allied with white supremacist elements in South Africa. As TCC national director, Phillips boasted, "We organize discontent" and "must prove our ability to get revenge on people who go against us."
>
> TCC links to the elite Catholic Tradition, Family and Property.[21]

The Tradition, Family, and Property groups (TFPs) operate worldwide. The organization was founded on the works of Plinio Corrêa de Oliveira, a wealthy right-wing Brazilian who used his resources to oppose the freedom movement in Latin America. The TFP opposes "liberal and egalitarian ideas, policies, and trends...that have undermined Christian civilization since the 14th century. Thus, in addition to supporting all official Catholic teaching, the group also argues for the need for authentic elites in society that raise, above all, the moral tone of general society."[22]

Building an American Christian Nationalist Theology

In his insightful and valuable book on the formation of the religious right, *The Theocons: Secular America under Siege*, Damon Linker concluded that while Protestant evangelicals played an important role, the vocabulary and validation for the movement derived from the Roman Catholic tradition of church as a tool to uphold the authority of the state.

> [Theoconservatism] maintains that a secular society is both undesirable and unsustainable, since the US for most of its history was a thoroughly Christian nation. It was founded on absolute moral principles that made no sense outside of a religious context. However, liberal elites in the nation's educational system and media were responsible for the secular drift of American culture since the 1960s, as they consciously foisted their corrupt views on the nation. The practical results of this "secularization" are a sex-saturated popular culture, the collapse of important social institutions such as traditional marriage, a separation of law from religiously-based moral principles, and the rise of a "culture of death" (abortion and euthanasia). The only solution is to bring America "back" into line with the moral strictures of biblical religion, and this can be achieved through the political process, by the election of "Christian" politicians who will advance religion in public life, by conservative judicial appointments, constitutional amendments, and popular referenda like anti-gay marriage initiatives.
>
> [Theoconservatism] joined together the intellectual heft of Catholicism with the zealous religiosity of the evangelicals, overcame much of the mutual suspicion and animosity of the two communities, and empowered the ideological agenda of the theocons. Catholics and evangelicals became allies and friends in an "ecumenism of the trenches" (Colson) in the culture war against moral anarchy.[23]

Convincing fundamentalist Protestants they should work with Catholics was a difficult task as they were historically suspicious of "papists" not only on doctrinal issues but from the very founding of their faith traditions as a "protest" against the corruption and excesses of the Roman Church. One of the leading arguments against permitting the earlier in-migrations of Catholics, as well as the candidacies of Al Smith and John F. Kennedy, was their alleged fealty to a foreign power which precluded them from being loyal and patriotic Americans. The neo-Catholics (the term was first used on the *Catholic Apologetics International* website) would use the Moral Majority, the Christian Coalition, Council on National Policy, Family Research Council, Eagle Forum, Focus on the Family and other such organizations not only to elect Republicans, but also in a broader context to homogenize religious-speak and issues into a "Christian Nationalism" which would overcome denominational differences and unify right-wing Catholics and Protestants.

Some have concluded that this Catholic/Protestant coalition was the creation of the Vatican and/or American Catholic bishops. The Vatican's willingness to politically ally with American Protestants will be covered in subsequent chapters, but in fact, Catholic hierarchs were bought and paid for the same as Protestant leaders. The Knights of Malta and Opus Dei are, after all, organizations run by the laity not the clergy.

The successive "Christian Nationalist" groups which gained national prominence are too numerous to mention, but their positions, presentations and funding were provided by the same think tanks and the following foundations: Sarah Scaife, Castle Rock, Lynde and Harry Bradley, John M. Olin and Sun Myung Moon. The goal was the same—to cast Republican positions as moral and moderate and Democratic positions as immoral, fiscally irresponsible, cowardly and/or unpatriotic. Their goal was to discredit thoughtful dissent as well as the values exemplified by the life and teaching of Jesus Christ. "Brainwashing" may be a term no longer popular, but it best describes how more than a third of Americans even in 2008 could believe that presidential candidate, Barack Obama, was a Muslim and "palled around with terrorists."

As lawyer and journalist Frank Cocozzelli put it, "Unadulterated obedience appears to be the common themes in both the religious and secular spheres of radical movement conservatism. And a citizenry that more easily submits to religious authority will be less likely to question governmental authority."[24]

Abortion

The Catholic Church's opposition to birth control and divorce—the more obvious "family values"—weren't suitable for an inter-denominational effort since these were acceptable to most Americans. American parents may have been extremely concerned about sex and violence in the media, but any constraints in that area would cut into the profit margins of the emerging multi-media conglomerates. Opposing legal abortion, however, would have no adverse personal consequences for a male-only Catholic hierarchy and the almost exclusively male fundamentalist leadership. Even if they were successful in overturning *Roe v. Wade*, their income and connections would always provide access to private clinics for their wives, daughters and girlfriends.

As George Lakoff noted:

It is important to understand that conservative opposition to abortion is not just an overriding respect for all life. If it were, conservatives would not favor the death penalty. Nor is it a matter of protecting the lives of innocent children waiting to be born. If it were, conservatives would be working to lower the infant mortality rate by supporting prenatal care programs. The fact that conservatives oppose such programs means that they are not simply in favor of the right-to-life for all the unborn. Instead, there is a deep and abiding, but usually unacknowledged, reason why conservatives oppose abortion, namely, that it is inconsistent with Strict Father morality.[25]

Opposing abortion fit the world-view of men who wanted control over women and the women who wish to be dominated. It was "justice" that "loose women" should suffer the consequences (pregnancy) for sexual indiscretions, not men, and that the "greatest sinners" would no longer be males who murder, maim and torture, but women who have abortions.

In the early 1970s, while *Roe v. Wade* was making its way through the judicial system, public debate centered on

- whether women should have to suffer permanent harm or death in self-administered or back-street procedures;

- when does human life (or personhood) begin—at conception, after the fertilized ovum becomes implanted in the uterus, the inception of brain waves, viability outside the womb;

- is abortion a public or private matter.

When records from states which had already liberalized their laws showed the risk to women's life and health improved, public opinion generally conceded this was a matter better left between a woman and her physician and polls have showed the majority of Americans agree that abortion should be legal in at least some circumstances ever since.

What the subject of abortion definitely was not was an issue which divided Republicans and Democrats

In the late 1960s and '70s, before positions hardened and the lines were clear, elected Democrats favored abortion restrictions in roughly the same numbers as their Republican counterparts; Republican governors Ronald Reagan (his libertarian instincts winning out) and Nelson Rockefeller (population control was a family cause) signed the most liberal pre-*Roe* abortion laws in the country; Jesse Jackson compared abortion to slavery, while Missouri Congressman Richard Gephardt was a

"Democrat for Life." Five of the seven justices joining in the *Roe* opinion were Republican appointees.

In writing the majority opinion for *Roe v. Wade*, Justice Harry Blackmun had included an analysis of historical precedents favoring safe abortion from the Persian Empire, Roman and English statutory law, common law and American law as well as positions of the American Medical Association, the American Public Health Association and the American Bar Association.

Few could have predicted in 1973 that abortion would become *the* major issue in partisan politics especially when, at the time, it was a topic most politicians hoped to avoid. Even the official Roman Catholic response to *Roe v. Wade* was muted. The Vatican's "Declaration on Procured Abortion" issued in 1974 included the following footnote.

> 19. This declaration expressly leaves aside the question of the moment when the spiritual soul is infused. There is not a unanimous tradition on this point and authors are as yet in disagreement. For some it dates from the first instant; for others it could not at least precede nidation [when the fertilized ovum is implanted in the womb]. It is not within the competence of science to decide between these views, because the existence of an immortal soul is not a question in its field. It is a philosophical problem from which our moral affirmation remains independent for two reasons: (1) supposing a belated animation, there is still nothing less than a human life, preparing for and calling for a soul in which the nature received from parents is completed, (2) on the other hand, it suffices that this presence of the soul be probable (and one can never prove the contrary) in order that the taking of life involve accepting the risk of killing a man, not only waiting for, but already in possession of his soul.[26]

Since the presence of a soul could neither be proved in the affirmative, the lack of "unanimous tradition" in Christianity referred to differing opinions of Church leaders throughout history. Many early Christians categorically opposed abortion ("The Teaching of the Twelve Apostles" written ca. 150, Athenagoras, Tertullian, Basil of Caesarea and Jerome). Augustine of Hippo wrote ca. 415 that early abortion should not be regarded "as homicide, for there cannot be a living soul in a body that lacks sensation due to its not yet being fully formed." Augustine believed that "hominization" took place at forty days after conception for males and eighty days for females.

During medieval times, Bede of England and Irish texts also differentiated between abortion before the "fortieth day" of gestation, and "after the flesh has formed" in instructing priests what penance should be applied if this sin is confessed.

Thomas Aquinas, *On the Truth of the Catholic Faith*, book II, ch. 89, reflected the influence of Aristotle's views on human development: "The vegetative soul, which comes first, when the embryo lives the life of a plant, is corrupted, and is succeeded by a more perfect soul, which is both nutritive and sensitive, and then the embryo lives an animal life; and when this is corrupted, it is succeeded by the rational soul introduced from without [i.e., by God]." This "delayed hominization" view was confirmed as Catholic dogma by the Council of Vienne in 1312.

By the nineteenth century, however, the all-male Vatican opposed all abortions, even to save the life of the mother.[27]

Neo-Catholics would be successful in convincing their followers that the rights of and care for a zygote, blastula, embryo and fetus would supersede the rights of and care for every post-birth human being while war, torture, raping and sodomizing children, intentional poverty, depriving people of healthcare and all the ensuing death and suffering resulting from their policies would be excused, justified and endorsed. By framing a legitimate moral issue as "us against them", black and white, all who disagree are not only murderers but un-patriotic Americans bent on destroying families, communities and country.

By focusing attention on abortion, the neo-Catholics were able to deregulate big business, eliminate worker and consumer protections, lower taxes for the wealthy and privatize and fund those government programs which poured tax dollars into their pockets. In no other majority Catholic or Christian nation in the world is abortion accepted as the most vital issue necessary to their society's commonweal. That the Republican Party did so in the United States is testimony to the neoconservative success in using that issue to consolidate the American religious right.

Support for Israel

Neo-Catholics support a hyper-militarized Israel, not because the Holy See has any strategic interest in the Middle East other than protecting the religious freedom of Catholics and its relatively small number of properties, but because they accept the neoconservative argument that Israel was a necessary extension of US domination of the Middle East.

In contrast, defense of the State of Israel had been a religious issue for evangelicals since 1947. Believing in the inerrancy of the Bible, they considered a Jewish homeland as the fulfillment of God's promise to Abraham that the descendents of his son, Isaac, should rule Palestine.

Israel's existence, however, did not create sufficient justification for its incessant breaches of international law, or for its immediate 1949 and subsequent 1967 expansions beyond its original 1948 UN-mandated borders. So after the 1967 Six-Day War, the Israeli government began sending representatives to liaison with Christian conservatives and hosting trips to the Holy Land for fundamentalist leaders. In return, these Americans gave their financial and vocal support for Israeli settlements in the occupied territories.[28]

To instill an element of urgency and heightened belligerence, the religious right legitimized and made centrist a fringe belief that the end of the world was imminent and the occupation of the Holy Land by Jews was necessary before the second coming of Jesus. Known as dispensationalism,

> it offered a system for recognizing, through a literal reading of Scripture, the whole of human history—past, present, and future—explained in seven Biblical ages, or dispensations....
>
> The spectacular dénouement of the seventh, and final, dispensation includes the rapture (sudden heavenly ascent) of saved Christians, followed by a seven-year tribulation during which the Antichrist and a false prophet will install a one-world religion and the forces of good and evil will clash mightily. After the defeat of the False Messiah, Jesus Christ will return to earth and reign in glory for a thousand years, before engaging Satan in one last battle, at Armageddon.[29]

Hal Lindsey's enormously successful book, *The Late Great Planet Earth*, predicted the end would come within a generation of Israel's statehood. Both Jerry Falwell and Pat Robertson were dispensationalists. Falwell wrote, "It is apparent, in light of the rebirth of the State of Israel, that the present day events in the Holy Land may very well serve as a prelude or forerunner to the future Battle of Armageddon and the glorious return of Jesus Christ."[30] This belief became even more popular after the introduction of the *Stay Behind* books by Tim LaHaye, one of the first leaders of the Moral Majority.

There are many variations of this scenario within the Christian right-wing based upon which passages—usually from the books of Daniel, Matthew and Thessalonians—are used. But all include some personal interpretation of the allegorical last book in the New Testament, the Book of Revelations or the Apocalypse. The text relates the dream or fantasy of a man known as John traditionally thought to be exiled to the Greek island of Patmos due to persecution of Christians during the reign of the Roman emperor, Domitian (81-96 AD). Therefore, it is generally agreed by scholars that such symbolic references as the harlot (or whore) Babylon, refers to Rome, the city built on seven hills. John's writings barely gained enough support to be included in the official canon known as the New Testament when Church officials gathered in the latter half of fourth century to decide which texts would or would not be included. Nevertheless, for over seventeen centuries, people have used Revelations to announce the end of the world was imminent.

Currently, "over one-third of those Americans who support Israel report that they do so because they believe the Bible teaches that the Jews must possess their own country in the Holy Land before Jesus can return."[31]

CHAPTER 5

TWO POPES NAMED JOHN PAUL

John Paul I

Pope Paul VI died of a heart attack on August 6, 1978. He had asked that his funeral be simple with no catafalque and no monument over his grave. Cardinal Albino Luciani was elected quickly on the third ballot as his successor. Vatican insiders said he represented a compromise between the progressive and conservative factions. After the ballots were counted, Cardinal Pironio stated, "We were witnesses of a moral miracle."

In his first public address, Luciani explained why he chose to be called John Paul, the first pope with a double name. "I have neither the 'wisdom of the heart' of Pope John, nor the preparation and culture of Pope Paul, but I am in their place. I must seek to serve the Church." He took "Humilitas" as his personal motto and quickly became known as "The Smiling Pope" for his natural friendliness and good humor.

Luciani was born in the region of Veneto in 1912 and was raised in a poor family. His birthplace, Vittorio Veneto, is a small city situated in the northeastern part of the Italian peninsula. It is famous for a battle fought in 1918 when the Italians were victors over the Austro-Hungarian army bringing World War I to an end. Its incorporation into the nation was the final step in the unification of Italy. The seminary Luciani attended later became a sanctuary for members of the resistance during World War II. Pope John XXIII named him bishop of Vittoria Veneto in 1958. Upon his elevation, he refused all gifts with the words, "I came without five lire. I want to leave without five lire."

In 1962, two priests in Luciani's diocese cheated their parishioners out of money. In stark contrast to other prelates' handling of scandal and malfeasance, Luciani called a meeting with his priests and told them:

> It is true that two of us have done wrong. I believe the diocese must pay. I also believe that the law must run its due course. We must not hide behind any immunity. In this scandal there is a lesson for us all. We must be a poor

Church. I intend to sell our ecclesiastical treasure. I further intend to sell one of our buildings. The money will be used to return every single lira that these priests owe. I ask for your agreement.[1]

Luciani was named patriarch of Venice in 1969 by Paul VI and cardinal in 1973. As Archbishop of Venice, he requested a low-interest loan from the Banca Catolica del Veneto to build special work centers for the mentally retarded and handicapped. This was a "Catholic" bank where the IOR was the majority shareholder and the principal depositors were religious and charitable organizations. Luciani was refused a loan at special interest rates because, he was told, the bank had been sold by Bishop Paul Marcinkus to Roberto Calvi without consultation of the local clergy and with all the profits kept by the Vatican Bank.[2]

Luciani discreetly asked questions. Bishop Giovanni Benelli, Undersecretary of State for the Holy See, explained to Luciani the relationship between Michele Sindona, Calvi and Marcinkus and that there was no point in complaining to the pope; Benelli had already tried.[3] Subsequently, Benelli lost his Vatican position and was sent to Florence in 1977.

When he was elected pope on August 26, 1978, Luciani refused the traditional triple golden tiara and "Papal Coronation" for a more modest inauguration Mass. He declined to use the portable throne borne on the shoulders of twelve footmen. He would not use the royal "we" and instead used the singular pronoun in referring to himself. (Vatican officials, however, rewrote his speeches before publication inserting the plural pronoun.) He asked the office of the Secretariat of State not to invite the leaders of Argentina, Chile and Paraguay to his inaugural Mass, as a reproof for the conduct of their governments. Unfortunately, Cardinal Jean-Marie Villot, Paul VI's secretary of state asked to stay on by the new pope, had already sent out the invitations.[4]

On August 27, Luciani instructed Villot to undertake a thorough investigation of the entire financial operation of the Vatican. Italy's leading economic periodical, *Il Mondo*, addressed a long, open letter dated August 31 to the new pontiff accusing the Vatican Bank of assisting Italians to evade taxes and the illegal transfer of Italian capital to other countries. The editor noted the relationship of IOR directors with

the most cynical financial dealers in the world, from Sindona to the bosses of the Continental Illinois Bank in Chicago (through which, as Your Holiness's advisers can tell you, all of the Church's investments in the United States are handled)....

Marcinkus is the only bishop in the world who is on the board of a lay bank, which incidentally has a branch in one of the great tax havens of the capitalistic world. We mean the Cisalpine Overseas Bank at Nassau in the Bahamas."[5]

Reporter Mino Pecorelli, a former P2 member, wrote a newspaper article, "The Great Vatican Lodge," published on September 12. He named 121 prelates who were members of P2 including Villot, Marcinkus, Cardinal Sebastiano Baggio, prefect of the Curial bishops, and Archbishop Agostino Casaroli, whom Pope John Paul II would later elevate to cardinal and secretary of state. On September 27, John Paul I asked Baggio to take the position he vacated in Venice. Baggio refused. Luciani had also asked for the resignation of Cardinal John Cody of Chicago,[6] the only American hierarch ever subjected to an FBI investigation for financial malfeasance and he also refused.[7]

On September 28, John Paul I informed Villot he was planning to remove not only Marcinkus, but also other members of the Curia. He also intended to end the association of the Vatican Bank with Roberto Calvi. After speaking with Villot, John Paul I phoned Cardinal Giovanni Colombo at 8:45 p.m. in Milan and discussed the changes he intended to make. "Of the phone conversation, Cardinal Colombo has said, 'He spoke to me for a long time in a completely normal tone from which no physical illness could be inferred. He was full of serenity and hope. His final greeting was, 'Pray.'"[8]

After only 33 days as pontiff, Albino Luciani was found dead in his chambers the morning of September 29, 1978. Villot took immediate control of news releases. Thinking it unseemly to report that the nun who brought Luciani his morning coffee every day was the first to discover the pope was dead, Villot stated a priest-secretary discovered the body. The first Vatican announcement as to the cause of death claimed it was due to an accidental overdose of medicine; later the official cause was changed to a heart attack. Luciani's personal physician and family members refuted this, claiming the pope was in excellent health. Villot ordered the papal apartment stripped of all traces that Albino Luciani had ever lived there, including his personal effects, papers, notes and documents. The pope's body was embalmed within a day of his death with no blood being drawn and before an autopsy could be performed. The Vatican press office claimed that a post-mortem was prohibited under Vatican law although in 1830 an autopsy had been performed on the remains of Pope Pius VIII which showed evidence he had been poisoned.

Having read the newspaper exposés and being familiar with centuries of Vatican intrigue, most Italians had an immediate conviction the pope had been murdered as did many others throughout the world. Even cardinals who gathered in Rome to elect Luciani's successor "were clearly frightened."[9]

David Yallop, a well-known British crime reporter, was asked by a Vatican official (who remained anonymous) to investigate the pope's suspicious death. After years of exhaustive research and personal interviews, Yallop wrote the seminal book, *In God's Name: An Investigation into the Murder of Pope John Paul I*, about the death of Luciani and the Vatican Bank scandal which he claimed was the cause. Yallop came to the conclusion the pope had been poisoned and narrowed down the suspects to the six men who would immediately gain from Luciani's death: Marcinkus, Villot, Cody, Calvi, Sindona and Licio Gelli.

When Yallop's book was published in 1984, it created a sensation including renewed demands that John Paul I's body be exhumed. In response, Pope John Paul II's public relations maestro and Opus Dei numerary, Joaquin Navarro-Valls, contacted renowned author and former seminarian, John Cornwell, to write a book refuting Yallop's. Cornwell was told he would be free to do his own investigation and draw his own conclusions, but he was steered towards those officials who were "available" to grant interviews and denied access to others. Almost ten years after the fact, the Vatican press office was able to produce "documents" for Cornwell which no one else had seen until then. Navarro-Valls, a physician by training, provided Cornwell with medical records and testimonials which mysteriously appeared years after Luciani's death attesting to his ill-health. Not surprisingly, Cornwell's 1989 book, *A Thief in the Night: the Mysterious Death of Pope John Paul I* stated John Paul I's death was from natural causes. Cornwell concluded Luciani was lonely, troubled and sick.

While it is true that John Paul I had no allies in the Curia, this holy and amiable man had friends all over the world. His niece lived in Rome and would come for dinner on occasion and he kept in touch with his siblings and other members of his extended family. Luciani was unconcerned when urbane Roman prelates said he was stupid and called him the "Peter Sellers" of the Vatican because his public speeches were not in the intentionally obtuse "Vatican-speak" of the other hierarchs. He told simple stories using Pinocchio, Topo Gigio or some other beloved fictional character, to make his point. After all, hadn't Jesus spoken in parables using people, places and things familiar to his listeners? Those who had no reason to be jealous recognized Luciani's brilliance and communication skills.

Based on Navarro-Valls' information, Cornwell concentrated on Luciani's minor ailments (he was 66 years old) even though the cardinals who elected him saw no signs of infirmity. In fairness, Cromwell did quote Fr. Lorenzi, Luciani's secretary, who said, "He [the pope] told us many times, 'I am enjoying a deep peace of mind. I am light as a feather. I am not overburdened. I am not unhappy.'"[10].

A more recently published book, *The Death of the Pope* by Luis Miguel Rocha, a Portugese author and scriptwriter, states John Paul I was smothered with his own pillow. Another recent publication, *Murder in the Vatican: The Revolutionary Life of John Paul and the Vatican Murders of 1978* by Lucien Gregoire linked Luciani's murder to the mysterious deaths of other liberal prelates around the same time.[11]

To say Pope John Paul I was murdered leads to the obvious question: What would be the point of eliminating one pontiff unless the murderer(s) were sure the next would be more cooperative? The alternative would be to keep killing popes until the right one came along.

And the Winner Is… Wojtyla!

An article relating the history of the Polish Roman Catholic Pastoral Mission of the Church of the Nativity at 245 Linden Street in San Francisco noted: "After its creation, the Pastoral Mission hosted a number of visitors, among them: Bishop Wladyslaw Rubin, and Cardinal Karol Wojtyla from Kracow. Wojtyla came to San Francisco in 1978 shortly before he was elected pope."[12] Yet, unlike his other travels, there is no mention of a trip to the US in 1978 in Pope John Paul II's official Vatican biography, leaving open to speculation why the soon-to-be pontiff's presence in California is considered secret.

At the time of the death of Pope John Paul I, Wojtyla was back in Krakow and the news was brought to Wojtyla by one of his aides while the cardinal was having breakfast. As noted by Polish émigré and foreign and Washington correspondent for the *New York Times,* Tad Szulc, one priest remembered, "Wojtyla sat in silence for a moment, then said, 'God works in mysterious ways. Let us bow our heads before them.'" In his article for the *Newsweek Society,* Szulc continued, "The following day, the cardinal asked his chauffer to stop the car in a secluded area. He sat in the car for a long time, busily writing letters on his lap desk. As an assistant remarked later, 'It was as if he wanted to wind up all his affairs here, not leaving behind anything undone.'"[13] Before leaving for Rome, Wojtyla uncharacteristically wrote a demand for the end of communist censorship of the press. The sudden death of Luciani made the health of the next pope an issue and Wojtyla left Poland on October 3, 1978, with an electrocardiogram in his briefcase as proof of his physical fitness.[14]

In the days following the funeral of the last pope until the conclave to elect a new one, cardinal-electors gather informally, meet potential candidates and discuss the contenders. Wojtyla had three vocal supporters: his close friend, Bishop Andrzej Deskur of Poland, and Cardinals Krol of Philadelphia and König of Austria.

Deskur, a chaplain in the Knights of Malta, attended the same Krakow seminary with Wojtyla. He had worked in the Vatican since 1952 mostly in communications as a member of the Vatican Cinema, Radio and Television Commission and later as president of the Pontifical Council for Social Communications. In Rome, Deskur was Wojtyla's "closest confidant."[15] During the interregnum, Deskur introduced Wojtyla to other influential hierarchs and guided his campaign. This requires delicacy since anyone who openly appears to want to be pope is automatically disqualified. Deskur hosted several social events for Wojtyla, as did Cardinal Cody from Chicago.[16]

Cody would not be the only Chicagoan in the conclave. Not everyone "sealed" inside the Sistine Chapel are voting cardinals so even if ballots are kept secret, the cardinals' conversations and comments are subject to being overheard. In this conclave, there were 88 others authorized to be there including Monsignor (later Cardinal) Edward Egan. Egan was ordained in Chicago and from 1964 to 1972 had been assistant chancellor, co-chancellor and secretary to Cody. In 1972, he went to Rome as a judge in the Roman Rota. Egan's job at the conclave was to check all materials entering or leaving the voting area.[17]

Wojtyla's second sponsor, Cardinal John Krol of Philadelphia, was the son of Polish immigrants. He had been elevated to cardinal in the same ceremony alongside Wojtyla. Besides the same nationality, they shared the same conservative ideology. Krol took every opportunity in the pre-conclave gatherings to promote Wojtyla since his election with Krol's support would bolster the Philadelphian's importance among American hierarchs. It was widely known that Pope John Paul II often consulted with Krol who enjoyed his status as friend of the great pontiff.[18]

Franz König, the third sponsor, had been Archbishop of Vienna since 1958. He had an excellent reputation and great influence among European prelates. He had also developed ties with Opus Dei. König went with Wojtyla to their Roman headquarters at Villa Tevere "to pray before the tomb of Escriva" just days before the conclave.[19] Supporters and members of Opus Dei, believing that Wojtyla would restore "Catholic Europe," came prepared to do their part.[20] Opus Dei priest (later Bishop and Vice President of the Pontifical Commission for Latin America) Cipriano Calderon Polo of Spain brought hundreds of copies of a book of Wojtyla's reflections which the cardinal had presented at a 1976 Lenten retreat. After being sequestered, König provided each of the other electors with the book. "Wojtyla, rooming in cell 91, brought with him a Marxist journal."[21] After the election, König cast himself in the role of Wojtyla's "king-maker." But it was an incredible series of events just before the conclave which proved to be the significant factor.

Knowledgeable reporters identified Cardinals Giovanni Benelli of Florence and Giuseppe Siri of Genoa as the leading candidates of the second 1978 conclave. They received most of the press attention and it was widely predicted one or the other would be the next pope. Benelli joined the Curia in the Secretariat of State and became a papal nuncio (ambassador) at a relatively young age. For the next ten years, he worked closely with Paul VI and was considered a top prospect to succeed him. However, in the August 1978 conclave following Paul VI's death, he had asked that his name be withdrawn in support of Cardinal Albino Luciani of Venice. Benelli considered Luciani as less divisive and knew he had the support of the Third World cardinals.[22]

Siri had actually received enough votes to be elected in 1958 and 1963 when he was the US-backed favorite. When told that Catholics under Soviet occupation would suffer greater persecution because of his staunch anti-communism, Siri withdrew himself as pontiff-elect.

Siri came to both 1978 conclaves as the heavy favorite of the right wing of the Roman Curia and the numerous other cardinals who thought the changes made after the Second Vatican Council had gone too far in promoting participation by the laity, changes in the liturgy and an ecumenical dialogue with other religions. The Vatican II documents had stressed a model of Church as an inverted pyramid—"the people of God" on top and the clergy, bishops, and the pope in descending order beneath as "servants" of the people—obviously contrary to the "pope as monarch" faction.

"On the eve of the ceremony to seal the 111 electors into the Sistine Chapel, an extraordinary set of maneuvers hardened all the lines."[23] A reporter for Turin's *Gazzetta del Popolo* newspaper arranged an exclusive interview with Siri. As the story goes, he promised Siri the article would not be published until after the cardinals were sequestered. In his interview, Siri "ridiculed John Paul I, spitefully attacked the secretary of state, Cardinal Jean Villot, and insulted the interviewer in terms that do not draw favorable comparison to a wise and kind shepherd."[24] The reporter claimed that Benelli convinced him to print the interview immediately. In the morning, before the electors entered the conclave, the newspaper "mysteriously appeared on their doorsteps. With that, Siri's chances were dead. But Benelli's move backfired, too. 'As it turned out,' says Fr. Francis X. Murphy, a veteran Vaticanologist, 'their acrimonious rivalry insured the election of a non-Italian Pope.'"[25]

While reports differ as to the exact numerical results on each successive ballot, all agree that Benelli and Siri led on the first round with Wojtyla receiving only a handful of votes. Meanwhile, Villot was doing his best to disparage Benelli and Siri.[26] "That night at the dinner table and in smaller bedtime meetings in their cells, several cardinals argued that the infighting among the Italians necessitated a compromise choice from outside the Italian ranks."[27] By late afternoon on the following day, Wojtyla had received enough votes to be pope. "From the moment the cardinal chairman announced his election, [Wojtyla's] presence of mind had been astonishing....He seemed perfectly self-possessed as he received congratulations...calm, serene."[28] Some said the former actor put his head down and wept. *Newsweek* reported, "He was only composing his answer in Latin suitable for the occasion." *Newsweek* also reported, "In the aftermath, Benelli was less suave than usual with the press, and Siri was openly bitter."[29]

Benelli and Siri had more than enough reason. The idea that two senior churchmen with years of experience, who had previously sacrificed their papal ambitions for the good of others, would speak and act in such a manner strains credulity. Nor did anyone offer an explanation as to how a Turin newspaper turned up on Roman doorsteps at the most propitious hour.

For most of the world, the election of Cardinal Karol Wojtyla on October 16, 1978, was a shock. The Vatican had issued a press guide with biographies of thirty-six possible successors to John Paul I and strikingly, Wojtyla was not one of them.

Fr. Andrew Greeley, a best-selling American author and sociologist, was part of the crowd in St. Peter's Square when the announcement was made. "In response to the name Karol Wojtyla (Voy-TIH-wa), came a stunned silence, with just a smattering of hand-claps. Most people in the piazza don't seem to know who he is." Greeley described the multitude as "angry, confused, sullen." A man asked him if the new pope was black. When Greeley responded he was a Pole, the man "pounded his head in astonishment."[30]

The response at the Archdiocese of Brooklyn to the radio announcement was, "Who?" Monsignor (later Cardinal) Anthony Bevilacqua considered himself knowledgeable about the candidates and ecclesial politics. Yet he and the others gathered in his office looked at each other dumbfounded. "Nobody knew who he was," Bevilacqua recalled. "Someone thought he was an Oriental. It sounded like a Chinese name."[31]

There was amazement even in Poland. The government's minister of religious affairs, Kazimierz Kakol, was in the middle of a press conference. Coincidentally, the topic was church-state relations. After hearing the news on the radio, a worker rushed a hastily written note to the official. "It seemed so unrealistic that I left the room to check it out," said Kakol. He came back and made the announcement to the reporters who covered religious news. "Their first reaction to the name Wojtyla was, Who?"[32]

Yet it was no surprise to a small group of insiders. Secretary of State Cardinal Jean Villot had confided to his secretary shortly before the death of Paul VI that Wojtyla would be the next pope. Cardinal Pignedoli was told by Krol forty-eight hours before the conclave that "the Pole" would be elected. After the first day of balloting, König asked Stefan Wyszynski, former chaplain of the Polish resistance fighters and the cardinal primate of Poland, "Will we elect a Polish pope?" Wyszynski replied that he was needed in his own country, unaware that anyone considered Wojtyla as a serious candidate.[33] But a friend of Deskur, Marek Skwarnicki, told friends in Krakow as the conclave began that he was preparing background information because he was certain Wojtyla would be elected.[34]

Deskur suffered a debilitating stroke two days before the conclave began which would leave him paralyzed for the rest of his life. The day after Wojtyla was elected, the world witnessed what would be the hallmarks of the new regime—John Paul II's love of publicity, sense of theatrics, and a fawning press. Rather than slipping out quietly to visit his friend in the hospital, the new pope was driven out of the Arch of the Bells into St. Peter's Square in an open car. One reporter gushed, "It mattered not to Karol Wojtyla that he had just been elected Pope. He would be there for his friend."[35]

During the week following the conclave, the new pontiff was informed of the personnel changes his predecessor wanted to make and why. Cardinals Benelli, Felici and others showed Wojtyla evidence of the illegal Vatican Bank transactions. He was given the names of his highest-ranking prelates who were members of P2 and was told the extent of Cody's corruption.[36] Yet the new pope left assassins and international terrorists in control of the IOR. Had he followed through on Luciani's directives, the subsequent murders of honest Italians may have been prevented. When Villot died less than five months after Wojtyla's election, he was replaced with another member of P2, Archbishop Agostino Casaroli, as Vatican secretary of state.

The Bank of Italy had begun its investigation into Calvi and the Banco Ambrosiano in 1978. Its initial report was sent to a Milanese magistrate, Judge Emilio Alessandrini. Alessandrini was gunned down in his car January 29, 1979.[37]

The journalist, Mino Picorelli, who had written the article listing the names of Vatican officials who were members of P2, said he would expose Gelli's links to the CIA and the assassination of former Italian prime minister, Aldo Moro.[38] He was shot to death on March 20, 1979. The former prime minister and "senator for life" Giulio Andreotti, along with five others, was charged with the murder but later acquitted.[39]

In July 1979, a Milanese lawyer, Giorgio Ambrosoli, commissioned by the Italian court to liquidate Sindona's holdings was shot to death. A Rome security agent, Lt. Col. Antonio Varisco and his driver; and a Palermo police official, Boris Giuliano, were also gunned down. All three had been working together to trace Sindona's laundering of drug-trafficking profits through the Vatican Bank. In October 1979, a bomb exploded in the apartment of one of their witnesses, Enrico Cuccia, and another witness, Rosario Spatola, disappeared. [40]

In late 1981, Carlo De Benedetti, head of Olivetti (business machines), became deputy chairman of Banco Ambrosiano at Calvi's request to lend the bank respectability and restore some confidence. Little more than a month later, De Benedetti left after learning P2 was planning his murder.[41]

The general manager of the Banco Ambrosiano, Roberto Rosone, was shot in front of the building on April 27, 1982. Rosone was thought to be behind a letter signed by the bank's shareholders and sent to Pope John Paul II pleading for his help—which was ignored—against the "powerful groups in the international underworld" running the Vatican Bank. Luckily for Rosone, the bank guards returned fire and he survived with crippling wounds.[42]

Calvi was arrested in May 1981 but was allowed to remain free on bail until his trial. Calvi pleaded with an Opus Dei official to keep him and the Banco Ambrosiano from ruin according to sworn statements by his family.[43] Opus Dei agreed to buy the Vatican's shares, but Marcinkus nixed the deal fearing that any influx of Opus Dei money would result in him being replaced as head of the Vatican Bank, which eventually happened anyway.[44]

Calvi's private secretary, Graziella Corrocher, was "suicided" from a fourth-floor window of Banco Ambrosiano on June 16, 1982.

The next day, Calvi was found hanged from the Blackfriars Bridge in London. Bricks had been placed in his pockets, possibly to tie his murder to the Freemasons. However, members of the Mafia were eventually charged, Calvi having lost a great deal of their money also. Within hours of the news of Calvi's death, there was a run on Banco Ambrosiano and the IOR.[45]

On October 2, 1982, Giuseppe Dellachia, an executive of Banco Ambrosiano, was also "suicided" from one of the bank's windows.[46]

On November 28, 1982, John Paul II established Opus Dei as a "personal prelature," meaning for the first time in the two-thousand-year history of the Church, an "official" Roman Catholic organization could operate a global network independent of any interference by local bishops and answerable only to the pope.

For the next two years, the Vatican negotiated with the Italian government and a consortium representing international banking interests. In May 1984, a multi-national commission found the Vatican Bank jointly liable for the crash of the Banco Ambrosiano and was accused of serious malfeasance.[47] The Italian government agreed to pay less than two-thirds of the reparations and the Vatican agreed to pay $312 million which knowledgeable sources maintained came from Opus Dei. Opus Dei expert, Michael Walsh, suggested the organization also agreed to pick up 30 percent of annual Vatican expenditures.[48]

The Vatican claimed the payment was made "on the basis of non-culpability" but "in recognition of a moral involvement." The Vatican had made huge profits and had purchased political influence through the vast sums channeled through the Bahamas, Latin America and Solidarity, the Polish labor union. The principals—Gelli, Calvi, Sindona and Marcinkus—had directed payments to military regimes in Argentina, Uruquay and Paraguay. The Vatican was actually only repaying a fraction of the $1.4 billion which was lost.[49]

The Italian government did extract some justice from the sordid affair. A revised concordat was signed in 1984 declaring the Catholic Church was no longer the official government-funded religion of Italy. Clergy salaries would no longer be paid directly by the state and religious education in public schools was no longer obligatory but optional.

Beginning in 1982, Marcinkus remained within Vatican City State to avoid Italian justice. When a magistrate rescinded his indictment in 1989, Marcinkus retired to Sun City, Arizona, and administration of the IOR was given to laymen close to Opus Dei.[50] In 1993, a civil court in Switzerland tried to obtain an accounting of his affairs while he was president of the IOR. The US State Department upheld Marcinkus' "functional immunity" as a "member of the Consulta of the State of Vatican City" and the order demanding his testimony was dismissed.[51] Marcinkus died from natural causes at the age of 84 in February 2006.

Sindona, however, had been "suicided" by strychnine in his coffee in March 1986 while he was incarcerated in Italy.

As a testament to who held the ultimate power, as of this writing Licio Gelli is living a happy retirement in his Tuscan villa.

CHAPTER 6

JOHN PAUL II AND LATIN AMERICA

"We have no temporal goods to exchange, no economic interests to discuss. Our possibilities for intervention are specific and limited and of a special character. They do not interfere with the purely temporal, technical and political affairs, which are matters for your governments."

Pope John Paul I
Address to the Vatican diplomatic corps[1]

Liberation Theology

The Roman Catholic Church has been allied with Latin American governments since the Spanish and Portuguese conquistadors. Class distinctions were decided largely by race—the rich being of European stock, the poor being from indigenous tribes in most countries or descendants of slaves in others or of mixed heritage. Most clergy and every prelate were members of the very small wealthy class or the middle class where it existed. Church-sponsored schools and seminaries were run primarily for the benefit of the elites and Church resources went first to maintaining parishes for the rich. Clergy and religious taught that subservience of the many for the benefit of the few was the will of God and the poor would find their reward in another life. "A kingdom of God that would claim to be fully real on earth before Christ comes again would be only a snare and a delusion," wrote Franciscan Bonaventura Kloppenborg (*Temptations for the Theology of Liberation,* 1974). Church and state were of one mind.

Pressures began building within the Church in the 1960s. High society's post-war generation produced fewer sons interested in a priestly vocation. The Church, averse to ceding any authority to the laity or lower class, found itself short-staffed; but as long as Roman Catholicism was the predominant religion, there was little reason for concern. However, when Protestants began successfully evangelizing in Latin America, home to half of the world's Catholics, some bishops and priests began a process of self-examination.

During the same period, Latin American economies had prospered in the post-war era and even the lower classes caught a glimmer of hope that their lives could improve. When the economies faltered, the urban and landless rural poor suffered the brunt of the downturn, becoming increasingly aware of their exploitation. Those who protested were persecuted by both the government and the Church. US foreign policy continued to favor the rich while Marxists appealed to the destitute with a promise that, under communism, a nation's wealth would be more equitably distributed.

In response to the growing unrest, even more threatening after the Soviet sponsorship of Cuba, governments changed from laissez-faire (as long as the rich got richer) oligarchies to right-wing military dictatorships installed through a collaboration among multi-national corporations, the CIA, the Confederation Anticomunista Latinoamericana (CAL)—the Latin American branch of World Anti-Communist League—P2, other neo-Nazis, the Knights of Malta, Opus Dei and organized crime which was running the Western Hemisphere's drug trafficking.

Archbishop Aloisio Lorscheider of Brazil warned,

> We are seeing institutionalized violence in the form of extremely strong repression. The rationale of security is not acceptable when it means destroying human beings. This is the socially critical and prophetic position that the Church takes in the light of the gospel in its fight against sin. We also believe that the economic system does not take sufficient account of the need for respect and development of the human being but emphasizes money and profits instead.
>
> We hope...the Church will assume a stronger stand in today's society in support of the development of the Latin American people, or what we describe as the liberation of every human being to become an active agent in his or her destiny.[2]

This call for the "liberation of every human being" became known as "liberation theology." It was termed a "theology" because the image of the brutalized and oppressed Latin American was superimposed on the persecuted and crucified Jesus who understood their suffering. The movement was carried forward by socially-aware churchmen and women religious.

There was a backlash from conservative factions. For example, in August 1966, Fr. Felix Morlion, leader of the Pro Deo organization originally financed by Donovan's OSS, arranged a meeting between American oil tycoon, H. L. Hunt, who had helped organize the CAL chapter in Guatemala,[3] and a Vatican representative. Hunt was asked to fund Catholic anti-communist operations in Latin America. Per Hunt,

> "I was approached by Cardinal Paolo Marella, who said he spoke for the pope and asked if I would supply

members of my Youth Freedom Speakers' movement who spoke Spanish to be sent south [to Latin America] to engage in speechmaking and activities. I was told the pope was thinking in terms of 11 million dollars a year support for the entire movement against communism in Spanish-speaking countries."....

The project was run from the Asian Speakers Bureau in New York with the Free Pacific Association, Inc., a front for Rev. Moon's Unification Church. A key figure in this papal concern over Leftist threats to the Vatican's greatest stronghold was the Rev. Felix A. Morlion, who was present at the original discussions.[4]

The 1968 conference of Latin American bishops in Medellin, Colombia, was something of a miracle. *Concejo Episcopal Latinoamericano* (CELAM) met to study and implement the principles promulgated by the Second Vatican Council (1962-1965). The result was astonishing for a faith-group traditionally aligned with the oligarchs.

The documents produced at the conference began with a declaration acknowledging the suffering of the poor: "The misery that besets large masses of human beings in all of our countries... expresses itself as injustice which cries to the heavens." Political reform was a "pre-requisite" for change to systems which "favor privileged groups." The Church must educate the people "for the purpose of bringing Christians to consider their participation in the political life of the nation as a matter of conscience." Drawing on the Vatican II document, *Constitution on the Church in the Modern World*, the group affirmed the right of bishops to take collective action independent of Rome, the necessity of cooperating with other religions, and that the "People of God" were not just the clergy and hierarchy. Medellin called for the establishment of small base communities so that the "downtrodden... might come to know their rights and how to make use of them." The Medellin documents became "a rallying cry for social reform in Latin America as well as a precedent for Catholic Churches in other developing regions."[5]

The CIA recognized liberation theology was a threat to US exploitation of the region's resources. As Archbishop Lorscheider pointed out, "Oppressive regimes are afraid of a conspiracy against the established order and we are questioning that established order."[6] Under orders from Director of Central Intelligence Richard Helms (1966-1973), the agency trained and financed police departments in the torture and murder of bishops, priests and nuns—some of them US citizens—who championed the cause of the poor while increasing financial support for the clergy and prelates it had routinely used as agents and informants.[7] The conservative hierarchs were able to conceal their funding through the Knights of Malta and Opus Dei financial networks. Schools, print shops and radio stations were shut down. They justified their actions as "fighting communism." The viciousness intensified when the "strategists of tension" lost support in Europe with the end of the Greek, Portuguese, and Spanish dictatorships and they redirected their resources to bolstering the neo-fascist-style governments in Latin America in the 1970s.[8]

CELAM met again in Bogota in 1976 to review the 1968 Medellin documents and continued to protest against oppression, especially the violation of human rights. The bishops' document from this conference noted:

> Many of these [violations] are accompanied by increased militarism. But even in those [countries] that are not governed by the military, there has been a failure to encourage a fair distribution of wealth or a lessening of the tremendous social and economic differences which were denounced at Medellin. While it is true that many of these evils are common to all mankind, there can be no doubt that they have been exacerbated in our continent because of its past and present economic dependence, political confusion and social injustice.

"It is no longer enough for a bishop to criticize," added Renato Poblete, a Chilean Jesuit who was the executive secretary of CELAM's Social Action Department. "There must be action, and that is why the bishops are rereading the Medellin documents—to push ahead."[9] Although the bishops feared that retaliation against their followers would be worse than that against themselves, unlike Pope Pius XII, they also knew that silence was not possible.

> "With all its current limitations, the Church is the only surviving institution in the military regimes that offers some hope of change. Its task is to reach the mass of the people in its evangelization and renewal programs," writes Fr. Brian Smith, S.J., since "awakening in them a sense of personal dignity, hope and confidence that they can change their fate will be crucial not only for the vitality and integrity of the Church as a gospel community, but also for the future shape of Latin American societies."[10]

Guided by the spirit of Medellin and Bogota, the Church was changing from the bottom up. However, the Protestant denominations were successfully using local leaders from the lower classes and they were able to respect and incorporate the peoples' own cultures into their evangelization and worship services. In contrast, Eurocentric Roman Catholicism historically had been unwilling to learn or adopt from the indigenous and African cultures or encourage vocations from the sub-classes. The CELAM Mission Department studied the best methods to communicate with the non-white majority and incorporate native, rather than foreign, spirituality. Programs to encourage priestly vocations were less successful. Latin Rite Catholicism requires an unmarried clergy and many indigenous societies view marriage as a prerequisite for a position of authority. Catholic lay persons, however, were trained as catechists and leaders in the base communities. More Catholic schools redirected their efforts to reducing illiteracy among the masses.[11]

Right-wing Retrenchment Under John Paul II

Where would the pope who was a firm advocate of human rights in Poland stand on liberation theology? It is important to note that the first of Wojtyla's 104 international trips was to Latin America—not the US or Poland.

Encouraged by the success of their sponsors in electing Karol Wojtyla, the "connected" hierarchs took back the upper hand. Colombian Cardinal Alfonso López Trujillo planned the next CELAM conference to be held in Puebla, Mexico, in 1979. López Trujillo had spent many years at an Opus Dei center for priests in Rome and was an ardent supporter.[12]

Asked about the Puebla conference in a 2004 interview, López Trujillo recalled that during his brief papacy John Paul I had shown great interest in the meeting. In his remarks, López Trujillo not only maintained the canard that Luciani was in poor health but he also confirmed Opus Dei's participation in the election of his successor:

> He [Pope John Paul I] was preparing his inaugural television message for the Conference....He had planned the recording in two parts, because—I found out afterwards—he wasn't used to speaking for long at a time....It was tiring for him to speak at length, because he had had lung problems.
>
> I was in Rome for the beginning of the pontificate of John Paul I and...I met Cardinal Wojtyla....He asked me questions about the Conference in Puebla....
>
> When the white smoke announced the election of Cardinal Wojtyla, I was near the obelisk in Saint Peter's Square. I was in the company of Father Cipriano Calderon [the priest ordered by Opus Dei to distribute Wojtyla's book], who *oddly enough* was carrying the collection of spiritual exercises preached by the Archbishop of Krakow to the Roman Curia.[13] (emphasis added)

In a working paper for the 1979 Puebla meeting, López Trujillo expressed support for the dictators: "These military regimes came into existence as a response to social and economic chaos. No society can admit a power vacuum. Faced with tensions and disorders, an appeal to force is inevitable." López Trujillo wrote to a colleague in the social action department at CELAM: "Prepare your bombers for Puebla" and "get into training just like boxers before entering the ring for a world match."[14]

The first exposition outside of Italy of John Paul II's ideology would come at Puebla. With the pope's strong defense of freedom and liberty for Poland, his sympathetic statements to those who suffered from political oppression in communist Eastern Europe, his declarations of compassion for the poor and his endorsement of the Second Vatican Council, supporters of liberation theology naively looked forward to the pope's attendance with great anticipation.

In his speech to the bishops, John Paul II first affirmed the Medellin documents and then gave an ominous warning of what was to come:

> This Third Conference...will therefore have to take as its point of departure the conclusions of Medellín...but without passing over the incorrect interpretations at times made and which call for calm discernment, opportune criticism and clear choices of position.

Referring to López Trujillo's work, he continued,

> In your debates you will find guidance in the working draft, which was drawn up with great care so that it might serve as a constant point of reference.

The pope chided liberals for neglecting their "religious" duties by seeking civil means to provide a decent life for others. He noted they gathered "not as a parliament of politicians" but rather as teachers "not of a human, rational truth but of the truth that comes from God." He warned them against "re-readings" of the Gospel which were the product of "theoretical speculations" because they sow "confusion." Moreover, it was against the Church's teachings to "depict Jesus as a political activist, as a fighter against Roman domination and the authorities, and even as someone involved in the class struggle."

John Paul II went into a lengthy discourse as to why he expected the assembled episcopate to be obedient to him including a reminder that in obeying the "sacred magisterium" (i.e. himself) they were "not accepting the word of human beings but the authentic word of God." The pope even acknowledged,

> In some instances an attitude of mistrust is fostered toward the "institutional" or "official" Church, which is described as alienating. Over against it is set another people's Church, one which is born of the people and is fleshed out in the poor. But let us face the fact: If the Gospel proclaimed by us seems to be rent by doctrinal disputes, ideological polarizations, or mutual condemnations among Christians...how can those to whom we address our preaching fail to be disturbed, disoriented, and even scandalized?"

Finally, the pope made it clear he expected bishops, priests and religious to be "docile and trusting."[15]

John Paul II's intellectual framework for the denunciation of liberation theology had been provided by the West German bishops who, even before Wojtyla's ascension, had been agitating against the "socialist" tendencies of the clergy in Latin America. They had been especially upset when some South American bishops, most notably Peruvian and Brazilian hierarchs, specifically denounced the greed of foreign capitalism. The German-Polish alliance in the Vatican claimed protests against military regimes and their multinational corporate allies were proof of Marxist tendencies, though the Latin Americans strove for no more than the same basic rights already enjoyed in West Germany and which were being sought with great fanfare for the Poles.[16]

The real concern among these prelates is that liberation theology threatens hierarchical control of the Catholic Church as much as it does civil dictatorships. To counter its influence, John Paul II et al responded by conjuring up the Bolshevist boogey-man. Similar to other neocon errors—i.e. repeated endlessly until it becomes "fact"—the mainstream media to this day routinely refers to liberation theology as "Marxist." This pejorative has been repeated so often for so long that no one questions the basic illogic in asserting that a theology founded on Gospel principles could rightly be described by an intensely atheistic ideology. Marx called religion the opiate of the people whereas liberation theology calls for a community alive with love and compassion, believing in both God and social justice. The excuse posited by Pius XII apologists—when the choice is between fascism and communism, fascism is the lesser of the two evils—was repeated by John Paul II supporters who claimed the choice was between military dictatorships and communism. The choice, however, for an institution which claims to be a politically neutral follower of Jesus Christ should be in favor of human rights—especially for the poor, marginalized and outcast—whatever the secular form of government or economic system.

John Paul II set out to eradicate liberation theology, punish its proponents, disband the base communities, and declare Latin America safe for foreign capital. As each prelate died, retired or was forced to retire, men loyal to the pope's political ideology were appointed to rule dioceses, seminaries, formation centers, schools and Church-controlled charities. In so doing, the pope not only deprived himself of independent and knowledgeable counsel, but struck at the already shaky moral foundation of his institution by installing men like himself who sought and received support from the rich and powerful.

The Neoconservatives Confront Liberation Theology

The Santa Fe Report, prepared for the war-mongering Council for Inter-American Security, was presented in 1980 to the Republican Platform Committee. It stated, "US foreign policy must begin to counter (not react against) liberation theology as it is utilized in Latin America by the 'liberation theology' clergy." To support this policy, the Institute on Religion & Democracy (IRD), an "ecumenical" organization, was established in 1981 with funding from the usual foundations: Scaife, Bradley and Olin. Its purpose was to counter not only liberation theology but also the peace and social reform positions of mainline Protestant religions—Presbyterian, United Methodist and Episcopal—as well as liberal Catholics in the US. The IRD was established under the direction of Catholics Michael Novak, Mary Ellen (Mrs. Robert) Bork, George Weigel and Rev. Richard J. Neuhaus, a Lutheran minister who would convert to Catholicism.[17] The institute's mission statement offered an alternative position against clergy who "have thrown themselves into multiple, often leftist crusades—radical forms of feminism, environmentalism, pacifism, multiculturalism, revolutionary socialism, sexual liberation, and so forth."

When the IRD wasn't criticizing the Protestant denominations for being soft on communism, it was charging that they were anti-Semitic and anti-Israeli. For its part, the IRD has long echoed the policies of the Likud Party militarists and right-wing Zionists. In addition to the Protestant denominations, the IRD considers the National Council of Churches (NCC) and its counterpart World Council of Churches to be instruments of liberalism and secularism.[18]

The IRD organized a propaganda drive against religious activists who led domestic opposition to US aid to the military regimes in Latin America. The IRD campaign was highly successful, even reaching the pages of the *Reader's Digest* from where it was picked up by *60 Minutes*. Novak's responsibility was maintaining this quasi-governmental religious organization's communications with the Vatican.[19]

John Paul II Tours Latin America

The following countries merited the particular attention of a papal visit. Politicians in many parts of the world seek "photo-ops" with Catholic prelates, hoping that their position as moral leaders of large segments of the population will somehow legitimize the politician and be viewed as an endorsement. The presence, however, of the "superstar" pope with his own international press corps was the greatest "seal of approval" a government could hope for. That Pope John Paul II would travel thousands of miles to any country amid all the pomp and circumstance of a papal visit was a feather in the cap of any world leader. Not coincidentally, the Latin American countries visited by John Paul II were also areas where dreadful human rights atrocities had occurred, were ongoing or were being planned for the future.

When reading about this period in Latin America, it is also important to remember that profits from narcotics trafficking constituted a major segment of Vatican Bank deposits and that cocaine production and dealing had become the lifeblood of organized crime in the Western Hemisphere. The epidemic of crack cocaine, a highly addictive form of the drug, began in the US in the 1970s, peaked in the mid-1980s, and was eventually replaced by heroin again in the 1990s.[20] As a result, crime in poor inner-city neighborhoods increased dramatically, reaching its worst between 1984 and 1990, decimating young African-American and Latino populations.[21]

Argentina

John Paul II made his first trip to Latin America after Puebla by visiting Argentina in 1982. The country had been one of the principle destinations for Nazi criminals escaping Europe via the Catholic "ratlines" and they had been welcomed by Juan Perón. Adolf Eichmann, who implemented the "Final Solution," is the most prominent example.

Perón went into exile in 1955 rather than face a possible coup but returned in 1973.

> Though many Argentines might not have understood the full picture in 1973, the reality was that Juan Perón had survived his 17-year exile in large part by becoming a political ward of Europe's neo-fascist elite. In the months ahead, Peron's patrons would use the frail leader as a cover for their infiltration of neo-fascist operatives and drug-tainted gangsters into South America....
>
> Joining him on the dais at the airport welcoming ceremony was a security detail including: Cuban-Americans from Alpha 66, gunmen from Italy's Ordine Nuovo, Croatian fascist Ustashi thugs and several Corsican gangsters who were involved in the infamous French Connection heroin ring.[22]

Pre-eminent among the "neo-fascist elite," Licio Gelli personally engineered Perón's election in 1974 which Perón acknowledged by kneeling at Gelli's feet. Perón appointed Gelli honorary Argentine consul in Florence and Gelli became one of his economic advisers.[23] It was the failures of the government formed by Peron's third wife and widow, Isabel, which precipitated the military takeover.

The 1976 junta which followed Peron brought about the bloodiest period in Argentine history.

> A carefully orchestrated campaign by conservative segments of the media, the support of the Argentine landowners and industrialists, and pressure from international financial circles created an image of the

generals as reasonable and honest men willing to shoulder the heavy burden of "saving" Argentina. Habeas corpus was undermined, censorship was extended to all spheres of life. The military, presenting itself as the defender of "tradition, family and property," considered any criticism of its rule as a sign of anti-Argentine, subversive behavior....

The internal enemy was [declared] more dangerous than enemies from abroad because it threatened the fundamental Western and Christian values of Argentine society.[24]

The junta assumed the posture as defender of the Church and the Catholic Bishops' Conference of Argentina (CEA) became their accomplices. In just one of the many accounts of Church complicity with the dictators,

Journalist Horacio Verbitsky recently published a book on the Catholic Church's involvement with the military dictatorship. In his book, *El Silencio* (*The Silence*), he reports that the Catholic Church actively participated in the 1976-1983 dictatorship while having full knowledge of the human rights violations being committed at the time. In the days leading up to the coup, representatives from the Catholic Church met with leaders of Argentina's armed forced and witnesses report they left each of these meetings smiling. On the eve of the March 24, 1976, coup, military leaders Jorge Videla and Ramón Agosti visited Archbishop Paraná Adolfo Tortolo and Monsignor Victorio Bonamín at the Catholic Church's Vicariato Castrense headquarters. A week later, Tortolo reported, "General Videla adheres to the principles and morals of Christian conduct. As a military leader he is first class, as a Catholic he is extraordinarily sincere and loyal to his faith." He also said that when confronting subversion, the military should take on "hard and violent measures."

However, it was during interviews in 1995 with former Marine captain Adolfo Scilingo in which he confessed to Verbitsky having led the "vuelos de muerte" or death flights, that Verbitsky realized the gravity of the Catholic Church's complicity with the military's human rights crimes. Scilingo, who was sentenced to 645 years in prison by a Spanish court, reported that the Catholic hierarchy approved drugging dissidents and dropping them from planes into the Atlantic Ocean during the "vuelos de muerte," as a Christian form of death. When Scilingo felt anguished after directing these death flights, he would seek counseling from military chaplains at the ESMA (Spanish acronym for the navy mechanics school), the largest clandestine detention center in Buenos Aires.[25]

During the junta's rule, the Catholic Church maintained secret lists of those who "disappeared." "Disappeared" refers to one of the many types of Nazi atrocities copied by Latin American dictators. In 1941, Hitler ordered the *Nacht und Nebel Erlass* (Night and Fog Decree) designed to make political enemies "vanish without a trace into the night and fog of the unknown." A victim who is murdered or publicly executed becomes a martyr and public opinion is galvanized against the perpetrators. But kidnapping plays on the hope that the victim may someday be found, causing the family to withhold public denunciation. Moreover, it is difficult to say what happened with certainty in the absence of physical evidence. The unknown creates its own terrors and takes a psychological toll on the victims' loved ones. "To presume the death of people you have not seen dead, without knowing the conditions of their death, implies that one has to kill them oneself. I believe that is one of the more subtle and complex mechanisms of torture for the relatives and for all the members of the community...To accept their deaths we have to kill them ourselves," Dr. Vicente Angel Galli, an Argentine psychiatrist, explained.[26]

One of the Catholic officials who had access to the lists of the disappeared was papal nuncio, Archbishop Pio Laghi, who visited the detention camps to bless the officers. "Laghi admitted giving communion to a general he knew to be involved in the massacre of five Irish Argentine priests and seminarians—this at the funeral Mass for the slain priests. In a speech given to the military in 1976 Laghi said, 'Christian values are threatened by an ideology [communism] that the people reject. The Church and the armed forces share responsibility. The former is an integral element in the process. It accompanies the latter, not only by its prayers but by its actions.'"[27]

The archbishop was particularly close to Admiral Emilio Eduardo Massera. They played tennis together almost every day. Massera was convicted in 1985 of human rights violations and again in 1999 for disappearances. He was also charged with abducting babies of women who went into labor or suffered involuntary caesarian births while in prison. Later, charges were also filed against Laghi in an Italian court, but he escaped prosecution on the basis of his diplomatic immunity.[28]

Shortly after Ronald Reagan won the 1980 election, the pontiff transferred Laghi to the Vatican's Washington DC nunciature (embassy).

John Paul II met with Reagan in Rome on June 7, 1982, then left for Argentina on June 10. During his visit, the pope refused to meet with human rights organizations and never referred to his Church's complicity in the barbarity.

The Argentines dominated the Latin American Anti-communist Confederation (CAL), the regional branch of the World Anti-Communist League. Its chairman, Argentine Suarez Mason, became one of Latin

America's chief drug traffickers. The drug connections between European right-wing terrorists and their Latin American protégés were arranged mostly by Licio Gelli. The September 1980 CAL conference approved the "Argentine solution" of death squads from Buenos Aires to Guatemala City to be financed in part through drug profits and in part, through the Banco Ambrosiano and Vatican Bank.[29]

Roberto Calvi and Gelli were in Buenos Aires when news of the death of John Paul I was broadcast in 1978. During their stay, financing was arranged for fifty Exocet missiles as requested by the Argentine navy.[30] Later, the missiles were used to sink two British ships during the Falklands/Malvinas war. The funds for the missiles had been passed from P2 through Bellatrix, one of the companies under Bishop Paul Marcinkus' control. In total, the Vatican Bank guaranteed loans worth millions to finance bogus Latin American companies which supplied arms to Argentina.[31]

The military junta, however, overestimated Reagan's support when they challenged Great Britain for control of the Falkland Islands. Reagan had no choice but to side with his ally, Prime Minister Margaret Thatcher, during the ensuing war in 1982. When the junta lost the war, humiliating their supporters, a civilian government was elected in 1983. During the junta's "Dirty War" against their own citizenry, an estimated 30,000 disappeared.

Nicaragua

John Paul II's third Latin American trip in March 1983 included stops in Nicaragua, Panama, El Salvador and Guatemala.

Nicaraqua had been ruled by the Somoza family dictatorship since 1933. Towards the end of the 1960s, a leftist rebel movement called the *Frente Sandinista de Liberación Nacional* (FSLN or Sandinistas) began a guerrilla campaign which finally overthrew Anastasio Somoza in 1979.

Before he left office, Anastasio Somoza played an important role in the Vatican Bank/Banco Ambrosiano Latin American activities. When the Bank of Italy began investigating Calvi in 1978, Calvi incorporated shell companies in Nicaragua at the invitation of Somoza and with his promise of secrecy. A year later when Somoza's position was threatened, Calvi moved his Nicaraguan operations to Peru under the aegis of "friendly" financiers.

A US-led coalition could not allow the Sandinista government to remain in power. The American Security Council created a film which summed up the ideological basis for war against Nicaragua. The film, titled "Tomorrow: Honduras...Venezuela, the Dominican Republic, Mexico...the United States," posited that the very survival of the US depended on driving the Sandinistas out.[32]

The flow of cocaine through Nicaragua to the US

was facilitated by a letter from CIA Director William J. Casey to Attorney General William French Smith less than two months after President Reagan authorized covert CIA support for the Nicaraguan Contras in mid-December 1981. Casey asked for an exemption for the CIA from a legal requirement to report on drug smuggling by agency assets and permission was granted by Smith in a February 11, 1982, letter. When Rep. Maxine Waters (D-Calif.) placed the letters into the Congressional Record in 1998, she stated that the Casey-Smith arrangement "allowed some of the biggest drug lords in the world to operate without fear that the CIA would be required to report their activities to the DEA and other law enforcement agencies.... These damning memorandums...are further evidence of a shocking official policy that allowed the drug cartels to operate through the CIA-led Contra covert operations in Central America."[33]

In October 1982, Reagan sent his roving ambassador, Gen. Vernon Walters, a Knight of Malta, to confer with John Paul II. While working for the CIA, Walters had been involved in some of its most notorious coups: Iran, 1953; Brazil, 1964; Chile, 1973. Walters helped set up CIA-backed Nicaraguan exile groups based in Honduras. The general advised the pope which of his priests were part of the Sandinista government.[34]

Five months later, John Paul II landed at the Managua airport. One of the dignitaries lined up to greet him was Fr. Ernesto Cardenal who held a ministerial post in the Sandinista government. In an incident captured on film, Cardenal bowed to kiss the pope's ring and Wojtyla shook his finger in the priest's face demanding the priest give up politics. Later the same day, at an open-air Mass, the pope was booed and jeered when he refused requests to pray for those who had died in Nicaragua's terrible civil war. Accustomed only to adulation, the pope shouted "Silencio!" three times.

[John Paul II] attacked the "people's church" as "absurd and dangerous," implying that the only role the Church had in Nicaragua was to oppose the Sandinistas. Such an outspoken repudiation of liberation theology...must have been well-received within the CIA.

The pope's condemnation of the Nicaraguan revolution coincided with a dramatic increase in border raids from Honduras by CIA-trained exile groups. But perhaps more damaging than the military actions was the psychological impact of the pope's refusing to pray for the souls of Nicaraguans killed by Somozistas, despite the pleadings of wives and mothers who wept openly before him. And insult was later added to injury when the pope did pray for six "suspected subversives" who had been executed by Guatemala's Protestant dictator Efrain Rios Montt....John Paul II had, in effect, given his blessing to the

CIA's campaign to destabilize the Sandinista government.[35]

The Archbishop of Managua (1970-2005), Miguel Obando y Bravo, was one of the leading critics of the Sandinista government and began cracking down on his liberal clergy for which he was rewarded in 1985 by being named the first cardinal from Central America. In a *Newsweek* article, Nicaraguan Msgr. Bismark Carballo, then living in exile, told reporters, "In Nicaragua, everyone receives money from outside. Obando's archdiocese openly took assistance from the US Agency for International Development in 1982, and when that was blocked he sought help from US Catholics and business executives."[36]

> The General Accounting Office, which was investigating the use of US humanitarian aid to the Contras [the US backed militia trying to overthrow the Sandinista government], unexpectedly found a signature card with Obando's name on it apparently linking the churchman to an account at BAC International, a Cayman Islands bank used by the [Central Intelligence] agency and the Contras....
> Sources say payments eventually went out through one of the many shell corporations that [Oliver] North and his colleagues set up to fund their various operations. North's cutouts, the sources say, funneled at least $125,000 to the Church through the Cayman account and banks in New York and Miami.[37]

Obando y Bravo was also funded by the Institute for Religion & Democracy (IRD).[38]

The cardinal was invited to Washington in January 1986 to ask Congress to provide more military aid for the Contras after the legislature had cut off funding the previous year.

After the Sandinistas lost the 1990 election, the Knights of Malta, particularly the chapter in Los Angeles, made huge donations to Nicaragua. SMOM members assisted in the delivery of three plane-loads of medical supplies from AmeriCares, a charity set up to aid only US allies, which arrived in Managua three days after the election. A charitable arm of the Knights of Malta, AmeriCares was founded in 1982 by J. Peter Grace, long-time president of the American Chapter of the Knights of Malta, chairman of W.R. Grace & Company, and chairman of the AmeriCares Advisory Committee until 1995. German SMOM members served as part of the ONUCA (Organizaciones Unidas de Centro America) peacekeeping force which watched the Nicaraguan borders to prevent Contra movements across the border with Honduras. Knight of Malta William Simon was chairman and Dame of Malta Clare Booth Luce was a member of the Nicaraguan Freedom

Fund (NFF), a fundraising organization set up in 1985 by Rev. Sun Myung Moon's *Washington Times* to raise funds for the Contras.[39]

Panama

John Paul II left Nicaragua and landed in Panama where Bishop Marcinkus and Roberto Calvi had set up dummy bank accounts to launder mob money and finance arms deals. Senator John Kerry's 1988 Subcommittee on Terrorism, Narcotics and International Operations concluded that,

> Throughout the 1970s and the 1980s....it is clear that each US government agency which had a relationship with [General Manuel Antonio] Noriega turned a blind eye to his corruption and drug dealing, even as he was emerging as a key player on behalf of the Medellin Cartel (a member of which was notorious Colombian drug lord Pablo Escobar).
>
> Noriega was allowed to establish "the hemisphere's first 'narcokleptocracy'".[40]

During the 1988 presidential debates, Gov. Michael Dukakis accused Vice President George H. W. Bush (a Washington tennis partner of Vatican nuncio Laghi[41]) of participating or "in some way being involved in the relationship between this government and Mr. Noriega and drug trafficking in Panama."[42]

The US had backed Noriega because he was sending arms to the Contras and El Salvador. Similarly, the Reagan administration also ignored drug smuggling by the Honduran military and the Contras.[43] Though the US was aware of Noriega's narcotics connection for two decades, his usefulness as a supplier of drugs and arms came to an end with defeat of the Sandinistas. The US government used his cocaine connections to indict him and Noriega refused to turn himself over to American authorities. Using the pretext of protecting US citizens threatened by Noriega and his supporters, President Bush ordered the invasion of Panama in December 1989. During the invasion, condemned by the Organization of American States and the United Nations General Assembly, to capture Noriega, the Pentagon reported at least 500 Panamanians, mostly civilians, and 24 Americans died. An Independent Commission of Inquiry on the US Invasion of Panama estimated Panamanian deaths at 1,000-4,000. More than 3,000 were wounded and thousands were left homeless.

Due to the strategic importance of the Panama Canal, 45 countries maintain an embassy or consulate in Panama City including Noriega's drug partners, Colombia and Nicaragua. Yet the only foreign government with which Noriega felt confident enough to seek refuge was the Holy See and he hid in the Vatican's Panama City mission expecting to be granted political asylum. Cardinal Angelo Sodano, John Paul II's second secretary of state, working behind the scenes with Bush, helped secure the surrender of Noriega to US forces on January 3, 1990.[44]

El Salvador

John Paul's next stop through Central America to support Reagan-backed military dictators was El Salvador. "In 1981, only weeks into the first term of Ronald Reagan, Secretary of State Alexander Haig assured Reagan that El Salvador is 'one we can win.'"[45] During the ensuing twelve-year civil war, in a country of only 5.5 million people, more than 75,000 Salvadorans were killed, one million fled the country, and another million were left homeless as they were forced into hiding.

Liberation theology had taken root in the lower echelons of El Salvador's Church causing right-wing assassins to encourage their countrymen to "Be a patriot: kill a priest." People found possessing a Bible or hymnal were shot or dismembered. The murders of several liberal churchmen and women are well-known to American Catholics. "The Christian base communities are the greatest threat to military dictatorships throughout Latin America," said Maryknoll Sister Ita Ford three weeks before she, two other American nuns and Jean Donovan, a lay missionary worker, were brutally raped and murdered by the Salvadoran National Guard on December 2, 1980.[46] Fr. Ignatio Ellacuría S.J. declared, "The struggle against injustice and the pursuit of truth cannot be separated nor can one work for one independent of the other," before he was gunned down along with five other Jesuits, their housekeeper and her daughter in November 1989 at the University of Central America in San Salvador. The Jesuits' brains were ripped out of their heads.

Latin America's most famous martyr is Archbishop Óscar Arnulfo Romero y Galdámez, the subject of a 1989 movie starring Raul Julia. Born as a member of the ruling class, he was chosen to be archbishop for his conservative beliefs and with the government's approval. Romero had a deep conversion experience when his good friend, Fr. Rutilio Grande S.J., was gunned down by government soldiers. "When I looked at Rutilio lying there dead I thought 'if they have killed him for doing what he did, then I too have to walk the same path,'" Romero later told the press. The archbishop became a fearless champion for the poor. "It is so striking that in his teachings Jesus had the poor in mind in a preferential way. In two of his speeches, the Sermon on the Mount and at Nazareth, he refers to the poor and to those who suffer," Romero said.[47] He railed against the government's murder and torture.

Romero attracted international attention.

> In 1978, the International Federation of Human Rights arrived in El Salvador, drawn by Monsenor Romero's denunciations. The Inter-American Commission of Human

Rights visited El Salvador in 1979, attracted by the voice of Monsenor Romero. Amnesty International chose El Salvador as the destination for its first large-scale mission to Central America because of Monsenor Romero. From Geneva the International Commission of Jurists, dedicated to promoting the rule of law and justice throughout the world, visited El Salvador to listen to the archbishop. A congressional delegation from the United States made its first investigation of human rights violations, motivated by the courageous words proclaimed each Sunday by Monsenor Romero from the Cathedral. Also, from Geneva, the Protestant Churches and other Christian denominations united in the World Council of Churches encouraged its Commission for International Concerns to accompany Archbishop Romero in his work. Shortly before his assassination, the British Parliament presented Monsenor Romero as its nominee for the Nobel Peace Prize.[48]

In a famous letter to Jimmy Carter, Romero wrote, "You say that you are Christian. If you are really Christian, please stop sending military aid to the military here, because they use it only to kill my people."

John Paul II twice sent delegations to Romero to pressure him to stop criticizing the government. When Romero went to Rome to plead with the pontiff to denounce the slaughter, he was left waiting for three days before being given a brief audience and a papal deaf ear. Salvadorans were being killed at the rate of 3,000 per month in 1980, the year of Romero's assassination.[49]

The archbishop was shot through the heart while saying Mass and his funeral, attended by over a quarter of a million people, was the largest public demonstration to date in Central America. The funeral was disrupted by a bomb-blast and shots fired from rooftops into the crowd. A 1993 UN Truth Commission report stated Romero was murdered by a right-wing death squad, two of its members being graduates of the School of the Americas, and masterminded by Roberto D'Aubuisson, founder of the Nationalist Republican Alliance (ARENA) Party.

Gerald Coughlin, a US citizen who married into a wealthy Salvadoran family, was the director of the Salvadoran Knights of Malta. Coughlin administered SMOM from the International Harvester building in San Salvador which doubled as the main SMOM warehouse in the country. SMOM and the US-based Family Foundation of America received a US Agency for International Development (USAID) grant to carry out rehabilitation programs in the Suchitoto area which had been selected by the military for a pilot repopulation effort. The government built "model villages" to replace those destroyed by the death-squads. Like the "strategic hamlets" in Vietnam, these villages were designed to control and pacify the local population. People in areas which supported the leftist guerillas were left without food, water and medical supplies. SMOM in El Salvador also received aid from its branches in France, Rome, and Venezuela.[50]

The *Washington Post* dated December 27, 1984 reported as follows:

> A private humanitarian organization called the AmeriCares Foundation, working with the Order of the Knights of Malta, has channeled more than $14 million in donated medical aid to El Salvador, Honduras and Guatemala over the last two years....
>
> Part of $680,000 in aid to Honduras went to Miskito Indians linked to US backed rebels fighting the leftist government in Nicaragua, according to a Knights of Malta official in Honduras. Much of the $3.4 million in AmeriCares' medical aid to Guatemala has been distributed through the armed forces as part of its resettlement program of "model villages" aimed at defeating leftist insurgents, said the official, Guatemalan businessman Roberto Alejos, co-chairman of the Knights of Malta in Honduras[51]

Alejos, owner of the sugar plantation where the counterrevolutionaries for the Bay of Pigs invasion were trained, was also head of the SMOM in Guatemala and the principal organizer of Guatemala's "Reagan for President" campaign.

The Knights of Malta benefited from free transport of their supplies. Retired General H. C. Aderholt, head of the 1,500-member Air Commando Association of Fort Walton Beach, Florida, delivered food and medicine to SMOM in El Salvador. Aderholt said his association also distributed $4.5 million in food and medicine to El Salvador provided by Pat Robertson's Christian Broadcasting Network and World Medical Relief. He said liberals in Congress had tried to tie his efforts "to some sinister plan with the CIA," which he said is incorrect.[52]

Archbishop Fernando Saenz Lacalle, brigadier general in the Salvadoran army and founder of Opus Dei in El Salvador, reigned until his death in 2008 from the restored Metropolitan Cathedral where the slain Romero preached for justice. He was elevated to archbishop by John Paul II in 1995 with the approval and praise of the ARENA ruling party and support from the US.[53] Sixteen years after the war, "conditions in El Salvador are as tenuous and as volatile as ever. This time, it is not open warfare but the slow agony of inequality, poverty and political repression."[54]

For decades, worldwide demand that Romero be declared a saint was ignored by the Vatican. Public pressure finally resulted in an opening of his case for beatification, but nothing further has been done.

Guatemala

The final leg of Wojtyla's 1983 tour was to Guatemala.

As was typical of the region, a little over two percent of the Guatemalan population owned 70 percent of the land and only a third of what was left was available for use by the other 98 percent. In this small country, American-owned United Fruit Company (UFCO) acted as an autonomous state within a state. The company controlled the utilities and rail systems, administered the country's only Atlantic port and monopolized most of the economy becoming the prototype of a "banana republic." When Colonel Jacobo Arbenz Guzman was elected president in 1951, he had begun a program of land reform, improved workers' rights and tried to break the United Fruit monopoly. The resultant US-CIA intervention plunged the country into chaos and kicked off decades of political turbulence not only in Guatemala but all of Central America. A succession of tyrants and brutal suppression followed until 1996.

The duration and brutality of the Guatemalan war shocked the world community. Guatemalan dictators were the first to use militia-controlled death squads which became so much a part of Latin American history. They were products of the CIA-military intelligence system and many members were graduates of the School of the Americas in Fort Benning, Georgia. "US-backed military regimes wiped out entire villages of Mayan Indians suspected of aiding the rebels, the survivors fleeing deeper into the mountains or neighboring Mexico. Death squads swooped down on students, union leaders and political dissidents whose mutilated bodies turned up in ditches or were never seen again." Recently declassified CIA documents prove this was known at the highest levels of the US government. "Murder, torture and mutilation are all right if our side is doing it and the victims are communists; I have literally heard these arguments from our people," Viron P. Vaky, the US Embassy's deputy chief of mission in Guatemala, wrote in a March 1968 memo to Washington.[55]

A United Nations-sponsored peace treaty was signed in December 1996. As part of the peace process, the UN had established a Commission for Historical Clarification (CEH) in June 1994 to record events of the "fratricidal war." In 1999, the commission stated that—in a country smaller than Tennessee—over 200,000 Guatemalans had been killed or "disappeared."

The CEH concluded the US-backed government and paramilitary groups "were responsible for 93 percent of the documented violations, including 92 percent of the arbitrary executions and 91 percent of forced disappearances." The report also noted the CIA's direct military support and training for Guatemalan army officials in tactics "committed with particular cruelty, with massacres representing their archetypal form." The report continued:

> In the majority of massacres there is evidence of multiple acts of savagery, which preceded, accompanied or occurred after the deaths of the victims. Acts such as the killing of defenseless children, often by beating them

against walls or throwing them alive into pits where the corpses of adults were later thrown; the amputation of limbs; the impaling of victims; the killing of persons by covering them in petrol and burning them alive; the extraction, in the presence of others, of the viscera of victims who were still alive; the confinement of people who had been mortally tortured, in agony, for days; the opening of the wombs of pregnant women and other similarly atrocious acts, were not only actions of extreme cruelty against the victims but also morally degraded the perpetrators and those who inspired, ordered or tolerated these actions.

According to the CEH report, the Catholic Church was in step with the US and their puppet tyrants, labeling anyone who challenged its authority as communists, though this changed somewhat after the 1968 Medellin Conference which led to some Guatemalan bishops announcing the Church would use its resources to help the poor.

However, Opus Dei, established in Guatemala in 1953 while the CIA was planning its initial coup, was still the dominant ecclesial faction. It maintained control of the Archdiocese of Guatemala City, the wealthiest and most influential of the country's fourteen dioceses.[56] Opus Dei differed from US policy only when it came to support of José Efrain Rios Montt, who was also pastor and member of the Council of Elders of the Church of the Word, an evangelical religion based in California. Ríos Montt (1982-83), lauded by Reagan as "totally dedicated to democracy" and trained at the School of the Americas, was especially close to the Reagan administration and was responsible for the worst atrocities of the war.[57] Resentful of the inroads being made by US evangelicals in the region, Opus Dei helped Oscar Mejia Victores defeat Rios Montt by coup.

Mejia Victores instituted even more oppressive economic measures creating another crisis. In November 1985, about 150 relatives of missing persons took over the Metropolitan Cathedral in Guatemala City. The papal nuncio and Christian Democratic Party candidate agreed to mediate, bringing to a close only the worst chapter of the civil war.[58]

As part of the reconstruction effort, AmeriCares shipped medicines and other goods concentrating their efforts in Guatemala's "model village". Alejos and other SMOM members provided AmeriCares with office space, transportation and storage facilities.[59]

While the UN truth commission agreed not to name names or provide evidence for criminal trials, a report titled "Nunca Mas" (Never Again), researched and prepared by Catholic clergy documenting crimes against humanity, specifically named over 1,000 individuals and military members responsible for the carnage. It was released on April 26, 1998, and Juan José Gerardi Conedera, Bishop Emeritus of Santa Cruz del Quiché, was bludgeoned to death in his garage just two days after he had presented the report to the public.

Fr. Mario Orantes, Gerardi's assistant who lived in the rectory with him, was initially charged with the crime. When human rights groups complained that Orantes' arrest was a smokescreen for the military's involvement, Orantes was released. Eventually two army officers, one being a graduate of the School of the Americas, were also accused in Gerardi's murder, but the re-arrest of Orantes in April 2000 suggested prosecutors were turning their attention back to suspects within the Catholic Church. Nine years after Geradi's death, the conviction of the two officers and the priest is still under appeal and no further arrests were made.[60]

As a repudiation of Bishop Emeritus Gerardi and the others who suffered unspeakable crimes in their efforts to expose and document crimes against humanity, Guatemala City's Archbishop Prospero Penados del Barrio brought a "cause of sainthood" to the Vatican in 2000 for a wealthy physician and Opus Dei supernumerary who died of cancer at age ninety-two. The archbishop requested the doctor be canonized based on a life of personal sanctity and for establishing the Pediatric Association of Guatemala.

CHAPTER 7

MAKING MOVIE ACTOR REAGAN "GOD'S MAN"

The 1980 Presidential Campaign

In 1980, Ronald Reagan would be running against an incumbent president who was also a Baptist Sunday School teacher. Fundamentalist and evangelical Christians may have objected to some of Carter's policies, but he still had the advantage, more or less, of being one of their own. As would be repeated in 2004 when George W. Bush was made to appear more "Catholic" than John F. Kerry, Ronald Reagan was to become more "Christian" than Jimmy Carter.

To show that the religious right was ready to hit the ground running in getting Reagan elected, Edward E. McAteer, a former sales manager for Colgate-Palmolive who left the company in 1976 to devote himself to neoconservative causes full time, formed the Religious Roundtable in 1979 to bring religious and political leaders together.[1] Pastor Jerry Falwell was an early board member and leading participant in their events. The National Affairs Briefing held in Dallas in the summer of 1980 and sponsored by the Religious Roundtable is considered a watershed of American politics. The star attraction was the appearance of Reagan who was introduced by a Southern Baptist pastor as "God's man." Reagan told the gathering of conservative Christian leaders, "I know you can't endorse me, but I endorse you."[2] Other speakers at the seminar included Senators Jesse Helms (R- N.C.) and William Armstrong (R-Colo.), former Texas governor John Connally, Phyllis Schlafly, head of the Eagle Forum credited with blocking passage of the Equal Rights Amendment and evangelists James Robison and Pat Robertson.

The Roundtable, the National Conservative Political Action Committee, The Conservative Caucus and the Moral Majority* were hugely successful. Fundamentalist and evangelical Protestants who were previously unengaged in civic activism were instructed how to wield political power. By demonizing Democrats, social conservatives were energized to vote in record numbers, now convinced they were saving their families and communities from those who wanted to destroy them. They opposed legal abortion, the Equal Rights Amendment, equal rights for homosexuals, and sex education in the schools but supported a strong national defense, were staunchly anti-communist and fought for "free enterprise" unfettered by government regulation.

(*The term "Moral Majority" collectively included the tax-exempt Moral Majority Foundation which educated voters; the Moral Majority Political Action Committee which raised money for candidates; Moral Majority Inc., the lobbying group for influencing legislation; and the Moral Majority Legal Defense Foundation, established to counter the American Civil Liberties Union.)

They, especially the Moral Majority, took credit for Reagan's election in 1980.

Foreign Backers

In 1974, Reagan declined a third term as California governor so his team could devote its energies to winning the presidency. Reagan lost the 1976 nomination to Gerald Ford, but this was just a practice run for the 1980 campaign because in 1976, Americans were appalled by the corruption of the Nixon administration and the Democrats were expected to win.

When Reagan made the announcement he would not run again for governor, Michael Deaver, one of Reagan's earliest and most valued staff members, formed a public relations firm with a fellow employee from the governor's office, Peter Hannaford, to advance Reagan's national candidacy. Deaver and Hannaford arranged Reagan's public appearances, marketed his radio program and oftentimes wrote his syndicated column. Their office became Reagan's de facto presidential campaign headquarters and a recipient of funding from the Taiwanese-founded World Anti-Communist League.

In 1977, Deaver and Hannaford registered with the Justice Department as agents for Taiwan. When Jimmy Carter normalized relations with the People's Republic of China in 1978, Reagan became his loudest critic. Reagan hinted that if elected president he would restore recognition to Taiwan. He also promised to sell Taiwan weapons, regardless of China's opposition.[3]

Representatives from Argentina and Guatemala also helped pay the Deaver and Hannaford firm's expenses.[4] While Carter objected to the abuses by the Argentine junta, "in one radio commentary, former California Gov. Reagan chastised Assistant Secretary of State Pat Darien for her human-rights protests, saying she should 'walk a mile in the moccasins' of the Argentine generals before criticizing them."[5] As regards the junta, Reagan admitted "that in the process of bringing stability to a terrorized nation of 25 million, a small number were caught in the cross-fire, amongst them a few innocents."[6]

Eventually all three countries officially hired Deaver as their Washington lobbyist.

Neoconservative propagandist Michael Ledeen had worked in Italy during the 1970s as a journalist for the CIA-financed Italian newspaper, *Il*

Giornale Nuovo, producing anti-communist propaganda. In 1980 he collaborated in "war games" with Francesco Pazienza, an agent of Italy's secret service (SISMI) and member of P2. When Pazienza was found guilty in 1985 in an Italian criminal court of political manipulation and protecting terrorists, court documents identified Ledeen as a paid SISMI agent during the same time he was being paid by the US government. During the 1980 presidential campaign, Pazienza leaked the damaging story about Billy Carter's Libyan ties to Ledeen, and Ledeen wrote the story for *The New Republic*.[7]

Other P2 members also helped Reagan's campaign. In April 1980, Licio Gelli wrote to Phillip Guarino, a senior member of the Republican National Committee, "If you think it might be useful for something favorable to your presidential candidate to be published in Italy, send me some material and I'll get it published in one of the papers here." Favorable comments about Reagan, placed by Gelli, appeared in publications owned by P2 members including the Vatican-controlled Rizzoli newspapers. Rizzoli was a massive publishing group with multinational holdings. Among their many magazines and newspapers was *Corriere della Sera*, Italy's most prestigious newspaper. "Other P2 members were planted throughout the television, radio, and newspaper media." In January 1981, Gelli was an honored guest at Reagan's inauguration. Guarino later observed, "He had a better seat than I did."[8]

The Iran Hostage Crisis

For all of Deaver's expertise in running the campaign, when Reagan lost the 1980 Iowa caucus, William J. Casey was appointed as campaign director. A Knight of Malta, Casey had worked for the OSS in Germany. After the war, he became well-known as a Wall Street attorney writing how-to guides on accounting and taxes. He reportedly coined the term "tax-shelter."[9] He made his own fortune as a venture capitalist, sometimes being sued for his questionable methods. He lost a 1966 race for Congress but continued to contribute heavily to other Republican candidates. Nixon rewarded him in 1971 by nominating him for chairman of the Securities and Exchange Commission where he avoided prosecution by "following the letter, if not the spirit, of the law." Beginning in 1974, he headed the Export-Import Bank for two years. Casey also supported various "charities" such as AmeriCares and the International Rescue Committee (IRC). The IRC was funded by foundations sponsored by AT&T, Mobil, Shell Oil and Proctor and Gamble, as well as the usual groups such as the Olin and Smith Richardson Foundations.[10]

The incident which most damaged Carter's chances for re-election was the Iran Hostage Crisis. A group of radicals, angry over US attempts to undermine the Iranian Revolution which had overthrown the US-sponsored Shah of Iran, took over the United States Embassy in Tehran on November 4, 1979, and 52 Americans were held as hostages. The longer the crisis continued without the safe release of the hostages, the more Carter was perceived as ineffective.

Gary Sick, Adjunct Professor of Middle East Politics at Columbia University, and Iran Specialist for the National Security Council in the Ford, Carter, and Reagan administrations, wrote a history of the Iran Hostage Crisis which appeared in the April 15, 1991, *New York Times*. According to Sick, in late February or early March 1980, Casey was contacted by Iranian agents and they met without the knowledge of the Carter administration. Carter had insisted on maintaining a total arms embargo with Iran and the agents made it clear to Casey the hostages would be released in return for promises of arms from a Reagan administration.

During further negotiations which directly undermined US foreign policy, Casey promised that the Reagan administration, once in office, would not only return Iran's US assets which Carter had frozen after the embassy takeover but also help them acquire badly needed military equipment and spare parts. The Reagan campaign gained an agreement from the Israeli government to make the clandestine arms deliveries to Iran. (Israel was agreeable to dealing with Reagan surrogates because Israel objected to Carter's dialogue with the Palestinians.) When the Iraqi's invaded Iran on September 22, 1980, Iran also approached the Carter administration with a guns-for-hostages trade. In their desperation, they were playing both Carter and Reagan for release of the hostages, but Carter refused to lift the embargo. US intelligence officers, unhappy with Carter's housecleaning of the post-Watergate CIA, were keeping the Reagan team informed of Iranian contacts with the White House as well as Carter's clandestine attempt to rescue the hostages which failed.

The Reagan-Bush campaign leaked information to the media that Carter was planning to obtain release of the hostages by providing arms to Iran to bolster his prospects for re-election. Not only did the publicity damage Carter's chances of negotiating in good faith with the Iranians, but the president's reputation was damaged for purportedly "dealing" with the enemy in contradiction of his own embargo.

During the third week of October, a series of meetings were held in Paris hotels with Casey, George H. W. Bush, Reagan's running mate and former CIA director, and high-level Iranians and Israelis to work out the details. The US team persuaded Ayatollah Ruhollah Khomeini not to release the American hostages until Reagan was sworn in. Once president, Reagan would have Israel deliver the military arms and spare parts which Carter had denied Khomeini. Between October 21 and October 23, Israel sent a planeload of F-4 fighter aircraft tires to Iran as a sign of good faith. On October 22, the hostages were separated and moved to different locations to make sure any further rescue attempts would fail. On January 15, 1981, Iran contacted Carter and a final agreement was reached. The hostages were released on January 21, 1981, minutes after Ronald Reagan was sworn in as president.

Within days of the inauguration, Israel began delivering substantial quantities of arms to Iran.

When shown the evidence that his life was endangered and his freedom delayed in the cause of election politics, one former hostage told Sick, "I don't want to believe it. It's too painful to think about it."[11]

Michael Deaver later told the *New York Times*: "One of the things we had concluded early on was that a Reagan victory would be nearly impossible if the hostages were released before the election.... There is no doubt in my mind that the euphoria of a hostage release would have rolled over the land like a tidal wave. Carter would have been a hero, and many of the complaints against him forgotten. He would have won."[12]

Infesting the Reagan Administration

Deaver was appointed as Deputy White House Chief of Staff under James Baker III. Within a short time, Deaver's clients—Argentina, Guatemala, and Taiwan—received the attention they had paid for. Reagan asked Congress to lift the embargo on arms sales to Argentina. Reagan had more difficulty persuading Congress to provide arms to Guatemala. During a May 4, 1981, session of the Senate Foreign Relations Committee, it was announced that the Guatemalan death squads had murdered 76 leaders of the moderate Christian Democratic Party including its leader. As pointed out by Peter Dale Scott in *The Iran-Contra Connection*: "When Congress balked at certifying that Guatemala was not violating human rights, the administration acted unilaterally by simply taking the items Guatemala wanted off the restricted list." Reagan also aided Guatemala by arranging the training of its officers in torture and repression.

Taiwan benefited when, despite Vice President Bush's promise to China in August 1982 that the US would reduce its weapons sales to Taiwan, arms sales to Taiwan increased to $530 million in 1983 and over a billion dollars in 1984.[13]

Deaver left the White House in 1985 to become an independent lobbyist and was convicted of perjury in 1987 based on testimony he gave to a congressional subcommittee and a federal grand jury investigating his lobbying activities.

In 1980 the *Heritage Foundation* published a 3000-page, 20-volume set of policy recommendations, *Mandate for Leadership*, which was presented to Attorney General Ed Meese a week after Reagan's election. Meese was quoted as saying that "the Reagan Administration will rely heavily on the Heritage Foundation." These recommendations included: rollback of minority programs, dramatic increase in military spending, and cutting taxes. In 1985 Heritage claimed that the Reagan administration's policy reflected 60 to 65 percent of HF's policy measures.

In 1984, *Heritage* published "Mandate for Leadership II," which recommended privatization of social security and denial of special educational funding for the handicapped.[14]

Reagan's "kitchen cabinet" of Heritage Foundation backers was headed by Joseph Coors and actually had office space in the Executive Office Building. "Embarrassed by the image of a covey of millionaires seeming to run parallel and sometimes conflicting personnel recruitment operations, senior White House staff produced legal opinions saying that it was illegal for a private group to occupy government property, in this case a White House office."[15]

The budding religious right was consolidating its power. The secretive Council for National Policy was formed in 1981 by Tim LaHaye, author of the "Left-Behind" series, with funding from Texas billionaires Nelson Bunker Hunt, Herbert Hunt, and T. Cullen Davis. CNP's roots reached into a community of connected activists who advocated for the imposition of Christian Nationalism. CNP's board and members list included Paul Weyrich, Edwin Feulner, and Holly Coors.[16] Among those who attended the group's first meeting in May 1981 were Richard Viguerie and Howard Phillips.[17]

The agenda of a meeting in Colorado Springs in 1982 listed Viguerie and fellow Catholics Terry Dolan, Pat Buchanan, Phyllis Schafley, Jeane Kirkpatrick (US Ambassador to the UN) and Frank Shakespeare—Knight of Malta, former president of CBS Television, director of the United States Information Agency, director of Radio Free Europe, vice president of Westinghouse, vice chairman of RKO General and member of the board of trustees for the Heritage Foundation—as speakers. Maj. Gen. John Singlaub ret. (a WACL operative on special operations in El Salvador at the time), Philip Trulock of the Heritage Foundation, and Joseph Coors were also listed as members of the Council. Other early supporters of the CNP included Fr. Charles C. Fiore, chairman of the National Pro-Life PAC, Knights of Malta J. Peter Grace and Lewis Lehrman, Howard Phillips and Lt. Col. Oliver North. As of 2006, Weyrich was still listed as CNP Secretary-Treasurer.[18]

Right through to the 2008 election cycle, this group—referred to as "the real leaders of the Republican Party"—has "met behind closed doors at undisclosed locations for confidential conferences to strategize about how to turn the country to the right. Details are closely guarded." Rules for attendees include, "The media should not know when or where we meet or who takes part in our programs, before or after a meeting." The membership is "strictly confidential." Guests may attend "only with the unanimous approval of the executive committee." In e-mail messages to one another, members are instructed not to refer to the organization by name, "to protect against leaks."[19]

Deploying the Papacy Against the USSR

The US had maintained consular relations with the Papal States from 1797 to 1870 and diplomatic relations with the pope in his capacity as head of the Papal States from 1848 to 1868, though not at the ambassadorial level.

The association was not without its difficulties. In 1848, Secretary of State Buchanan instructed the first chargé d'affaires in Rome to "carefully avoid even the appearance of interfering in ecclesiastical questions, whether these relate to the United States or any other portion of the world."[20] When the frigate, the USS Constitution, was at harbor in Gaeta in 1849, the ship's captain allowed Pope Pius IX, who was fleeing from the republican army which had captured Rome, to come aboard for three hours. The captain was later court-martialed.[21] Official ties lapsed with the loss of all papal territories in 1870.

President Franklin D. Roosevelt sent Myron C. Taylor as his personal representative to the Holy See in 1939. Taylor served until 1950. Roosevelt had the support of two American cardinals from different ends of the political spectrum. Chicago's Cardinal George Mundelein supported the New Deal and its call for social action. When Mundelein died, Taylor, under orders from Roosevelt asked Vatican Secretary of State Cardinal Luigi Maglione to consider Bishop Bernard Sheil, another social liberal, as Mundelein's replacement. His request was denied.[22]

New York's Cardinal Francis Spellman, the most powerful cleric in US history, maintained control of the US Catholic war effort during World War II. He was named head of the US military chaplains and was deeply involved in post-war measures against the Soviets. Spellman was also instrumental in the selection of South Vietnamese president and devout Catholic, Ngo Dinh Diem.

Each president following Roosevelt sent a representative to the Vatican. John F. Kennedy, the only Catholic president, reduced US relations with the Holy See to a minimum for which he was criticized in "quite undiplomatic" terms by the Vatican official closest to the US Embassy in Rome.[23]

Popes John XXIII and Paul VI favored détente with the Soviet Union, meaning the arms race was frozen and the Cold War remained as status quo. While the Carter administration was generally in sync with Vatican geo-politics before Karol Wojtyla's election, Carter's national security advisor, Zbigniew Brzezinski, took a more hawkish stance than other Democrats. While Carter was sincere in his interest in promoting human rights, Brezezinski saw their utility in advocating more of an interventionist role for the US in Eastern Europe, the Balkans and Afghanistan. Brzezinski, born in Poland, was interviewed after the death of John Paul II. He said he met the pope when Wojtyla was lecturing at Harvard in 1976. The two corresponded regularly after that. According to authors Carl Bernstein and Marco Politi, Brzezinski phoned the pontiff in 1980 to warn that the Soviets were preparing to invade Poland. John Paul II instructed the bishops in Western Europe to ask their governments to threaten the Soviets with isolation if they carried out their plan and the Soviets backed off.[24]

The Poles were euphoric when Karol Wojtyla was elected pope in 1978. When he traveled to Poland in 1979, he was received by immense and jubilant crowds. Wojtyla's presence acted as a catalyst in strengthening open opposition to the communist regime and the Solidarity movement flourished. When Lech Walesa signed the agreement with the Polish government legalizing Solidarity in 1980, it was with a souvenir pen from the pope's visit. The anxious Soviets were sure John Paul II had been elected through a plot hatched by Brzezinski since the statesman planned on undermining USSR control in the region by emphasizing human rights.[25]

The Soviets were also apprehensive about the huge amounts being raised for Solidarity especially from Polish and other Eastern European émigré communities around Detroit and Chicago. The Polish-American Cardinal Krol, the US prelate closest to the pope, spearheaded the effort to funnel dollars to Solidarity similar to the massive funding directed by Cardinal Spellman against the communists in the post-World War II era. The Knights of Columbus and other US Catholic organizations did what they could to ensure the defeat of the Soviet Union, support a restoration of the Church's pre-eminent position in a post-Soviet Eastern Europe, as well as provide aid to Latin American militias preventing any Soviet encroachment in the Western Hemisphere.

Fr. Konrad Hejmo, later identified as a Soviet informant, was called to Rome in 1979 to operate a Vatican news service ostensibly designed to evade Polish government censors. Within five years he would be asked to salvage conduits for secret funding to Solidarity which had closed when the Vatican Bank/Banco Ambrosiano consortium collapsed. "Envelopes of cash had come from big-time crooks, and Hejmo's orders were to clean it up, then hush it up."[26]

After Casey was named head of the CIA, the agency employed undercover operatives to lobby members of the Curia and spy on Vatican staff remaining from the previous pontiffs "who challenged the political assumptions of the US."[27] In addition, private and charitable organizations continually fed information to the Vatican from around the world at the same time American intelligence officials in Rome were providing their appraisals of people and events to the Vatican. This flow of information only increased when the US established full diplomatic relations with the Vatican in 1984. The extent to which American agencies and personnel provided intelligence to John Paul II and vice versa can only be guessed, but a later ambassador to the Vatican was convinced the CIA even supplied the Curia with background data on other members of the international diplomatic corps assigned to the Vatican.[28]

Within a month of Reagan's election, Archbishop (later Cardinal) Pio Laghi was assigned to Washington DC directly from his service in Buenos Aires. Described as a "charming if ambitious career diplomat... conservative because he is ambitious for his career," Laghi was mentioned as a candidate for Vatican Secretary of State.[29] The US had used Argentina as a training ground for right-wing militias and the archbishop had also served in Managua in the 1950s, so Laghi already had high level contacts in the Reagan administration.

In Washington, a close relationship developed between Laghi, Casey and fellow Knight of Malta Judge William Clark, Reagan's National Security Advisor and one of his earliest California supporters. Clark was referred to as Reagan's "closest spiritual partner."[30] "'Casey and I dropped into his [Laghi's] residence early mornings during critical times to gather his comments and counsel,' said Clark....On at least six occasions Laghi came to the White House and met with Clark or the president; each time, he entered the White House through the southwest gate in order to avoid reporters."[31]

On March 30, 1981, Ronald Reagan almost died after an assassination attempt by John Hinckley, a mentally-unbalanced loner. On May 13, 1981, John Paul II almost died after an assassination attempt by Mehmet Ali Ağca, a member of a right-wing Turkish group known as the Grey Wolves. When Reagan traveled to Rome to meet with John Paul II in June 1982, the two talked alone in the Vatican Library about the assassination attempts. Reagan said he told the pope: "Look how the evil forces were put in our way and how Providence intervened." The two men confided in one another they believed God had spared their lives for a special mission which they interpreted as the defeat of communism.[32]

While Wojtyla and Reagan met in private, P2 members Vatican Secretary of State Cardinal Agostino Casaroli and Archbishop Achille Silvestrini, Secretary of the Council for the Public Affairs of the Church, met with SMOM members, US Secretary of State Alexander Haig and Judge Clark.[33]

Reagan believed fervently in both the benefits and the practical applications of Washington's relationship with the Vatican....One of his earliest goals as president, Reagan said, was to recognize the Vatican as a state "and make them an ally." The pope himself, not only his deputies, met with American officials to assess events in Poland and the effectiveness of American actions and sent back messages—sometimes by letter, sometimes orally—to Reagan.

On almost all his trips to Europe and the Middle East, Casey flew first to Rome, so that he could meet with John Paul II and exchange information. But the principal emissary between Washington and Rome remained [SMOM member and ambassador at large, General Vernon] Walters, a former deputy director of the CIA who worked easily with Casey. Walters met with the pope perhaps a dozen times, according to Vatican sources. "Walters was sent to and from the Vatican for the specific purpose of carrying messages between the pope and the president," said former US Ambassador to the Vatican Wilson. "It wasn't supposed to be known that Walters was there. It wasn't all specifically geared to Poland; sometimes there were also discussions about Central America or the hostages in Lebanon."[34]

Following the June 1982 meeting, the two leaders and their teams agreed to openly aid the Solidarity movement in Poland, aiming to keep it alive as the wedge that would split the USSR's empire in Eastern Europe.[35]

Some European observers argued the pope's interest in Poland and opposition to communism had nothing to do with democracy since he ran his own organization as a tyrant. Swiss theologian Fr. Hans Küng, who was banned from teaching in Church-affiliated universities following an article in 1980 critical of the pope, described the internal atmosphere of the Church and the role of John Paul II as follows:

> [The pope] with dictatorial power directs his inquisition against unpopular theologians, priests, monks and bishops; above all, believers distinguished by critical thinking and energetic reform are persecuted in inquisitorial fashion....
>
> John Paul II (and his grand inquisitor Ratzinger) persecuted Schillebeeckx, Balasuriya, Boff, Bulányi, Curran as well as Bishop Gaillot (Evreux) and Archbishop Hunthausen (Seattle). The consequence: a Church of surveillance, in which denunciation, fear and lack of liberty are widespread. The bishops regard themselves as Roman governors instead of the servants of churchgoers, the theologians write in a conformist manner—or not at all.

His secular critics viewed Wojtyla's personal role in directing millions of dollars to Solidarity and providing worldwide media attention for the movement from another viewpoint:

> The Catholic Church is, after all, the largest single property owner in the world. Hence the Church supported bloody Latin American dictatorships, which upheld capitalist property, but opposed Stalinist regimes in the USSR and Eastern Europe that were based on nationalized property....
>
> The aim of the Vatican, however, was not to support the social demands of the workers. Rather, it sought to keep the movement under the influence of reactionary Catholic ideology and Polish nationalism, and ensure that it did not develop into an international challenge to the existing order. The Catholic hierarchy, whose experience in defending authority and order spanned one-and-a-half millennia, was highly aware that a popular movement such as that which had developed in Poland could not be tamed through passive means, but had to be actively influenced and turned in a different direction....
>
> Initially, there existed not only Catholic, but also

strong secular and socialistic tendencies in the Solidarity movement. These, however, lacked an effective perspective for opposing the Stalinist regime. The intervention of the Vatican contributed substantially towards bringing the movement under the control of the Catholic-nationalist wing around Lech Walesa—a man who combined his reputation as a militant workers leader at the Lenin Shipyard with a large dose of bigoted Catholicism.[36]

The US and the Holy See: Government to Government

The US and the Holy See announced the formalization of diplomatic relations on January 10, 1984. On March 7, 1984, the Senate confirmed William A. Wilson, already Reagan's personal envoy to the pope, as the first US Ambassador to the Holy See. The Holy See officially named Archbishop Pio Laghi, already the papal legate, as the first Apostolic Pro-Nuncio of the Holy See to the US. (The adjective "apostolic" means "papal," a reminder of the Church's claim that the pope and his prelates stand in direct succession to the original apostles. A "delegate" or "legate" is sent to a country which does not have formal diplomatic ties; a "nuncio" or "pro-nuncio" is sent to a country which does.)

Even before the announcement, there was opposition from the American Catholic bishops. A progressive group at the time, the US hierarchy preferred that a permanent and full diplomatic staff from Rome not be established in Washington DC.[37] Some Catholics feared it would enable the US government to exert influence over the American Church; non-Catholic opponents feared increased Vatican influence on the US government; both concerns proved to be valid. The National Association of (Catholic) Laity (NAL) joined Americans United for Separation of Church and State in seeking a court injunction. In its brief, the NAL cited "the potential for Government intrusion into the internal affairs of the Roman Catholic Church." The Justice Department responded that such fears were "pure speculation." Later, an archbishop claimed that Ambassador Wilson "gave a list of twenty or thirty troublesome [US] bishops to the Vatican" which Wilson denied.[38]

Wilson, a wealthy Californian, was among the group of businessmen who, in the 1960s, had urged Reagan to go into politics. He advised Reagan on his personal finances negotiating the $500,000 purchase of Reagan's ranch near Santa Barbara, and he led the fund-raising drive in California for Reagan's 1980 presidential campaign. "Vatican insiders said the appointment was primarily a 'feather in the cap' of a man who was less interested in diplomacy than in business....Over a period of years Wilson's usefulness was eroded by a lack of diplomacy."[39]

The Georgetown University archive of Wilson's papers lists correspondence between Wilson and Bishop Marcinkus as early as 1979 and lasting until Wilson resigned in 1986, as well as communications with Cardinal John Cody. After Wilson's arrival in Rome, Marcinkus found office space for Wilson in a prestigious building owned by the Vatican and occupied by highly-placed Curia members such as Cardinal Ratzinger.[40] "Wilson returned the favor by writing to then Attorney General William French Smith on Marcinkus' behalf, for which he received a rap on the knuckles from senior Justice Department officials. They feared that Wilson might involve Smith in an Italian government investigation of Marcinkus' links to Michele Sindona."[41]

Finding "Parallelism" on Abortion, Star Wars and Latin America

As governor of California, Reagan had signed one of the nation's most liberal abortion laws in 1967. As a sign of the growing conflation of Republican and neo-Catholic ideology, as president, Reagan favored a constitutional amendment to outlaw all abortions except those necessary to preserve the mother's life. At the 1984 United Nations International Conference on Population, the "Mexico City Policy" was implemented, named for the city which hosted the conference. The US announced that Agency for International Development (AID) funds would be withheld from any foreign non-governmental organization (NGO) which provided abortion-related information or services, even if these services are legal in their own countries and funded with their own money. The rule prevents NGOs from even participating in public debates or speaking out on issues concerning abortion. "American policy was changed as a result of the Vatican's not agreeing with our policy," Ambassador Wilson explained.[42]

AID also made a $20 million grant to Georgetown University, a Catholic institution, to review all international "natural family planning" projects. ("Natural family planning," or NFP, means a couple abstains from sexual intercourse during the woman's fertile period as their only means of contraception.) It gave a $6.8 million grant to Family of the Americas Foundation which promotes NFP in other countries, condemns contraception, and does not supply information on other methods.[43]

The US affected changes in Vatican policy, as well. The Pontifical Academy of Science had prepared a report taking a stand against the Reagan administration's Strategic Defense Initiative (Star Wars). Not only did Ambassador Wilson get the report suppressed but he said the reason was "so that the Holy Father would not make a statement that was not consistent with the way we saw things and the way we wanted things to happen."[44]

Wilson sat in on a meeting between US Secretary of State George Schultz and Vatican Secretary of State Casaroli. According to Wilson:

> [Schultz] explained the problems we are having in Nicaragua and how the Church could be helpful in certain aspects of that....We found that there are Catholic clergy who are very active in the matter of liberation theology in

a way that puts them either with or strongly against the current regime in Nicaragua. That is certainly relevant in political terms and hence of considerable interest here. And that interest would extend to the identity of the people, and how effective they are and what their following is, and what their followers are going to do about it, and whether this is being used by the current regime in a positive or negative sense. All of that is fair game.[45]

Wilson later denied giving the Vatican a list of Latin American clergy and religious the US wanted "removed."

In 1984 John Paul II met with Sen. Robert Dole (R-Kan.), who visited the pontiff on behalf of Reagan to discuss Central America. Dole gave the pope a letter from Reagan outlining his administration's strategy on Nicaragua. A second letter from the president on the same subject was delivered by the US embassy in Rome. The pope's response to the two letters was approval of Reagan's Nicaragua policy. Due to what a Curia official called a "gaffe," Reagan blurted out John Paul II's affirmative reply to participants at a State Department conference on religion. They immediately relayed it to the press, prompting a Vatican denial that the pope had given any endorsement of a "concrete plan" for Central America. Laghi, however, admitted a "parallelism in viewpoints" of the Vatican and the administration but insisted that there were no specific arrangements between the president and the pope.[46]

When Congress was considering a Reagan request for resumption of aid to the Contras in 1985, Reagan told news photographers that the pope "has been most supportive of all our activities in Central America." Ambassador Wilson also recalled discussing the matter with Nicaraguan Cardinal Miguel Obando y Bravo. "[O]ne of the big problems of the president is trying to get this aid package for the Contras through Congress. He finally made it, but it was over a few dead bodies that he got it done."[47]

Unmoved by the assassinations of Italians investigating the Vatican Bank scandal and providing a papal blessing to Latin American murderers and mutilators, John Paul II always maintained pastoral concern over his fellow-countrymen in Poland. When the US invoked economic sanctions against Poland to pressure the communist rulers, the pope worked for their elimination. In February 1987, a month after a meeting between Poland's dictator, Wojciech Jaruzelski, and the pope, Reagan lifted the sanctions. Reagan's foreign policy advisers agreed the change in policy towards Poland was a small price to pay for the pope's backing in Central America.[48]

Apparently some of John Paul II's foreign policy advisers were not as impressed by Reagan's support for the Vatican's positions. According to Ambassador Wilson, when a meeting was being arranged between the pope and the president in Fairbanks, Alaska, Reagan's staff wanted them to leave the airport in the same car. The president's aides were told, "The pope never rides in the same car with the head of a country. It would look like he was endorsing him. Then Kim in South Korea would want it, Marcos would want it, and Pinochet. We can't do it for the United States but not for other countries."[49] Placing Reagan in such dubious company was a Vatican slight to his leader that the gaffe-prone Wilson was dense enough to pass along.

Reagan used his friendship with Pope John Paul II to solidify Catholic support for the Republican Party. In addition to his several meetings with the pope, Reagan spoke before the Knights of Malta, the Knights of Columbus, the Heritage Foundation of Eastern Europeans, Catholic universities and other organizations. When the president visited Chicago's Holy Angels School to propose federal tuition aid for parochial schools, he affirmed that in order to attend that school both the children and their parents must be instructed in Catholicism. In an April 1982 speech before the National Catholic Education Association, Reagan made the incredible statement, "I am grateful for your help in shaping American policy to reflect God's will....And I will look forward to further guidance from His Holiness Pope John Paul II during an audience I will have with him in June."[50] Reagan and Bush even made it a point to visit the Polish-American Shrine of Our Lady of Czestochowa located outside of Philadelphia during the 1984 campaign.[51]

By the end of Reagan's two terms, 138 officials in his administration had either been convicted, indicted, or had been the subject of official investigations for official misconduct and/or criminal violations. The share of national income going to the wealthiest one percent of Americans nearly doubled from 8.1 to 15 percent and the net worth of the 400 richest Americans almost tripled.[52]

CHAPTER 8

JOHN PAUL II AND THE MEDIA

An actor and playwright in his youth, Pope John Paul II knows that the simplest gesture can move an audience. From a bold wave to his countrymen in communist Poland in 1979 to his quietly slipping a note in Jerusalem's Wailing Wall two decades later, this pope has always found ways to keep the world watching.[1]

Wherever Pope John Paul II went, it became a media event, with all the pomp and circumstance of a royal wedding, all the hype of a Super Bowl, all the uproar of a rock concert....He took center stage at a Hollywood theater, holding a conversation via satellite with thousands of young Catholics in four cities. This pope also came out with a music video, featuring him singing and reciting psalms and the Gospels.[2]

The coverage of Pope John Paul II's funeral, "noted the *Global Language Monitor,* far exceeded attention given to other events such as the South Asian tsunami, the Sept. 11 terrorist attacks, and the deaths of Ronald Reagan and Princess Diana. Within the first 72 hours of the pope's death there were about 10 times more news stories on John Paul II than were published in the same period on US President George Bush following his re-election last November... The Associated Press on April 12 reported that more than 9 million people in the United States either wakened early or stayed up late to watch the Pope's funeral (it started at 4 a.m. on the East Coast and 1 a.m. on the West Coast)."[3]

Karol Wojtyla understood his role and courted the press. During his first trip outside Italy in 1979 to the Puebla Conference, he was the first pope to directly answer reporters' questions. Even on vacation, he was available for photos showing him hiking and skiing. "It is well known from the beginning of his term of office that he, the 'mystic' liked to be depicted as someone deeply immersed in prayer. This too was part of his calculation."[4] Cast as God's own messenger—the ultimate and infallible religious figure—he made any politician with whom he shared a photo frame seem more acceptable.

Before the John Paul II-era, international journalists assigned to Rome had covered the Vatican as a sideline. Now, covering the pope was a full time job. "He tries to give the press a new lead each day," said Wilton Wynn, the former Rome bureau chief at *TIME Magazine.* "One day he visits those dying people in the slums of Calcutta. Another day the Dalai Lama, and another day he makes a speech against contraception."[5] "Contemporary VIPs were in and out of the Vatican all the time. Sport, show business and politics were woven into the cycle of holidays, episcopal visits, conferences and official events."[6]

As the world's press reported his carefully chosen words and broadcast every staged event, no group benefited more than US neoconservatives energized by Reagan's presidency.

> For neocons, promoting the cult of John Paul II not only attracted Catholics but also served to tighten the Evangelical/Catholic bond. A new nationwide poll has found that evangelicals view Pope John Paul II more favorably than either Rev. Jerry Falwell or Pat Robertson. The poll, conducted by Greenberg Quinian Rosner Research in Washington, found that Falwell's favorability ranking among evangelicals was only 44 on a 0 to 100 scale. Robertson ranked 54. The pope, however, came in at 59.[7]

The Reagan administration traded on its alliance with the world's most admired human being and GOP operatives synchronized Vatican and Republican "positions." Regardless of the ruthless suppression within his own organization or his support for some of the world's worst dictators, John Paul II carried the title "champion of freedom."

The pope knew to whom he owed his spectacular success and wrote, "We give thanks to God for the presence of these powerful media,"[8] a media created by corporate interests backed by the Reagan administration. Until 1980, the US media had been regulated so as to promote a free press and a diversity of opinion. In 1981, Mark Fowler, who served as communications counsel during Reagan's 1976 and 1980 presidential campaigns, was named head of the Federal Communications Commission (FCC), the federal agency charged with oversight of broadcast communications. He began a program of deregulation including extending television licenses from three years to five. By 1985:

- The number of television stations any single entity could own was increased to twelve.

- Guidelines for minimal amounts of non-entertainment programming were abolished.

- Guidelines on how much advertising can be carried per hour were eliminated.[9]

Increasing the number of TV stations any single entity could own permitted Capital Cities to purchase ABC, since Capital Cities was now allowed to combine the ABC affiliates it already owned with ABC's corporately owned-and-operated stations. CIA Director William Casey was one of the founding investors of Capital Cities. "Casey, in fact, may have actually held down the price of ABC stock at the time Cap Cities was acquiring it, by asking the FCC to strip ABC of its broadcast licenses in retaliation for negative reporting on the CIA."[10]

No change has had a greater impact on US politics than the elimination of the Fairness Doctrine in 1987. Adopted in 1949, the Fairness Doctrine viewed station licensees as "public trustees" and required they make every reasonable attempt to cover contrasting points of views. The FCC had also required that stations perform public service in reporting on crucial issues in their communities. Soon after he became FCC Chairman, Fowler stated his desire to do away with the Fairness Doctrine. His position was upheld by a 1987 District of Columbia Circuit Court decision, *Meredith Corp v FCC*, which ruled that the doctrine was not mandated by Congress and the FCC no longer had to enforce it. The FCC suspended all but two corollary doctrines at this time.[11]

Even in the age of the internet, Americans watch television on average four hours and thirty-five minutes every day. After 1987, candidates for office would have to buy time on television. Not only did this enrich the TV stations, but it led to campaign contributions as the defining criteria for a successful campaign. The requirement of purchasing TV time led to the reduction of a candidate's position on critical issues to "sound-bites"; since broadcast time is purchased in 30-second increments, the image became the message.

Concentration of the media into the hands of a few "gatekeepers" continued until it is now the situation that the largest and most influential newspapers, book publishers, magazines, television, radio and movies are currently controlled by ten multi-national corporations: AOL Time Warner, Disney, General Electric, News Corporation, Viacom, Vivendi, Sony, Bertelsmann, AT&T and Liberty Media.

One media mogul, Australian Rupert Murdoch (News Corporation), first gained fame in the US as the owner of sleazy supermarket tabloids. He expanded his international holdings to other outlets including two New York TV stations, the *New York Post*, and Fox Cable News known for its sophomoric and bellicose talk-show hosts. In January 1998, Murdoch and his wife at the time were inducted into the Pontifical Order of St. Gregory the Great, given to people of "good character" who have "promoted the interests of society, the Church and the Holy See."[12] In 2005 the Parents Television Council rated four Fox network programs as the most offensive prime-time shows. The group's president said he was alarmed the three Fox Sunday night comedies were being marketed as family friendly. "The top three worst shows all contain crude and raunchy dialogue with sex-themed jokes and foul language. Even worse is the fact that Hollywood is peddling its filth to families with cartoons."[13]

When John Paul II became pope in 1978, instant global television was in its infancy. "If it doesn't happen on television, it doesn't happen," the pontiff affirmed.[14] By 1987 an estimated one billion people watched the pope when 23 satellites linked him to16 countries in "A Prayer for World Peace." When Wojtyla visited Cuba in 1998, 3200 reporters and photographers were there to record the event.[15]

The Pope John Paul II Cultural Center

Not all efforts to exalt the pope were successful. The Pope John Paul II Cultural Center in Washington DC was described as "a presidential museum for the pope" from where propaganda regarding the cult of Wojtyla could be disseminated. "The pope chose Washington rather than Rome or Jerusalem, presumably because he expects the US to continue to be the world's most influential nation."[16]

Cardinal Adam Maida of Detroit discussed the project with Wojtyla before receiving his approval.

Maida established the foundation responsible for raising the funds and ultimately managing the center (he continues to serve as its president). Contributions flowed, according to news accounts from the 1990s: $3 million from the Knights of Columbus; more than $1 million each from special collections in the Chicago archdiocese and the Peoria, Ill., diocese; and nearly $1 million from parishioners in the diocese of Gary, Ind.

"Many bishops throughout the United States stepped up to the plate and invited us into their dioceses," recalled Peter deKeratry, who in 1999-2001 worked for the company hired by the center to raise funds. Eventually, said deKeratry, more than 70,000 individual donors contributed and $67 million was raised, still $8 million short of the final construction costs.[17]

The cardinal, while closing three dozen schools and dozens more parishes in the inner-city, put up $36 million in archdiocesan funds in loans for the center's construction and operation which were never repaid.[18] The $75 million building opened in March 2001. Six years later the project was a bust. There were never enough visitors or contributors to keep the center operating in the black.

Fatima

Perhaps the most egregious (for Catholics) self-promotion by

Karol Wojtyla was his appropriation of the "Third Mystery" of Fatima. For believers, on May 13, 1917, Mary, Mother of God, first appeared to three Portuguese peasant children near the town of Fatima. At the request of her bishop in 1941, Lucia dos Santos, the only survivor of the three "seers" and a cloistered nun, recorded in hand-written notes that the "Lady" had said, among other things, World War I would end but a larger and more terrible war would follow and that "Russia would spread her errors" but would eventually be converted. There was a third "secret" Lucia wrote down and gave to her bishop in 1944 with instructions that it be disclosed either in 1960 or after her death (she died in 2005), whichever came first. The bishop sealed the letter in an envelope and gave it to the Vatican in 1957.

For reasons never fully disclosed (Pope John XXIII said only, "It is not of my time"), the "Third Secret" was never revealed and speculation as to its message and why it was kept secret has covered the full range of doomsday scenarios. With his sense of the theatrical and savvy use of the media, with great fanfare and publicity, John Paul II announced in May of the US presidential election year 2000 that the "secret" would be disclosed after suitable preparation and an explanation had been prepared, and that he himself was the subject of the "secret." It was never mentioned why the entire corpus of the previously disclosed portions of the message from Fatima or the Marian messages from other apparitions such as Lourdes or Guadalupe could be revealed without the necessity of a Vatican "explanation."

> It is no coincidence that the pope, who is exceptionally confident about his own divine mission to restore the Church and in the guiding role of the Virgin Mary has allowed the contents of the Third Secret to be known in 2000, which he believes could herald a rebirth of the Church. The revelation will no doubt also add to his own charisma: the fact that an event in his life was apparently foretold by the mother of Christ will increase his already considerable kudos and authority."[19]

The pertinent part of Lucia's letter as related by the Vatican on June 26, 2000, after Wojtyla met personally with the nun is as follows:

> And we saw in an immense light that is God (something similar to how people appear in a mirror when they pass in front of it) a Bishop dressed in White (we had the impression that it was the Holy Father). Other Bishops, Priests, men and women Religious going up a steep mountain, at the top of which there was a big Cross of rough-hewn trunks as of a cork-tree with the bark; before reaching there the Bishop passed through a big city half in ruins and half trembling with halting step, afflicted with pain and sorrow, he prayed for the souls of the corpses he met on his way; having reached the top of the mountain, on his

knees at the foot of the big Cross he was killed by a group
of soldiers who fired bullets and arrows at him, and in the
same way there died one after another the other Bishops,
Priests, men and women Religious, and various lay people
of different ranks and positions.

John Paul II declared this revelation was a prophetic vision of
his being shot while riding through St. Peter's Square in his pope-mobile
on May 13, 1981, because the month and day were the same as the first
apparition. None of the other facts—other than he wore white—surrounding
the attempted assassination concurred with the letter. The would-be
assassin, Ali Mehmet Agca, was not a soldier but a member of a Turkish
right-wing gang. Archbishop Oscar Romero of El Salvador, however, was
shot through the heart March 24, 1980, as he was saying Mass in front of
a cross in a city in ruins from civil war. He was murdered by soldiers. At
the time of Romero's assassination, other clerics and religious were being
gunned down or worse in his country, as well as catechists and other lay
religious workers who were tortured, killed and dismembered.

Joaquin Navarro-Valls

What Michael Deaver did as a publicist for Ronald Reagan, Joaquin
Navarro-Valls would do for John Paul II.

Deaver was celebrated and scorned as an expert
at media manipulation for focusing on how the president
looked as much as what the president said. As Reagan's
chief choreographer for public events, Deaver protected
the commander in chief's image and enhanced it with a
flair for choosing just the right settings, poses and camera
angles....

Deaver's greatest skill "was in arranging what
were known as good visuals—televised events or scenes
that would leave a powerful symbolic image in people's
minds," former first lady Nancy Reagan recalled in her
memoir, *My Turn*.[20]

An Opus Dei numerary, Dr. Navarro-Valls, was named Director
of the Press Office of the Holy See in 1984 as the Vatican negotiated its
monetary settlement with the Italian central bank. Educated in Spain as a
psychiatrist, Navarro-Valls turned the sluggish Vatican press office into a
papal public relations machine. As a testament to his skills,

One just has to remember the endless perfect
images which the television produced during [the Pope's]
countless trips abroad, indulging in mass events and in

the cheers of the countless masses....The Pope was surrounded by cheering crowds of people; he stroked children and took babies into his arms. Added to that was now an all encompassing stage production: trips became a complete work of art. The "Pope Mobile" had to be everywhere. Altars and altar arrangements had to be constructed with perfection in terms of material, colour and shape, with the papal throne at the centre. Pictures of Assisi of all places show against a muted red background who among those present was the most worthy of them all; one could always feel a certain contrast between medium and message. The vestments were the right ones. They too had been carefully coordinated with regard to their colour and fall of the folds. Frequently hundreds of dignitaries appeared in the identical vestments (different ones each time). Then they wore identical mitres which as the years went by became bigger and bigger in order to drive home the gentlemen's claim to respect.

This was mightily impressive. We will never forget the cloak, once again exuberant in terms of colour and fall of folds, which the Pope was wearing as, at the beginning of the new millennium he opened the Holy Gate. It almost drowned his own body. Virtually ecstatic were the heaving vestments which the Pope wore during a beatification in Maribor (September 1999). Still present is the ecstasy of vermillion red which covered St Peter's Square on the occasion of the appointment of new cardinals in February 2001. Indeed this took place twice as if the handing over of the biretta and the ring required two separate ceremonies. No one was able to look through the exaggerated nature of this show. Weak when it comes to memory, the media thought that this had always been the case.[21]

The Press Office of the Holy See was funded in large part by the Republican-led Knights of Columbus, a male-only Catholic lay organization with over 1.7 million members in nine countries. Founded in the US in 1882 in response to anti-Catholic bigotry, the fraternal society offers life insurance and annuities to its members and their families. In 2006, it had $60 billion of life insurance in force, and $13 billion in assets.[22]

Though they contribute many hours of volunteer work, what the Knights do best is raise money for the Church. In 2003, they gave the pope a check for $2.5 million, "representing one year's interest from a fund established in 1981. [It] brought to more than $35 million the amount the Knights have given the pope during his pontificate" for his personal use.[23] When the Archdiocese of Boston was strapped for money in 2002, it mortgaged Cardinal Bernard Law's mansion and the chancery grounds to the Knights for $38 million.[24] In 2004, members contributed $195.6 million to their local parishes and dioceses. In addition, they have supported the Vatican's UN Permanent Observer Mission headquarters in New York City and the United States Conference of Catholic Bishops' support of a natural family-planning effort.[25]

The Knights provided the funds to modernize Navarro-Vall's operations. They had already paid for the Holy See's ability to beam programs via satellite and the charges for capturing the signal by TV stations in third-world countries. Beginning in 1985, they paid for the Vatican Television Center's mobile television studio for the taping, recording and worldwide transmission of Vatican ceremonies,[26] two production vans, a new transmitter for Radio Veritas and satellite transmissions of papal events through the Knights' Satellite Uplink Program.[27] They also paid for the computerization of several Vatican departments, renovations of St. Peter's, and papal travel expenses.

Navarro-Valls used his position to also advance Opus Dei. According to The New Yorker, in 1993 "Navarro-Valls' secretary called several Vatican correspondents, leading them to think that they would get an interesting story if they appeared at the spokesman's house a couple of months hence. But when the reporters arrived at the house they were treated to a recruiting film for Opus Dei."[28]

Not only was Navarro-Valls capable of shaping the message, he could fabricate a news story as well. Two noted Vatican reporters, Sandro Magister of www.chiesa and John L. Allen Jr. of the National Catholic Reporter, related the story of how Navarro-Valls issued a press-release in February 1996 about the pope's meeting with Guatamalan Nobel Peace Prize Winner Rigoberta Menchu, mentioning her clothes and details about their conversation even thought the meeting had never taken place.

One of the greatest challenges for Navarro-Valls, a former physician, was to hide Wojtyla's poor health for as long as possible. After showing off his athletic prowess and physical strength at the beginning of his reign, the pope's ego required the continued appearance of toughness and vibrancy. Even after the pope's first symptoms were diagnosed as Parkinson's disease in 1991, it was five years before the press would publicly note the pontiff's trembling left hand and another seven years before Navarro-Vall's officially acknowledged Wojtyla's illness. During the interim, Navarro-Valls would only admit the pope was suffering from an "extrapyramidal neurological disorder."[29]

Navarro-Vall's skill at deception was most evident in the aftermath of an Opus-Dei-related murder inside the Vatican. On May 4, 1998, at 9 p.m., the new commandant of the Swiss Guards, Alois Estermann, his wife and 23-year-old Vice Corporal Cedric Tornay were all found shot to death in Estermann's Vatican apartment. Estermann and his wife were members of Opus Dei and some feared that, as commandant, he would be privy to such secrets as the comings and goings of the pope, his Curia and their visitors. A year before he died, the young Tornay wrote his mother that he and two other guards were investigating the hold of Opus Dei on the Swiss

Guard including Estermann's attempts to recruit guards into the movement and warned her that this information could put him in danger.[30]

Within minutes of arriving at the crime scene, Navarro-Valls had the apartment sealed and the bodies immediately taken to the Gemelli Hospital morgue. Italian police were barred from investigating the crime. At around midnight and before any autopsies were completed, Navarro-Valls told the press that Tornay killed Estermann and his wife and then turned the gun on himself. He stated, "The information which has emerged up to this point allows for the theory of a 'fit of madness' by Vice Corporal Tornay," who was angered by being passed over for a decoration. In less than three hours Navarro-Valls was able to specifically deduce the frame of mind and motive of the alleged murderer. First thing the next morning, without any forensic evidence or official investigation, Navarro-Valls told the world's press the Vatican had a "moral certainty" that events had occurred exactly as he had reported earlier.[31]

The Vatican refused to release Tornay's body to his mother. In order to obtain an independent post-mortem, she was forced to literally steal her son's remains from a Church official in Switzerland where the body had been shipped for burial. A forensic autopsy done in Switzerland contradicted Navarro-Vall's reconstruction of the event.[32] Unfortunately, there will never be a public resolution in the case because John Paul II barred any outside investigation.

CHAPTER 9

THE NEO-CATHOLIC CHURCH

"Reform" of the US Episcopate

In the first half of the 1980s, the majority of US bishops, clergy and religious did not support the Republican Party. Many had personal ties to their fellow clergy/religious in Latin America suffering under the Reagan/John Paul II-supported military dictatorships. When the three American nuns and a lay missionary were kidnapped, raped and murdered by Salvadoran National Guardsmen on December 2, 1980, less than a month after Ronald Reagan's election, the atrocity occurred amid ongoing reports of massive human rights violations by the Salvadoran military, including numerous attacks on Church personnel. In November 1981, the US bishops issued a statement criticizing the military focus of the administration policy in Guatemala, El Salvador and Nicaragua. When Congress was considering Reagan's request to lift its ban on aid to the Contras in 1985, Archbishop James A. Hickey of Washington DC described US support for the Contra insurgency as "illegal and, in our judgment, immoral."

> According to one cardinal present at a meeting to prepare for a1985 synod of bishops in Rome, John Paul II opened the discussion by telling Chicago's Cardinal Joseph Bernardin that he did not understand why the US hierarchy was sending bishops to visit Cuba and Nicaragua or why the bishops did not "support your own president's policies in Central America". After hearing this salvo, [Cardinal] Sin, who was then deeply involved in the rising opposition to Ferdinand Marcos, rolled up his eyes as if to say, "Now we have to run our churches to please Reagan." The discussion ended after Bernardin made a reasoned reply, explaining the US bishops' position against the Contra war.[1]

After setting out to destroy liberation theology in Latin America, a "correction" in the American episcopate was next on the pope's agenda, not only for the long-term political goals and financial security of the Vatican but also of the Republican Party with its emerging neoconservative agenda.

Officially, the pope appoints all bishops, but in a worldwide organization with thousands of prelates, the papal legate or nuncio usually selects the candidates and has the greatest say in who is chosen. In considering candidates for bishop, questionnaires are sent to those who know the priest under consideration. The questionnaire used by the US pro-nuncio Laghi "asked about the priest's attitude toward 'social justice,'.... loyalty and docility to the Holy Father, the Apostolic See, and the Hierarchy as well as other questions regarding their orthodoxy."[2]

The Vatican will often assign an auxiliary bishop who can be controlled if the prelate-in-charge becomes objectionable.

> Especially noteworthy were three [US] appointees who had served as priests in Rome. Cardinal O'Connor, for example, accepted the appointment of Bishop Edward M. Egan [Cardinal Cody's protégé present in the last conclave] as his auxiliary in 1985 because the pope asked him to, despite the fact that the cardinal did not even know Egan. The cardinal, since he was not himself from New York, made it plain to his priests that if he were choosing an auxiliary himself it would be a New York archdiocesan priest. The same year, Archbishop Raymond G. Hunthausen of Seattle also accepted an auxiliary, Donald W. Wuerl, whom he did not request. Likewise David Foley was sent to Richmond as an auxiliary. These bishops had special faculties because Rome had lost confidence in the local diocesan bishops.[3]

John Paul II, with help from the Reagan administration, chose to make a special example of Hunthausen who had been especially critical of the Republicans. In 1975, he was elevated to Archbishop of Seattle where he was renowned for his devotion to the disadvantaged and for his positions on peace and justice. Hunthausen lived very modestly and cared for the poor and sick. When being introduced, the bishop would offer his hand with a simple "I'm Ray Hunthausen." He condemned the American lifestyle of "outrageous wealth and power," saying it invited nuclear war. An editorial in the *Seattle Post-Intelligencer* praised Hunthausen for his good works such as cleaning the filthy apartment of a man who could not care for himself. "There was the archbishop, dressed in work clothes, on his hands and knees wiping up the floor in the bathroom, no robes or bishop's miter to suggest the trappings of his office," the editorial said.

In 1982, Hunthausen withheld half of his income tax to protest the stockpiling of nuclear weapons exemplified by the Trident missile-equipped submarines located at the naval base on Puget Sound.

With Hunthausen's encouragement, the National Conference of Catholic Bishops (NCCB) issued "A Pastoral Letter on War and Peace" on May 3, 1983. It stated: "The good ends (protecting one's country, defending freedom, etc.) cannot justify immoral means (the use of weapons which kill indiscriminately and threaten whole societies)." The letter referred to the arms race as "one of the greatest curses of the human race" and called for the banning of nuclear weapons.

The West German bishops, led by Cardinal Joseph Hoffner of Cologne, denounced the American bishops for their position which condemned even nuclear deterrence. Paul Weyrich, founder of the Heritage Foundation and the Moral Majority, and his followers flooded the Vatican with criticisms of Hunthausen. "If we didn't know the pope agrees with us, we Catholics in the New Right would have serious conscience problems," stated Weyrich [4]

The attack on Hunthausen was not direct. Neo-Catholics focused on the archbishop's unorthodoxy as an excuse for the political assault. Hunthausen needed to be disciplined, they said, because there was too much democracy in his archdiocese and he had sanctioned all manner of liturgical innovations. But since many other US dioceses were guilty of the same practices, there was no convincing reason for Hunthausen to be singled out except for his peace activism.[5]

Using the Freedom of Information Act, the *National Catholic Reporter* obtained FBI documentation that showed the agency had been keeping files on Hunthausen and Detroit Auxiliary Bishop Gumbleton because of their antiwar activities. The FBI withheld six pages of information on Hunthausen on the ground that the material had originated at another unnamed agency, possibly US Naval Intelligence, which had also kept files on Hunthausen, or the CIA. Although the Gumbleton files dealt with his campaigns against the Vietnam war and racial inequalities during the late 1960s and early 1970s, the Hunthausen documents showed that he had been an object of surveillance through 1983 - the same period when the American bishops were preparing their controversial peace pastoral on nuclear war. Representative Don Edwards (D-Cal.), chairman of the House Judiciary Subcommittee on Civil and Constitutional Rights, told the *Reporter* that the investigation of the bishops "fits right into" a pattern of harassment of critics of the administration's foreign policy, citing nearly 60 cases of suspicious break-ins of offices belonging to groups opposed to Washington's Central American policy, including churches.[6]

In 1985, the IRS garnisheed the archbishop's wages to collect back taxes. Also in 1985, Cardinal Joseph Ratzinger issued a report on Hunthausen:

....It is important that clear and firm guidance be offered to those in the Archdiocese who seem reluctant to accept the Magisterium [Vatican authority] as capable of giving definitive direction in matters of faith and morals....

While efforts to encourage the laity to...assume their proper roles in the Church should continue, the unique ministry and office of the Bishop, as well as that of the priests who assist him, must never be obscured....It has been noted that in 1976 and in 1979, the Archdiocese of Seattle devised questionnaires to obtain information useful for the formation and conduct of Archdiocesan programs. Some, unfortunately, understood these questionnaires to be a kind of voting process on doctrinal or moral teachings....

A final question of pastoral practice pertains to ministry to homosexual men and women. The Archdiocese should withdraw all support from any group, which does not unequivocally accept the teaching of the Church concerning the intrinsic evil of homosexual activity.[7]

As much an act of public humiliation as one of control, John Paul II appointed Donald Wuerl, a loyal conservative, as auxiliary bishop of Seattle with special authority over the administration of the archdiocese including training priests. Hunthausen protested this encroachment on his authority. When Hunthausen revealed in September 1986 that he was being punished, Milwaukee's Archbishop Rembert Weakland, another leading liberal bishop, "did what is Just Not Done: He publicly criticized the Vatican, not only for stripping Hunthausen of authority but for its recent dismissal of Father Charles Curran, the liberal moral theologian at Catholic University."[8] Seattle Catholics, including 252 of the archdiocese' 280 priests, protested. A petition with more than 13,000 signatures urged the Vatican to restore Hunthausen's authority. The Canon (Ecclesial) Law Society of America expressed its concern to the NCCB and the Vatican, and voted 173 to 53 to question whether the Vatican's order to punish Hunthausen conformed to canon law.[9]

Pro-nuncio Laghi, who had to supervise the punishment, was furious when Hunthausen went public with the matter. "It made him look bad, and his defense had the same self-serving tone that he had used in Argentina to dismiss supplicants who wanted him to speak out against mass torture and murder. It wasn't his fault, he complained to the *New York Times*, if Americans had a 'Watergate complex' about Rome's desire to handle its affairs 'behind the door.'" In an unusual move for the Vatican, Laghi issued a public explanation. In a letter sent to US bishops two weeks before a scheduled November meeting in Washington DC, Laghi detailed the matters on which Hunthausen lacked the "firmness necessary to govern the archdiocese." Laghi also charged that Hunthausen had agreed to cede power to Wuerl and then reneged on the deal.[10]

The Last Hurrah for Progressive Prelates

The November 10, 1986, meeting of the National Conference of Catholic Bishops at the Capital Hilton Hotel was scheduled to debate the bishops' controversial pastoral letter on the economy. But the matter of the letter was upstaged by "the Hunthausen affair." When the conference opened, "That affair brought the American bishops as close to an open break with Rome as they have ever come. Not very close, as it turned out, but close enough."[11] In a closed-door meeting, the bishops began with a long ovation for Hunthausen but then gave him only three minutes to reply to Laghi's letter. Hunthausen distributed a lengthy statement protesting that he wasn't provided an opportunity to answer Ratzinger's accusations. The archbishop freely admitted some points, including the charge that he allowed Dignity, a group of Catholic homosexuals, to attend Mass in his cathedral. "They're Catholics too," he explained. "They need a place to pray."[12] Pointing out the many dioceses with similar practices, Hunthausen questioned why he was singled out.

The rest of the meeting confirmed this would be a turning point for the American episcopacy. At a reception one evening for the press, Rep. Robert K. Dornan (R-Cal.) showed up to castigate Cardinal Bernardin for his "seamless garment" doctrine which distressed neoconservatives. Bernardin taught a "consistent pro-life ethic" which included poverty, war and capital punishment as well as abortion as legitimate areas of concern, making the Republican's abortion-only position appear to be politically motivated.[13]

The pastoral letter on the economy to be debated at the meeting noted the moral failings in US capitalism:

> Vigorous action should be undertaken to remove barriers to full and equal employment for women and minorities....We urge that the principle of progressivity be a central guiding norm in any reforms of the tax system.... All of society should make a much stronger commitment to education for the poor....A thorough reform of the nation's welfare and income-support programs should be undertaken."

A lay group led by former treasury secretary William Simon issued a critical reply stressing not only the productivity of free-market capitalism but such traditional Catholic themes as the virtue of diligence and the necessity of strong families.

Archbishop Weakland responded to the Simon paper at a press conference calling it "libertarian" and saying the bishops preferred a more "communitarian" ethic. The bishops approved the letter by a vote of 225 to nine.[14]

Bishop James W. Malone's term as president of the NCCB was ending and he would be succeeded by Vice President Archbishop John L. May of St. Louis. The new president reproached the "Far Right" for their criticism of the bishops' peace and economics positions at a press conference. In the final order of business, the bishops had to choose a new vice president of their conference. Boston's Bernard Law, recently elevated to the rank of cardinal, proclaimed his candidacy as a representative of the conservatives by stating John Paul II would have been "irresponsible" if he had not clamped down on Hunthausen.[15] Law lost to Archbishop Daniel Pilarczyk of Cincinnati, a moderate, but his loyalty would later be rewarded by a promotion to Rome after he was run out of Boston in the wake the clerical sex-abuse scandal.

But at the close of the conference, Malone averred fealty to Rome. "The bishops of the United States wish to affirm unreservedly their loyalty to and unity with the Holy Father. The conference of bishops," he went on, "has no authority to intervene in the internal affairs of a diocese or in the unique relationship between the pope and individual bishops." The conference, he said, could not "review, much less judge, a case involving a diocesan bishop and the Holy See." Rome's decision regarding Hunthausen, he said, was reached "carefully and charitably," and "deserves our respect and confidence."[16]

That was the end of the progressive era of the Roman Catholic Church in the US. By punishing Hunthausen, Rome had sent a warning that social activism would no longer be tolerated and its allies in Germany and the US were provided symbolic support for the arms race.[17] When the NCCB meeting concluded in 1986, John Paul II had reigned for eight years and the American episcopate had already begun to reflect the politics of the new monarch. By the time Reagan left office, Laghi had been instrumental in the appointment of almost 100 American bishops, 12 of the country's 33 archbishops and the intimidation of the rest. Neo-Catholics were confident the new bishops would counter liberal Catholicism and influence the electorate to accept their platform instead.

The Neo-Catholic Papacy

Until John Paul II was elected, the world's bishops had taken encouragement from the Second Vatican Council calling for a new "collegiality" and mandating that bishops "jointly exercise their pastoral office" with the Vatican[18] For John Paul II, however, any authority which resided in a national association of bishops was a diminution of his own. Initially, the pope emasculated the strength and effectiveness of these groups by disregarding them. Later, he declared that only recommendations reached unanimously by national conferences could be submitted to Rome for his consideration. During his papacy, Wojtyla dealt directly only with the highest ranking archbishops and cardinals. If a gathering of bishops wanted anything from Rome, they would have to send a delegation like beggars to the king's court.

In his opening remarks at the 1986 NCCB meeting, Malone had noted "some persons" were questioning the "timeliness and utility" of the pope's scheduled US tour in September 1987. Malone asked for permission (which was denied) for American bishops to brief the pope in person about the situation he would face in the US.[19] John Paul II, however, who made more visits to the US than any other country except Poland, arrived with his own agenda. He publicly mischaracterized the previous NCCB position on nuclear weapons. "Edward L. Rowny, White House adviser on arms control, could thus state that the Reagan administration's defense policies were 'in harmony' with the pope's criteria but not with some positions adopted by the US bishops."[20] The pope raised the neoconservative banner: "All the great causes that are yours today....will succeed only if respect for life and its protection by the law is granted to every human being from conception until natural death," he stated at the Detroit Metro Airport.[21]

Abortion is not mentioned in the Bible. Nevertheless, neo-Catholics and evangelicals were united by the declaration that all human rights begin at the moment of conception. The Heritage Foundation issued position papers in 1980 and 1982 connecting abortion to the Declaration of Independence's "right to life" making the issue seemingly a cornerstone in the founding of the nation. Opus Dei institutes formulated the notion that hormonal methods of birth control (birth control pills, implants [norplant], injectables [depoprovera]) prevent the fertilized ovum (already a human being) from becoming implanted in the uterus and are therefore "abortifacients," making disapproval of birth control more palatable to their conservative Protestant brethren.

So successful was the religious right in linking birth control with abortion that 22 pro-life physicians and scientists, expressing a view already held by the American College of Obstetricians and Gynecologists,[22] felt compelled to write that hormonal birth control prevents ovulation or inhibits fertilization, not implantation. In their "Prolife Ob/Gyn's January 1998 Statement" they wrote:

> Currently the claim that hormonal contraceptives include an abortifacient mechanism of action is being widely disseminated in the pro-life community. This theory is emerging with the assumed status of "scientific fact," and is causing significant confusion among both lay and medical pro-life people. With this confusion in the ranks comes a significant weakening of both our credibility with the general public and our effectiveness against the tide of elective abortion....
>
> The "hormonal contraception is abortifacient" theory is not established scientific fact. It is speculation, and the discussion presented here suggests it is error....[23]

In the first six years of his pontificate, John Paul II's priority was defeating communism—real or imagined—and he made little mention of abortion other than including it in any enumeration of sins of the modern world ignoring the timeless and universal nature of the practice.

The 1983 revision of the Catholic Church's Canon Law, rewritten under the guidance of Opus Dei prelate, Msgr. Julian Herranz-Casado, included the punishment for abortion as automatic excommunication.[24] The following year, when Opus Dei paid IOR reparations to the Italian court, John Paul II moved abortion to first on his list of contemporary evils. A 1984 address to the medical faculty at Sacred Heart University in Rome was titled "Abortion, euthanasia, genetic manipulations are grave dangers of deviation for the doctor" and he referenced the Revised Code of Canon Law.

The Catholic Church had always stated males were justified to kill in defense of life or property but according to their law, females had no right to protect their own life or health. After *Roe v. Wade*, the NCCB issued a statement in 1974 reiterating their opposition to abortion. In 1975, they released the "Pastoral Plan for Pro-Life Activities" to encourage consideration of *Roe v. Wade* in the 1976 election but their document, "Political Responsibility Reflections on an Election Year," asked Catholics to consider a wide array of moral issues. It specifically stated that the bishops "do not seek the formation of a religious voting bloc."[25]

According to the NCCB website, there were no further official documents specifically on abortion until 1989.[26] The US bishops were following-up on John Paul II's Apostolic Exhortation, *Christifideles laici,* published in January 1989, urging lay Catholics to take an active role in anti-abortion politics.

John Paul II followed up his two visits to the US in the late 1980s with three more trips to the US in 1993, 1995 and his last in 1999 with the same recurring theme—abortion is the greatest evil of our time. Many of his major pronouncements during the 1990s centered on his other favorite topic—Catholics should obey their prelates as directed by their pope.

Obedience

The 1968 papal encyclical *Humanae Vitae* was clear that the only means of birth control approved by the Vatican was abstention from intercourse during a woman's fertile period. This meant that all traditional means of birth control (withdrawal, condom, cervical cap, spermicidal) as well as the newer hormonal methods were banned. In ignoring this ban, American Catholics for the first time felt unconstrained to question other doctrines and proscriptions as well. Obedience as a hallmark of Catholic life and practice was in jeopardy.

Cardinal Joseph Ratzinger—often referred to as the brains behind Wojtyla and the chief enforcer of orthodoxy—issued official Vatican documents assuming this would "force" Catholics into submission by the ancient tactic of threatening to declare them ineligible for heaven.

A special assembly was convened to begin work on a new catechism, "in order that all the Christian faithful might better adhere to it and to promote knowledge and application of it." The task was carried out by Ratzinger and twelve other prelates. In 1994, the official *Catechism of the Catholic Church*, where "the Christian faithful find directives for the renewal of thought, action, practices and moral virtue," was published. Paragraph 85 states: "The task of giving an authentic interpretation of the Word of God...has been entrusted to the living, teaching office of the Church *alone* (emphasis added) ....This means that the task of interpretation has been entrusted to the bishops in communion with the successor of Peter, the Bishop of Rome." Paragraph 87 adds: "Mindful of Christ's words to his apostles, 'He who hears you, hears me,' the faithful receive with docility the teachings and directives that their pastors give them in different forms."

The Vatican issued an instruction, Ad Tuendam Fidem (To Defend the Faith), in 1998 announcing the Code of Canon Law was being amended to more firmly assert Church authority by adding penalties for disobedience. The following paragraph was added to Canon 750:

§2. Furthermore, each and every thing set forth definitively by the Magisterium of the Church regarding teaching on faith and morals must be firmly accepted and held; ...anyone who rejects propositions which are to be held definitively sets himself against the teaching of the Catholic Church.

Canon 1371 was also revised:

The following are to be punished with a just penalty:

§1. a person who...teaches a doctrine condemned by the Roman Pontiff, or by an Ecumenical Council, or obstinately rejects the teachings mentioned in canon 750 § 2, or in canon 752 and, when warned by the Apostolic See [the Vatican] or by the Ordinary [the bishop], does not retract;

§2. a person who in any other way does not obey the lawful command or prohibition of the Apostolic See or the Ordinary or Superior [of a religious order] and, after being warned, persists in disobedience.

In a 2000 declaration, *Dominus Iesus* (Jesus is Lord), Ratzinger further asserted the truths about Jesus Christ exist "in their fullness in the Catholic Church and, without this fullness, in the other communities [religions]." Above all else, it must be firmly believed that "the Church, a pilgrim now on earth, is necessary for salvation..."

Homosexuality

As abortion, performed out of public view, was not an issue in the US until it was legalized in 1973, gays and lesbians remained in the "closet" until the American Psychiatric Association removed homosexuality from their list of mental disorders in 1974 and they began to demand their equal rights.

Fundamentalists, who understand the Bible (except for the parts with which they disagree) as God literally speaking directly to them, pushed back declaring that God considered homosexuality to be an "abomination."

The Catholic Church hadn't given much attention to the subject since all sex outside of marriage was sinful. Homosexual acts were forbidden but so were fornication, adultery and masturbation. Gays and lesbians were supposed to remain as chaste as any other unmarried Catholic. But neo-Catholics were forced to find common ground with fundamentalists and evangelicals to whom the matter was so important.

By comparison, the NCCB issued a statement in 1976, "To Live in Christ Jesus," which said, "Homosexuals, like everyone else, should not suffer from prejudice against their basic human rights. They have a right to respect, friendship and justice. They should have an active role in the Christian community."[27]

However, in 1986 Ratzinger's Confraternity for the Doctrine of Faith issued a "Letter to the World's Bishops on the Pastoral Care of Homosexual Persons" opposing any type of civil-rights legislation. It "has a direct impact on society's understanding of the nature and rights of the family and puts them in jeopardy." When such legislation is introduced, "neither the Church nor the society at large should be surprised when other distorted notions and practices gain ground, and irrational and violent reactions increase."[28]

In the first 1994 edition of the *Catechism of the Catholic Church*, paragraph 2358, read: "The number of men and women who have deep-seated homosexual tendencies is not negligible. They do not choose their homosexual condition; for most of them it is a trial." In 1997, the *Catechism* was revised so that the second sentence was changed to, "This inclination, which is objectively disordered, constitutes for most of them a trial."

Education

While Catholics had long enjoyed (and funded) a separate school system in the United States, with the rise of religion as a significant part of the Republican agenda, the practice of private schools grew among evangelicals as well—but now with a claim on public funding. In his prophetic book *Catholic Bishops in American Politics* (1991) Catholic writer Timothy A. Byrnes called the US episcopate:

> the "most focused and aggressive political leadership" ever exerted by the American Catholic hierarchy. This political campaign, which has been organized around the issues of abortion and certain forms of birth control, has wider implications. The ability to control political and judicial offices on one doctrinal issue can and will be used on other matters, such as aid to parochial schools to the neglect of public schools and use of welfare legislation to provide funds for the charitable activities of churches, among others.[29]

Public funding of private/parochial schools, once mostly a Catholic concern, was now an issue for all in the religious right as well. Especially in the South, other Christian denominations were building their own religious "academies" to keep their children out of integrated schools. In 1979 the Heritage Foundation actually proposed an "Anti-Busing Constitutional Amendment." The think tank followed with position papers favoring tuition tax credits and direct payment of tax dollars as vouchers for parents to pay private school tuition. Not only did these schools keep whites separated from blacks, but they also reinforced the political and social values of Christian Nationalism.

The new national interest in government support for religious schools was enthusiastically welcomed by the Catholic hierarchy. With the vast majority of American Catholics rejecting Rome's positions on birth control and divorce, prelates hoped increasing enrollment in their schools would create more obedient followers.

At a March 1989 papal conference with top-level-only US hierarchs titled, "Evangelization in the context of the culture and society of the United States with particular emphasis on the role of the bishop as teacher of the faith," the episcopate was charged with the "formation" of Americans by providing "authentic" Catholic education.

The NCCB issued a document in 1990, "In Support of Catholic Elementary and Secondary Schools." The bishops stated their responsibility was "to ensure total Catholic education in all phases for all ages." Philadelphia Cardinal Anthony Bevilacqua asked that the document "emphasize faithfulness to the Magisterium."[30]

Many bishops stopped funding the urban parochial school system which had educated European immigrants and their progeny but now educated African-Americans and Hispanics. While there had always been academies run by religious orders for the wealthy, they had at least taught the rich should care for the poor. Often, donations from these upper-class institutions had been used to offset tuition for poorer parish schools, but this source of financial aid was stopped.[31] Instead, the bishops, with new sources of financing from their political allies, built their own schools in well-to-do suburbs following the Opus Dei model of recruiting from the professional and executive classes. And whereas Catholic schools had once emphasized a solid secular education based on intellectual dexterity and curiosity, the new schools laid down orthodox doctrine combined with an obeisance to prelates and John Paul II bordering on idolatry.

Research completed by Cornelius Riordan, a sociologist from Providence College in Rhode Island, indicated that the socioeconomic composition of students in Catholic schools changed dramatically between 1972 and 1992. Riordan found that the proportion of students in the highest socioeconomic quartile increased from 29 percent to 46 percent between 1972 and 1992....The bottom line is that Catholic schools are serving an increasingly elite socioeconomic population of students, a trend that holds true across racial and ethnic categories....

The bishops asked in 1990 that new initiatives be launched to secure financial assistance from both public and private sectors in order to help Catholic parents struggling with the cost of church schools. This goal suggests that fiscal assistance lies in the direction of third-party intervention—tuition vouchers and/or endowments.... Obviously the requested assistance would be a multibillion dollar effort. [Catholics] must also take tuition vouchers seriously and actively seek access to public tax dollars.[32]

In the US Supreme Court ruling, *Lemon v. Kurtzman* (1971), the eight-justice majority had disallowed public support for private schools. In subsequent challenges to taxes being used for religious schools, neo-Catholic Justices Antonin Scalia and Clarence Thomas consistently sided with providing government funding. Those against government funding argued that public schools serve the entire community by creating a literate populace able to participate in democratic government and capable of adding to the economic well-being of the entire nation. They pointed out the injustice of using public money to subsidize a wealthier minority.

A study of the way a voucher program would work in Pennsylvania based on $900 for each student in the state revealed that, because private schools are generally located in wealthy neighborhoods, "two thirds of the funds authorized by this plan would flow into the eight Pennsylvania counties with the highest per capita incomes, while none of the funds would go to the state's poorest counties." This means that the state's poorest counties would be paying additional taxes to support the richest counties.[33]

Private schools also create indifference on the part of their students' parents to the quality of government-provided education as well as fostering elitism and racism by encouraging children to consider themselves as "set-apart."

Not only elementary and secondary schools, but also specifically neo-Catholic colleges and universities sprang up during the neoconservative era. In order to counter the academic freedom offered by established schools like Notre Dame and Georgetown, new institutions such as Ave Maria University, Holy Apostles College & Seminary, John Paul the Great Catholic University, Our Lady Seat of Wisdom Academy, Southern Catholic College, Wyoming Catholic College, Christendom College, The College of Saint Thomas More, Thomas Aquinas College, The Thomas More College of Liberal Arts, University of Dallas, and the University of St. Thomas in Houston, Texas, were founded and financed by the Republican nouveau riche. New funding was made available to the already established but right-leaning Aquinas College (Nashville), Franciscan University of Steubenville, Belmont Abbey College, Benedictine College, the Catholic University of America, DeSales, Mount St. Mary's and St. Gregory's universities.

In an effort to put Catholic institutions of higher learning under some sort of hierarchical oversight, John Paul II issued a ruling, *Ex Corde Ecclesiae (From the heart of the Church)*, in 1990. It stated that theology professors must obtain permission from their bishop to teach, faculty and boards of trustee vacancies must be filled by "faithful Catholics" (as determined by the bishop), and presidents must take an oath of fidelity to the Church upon assuming office. To their credit, the US bishops didn't approve the regulations until 1999 when the pope ordered them to do so. In the meantime, a vigilante group of young Republicans called the Newman Society began to monitor Catholic colleges for any deviation from the neo-Catholic party line, and what became known as the "orthodox patrol" would harass pastors and bishops if they witnessed any "misstep" in their local parishes and dioceses

The Neo-Catholic Episcopate

The primary focus of the National Catholic Conference of Bishops became abortion but the word actuality served as "code" for the comprehensive list of changes needed to complete the neoconservative transformation of government begun under Reagan. In 1989 the NCCB issued its first "Resolution on Abortion":

> At this particular time, abortion has become the fundamental human rights issue for all men and women of good will....Our long and short range public policy goals include: federal and state laws and administrative policies that restrict support for and the practice of abortion; continual refinement and ultimate reversal of Supreme Court and other court decisions that deny the inalienable right to life.

Equating the Republican Party with an anti-abortion program meant that every Catholic parish, charity and non-profit would maintain their Internal Revenue Code 501 (c) (3) tax-free status while conducting the most blatantly partisan political advocacy in the nation's history. For the past thirty years, every statement of a "pro-life" position has been construed as support for a GOP candidate.

According to John M. Swomley, "the bishops have created the impression that they speak for 59 million Catholics, which makes them a formidable political force, able to influence or intimidate presidents and other public officials."[34] While residents of the Northeast and Midwest with large Catholic populations were accustomed to the obligatory photo-ops of local politicians shaking the cardinal's hand, national politicians before Reagan had maintained their distance. With Protestant leaders of the religious right supporting the Reagan/John Paul II alliance and the new "Christian" political action groups—which Wojtyla praised as American ecumenism—rank-and-file fundamentalists were less suspicious of Catholicism. Catholic prelates became important not only for their influence on Catholics but as useful tools for imparting an aura of moral respectability to every Republican politician. More than for any other denomination, when a Catholic prelate speaks, the US media provides a deferential platform for whatever he has to say.

Within a month after George H. W. Bush took office, he included all five of the US cardinals in meetings at the White House and Cardinals Bernard Law of Boston and John O'Connor of New York were invited for overnight visits at the White House.

> In 1989, Law attacked what he called "slanderous allegations" when the *Boston Globe* alleged he had struck a deal with President George H. W. Bush. The *Globe* article said that Bush had requested Law's silence on the administration's lack of response to the murders of six Jesuits and two women in El Salvador. In exchange for silence, the *Globe* said, Law and other US cardinals would receive the president's support of Catholic issues such as tax money for church day cares, prayer in public schools and opposition to abortion.[35]

Also in 1989, Law went to Spain to ordain 19 Opus Dei priests.

"In the late '80s and early '90s, Law often consulted with President Bush. Law's friendship and weekly consultations with John Sununu, a conservative Catholic serving as Bush's chief of staff, were often noted in the media."[36] Bush appointed Law as chairman of the Commission on Legal Immigration in 1992. Doug Wead, a special assistant to the president, could now claim that George H. W. Bush "has been more sensitive and accessible to the needs of the Catholic Church than any president I know of in American history....We want the Church to feel loved and wanted, and we want them to have input." Wead also boasted "this administration has appointed more Catholic cabinet officers than any other in American history."[37]

The Catholic Campaign for America (CCA), founded in 1989, had as original board members William L. Bennett, Reagan's Secretary of Education who often appeared along with Bob Dole promoting federally funded school vouchers, Mary Ellen Bork, former New York Governor Hugh Carey and Corpus Christi Bishop Rene Gracida with support for Republican candidates its major focus.

Gracida, president of a controversial multimillion-dollar foundation, was accused by the Texas state attorney general in 1996 of funneling more than $100 million to his diocese in 12 years, and was charged with "manipulating the grant process" and breaching his fiduciary duty. According to the suit, Gracida's involvement in the fund was rife with conflicts of interest and improprieties, including the diversion of funds for the purchase of a for-profit television station, KDF-TV, Channel 13, the Fox network affiliate in Corpus Christi.[38]

Other CCA members included presidential candidate Patrick

Buchanan whose role was to influence the Republican platform, and other key figures in the Christian Coalition as well as Pat Robertson's American Center for Law and Justice.

A 1992 newsletter by the CCA declared that "separation of church and state is a false premise that must finally be cast aside."[39] The CCA's main targets for criticism were Catholic bishops who didn't actively support their agenda.[40]

In an April 3, 1992, speech at the neo-Catholic Franciscan University of Steubenville, Ohio, Cardinal John O'Connor of New York declared,

> "The fact is that attacks on the Catholic Church's stance on abortion, unless they are rebutted effectively, erode church authority in all matters, indeed the authority of God himself." He said, according to the April 9 edition of his newspaper, *Catholic New York*, "Abortion has become the number one challenge for the Church in the United States because... if the Church's authority is rejected on such a crucial question as human life... then questioning of the Trinity becomes child's play, as does questioning the divinity of Christ or any other Church teaching."[41]

At the 1992 Republican Convention in Houston, Buchanan gave voice to the neo-Catholic militancy:

> My friends, this election is about... what we stand for as Americans. There is a religious war going on in our country for the soul of America. It is a cultural war, as critical to the kind of nation we will one day be as was the cold war itself....
>
> George Bush is a defender of the right to life, and a lifelong champion of the Judeo-Christian values and beliefs upon which this nation was built....
>
> The agenda Clinton & Clinton would impose on America—abortion on demand, a litmus test for the Supreme Court, homosexual rights, discrimination against religious schools, women in combat—that's change, all right. But it is not the kind of change America wants. It is not the kind of change America needs. And it is not the kind of change we can tolerate in a nation that we still call God's country.

By 1993 the NCCB's Secretariat for Pro-Life Activities was the best-funded of the bishops' thirteen secretariats and committees, more than three times the next largest budget, that of the Secretariat for Ecumenical and Inter-Religious Affairs, and four times the budget of the Secretariat for

Laity, Women, Family, and Youth.[42]

On March 25, 1995, John Paul II issued an encyclical, *Evangelium Vitae (The Gospel of Life)*, instructing Catholic lawmakers and justices that they were required to oppose any laws or proposed laws which permit abortion under any circumstances. Specifically, the pope warned: "In the case of an intrinsically unjust law, such as a law permitting abortion or euthanasia, it is never licit to obey it, or take part in a propaganda campaign in favor of such a law, or vote for it." It was a message directed to the heart of the political process.

The CCA held its first national conference in November 1995. Participants included Bennett, Domino Pizza mogul Thomas Monaghan and Fr. Michael Scanlan of the Franciscan University in Steubenville. Another attendee was Rep. Henry Hyde (R-Ill.) who, as a senior member of national security oversight committees in the 1980s and early 1990s, had helped cover up the immoral and illegal Iran Hostage and Iran-Contra deals as well as other misdeeds committed by the Reagan-Bush administration.[43] Workshops were conducted on how to disseminate views on abortion, the media, family-planning, and educational reform. Washington DC's Archbishop James Hickey read a letter from John Paul II extending his blessings on the group. Ralph Reed, head of the Christian Coalition, told the assembly that he "sees in the emerging Evangelical-Catholic partnership the key to the future of American politics....The Catholic Campaign for America will likely become an important player in the increasingly crowded field of religiously-based public policy organizations."[44]

George H. W. Bush, received a "rousing welcome" in January 1996 at a Knights of Columbus convention with "many of the attending clergy and bishops and including Cardinal John O'Connor, prominently present. The gathering was only one of many at which Catholic bishops provided meetings and photo opportunities with Republican politicians."[45]

The 1996 Presidential Campaign

In April 1996, during the presidential primaries, the NCCB's Secretariat for Pro-Life Activities placed a full-page advertisement in the *Washington Post* urging President Clinton not to veto a bill banning partial-birth abortion. In what the *New York Times* referred to as "an unusual joint statement that carried a scarcely veiled political threat," eight US cardinals along with Bishop Anthony Pilla of Cleveland, president of the NCCB, "promised to make their outrage a public issue among American Catholics."[46]

And they did. The bishops led a nationwide postcard campaign directing every parish-registered Catholic to contact their representatives to override the Clinton veto. The Archdiocese of St. Louis even forbade Catholic school students from hearing Clinton speak in suburban St. Louis on May 17, 1996.[47] No campaign of this scope and expense had been undertaken in the name of the Catholic Church on any other issue or topic up to then in the nation's history. When the bishops held their next semi-annual meeting in June, Pilla, departing from the custom of presidential addresses given only at the autumn meeting, gave a major talk about the bishops' proper role in the upcoming election. He exhorted his fellow prelates to step up their role as "teachers" even if accused of partisanship.[48]

Republican presidential candidate Robert Dole climbed on board:

> After winning the Republican primaries, Robert Dole made a major speech to the Catholic Press Association's annual convention in Philadelphia on May 23, in which he endorsed "school choice," which involves the funding of parochial schools through tuition tax vouchers.... Immediately following that speech, Dole had a 20 minute meeting with Cardinal Anthony Bevilacqua....
>
> On July 18, Dole spoke to a Catholic audience at Cardinal Stritch College in Milwaukee where, according to the *New York Times*, he emphasized his proposal for "vouchers paying $1,000 a year in tuition for pupils in grades one through eight and $1,500 a year for high school students. States that had adopted voucher programs would apply for federal assistance" and the "federal government would provide $2.5 billion a year to be matched" by the state.[49]

Within a week of the bishops' June 1996 meeting, Dole appeared on the front page of the *New York Times* in a photo with Cardinal O'Connor. According to the *Times*, Dole had commented days earlier that Republicans should be more tolerant of other views on abortion. In exchange for support from the cardinal, Dole agreed to a strong anti-abortion party platform. "The cardinal's blessing, coming when it did, was a blatantly partisan political act."[50] Dole attacked Clinton's partial-birth abortion veto and, in the context of abortion, the presidential candidate said: "Though not a Catholic, I would listen to Pope John Paul II."

Dole chose Hyde as head of the Republican platform committee. Hyde, according to the *National Catholic Reporter,* had invited Catholics to help him develop the party's 1996 platform. In an open letter he wrote: "Catholics are a powerful voice of moral authority and fulfill a growing leadership role in the Republican Party," noting that there were nine US senators, 55 members of the House, and nine governors who were both Republican and Catholic. His letter also stated, "As a Catholic, I believe the basic principles of Catholic teaching are philosophically and morally aligned with those of the Republican Party."[51]

At the August 1996 Republican Convention, Hyde and Ralph Reed joined together to make sure Dole did not allow pro-choice Republicans to change the official platform which stated, "The unborn child has a fundamental individual right to life which cannot be infringed. We support a human life amendment to the Constitution and we endorse legislation to make clear that the Fourteenth Amendment's protections apply to unborn children. Our purpose is to have legislative and judicial protection of that right against those who perform abortions." [52] Social liberals such as California Gov. Pete Wilson and Massachusetts Gov. William Weld argued to remove the Human Life Amendment plank from the platform but the neoconservatives held. *New York Times* columnist Anthony Lewis noted: "What matters is the rise of a religion-based party, one in which the dominant forces see all issues through the lens" of religion. He deplored the idea of a "single religious outlook . . . dominating a major party."

The US bishops issued a document in 1998 titled *Living the Gospel of Life*: "The arena for moral responsibility includes not only the halls of government, but the voting booth as well."

After the collapse of the Soviet empire, John Paul II turned his attention to more pastoral and less political concerns while not repositioning the Vatican's support of right-wing governments. He was free to examine moral and ethical issues outside the framework of the Cold War. The more he became incapacitated by illness, the more Navarro-Valls limited his contacts with journalists.

In 1990, Pio Laghi was replaced by Archbishop Agostino Cacciavillan, exposed by the Italian police as a member of P2. To maintain the Vatican/Republican interests in Latin America, Cacciavillan was also appointed as the Holy See's permanent observer to the Organization of American States while serving as pro-nuncio to the US. In 1998, Cacciavillan was replaced by the Colombian Archbishop Gabriel Montalvo who had worked in Bolivia, Argentina, El Salvador, and had been the pro-Somoza nuncio in Nicaragua.

President Bill Clinton appointed former Boston mayor and president of the US Knights of Malta, Raymond Leo Flynn, as American ambassador to the Vatican. [53]

CHAPTER 10

NEO-CATHOLIC PROTAGONISTS

The New Oxford Review is a magazine founded in 1977 by laymen which promotes orthodox Catholicism. It took its name from the nineteenth-century Oxford Movement and is staunchly anti-abortion and anti-gay. The publication has a macho, no-nonsense approach proclaiming, "If you hunger for the red-meat of Catholicism, subscribe!" Shortly after it began publication,

> The *NOR* was contacted by a neocon foundation—right out of the blue. The foundation wanted to give us money—'free' money. A fellow flew out from the East Coast and asked me (the Editor) to meet him for drinks in a San Francisco restaurant—on him. Sure! (We were desperate for money.) He told me he would fund us regularly—if we would support corporate capitalism and if we would support a militaristic US foreign policy.[1]

While *NOR* editor, Dale Vree, declined the offer—"It was patently obvious that our religious mission would be compromised, that the whole idea was to make us a front group for the neocon agenda"—other Catholic journalists did not. From the early 1980s, Christian National apologetics would be dominated by three men: Michael Novak, George Weigel, and Richard John Neuhaus. Their names would appear on the boards of dozens of think tanks, foundations, publications and political/religious organizations. They challenged any religious leader critical of a militaristic American foreign policy and "unduly attached to the welfare state."[2] Like Wormtongue in *Lord of the Rings*, they used flattery and feigned obeisance to papal and episcopal authority to convince others that the Republican platform was the only "authentic" position possible for "faithful" Christians. They served their paymasters by advocating for unbridled corporatism and portrayed American imperialism as a Christian crusade with a messianic vision of US world power. Their writings provided a "moral" rationale utilized by Dick Cheney, Paul Wolfowitz, Donald Rumsfeld, William Kristol et al when they launched the Project for a New American Century.

Michael Novak

Novak, like other promising seminarians, was sent to study in Rome where he earned a degree in theology from the Pontifical Gregorian University in 1958. Instead of becoming a priest, Novak began his writing career as a correspondent during the Second Vatican Council (1962-65) and wrote a book, *The Open Church*, based on his experience. With additional degrees in history and philosophy of religion, Novak has always referred to himself as a "theologian" as Josef Mengele always referred to himself as a "physician."

In *A Theology for Radical Politics* (1969), Novak lauded the leftist student movement which he stated advanced the renewal of the human spirit rather than just reforming social institutions. Novak changed sides during the 1970s but continued using "religious" principles to advance his newfound right-wing ideology. Novak's main function in neoconservative thought was to provide a religious context for rapacious capitalism and the accumulation of wealth by an elite few at the expense of the many. "In an article published as part of a Pfizer-sponsored 'advertising series' on public policy questions, Novak (who has served on Pfizer's board of directors) traced the origins of the modern corporation to the Benedictine monasteries whose trading networks constituted the 'West's first transnational corporations.'"[3]

In 1978, the same year Karol Wojtyla became pope, Novak was asked to join the American Enterprise Institute for Public Policy Research (AEI), a think tank originally founded in 1943 to promote big business and continues to specialize in the globalization of American interests through financial and militaristic means. During the period of neoconservative organizational formation, it grew from a group of twelve resident "thinkers" to an organization with 145 resident scholars, 80 adjunct scholars and a large support staff through funding by the Howard Pew Freedom Trust, financed by the Sun Oil company.[4] Between 1985 and 2004, AEI reported income of $42,342,101, the Lynde and Harry Bradley and Sarah Scaife Foundations among its donors, while Novak received $1,527,397 in support from the Olin and Bradley foundations during the same period.[5]

Novak defended an unfettered market place as the Christian ideal and AEI emerged as one of the leading architects of the George W. Bush administration's policies. More than twenty AEI alumni and visiting scholars and fellows have served either in a Bush administration policy post or on one of his government's many panels and commissions. Lynne Cheney, wife of the Vice President, is an AEI senior fellow. AEI members currently include Newt Gingrich, former speaker of the House; Richard Perle, Reagan's former deputy secretary of defense; and Michael Ledeen, involved in the transfer of arms to Iran during the Iran-Contra affair.[6] Other AEI-featured neoconservative "experts" included John Bolton, David Frum (credited with writing Bush's infamous reference to the "axis of evil" into his State of the Union address), Irving Kristol and Paul Wolfowitz (deputy-secretary of defense under Rumsfeld), all of whom (along with Richard Perle) were to be implicated in the push for war against Iraq.[7] Dick Cheney chose the AEI as the locale for his "Defense of Torture" speech on May 21, 2009.

Novak served in a number of government posts during the Reagan presidency. He wrote for *The National Review.* He was also a board member of the Capital Research Center (anti-union, anti-green, anti-government assistance for the poor) and Center of the American Experiment, another neocon think tank. Novak has also contributed articles to the Heritage Foundation and was one of the founders of the Institute on Religion & Democracy (IRD).

Novak launched his own magazine, *Catholicism in Crisis,* in 1982 to argue against the peace and economic positions of the US episcopate and promote the idolization John Paul II. He rejected the pastoral peace letter of the National Conference of Catholic Bishops as "seriously flawed both as a political document and as a religious one. 'They are overreaching,' he said. 'The desire to speak like prophets is sometimes only hubris....The laity is supposed to lead in Christian reflection on this-worldly matters."[8]

Later known simply *as Crisis*, the magazine was published by the Morley Publishing Group which is funded by the Olin, Lynde and Harry Bradley and Carthage Foundation which is part of the Scaife group. The magazine's contributing editors and publication committee would become a who's who of neo-Catholicism including George Weigel, William Bennett, J. Peter Grace, William E. Simon, Alexander Haig, former baseball commissioner Bowie Kuhn, Reagan speechwriter Peggy Noonan, and Paul Weyrich among them.[9]

The thrice-married former Baptist minister and Catholic convert, Deal Hudson, became editor in 1995.

Hudson further boosted circulation through improved professional direct mail solicitations and raised the magazine's profile by hosting radio and television programs on the Eternal World Television Network (EWTN). The drably designed monthly became a four-color glossy and established an Internet presence. Fundraising was no longer a matter of last-ditch solicitations to stave off financial disaster, but a series of well-planned and well-attended 'partnership dinners,' golf outings, and cruises.[10]

John Paul II wrote an encyclical, *Centisimus Annus* on the hundredth anniversary of *Rerum Novarum*, an encyclical written by Pope Leo XIII in 1891 and the first time a pope had addressed social issues. John Paul II differentiated between a free market in which "the well-being of the whole person comes before simple material comfort and the common good before individual desire." Novak, in his book, *Catholic Ethic and the Spirit of Catholicism*, dismissed the pope's understanding of capitalism as "early" or "primitive." The differences between his and John Paul II's positions, he wrote, were merely terminological, "probably because of European emotional resistance to the word 'capitalism.'"[11]

After John Paul II died, Novak reminisced:

I do recall praising the pope for the good words he had put into his recent letter-to-the-world, *Centesimus Annus*. As we were leaving, he told me he liked very much the article of mine... on the theme of the shift in the pope's understanding of "capital" from *Laborem Exercens* (1981) and the 1991 letter ten years later. "You understand my thought very well," he said generously—words that have warmed my heart ever since, in many a cold and difficult season.[12]

In 1992, Novak wrote an article for *Crisis* titled "Abandoned in a Toxic Culture" in which he charged the "liberal elite" who controlled the media with being "radically Christophobic," and "waging a form of total warfare to destroy every vestige of cultural support for Christian faith and morals." He concluded that Catholics should not only be in union with the pope, but should also "doubt the legitimacy" of the newly elected Clinton government. Continuing the theme of persecution, in another *Crisis* column Novak asserted:

[N]o one can be a Catholic in our culture without being battered daily. Practically everyone in our society defines herself or himself against the Catholic Church. Most feminists surely seem to. When ACT-UP acts up, as often as not they do it in a Catholic church. Even in a more benign sense, what do Protestants "protest" if not the deformations of Rome, and from what are the Enlightened "enlightened" if not from the Dark Ages of you-know-who?[13]

When economists noted the increasing wealth of only a small top percentile of the US population, Novak argued they suffered from the "green worm of envy." "Envy never travels under its own name; it prefers prettier names, good names to which it has no right: 'justice,' 'fairness,' and the like."[14]

George Weigel

George Weigel, who also calls himself a theologian, actually was one for awhile. Like Novak, Weigel studied for the priesthood and received a B.A. at St. Mary's Seminary and University and an M.A. at the University of St. Michael's College, Toronto. In 1975, Weigel moved to Seattle where he was an assistant professor of theology and an assistant (later acting) Dean of Studies at the St. Thomas Seminary School of Theology. In 1977 Weigel became a scholar-in-residence at the World Without War Council of Greater Seattle, "a somewhat conservative group, despite its name—and wrote critically of the anti-Trident submarine protests of Seattle Archbishop Raymond Hunthausen."[15] Like Novak, Weigel would later excoriate fellow-Catholics who disagreed with their bishops.

During the Reagan administration, Weigel was a member of the Institute on Religion & Democracy and other groups connected to the CIA and the Contras which sought to counter religious advocacy for peace in Latin America. In 1984-85, Weigel was a fellow of the Woodrow Wilson International Center for Scholars in Washington DC. From 1989 through June 1996, Weigel was president of the Ethics and Public Policy Center (EPPC) following Hillel Fradkin who, as president of EPPC, had directed the center's Islam and Democracy program, the Jewish Studies program, and the Foreign Policy program. Fradkin was also vice president from 1988 to 1998 of the Lynde and Harry Bradley Foundation and had previously worked as a program officer at the Olin Foundation.[16] Weigel served on the National Committee of the Catholic Campaign for America and is a charter member of the Project for the New American Century.

Professor of political science, Ernest Lefever, had founded the EPPC in 1976 to justify corporate greed. Several EPPC scholars and associates served in the George W. Bush administration. Members of the EPPC's Policy Advisory Board include Irving's son, William Kristol, and Novak. Most of EPPC's funding comes from the Olin, Bradley, Smith Richardson and Scaife foundations. The center is also supported by the Castle Rock (Coors) and Earhart (White Star Oil) foundations.[17] Between 1985 and 2004 the EPPC reported income of $12,535,574.[18]

In a 1995 essay, Weigel asserted that the "culture war" and the "celebration of 'autonomy' as the highest of democratic values" posed "the greatest threat to the integrity of the American experiment since the days before the Civil War."[19] As for his fellow Catholics who didn't share his own requirement of obedience to all Church teachings: "'Cafeteria' Catholicism is simply unserious. The Catholic faith is not a smorgasbord down which you can walk, saying, 'That looks good,' 'That doesn't look so good.' It's a complete package... I mean, with particular reference to the moral teaching of the Church, dissent on what are settled matters of Catholic moral doctrine, with specific reference to the Church's sexual ethic [abortion, birth control, homosexuality]."[20]

Weigel wrote a hagiography of Karol Wojtyla, *Witness to Hope: The Biography of Pope John Paul II,* published by HarperCollins (owned by Rupert Murdoch's News Corporation) in 1999. It portrayed the pope as the world's most courageous defender of human rights and his every utterance as if from Mt. Sinai. The book interpreted John Paul II's ideology in view of, and in agreement with, Republican Party "principles." The goal was to equate a vote for the GOP as a vote for the pope. As Wojtyla's illnesses restricted his travel and his inner circle kept him more and more isolated, Weigel represented himself as the pre-eminent interpreter of the pontiff's views.

When it was reported that the Pope John Paul II Institute—a second one in Lublin, Poland—would publish Wojtyla's academic papers stating his sympathetic view of Marxist thought in relation to the marketplace and a critique of Western capitalism, Weigel wrote a letter to the publisher dismissing what he called an "alleged Wojtyla text" and claiming the pope "did not regard the work as his own," a position rejected by academic and literary experts. Demonstrating post-communist Polish solidarity with neo-Catholic Americans, Lublin Archbishop Jozef Zycinski declared "support for the views of George Weigel" over the actual words of the pope. Wojtyla might have shown "social sensitivity," the archbishop explained, but this shouldn't to be "identified with the position of the left." Zycinski had worked with Weigel on "Free Society" summer schools in Poland, alongside Novak and Fr. Richard John Neuhaus.[21]

Richard John Neuhaus

Neuhaus was a Lutheran minister and, like Novak, a liberal whose conversion to neo-conservatism coincided with the flood of money available to the religious right. (Neuhaus admitted to receiving a "princely salary."[22])

Neuhaus joined the American Enterprise Institute (AEI) in 1975 during its transformation into a neocon think tank. He was part of a project to break down the wall separating church and state. Neuhaus promoted government funding for religion by referring to Christianity as a "mediating structure" in the community. Among the recommendations published in AEI's *Empower People: The Role of Mediating Structures in Public Policy* were government-funded school vouchers and an end to affirmative action policies.

In 1981 Neuhaus wrote the founding document for the Institute on Religion & Democracy. The IRD is funded by the Richard Mellon Scaife, Howard Ahmanson and the Bradley, Coors, Smith-Richardson, Randolph, and Olin foundations and reported an income of $8,387,500 from 1989 through 2005.[23]

Since the late 1970s, Neuhaus has espoused the replacement of liberal secularism with Judeo-Christian morality in "the public square." His 1984 book, *The Naked Public Square,* with a blurb on the cover by Weigel, provided much of the vocabulary for the religious right's increasing political power. Like Novak, Neuhaus depicted capitalism as having a virtuous role and he became religion editor of *The National Review.*

Neuhaus proposed in his book, *The Catholic Moment,* his sequel to *The Naked Public Square,* "that the Catholic Church is the right one to spearhead a drive for Christian reunification and the Church is best-suited to offer moral guidance for the development of public policy."[24] Neuhaus declared Catholics as most qualified to assume a leading role in revitalizing American culture and that non-Catholics were ready to listen to them.[25] Weigel agreed: "The Roman Catholic Church has arguably been the most influential religious community of the past ten decades in shaping the world the twenty-first century will inherit" (he meant it in a good way), and he named John Paul II as "the twentieth century's seminal figure"[26]

With funding from Bradley, Olin, Carthage, Castle Rock and Scaife foundations,[27] Neuhaus established the Institute on Religion and Public

Life, "an interreligious, nonpartisan research and education institute whose purpose is to advance a religiously informed public philosophy for the ordering of society." The institute's main activity is the publication of the journal, *First Things*, begun in 1990. Novak and Weigel are board members. Neuhaus, who became a Catholic priest in 1991, in turn served on the board of the AEI and the EPPC.

During the July 1992 Democratic Convention, Weigel as president of the Ethics and Public Policy Center, and Neuhaus as president of the Institute on Religion and Public Life, placed a full page advertisement in the *New York Times* stating, "Over the next months and years, the American people will confront again the question that Lincoln posed at Gettysburg: whether a nation conceived in liberty and dedicated to human equality can long endure. In this generation, the issue pressing that question on our consciences is the issue of abortion."[28]

Neuhaus kept up a running commentary against the *New York Times*, using it as a whipping boy for the purported ills of the liberal left:

> On almost every issue of great moral and cultural consequence - abortion, euthanasia, eugenics [stem-cell research], parental choice in education [school vouchers], cooperation between church and state [government funded religion], the normative status of marriage and family [no gay marriage], the authority of tradition [obedience], the arts in service to beauty and the mind in service to truth - the Catholic Church is on one side and the *New York Times,* along with most of the media, on the other....
>
> Early every morning will be delivered, to a relatively small percentage of the population, the latest instructions on how we do things here. Then the Church and the people will get on with their business. This is not to say that the Times is unimportant. There are people, including people of influence, who, in touching docility, accept the daily instruction on how and what to think[29]

Due to his Protestant background, Neuhaus played an important role in uniting evangelicals and Catholics. In 1994, Neuhaus published a proclamation, "Evangelicals & Catholics Together: The Christian Mission in the Third Millennium."

> ....In some cultures, that mission encounters resurgent spiritualities and religions that are explicitly hostile to the claims of the Christ. Islam, which in many instances denies the freedom to witness to the Gospel, must be of increasing concern to those who care about religious freedom and the Christian mission....
>
> We contend together for a renewed appreciation

of Western culture. In its history and missionary reach, Christianity engages all cultures while being captive to none.

The proclamation advocated a US foreign policy which "reflects a concern for the defense of democracy and, *wherever prudent and possible*, the protection and advancement of human rights."(emphasis added)

According to "Evangelicals & Catholics Together," abortion was still the gravest threat to the commonweal and what the country needed more than ever was government-supported religious schools and a "market economy." Acknowledging parental concerns, the proclamation included a statement against pornography but stated "antireligious bigotry" was a threat equal to the violence and "sexual depravity" in the media. The proclamation was signed by Fr. Avery Dulles, S.J., (son of Secretary of State John Foster Dulles, a Presbyterian), and Bishop Francis George, both future cardinals. Other signers included Weigel, Novak and Cardinal O'Connor. The most notable evangelicals listed were Pat Robertson and Charles Colson, former chief counsel to President Richard Nixon.[30]

In the same spirit, Pat Robertson's Christian Coalition made a highly publicized launch of the Catholic Alliance in 1995. Neuhaus supported the Alliance but it never became as influential as Robertson and co-founder, Ralph Reed, had hoped.[31]

Speaking at a gathering of US bishops in 1994, Neuhaus exhorted them to take a more public role in supporting the neocon agenda adding that clergy and laity also had to "unhesitatingly accept [their] responsibility to remedy a culture that is descending into decadence and disarray." Adding the pro-forma fear factor, Neuhaus ended with, "At the edge of the Third Millennium maybe the springtime is at hand; maybe the long dark winter has just begun. We do not know."

By 1996 Neuhaus had adopted an even more critical tone. In September, after the Senate had failed to override President Clinton's veto of the partial-birth abortion ban, he offered the following comments: "It is not hyperbole to say that we are at a point at which millions of conscientious American citizens are reflecting upon whether this is a legitimate regime. That is the solemn moment that we have reached."....

In November 1996 Neuhaus produced a provocative issue of *First Things*, a colloquium on judicial activism entitled "The End of Democracy?" In his introduction, he reiterated what he had said in September about the questionable status of the American regime, even alluding to Hitler's Germany: "America is not and, please God, will never become Nazi Germany, but it is only blind hubris that denies that it can happen here and, in peculiarly

American ways, may be happening here." That issue of *First Things* thrilled some readers and infuriated others. (Three members of the journal's board were so upset by Neuhaus's incendiary language that they resigned.)[32]

Damon Linker worked under Neuhaus at *First Things*—first as associate editor then as its editor from May 2001 to February 2005. In a critique entitled "The Christianizing of America" Linker wrote:

> The one [Catholic writer] who has exercised the greatest influence on the ideological agenda of the religious right is Richard John Neuhaus....Any attempt to come to terms with the religious challenge to secular politics in contemporary America must confront Neuhaus's enormously ambitious and increasingly influential enterprise....
>
> That America toward which Richard John Neuhaus wishes to lead us is an America in which eschatological [the final events in the history of the world] panic is deliberately channeled into public life, in which moral and theological absolutists demonize the country's political institutions and make nonnegotiable public demands under the threat of sacralized revolutionary violence, in which citizens flee from the inner obligations of freedom and long to subordinate themselves to ecclesiastical authority, and in which traditionalist Christianity thoroughly dominates the nation's public life.[33]

An article in the *Houston Catholic Worker* (the Catholic Workers are lay persons dedicated to helping the poor) responding to the neo-Catholics noted:

> The problem with Michael Novak and fellow neoconservatives George Weigel, Fr. John Neuhaus and Fr. Robert Sirico is this: They use Catholicism as window dressing to promote an economic system based solely on self-interest, a system that has nothing to do with the Gospel or Catholic social teaching. They replace the heart of Catholicism with Adam Smith and Max Weber (virtue comes to society only through self-interest; the Gospel is a private affair).[34]

Rev. C. John McCloskey III

"The bloody rise of theologically inspired politics" was advocated by Rev. C. John McCloskey III, foremost US Opus Dei spokesman and former stockbroker. As head of the Catholic Information Center, an Opus Dei institute located at 1501 K Street just two blocks from the White House, McCloskey is best known for converting high-profile conservatives to Roman Catholicism—Supreme Court nominee Robert Bork, Republican Sen. Sam Brownback of Kansas, TV commentator Lawrence Kudlow, publisher Alfred Regnery, politician Lewis Lehrman, Tyco counsel Mark Belnick and columnist Robert Novak.

When McCloskey was ordained in Rome in 1982, he wrote, "Priests are warriors for Jesus Christ. They are the Navy Seals, the Army Rangers, and the Green Berets of the Catholic Church, and I'm proud to serve among their ranks." He worked as associate chaplain at Princeton University's Aquinas Institute from 1985 to 1990 when he was dismissed for "being overly aggressive in recruiting and impinging on academic freedom."[35]

McCloskey took over the Center's operation in 1997 as the Republican's K Street Project, named for the street in Washington DC where the largest lobbying firms have their headquarters, was picking up steam. The K Street Project was founded in 1995 by Grover Norquist, a GOP strategist, and then-House majority whip, Tom DeLay, to pressure Washington lobbying firms into providing party hacks with high-paying jobs. In return, the lobbyists were given access to Republican senators, representatives, administrators and regulators—in effect placing a huge "for sale" sign over the government especially after the 2000 election. During the George W. Bush administration lobbyists became known as "the fourth branch of government" for their ability to buy legislation and regulations favorable to big-money interests and for providing employment to discredited public officials after their government work was exposed as inept, shoddy and/or corrupt.

McCloskey is on the Board of Advisors for the IRD and is a fellow at the Faith and Reason Institute located at 1413 K Street, another neocon think-tank funded by the Earhart and Bradley foundations. Novak and Neuhaus have been guest presenters at the Catholic Information Center.

One of McCloskey's functions was to goad Christians into a religious war with Islam. McCloskey wrote that unlike previous wars of the twentieth century,

> ...the present world conflicts reflect instead radically distinctive ways of looking at the ways man worships God or what gives meaning to life. The world, in short, is divided between a Western one and a non-Western many. As we are of the West and the West represents largely the continued existence of Greco-Roman civilization as 'baptized' by Christianity down to our own time, the question is whether the moral resources of the West and hence its willingness to fight are so depleted that they will be overcome by the "non-Western many."[36]

Provocation for a Christian holy war against Islam was and is a common theme for the religious right as a replacement for their holy war against the godless Soviets after the dissolution of the USSR. Since 1990, *The Remnant,* a US Catholic newspaper sharing many of the same goals as Opus Dei such as the restoration of Roman Catholic dictators, organizes an annual "pilgrimage" to France in hopes of creating young zealots capable of violence. The paper advertises, "This Pilgrimage dates back to the middle ages [and] is extremely difficult! It is a 72-mile, 3-day walk from Paris to Chartres—through woods and fields and over blacktop highways and country roads. Pilgrims sleep outside, in floor-less tents. They eat soup, bread and water. They develop horrible blisters and they suffer unbelievable fatigue." Editor Michael J. Matt reported at the conclusion of the 2005 "3-day walk into the past that is the Catholic training ground for the future,"

> A thousand children and young adults, many with feet freshly bandaged after the grueling march, knelt on the ground. The look on their faces was the same from one to the next—serene but deadly serious. It wasn't difficult to imagine them just then with bloodied swords secured to their belts and soiled red crosses emblazoned across their chests, having just limped in from the battlefield. And why not…these were no less the crusaders than the ones of old about whom we read in history books; they too fight for the survival of the old Faith and for the protection of the holy places, especially those inside their hearts. They were cross-bearers in every sense of the word and it was a privilege to pray with them!
>
> In the past, knights were called upon to protect the pilgrims on their way to the holy places. It seems that we have need once again of just such "pilgrim-soldiers" who will see to it that these holy "marches toward the light of God" are not shut down by the diabolical hands of Moslems, democratic governments, Jesuits who've lost the Faith, and the rest of the worldly rabble.[37]

When Clinton was elected president, the neo-Catholics threatened civil war to take by force what they were unable to accomplish with the ballot. Novak's assertion that "the liberal elite were waging total warfare to destroy every vestige of Christian faith and morals," Weigel's same warning of the internal "threat to America," Neuhaus' questioning whether a duly-elected US government was a "legitimate regime" he equated with Nazi Germany, were calls-to-arms. In an article appearing in *Catholic World Report* titled "2030: Looking Backwards," McCloskey assumes the persona of an American priest reminiscing with another cleric in the year 2030 over past events using the standard religious right code words:

In retrospect, the great battles over the last 30 years over the fundamental issues of the sanctity of marriage [homosexuality], the rights of parents [tax supported schools], and the sacredness of human life [abortion] have been of enormous help in renewing the Church and to some extent, society. We finally received as a gift from God what had been missing from our ecclesial experience these 250 years in North America—a strong persecution that was a true purification for our "sick society." The tens of thousands of martyrs and confessors for the Faith in North America were indeed the "seed of the Church" as they were in pre-Edict of Milan Christianity.

The final short and relatively bloodless conflict produced our Regional States of North America. The outcome was by no means an ideal solution but it does allow Christians to live in states that recognize the natural law and divine Revelation [as interpreted by Christian Nationalists], the right of free practice of religion [government supported religion], and laws on marriage, family, and life that reflect the primacy of our Faith. With time and the reality of the ever-decreasing population of the states that worship at the altar of the culture of death [abortion], perhaps we will be able to reunite and fulfill the Founding Fathers of the old United States dream to be "a shining city on a hill."[38]

When talking with the secular press, however, McCloskey was a little more guarded about advocating for civil war:

Do I think it's possible for someone who believes in the sanctity of marriage, the sanctity of life, the sanctity of family, over a period of time to choose to survive with people who think it's OK to kill women and children or for—quote —homosexual couples to exist and be recognized? No, I don't think that's possible. I don't know how it's going to work itself out, but I know it's not possible, and my hope and prayer is that it does not end in violence. But, unfortunately, in the past, these types of things have tended to end this way. If American Catholics feel that's troubling, let them. I don't feel it's troubling at all.[39]

McCloskey meant for orthodox Catholics specifically, not just Christians at large, to be the victors. In one of his columns, he congratulated the author who wrote:

Thus the Protestant revolt took power in what had

been provinces beyond the gates of Rome, in countries with fewer centuries of high civilization and Christianity: the Nordic Countries, northern Germany, parts of old Helvetia (Switzerland), parts of what became the Netherlands. All the barbaric peoples who had gaped and mocked at the legions of Rome and later plundered Rome's empire now rose again in a new barbarian assault against Roman authority.[40]

McCloskey is also anti-immigrant, ("...whether the majority of Hispanics will form almost a separate region within the United States, resulting in a 'Balkanization' of America..."), pro-death penalty ("...the perpetual teaching of the Church is that capital punishment is something that can be imposed by the state"), and anti-democracy ("*Americanism* could be defined simply as 'the basic harmony of American democratic ways with Catholicism'" which McCloskey termed both a "disorder" and a "heresy").

Opus Dei used the notoriety provided by the publication and filming of Dan Brown's *The Da Vinci Code* to portray themselves as a benign organization whose only goal is the "personal sanctification" of their members. Yet we know at least two men close to McCloskey were willing to commit treason and betrayal.

The most notorious traitor in recent history is Opus Dei member Robert Hanssen, an FBI agent convicted on July 6, 2001, for selling US intelligence to the Russians. A regular visitor to McCloskey's K Street Center, Hansen also "had spent several years directing the bureau's notorious Reagan-era probes of American liberal and peace organizations....What this often meant in practice was the harassment and sometimes the smearing of Americans engaged in lawful political activity [including] Catholic adversaries of Opus Dei."[41]

In 1997, Hanssen fed columnist Robert Novak—one of McCloskey's celebrity converts—information which Novak used to accuse the Clinton administration's attorney general, Janet Reno, and the Justice Department of covering up campaign finance irregularities. An Accuracy in Media report questioned, "What could explain Hanssen's use of Bob Novak to expose it, rather than going through normal channels?" A follow-up question might be, "Of all the Washington reporters, why did Hanssen bring the information to Novak?"

When the George W. Bush administration leaked the identity of an undercover CIA operative to seven journalists in retaliation for her husband, US diplomat Joseph Wilson, challenging the president's veracity in the *New York Times*, it was Novak who first made the name, Valerie Plame, public on July 14, 2003. Novak even admitted in a subsequent column that a CIA official had specifically asked him *not* to use Plame's name. Plame and her associates, foreign and domestic, were compromised and/or endangered. *The Washington Post* reported:

A former diplomat who spoke on condition of anonymity said yesterday that every foreign intelligence service would run Plame's name through its databases within hours of its publication to determine if she had visited their country and to reconstruct her activities.

Plame's cover as an "analyst" for Brewster-Jennings & Associates, a dummy company set up for use by CIA operatives, was also first made public by Novak thereby jeopardizing the lives of the other agents using the same cover.[42]

In a later interview, Plame pointed out the detrimental ripple effect Novak's columns had on all US global intelligence operations because they revealed that Bush administration officials were capable of disclosing classified information and state secrets for political gain. In grave danger from credible threats against her life, and with a refusal by the Bush administration to provide them with security, Plame, her husband and their children were forced to relocate to Mexico.[43]

Novak, however, thought it was all a hoot. "In March [2004], at the ultimate Washington insider event—the annual Gridiron Club dinner—Novak starred in a skit about the Plame leak. Dressed in a top hat and cut-away coat, the columnist hammed it up in front of an audience of his peers, crooning to the tune of 'Once I Had a Secret Love.' Novak sang off-key about outing 'a girl spy' thanks to 'a secret source who lived within the great White House.'"[44]

Novak was a frequent contributor to *First Things* and *National Review.* He was a member of the Catholic Advisory Board for the Tom Monaghan's Ave Maria Mutual Funds. Novak's son is director of marketing for Regnery Publishing (owner Alfred Regnery being another McCloskey convert), the company that published *Unfit for Command,* the Swift Boat Veteran's book which tried to discredit John Kerry's war record, but was later proved to be, as Sen. John McCain stated, "dishonest and dishonorable." Novak used his column and television appearances to disseminate the Swift Boat claim that Kerry had lied his way into receiving medals in Vietnam. Regnery also published Novak's newsletter.[45]

Rev. Frank Pavone

Pavone is head of Priests for Life (PFL), an overtly political organization since its founding in 1991. In 1993, Cardinal O'Connor named Pavone as its leader and PFL headquarters was moved to Pavone's home base on Staten Island, New York. The PFL organization provides an extensive collection of photos of both live and aborted fetuses via the internet. Membership is for bishops and priests but there is also a lay auxiliary membership. The primary mission is to politicize and mobilize Catholic clergy and its tactics are often aggressive.[46]

In 1995, Pavone chose as his closest partners not other Catholic clergy but the founders of a politically connected Pentecostal Washington DC church. Twin brothers Paul and Rob Schenck, termed "completed" Jews by the religious right meaning they were born Jews and became Christians, had furnished the seed money for the American Center for Law and Justice and Paul was the executive vice president. The three served as founders, executives or board members of at least half a dozen other anti-abortion groups including Randall Terry's Operation Rescue. Rob Schenck also has a history of arrests regarding abortion clinics.[47] [48]

PFL has the unusual practice of paying "grants and allocations" to other organizations rather than just receiving them. In 2003, Priests for Life was granted NGO (non-governmental organization) status by the United Nations coinciding with the fact its largest beneficiary that same year was the Vatican's Pontifical Council for Justice and Peace. The council's president, Cardinal Renato Martino, sits on the PFL's Episcopal Board of Advisors. Pavone is an official of the Pontifical Council for the Family,[49] the Vatican dicastery (department) most closely associated with Opus Dei.

The PFL web site lists several auxiliary organizations, including Deacons for Life, headed by Keith Fornier. Fornier was an advisor to publisher Steve Forbes, a Republican presidential candidate in 1996 and 2000, and first executive director of Pat Robertson's American Center for Law and Justice, founded to provoke and support legal challenges to the separation of church and state.[50]

In 2001, PFL launched an advertising campaign aimed at women who had had abortions. Because it politicized the help it offered women, the campaign was quashed by some US bishops in their respective dioceses. Cardinal Egan ordered Pavone to stop running PFL and return to parish work because of his close connection to Joseph Schiedler, convicted of extortion and threats of violence at abortion clinics, but Pavone continues as national director of PFL. Disappointed by his continued failure to recruit other priests in large numbers, Pavone accepted an invitation in 2004 by Bishop John Yanta, head of the Diocese of Amarillo in the Texas Panhandle, to institute his own seminary and establish a new community of priests, [51] the Missionaries of the Gospel of Life.[52] The effort failed but Pavone stayed on in Texas.

For fiscal year 2005, Charity Navigator gave Priests for Life a less than 50 percent rating based on administrative and fundraising expenses totaling more than 30 per cent of its outlays. Executive Director Anthony De Stefano was paid $168,641 in addition to other compensation received from affiliates.

Rick Santorum

Although Kansas Sen. Sam Brownback became a Catholic under McCloskey's sponsorship, no elected US official has been closer to Opus Dei or more committed to Christian Nationalism than Pennsylvania Sen. Rick Santorum. Santorum led the US delegation to a week-long celebration in

Rome honoring Josemaria Escrivá in January 2002. "The extent of the power and prestige of Opus Dei in today's Catholic Church was on full display during a high profile Jan. 7-11 congress here marking the 100th anniversary of the birth of founder Josemaria Escrivá."[53] Over a thousand international right-wing Church and government officials attended who "echoed the call for unity between faith and politics," per the *National Catholic Reporter.*

> Santorum was a forceful champion of this view. He told *NCR* that a distinction between private religious conviction and public responsibility, enshrined in John Kennedy's famous speech in 1960 saying he would not take orders from the Catholic Church if elected president, has caused "much harm in America. All of us have heard people say, 'I privately am against abortion, homosexual marriage, stem cell research, cloning. But who am I to decide that it's not right for somebody else?' It sounds good," Santourm said. "But it is the corruption of freedom of conscience."
>
> Santorum told *NCR* that he regards George W. Bush as "the first Catholic president of the United States. From economic issues focusing on the poor and social justice, to issues of human life, George Bush is there," he said. "He has every right to say, 'I'm where you are if you're a believing Catholic.'"[54]

A report released by Political Money Line listing trips for members of Congress funded by outside groups showed the Opus Dei Pontifical University of the Holy Cross Foundation paid $2,000 for Santorum to give a speech during the January 2002 event. Sounding a bit defensive, his spokeswoman, Christine Shott, "stressed that most of Santorum's trip was taken up mostly by meetings with embassy and Italian officials on matters relating to homeland security."[55]

Santorum will best be remembered for his leadership in the K Street Project. Elected to the Senate in 1994, Santorum was the Senate liaison. His infamous Tuesday-morning meetings to review which Republicans would fill which openings in the lobbying firms and to do what he could to grease the wheels of political corruption continued even after the Jack Abramoff scandal broke.

During the 2000 presidential campaign, Bush referred to himself as a "compassionate conservative." In a show of solidarity with Bush, Santorum helped sponsor the Good Neighbor Initiative, a fund-raising drive that netted $700,000, mostly from big corporations, to do good works in Philadelphia.[56] After the president's inauguration, Santorum transformed his group into a charity, the Operation Good Neighbor Foundation.

According to its web site, the Senator's charity

has doled out $474,000. But public records show that the group has raised considerably more than that since its inception in 2001. A review of federal tax returns filed by the foundation for 2001, 2002, and 2003 shows that the charity spent just 35.9 percent of the nearly $1 million raised on its charitable grants, while spending 56.5 percent on expenses like salaries, fund-raising commissions, travel, conference costs, and rent.[57]

Gary Ruskin of the Congressional Accountability Project, a good-government group, questioned why Operation Good Neighbor would hire lobbyists and political operatives instead of charity professionals. "It looks like another pocket to fill," Ruskin said, adding: "Senator Santorum is obviously a man with many pockets."[58]

The *Philadelphia Daily News* reported the largest individual contributor to Operation Good Neighbor was a real estate developer who made his donation at the same time Santorum was trying to secure $8.5 million in federal funding for one of the developer's projects. The paper further reported that in addition to donating to Santorum's charity, officials from Preferred Real Estate and their spouses made donations to Santorum's re-election campaign and to America's Foundation,[59] Santorum's PAC whose stated purpose was to assist other political candidates.

"In far too many families with young children, both parents are working, when, if they really took an honest look at the budget, they might find they don't both need to," Santorum wrote in his 2005 book, *It Takes a Family: Conservatism and the Common Good*. Most working parents, however, don't have Santorum's resources. After buying a home in northern Virginia, America's Foundation listed payments such as "dozens of trips to the Starbucks in Leesburg, a number of stops at fast-food joints, and purchases at Target, Wal-Mart, and a Giant supermarket in northern Virginia, although a Santorum aide defends those charges as legitimate political costs." America's Foundation gave just 18.1 percent of its money to other candidates in a recent five-year period. The biggest source of income for America's Foundation is industry PAC's—banking, insurance, health care, and pharmaceuticals.

Santorum has always run as a "moral values" conservative, but America's Foundation has accepted donations from gambling, tobacco and liquor interests. In October 2004, Santorum voted in committee to kill a provision allowing the Food and Drug Administration to regulate the tobacco industry. In April 2005, the senator introduced legislation that would halve the federal excise tax on beer. A study by the Center for Responsive Politics found Santorum was first among all 535 members of Congress in raising money from lobbyists for his regular campaign fund.[60]

Santorum was given a standing ovation at the first National Catholic Prayer Breakfast in April 2004. "'The greatest power the devil has,' Santorum said, 'is lies.' Those 'lies,' said Santorum, allow 'the greatest country in the world' to be a 'land so blessed' and yet 'soulless, vacuous and empty of His spirit.'"[61]

CHAPTER 11

THE 2000 PRESIDENTIAL CAMPAIGN

The Catholic Task Force

While the GOP could count on carrying the South in the 2000 presidential campaign, electoral votes from the heavily-Catholic states of Pennsylvania, Ohio, Michigan, and Illinois were essential. The Republican National Committee's Catholic Task Force, first formed in 1996, was revitalized in February 1999 and chaired by Colorado businessman, Jim Nicholson, later appointed by George W. Bush as US Ambassador to the Vatican. It had 93 members, including 27 members of Congress, and was headed by Thomas Melady, former ambassador under Presidents Nixon and George H.W. Bush including a posting as Bush's ambassador to the Vatican. Members included William Barr, attorney general under Bush; Alexander Haig, secretary of state in the Reagan administration; former Baseball Commissioner Bowie Kuhn, Rep. Bill Archer, R-Tex.; Rep. Henry Hyde, R-Ill.; Sen. Rick Santorum, R-Pa.; John Klink, an advisor to the Vatican's United Nations mission; and Peter Flanigan, a trustee of the John Olin Foundation.[1]

The Task Force planned for the campaign by using information in an article appearing in *Crisis* magazine written by pollster Steve Wagner and based on surveys conducted by Princeton University political scientist Robert P. George. George served on the board of directors of the IRD, the EPPC, the Catholic League for Religious and Civil Rights, and the anti-gay Alliance for Marriage. He would become a regular adviser to George W. Bush on Supreme Court nominations, stem cell research and the faith-based initiative. *The Nation* magazine reported, "Bush's operative, former Republican National Committee chief and chief Enron lobbyist Ed Gillespie, also a right-wing Catholic, chose George and others to teach Bush how to 'speak Catholic.'" According to *Crisis* magazine, "If there really is a vast, right-wing conspiracy, its leaders probably meet in George's basement."[2]

Conducted during a two-year period, the surveys concluded that Catholics who attended Mass frequently would most likely conform to Lakoff's "strict father" metaphor and align with evangelicals over "moral values." The study concluded "that Bob Dole might actually have won the

1996 Presidential election if he had attracted more Catholics in just a handful of states."[3] *Crisis* editor Deal Hudson sent the results to all the Republican presidential candidates' headquarters but "according to GOP strategist, Grover Norquist, Karl Rove was the only one to show interest. Rove invited Hudson and 20 prominent Catholics to two meetings in September, 1999, and May, 2000."[4]

Karl Rove was a political operative schooled in dirty tricks. Bush Senior chose Rove as chairman of the College Republicans in 1973 and then hired him as a special assistant to the Republican National Committee. It was during this time the elder Bush introduced Rove to his son, George W. Rove moved to Texas in 1976 when he married a Houston socialite. In 1977, Rove got a job as executive director of the Fund for Limited Government, a political action committee (PAC) in Houston formed by James A. Baker, later George H.W. Bush's secretary of state. The PAC was the foundation of the Bush-for-President campaign of 1979-1980 resulting in Bush's vice-presidency. In 1981 Rove started a direct mail consulting firm, Karl Rove & Co., in Austin. Rove ran his consulting business until 1999, when he sold the firm to take a full-time position in George W. Bush's presidential campaign. Between 1981 and 1999, Rove worked on hundreds of political campaigns. It was estimated Rove won 34 of the 41 races where he was the primary strategist.[5]

In its January 2000 mission statement, the Catholic Task Force claimed, "We have studied the political record of all major political parties and we believe that the Republican Party is closest to the teachings of the Catholic Church," a fallacious assertion which remained unchallenged by the hierarchs but not all Catholics.

> As researchers who have examined the religious factor in the US Congress, we decided to examine the Republican claims. Our extensive analysis, which included consulting many experts on Congressional votes in relation to Catholic teaching, shows clearly that, aside from the Republican Party's antiabortion stand, and its support for educational vouchers and funds for Catholic schools, the party's claim to best represent Catholic views is greatly exaggerated. In virtually every other area of concern to Catholic leaders and to Network, the Catholic social justice lobby, support by Democrats in Congress for positions aligned with Church teaching far outranks support by Republicans. These areas include raising the minimum wage, housing assistance, restricting the death penalty, health insurance, increased Medicaid eligibility, patients' bill of rights, cuts in military spending and support for peacekeeping efforts.[6]

Notre Dame University President Theodore Hesburgh noted that those Catholics who made opposition to legal abortion their political priority would find themselves supporting candidates who disagreed with 95 percent of the bishop's pre-1990 social justice agenda—the commitment to alleviating poverty, to demilitarization, to affirmative action, to ending capital punishment. Although these issues were no longer of concern to the most recently appointed prelates, there was still a moderate faction in the United States Conference of Catholic Bishops (changing their name in 2000 from the National Council of Catholic Bishops) which urged a "more generous immigration policy", a special concern for the poor and vulnerable and reform of the health care system "rooted in values that respect human dignity." But while the USCCB had denounced other groups for misrepresenting themselves as "Catholic," they never challenged the GOP's Catholic Task Force for claiming the title. According to Hudson, their only objection was that the bishops thought they alone should be consulted on policy issues.[7]

Priests, bishops, archbishops and cardinals aligned themselves with, and curried friendship with, Task Force members although the Task Force declared itself blatantly partisan and its goal as strictly political. It was what it claimed to be: "A leadership of dedicated lay Catholic Republicans whose mission is to influence the Catholic vote in favor of Republican candidates in 2000."[8]

The 2000 Neo-Catholic Campaign

George H. W. Bush was a stellar student-athlete at Andover and Yale. George W. Bush, was a mediocre performer, at best. The elder volunteered for combat in World War II, flew missions off aircraft carriers and parachuted from a burning plane. During the Vietnam War, the younger Bush slipped past other applicants to snare a treasured spot in the Texas National Guard.

Though both enjoyed privileged backgrounds—coming from blue-blood Yankee stock—the elder George Bush struck out for Texas after college and ran a moderately successful oil business. He entered politics, won a House seat and built a sparkling résumé of high-profile posts, including UN ambassador and CIA director. The younger Bush partied through his 20's and 30's. He could be surly when drunk. He also lost investment money forked over by his father's friends.

But not all the contrasts with his father are unfavorable for the Texas governor. Journalists who travel with the younger Bush marvel at his ease with crowds, his common touch, his unwavering "compassionate conservative" mantra, and even his charisma.[9]

Rove had handled Bush's 1994 gubernatorial race against incumbent Gov. Ann Richards. During the campaign, pollsters called voters to ask such questions as whether people would be "more or less likely to vote for Governor Richards if [they] knew her staff is dominated by lesbians." During the 2000 Republican primary campaign in South Carolina, voters were polled with the question, "Would you be more likely or less likely to vote for John McCain for president if you knew he had fathered an illegitimate black child?"[10]

> This year [2000], spurred by an unexpectedly contentious Republican primary, the nation is witnessing a 180-degree turn on the historic Kennedy confrontation. This time, it is a worried Protestant candidate from Texas, Gov. George W. Bush, who is now daily seeking out Catholic forums and photo ops, replete with church banners and Roman-collared clerics, to assure one and all his presidency would not be an instrument of a dominant religious group—evangelical Protestantism.... "The running joke here is whether Governor Bush will join the Knights of Columbus by primary day," noted John C. Green, director of the Bliss Institute of Applied Politics at the University of Akron.[11]

Bush made only one misstep vis-à-vis the Catholic vote during the primaries by appearing at Bob Jones University in early February. The fundamentalist Christian school which banned interracial dating had declared Catholicism a cult and the pope was sometimes referred to as Satan. This was Bush's first appearance in South Carolina after a 19 point loss to Sen. John McCain in New Hampshire and only ten days before the New York primary. Because of the ensuing uproar in the heavily-Catholic state, Bush wrote a letter to New York's Archbishop John O'Connor. "On reflection, I should have been more clear in disassociating myself from anti-Catholic sentiments and racial prejudice. It was a missed opportunity, causing needless offense, which I deeply regret," Bush wrote without actually apologizing for his visit. "Officials with the Bush campaign said that the letter to Cardinal O'Connor was inspired in part by the Bush family's longstanding friendship with the cardinal."[12]

Less than a month later, in an effort to further assuage any lingering hurt feelings among Catholics, House Speaker Dennis Hastert (R-Ill.) reversed his earlier decision to appoint a Protestant minister as chaplain for the House of Representative and for the first time in history a Catholic priest was named to the post. One of the Rev. Daniel Coughlin's first acts was to deliver the sermon at a Mass sponsored by the Republican National Committee where he endorsed Republican-sponsored revisions to the tax code.[13]

In June 2000, the GOP announced it was increasing its Catholic outreach in Florida, New Jersey, and Louisiana in addition to the key Rust Belt states. Nicholson announced, "We're shifting into high gear in our efforts to engage Catholic voters. We believe, based on solid research, that Catholic voters are especially inclined this year to support Republican candidates, and we intend to do everything we can to realize this potential." Steve Wagner, who had written the *Crisis* article, was named executive director of the Catholic Task Force and Brian Tierney (Tierney Communications) of Philadelphia was appointed as chair.

Tierney was a powerful public relations figure with close ties to Cardinal Anthony Bevilacqua, the prelate who succeeded Wojtyla's friend, Cardinal Krol, in Philadelphia when Krol resigned due to poor health in 1988. Tierney's firm represented the archdiocese in its battles with the *Philadelphia Inquirer* when reporter Ralph Cipriano investigated the diocese's big expenditures on an elaborate video-conferencing center and $200,000 to refurbish Bevilacqua's beachfront summer residence at a time when the diocese was unable to save parishes and schools in poor neighborhoods. Bevilacqua's response throughout was the standard, "he would not allow any news organization to unjustly malign the Catholic Church."[14]

Tierney was also a key organizer for the Republican Convention in Philadelphia where blatant appeals were made for the Catholic vote.

> Looking heavenward from the floor of Philadelphia's First Union Center, delegates spotted a large white banner that appeared on the last evening of the convention. Bright red letters declared "Catholics for Bush" on the unauthorized, hand-painted sheet, hanging from a plush skybox the GOP provided for its Catholic Task Force. Party strategists believe that Catholic swing voters will provide Bush with his margin of victory. According to Steven Wagner, the Task Force's executive director, George W. Bush has strengthened his appeal to Catholic voters in the last few weeks, even though he didn't pick a Catholic as his running mate. "With the selection of Dick Cheney, the ticket has responded to the call of the bishops to stand unambiguously for the life of the unborn," Wagner explains. Deal Hudson, editor of *Crisis* magazine and an informal adviser to the Bush campaign, agrees that any doubts about Bush's commitment to the pro-life cause should be eliminated with his selection of a pro-life running mate, and his acceptance-speech pledge to sign a ban on partial-birth abortion.
>
> The Task Force wanted this year's convention to have a visible Catholic presence, and a steady stream of the city's priests was hosted in its crowded skybox each night. Some of them periodically visited delegates on the convention floor. Cardinal Bevilacqua of the Archdiocese of Philadelphia delivered the closing prayer of the convention.[15]

When Catholics Al Smith and John F. Kennedy were running for president, both the candidates and the American hierarchy would have quickly rejected any suggestion the bishops had interfered in those campaigns. Both Smith and Kennedy had assured the public they did not take directions from the Church and both insisted on a strict separation of church and state. Yet in 2000, Catholic prelates lined up to show their support of George W. Bush and the candidate was eager to show he relied on their advice and sought their endorsement.

Bush visited Philadelphia churches and posed for pictures with Bevilacqua during the campaign.[16] Tierney, rewarded with a knighthood in the Papal Order of St. Gregory the Great, put together a list of three million Catholics for a direct-mail and phone political campaign including the State of Florida. Bevilacqua energized his flock with a "voters guide" circulated throughout his 283 parishes. His political involvement was described by the *Philadelphia Inquirer* as "heralding a new era in Catholic activism."[17]

In late September, Bush met with Cardinal Roger Mahony of Los Angeles. In October, Bush had a private meeting with Cardinal Edward Egan, chosen to replace O'Connor who had died in May. Nine days later, Egan released a pastoral letter urging Catholics to vote for those "who share our commitment to the fundamental rights of the unborn." On October 26, Bush met with Pittsburgh Bishop Donald Wuerl (formerly Archbishop Hunthausen's administrator), and returned to Pennsylvania to meet with Bevilacqua on the last weekend before the presidential election. "All in all, according to Tierney, Bush met with more than a dozen bishops during the campaign."[18]

Bush also met with Fr. Frank Pavone, head of Priests for Life (PFL), which ran a full-page ad in the *New York Times* with Pavone's "brazen and open endorsement of Bush."[19] In total, PFL spent $1 million on advertising to convince Catholics to vote Republican[20] and sent a package of campaign information to every US Catholic parish encouraging each one "to form a committee which deals in some way with the abortion issue." The package included bulletin inserts, camera-ready documents of the USCCB, their own brochure *Caesar Must Obey God,* and audio tapes titled "Does the Church Have a Political Role?" and "Challenging Government Leaders to Defend Life."[21]

Fr. Richard John Neuhaus claimed an allegation was made in *The New Republic* "that my friends and I, in league with certain evangelical Protestant co-conspirators, have captured the Bush campaign." Neuhaus didn't refute the claim but only modestly responded, "My influence is much exaggerated."[22] During the campaign, Bush repeatedly used the vocabulary of the religious right to connect with "values" voters: "compassionate conservatism," in part to appeal to those Christians still concerned with poverty issues; "sanctity of marriage," so as not to sound outright homophobic and yet convey a homophobic message; and "culture of life," strictly tailored to mean the protection of the unborn supersedes the right to life of the mother.[23]

While governor, Bush wrote the introduction to Marvin Olasky's book, *Compassionate Conservatism: What it is, What it Does, and How it*

Can Transform America released in time for the Republican convention. "Marvin is compassionate conservatism's leading thinker," Bush wrote. Some Republican women were concerned about Bush's endorsement because Olasky had written in his newsletter: "God does not forbid women to be leaders in society, generally speaking, but when that occurs it's usually because of the abdication of men." But this had little effect on the voters who favored Bush. More importantly, Olasky supported a "faith-based initiative" so that even social assistance tax dollars could be diverted to Republican cronies.[24]

Bush's "culture of life" record regarding the death penalty in Texas briefly became a campaign issue. During his term as governor, Texas executed 152 prisoners, forty in the year 2000. "It is a serious indictment of Bush that as Texas governor he acted as death's cheerleader, never questioning a system in which defense lawyers have nodded off in the courtroom, where death sentences have been rendered on the basis of one eyewitness and where every effort has been made to accelerate the process" wrote Richard Cohen of the *Washington Post* in June 2000.[25]

Cohen also reported in October 2000 that one of the execution chamber's "tie-down team" members, Fred Allen, had to prepare so many people for lethal injections during 2000, he quit his job in disgust. A former Texas Department of Public Safety officer, a devout Roman Catholic, told this reporter that evidence to the contrary, Bush was more than happy to ignore DNA data and documented cases of prosecutorial misconduct to send innocent people to the Huntsville, Texas lethal injection chamber. He said the number of executed mentally retarded, African Americans, and those who committed capital crimes as minors was proof that Bush was insensitive and a "phony Christian."[26]

Already a declared presidential candidate in August 1999, Bush gave an interview which wasn't widely reported until the 2000 campaign. Born-again Christian, Karla Faye Tucker, a convicted murderer who had led a prison ministry, appeared on the *Larry King Show* just prior to her 1998 execution. In an interview with *Talk* magazine, Bush mentioned he had seen the show. "I watched his interview with her, though. He asked her real difficult questions, like, 'What would you say to Governor Bush?'" The *Talk* reporter asked how she answered. "Please," Bush whimpers, his lips pursed in mock desperation, "don't kill me."[27]

Bush had ignored John Paul II's personal and specific plea to spare the life of Karla Faye Tucker. During a visit to St. Louis, Missouri, in January 1999, the pope said, "I renew the appeal I made most recently at Christmas for a consensus to end the death penalty, which is both cruel and unnecessary."[28] The 1997 edition of the *Catechism of the Catholic Church* states that the death penalty was wrong unless needed to protect the public safety, which is never the case in the US.

Cafeteria Catholicism as regards capital punishment, however, was justified by the neo-Catholics. Ralph McInerny, cofounder of *Crisis* magazine who served on George W. Bush's Committee on the Arts and Humanities, wrote, "George Weigel told me recently that he was seeing the same assumption spreading about the death penalty. It is widely believed that the Church condemns [it], no exceptions....But that is not the teaching of the Church."[29] Michael Novak praised the execution of Saddam Hussein as "that noble achievement now an imperishable marker in the history of the Middle East."[30] An April 2000 article in *First Things* stated: "In relatively recent times questions have been raised within Christian circles concerning the death penalty....In thinking about what it means to be pro-life, Christians must, to begin with, distinguish between protecting innocent life and protecting society against murderers."[31]

Neoconservatism had once again trumped Catholic teaching. The definition of "pro-life" was revised to include the adjective "innocent" to accommodate the Republican presidential candidate's record on the death penalty.

Looking Ahead to 2004: Goodbye Evangelicals, Hello Catholics

In the long struggle which followed election 2000 to decide who won, the outcome was ultimately determined through the intervention of the US Supreme Court which denied Gore a recount of ballots. The Catholic judges who voted in favor of Bush later denied having any personal bias in the decision although Clarence Thomas's wife Virginia was working on the transition to a Bush presidency at the Heritage Foundation and Antonin Scalia's son, Eugene, was a partner at the law firm of Theodore Olson who represented the Bush campaign before the Court.[32]

Vice President Al Gore actually won the popular vote. He carried the Catholic vote 50 percent vs. 47 percent for Bush. While 50 percent of the national electorate voted in 2000, the Catholic turnout was 57 percent. Catholics who attended Mass at least once a week favored Bush over Gore by 63 percent to 30 percent.[33]

By post-election 2000, it was clear that the fundamentalist/evangelical vote was maxed out—there were few who weren't already voting straight Republican tickets. To avoid losing again in 2004, Rove knew his Party would need to garner a larger Catholic vote.[34] Also, while the two largest and best-known organizations of the religious right had gone bust—Jerry Falwell's Moral Majority and Pat Robertson's Christian Coalition—the United States Conference of Catholic Bishops wasn't going anywhere.

Immediately after the 2000 election Bush began meeting with Catholic bishops and adopted Catholic themes and rhetoric in speeches. Under Rove's direction, his staff instituted a weekly conference call with an informal group of Catholic advisers. The Republican National

Committee set up [another] Catholic task force. In a March 22, 2001, speech honoring Pope John Paul II to an audience including Cardinals Adam Maida and Theodore McCarrick, Bush adopted the language of Catholic leaders: "In the culture of life, we must make room for the stranger. We must comfort the sick. We must care for the aged.... We must defend in love the innocent child waiting to be born."[35]

In February 2001 the New Jersey bishops issued a letter stating, "We applaud that the majority of Catholic voters in our state cast their ballots for the major party candidate who publicly stated his support of a ban on abortions..." Bush held meetings with Bishops Rigali in St. Louis, Wuerl in Pittsburgh, and with Boston's Cardinal Law after which Law announced, "To be more successful in transforming our culture in the United States it is absolutely essential that we be consistently and unambiguously pro-life." On the same day as Law's statement—April 18, 2001—the new Republican National Committee chairman, Jim Gilmore (replacing Jim Nicholson), announced a new National Catholic Leadership Forum to begin planning strategies for the 2002 and 2004 elections.

The first public event for the Forum was Mass on April 24, 2001, followed by a luncheon. The announcement stated,

> This event will include briefings on past efforts to get out the Catholic vote, insight from the White House, panel discussions on what we can do. These presentations will be given by people such as Mel Martinez (Secretary of HUD), Karl Rove (White House Chief of Staff), Rep. Chris Smith (NJ), Fr. Frank Pavone (Priests for Life), Raymond Arroyo (EWTN), and Deal Hudson (*Crisis Magazine*). Please join other Catholics interested in making a difference in the politics of the United States at this event. Pass the word and invite other Catholics.

On his first post-inaugural trip to New York City, Bush went to St. Patrick's Cathedral on July 10, 2001, to present the Congressional Gold Medal to the late Cardinal John O'Connor. Later in July, Bush traveled to Castel Gandolfo, the pope's summer palace, to meet with John Paul II. The meeting included Vatican Secretary of State Cardinal Angelo Sodano and National Security Advisor Condoleezza Rice.

Following his trip, Bush announced he was appointing Nicholson as ambassador to the Holy See, a relatively unimportant diplomatic posting under Clinton. "Nicholson seems on track to be the most powerful ambassador to the pope in US history....Gone are the days of relative quiet under [Clinton appointee] Corrine (Lindy) Boggs, an octogenarian and classic Southern dame," noted the *National Catholic Reporter*. In the same article, Nicholson told the weekly newspaper that Bush saw official US-Vatican ties as a way to secure the Catholic vote in 2004. "No president in recent American history has taken such a strong interest in the 'Catholic vote' as Bush. We increased the Catholic vote by 10 percent in the election of 2000 compared to 1996," Nicholson said. "We got lists of Catholics and mailed to them, telephoned them. I think President Bush's positions are appealing to Catholics."[36]

Although Catholics had declined slightly as a percentage of the general population (22 percent) since the 1960s, 27 percent of the national electorate in 2004 would be Catholic voters.[37] Of greater importance, Catholics were above their national average in the most important swing states, including Florida, Iowa, Minnesota, Nevada, New Hampshire, New Mexico, Pennsylvania and Wisconsin."[38]

Neo-catholics were appointed to important positions in the new Bush administration: John Negroponte, Ambassador to the UN; Fr. Robert Sirica, Bush's advisor on the Catholic vote; Anthony Principi, Veterans Affairs Secretary; Mel Martinez, Secretary of the Department of Housing and Urban Development (in appreciation of the support from Florida's Cuban-Americans); Tommy Thompson, Secretary of Health and Human Services; and Peter Wehner, White House speech writer, among others.

> One particularly shocking appointment is that of a Vatican insider, Joseph Klink to head the State Department's Bureau of Population, Refugees and Migration instead of Secretary of State Colin Powell's choice of a career State Department official. Klink, who holds dual Irish and American citizenship, represents the Vatican at United Nations conferences on social issues and has represented it on the executive board of UNICEF from 1998 to 1999. A *New York Times* account said, "His resume lists his current job as advisor to the Permanent Observer Mission of the Holy See to the United Nations." It is highly unusual for any government to let the Vatican determine this choice, but the *Times* account said the nomination of Klink "comes at a time when the White House is assiduously courting Roman Catholics, a group President Bush's political advisors believe may be pivotal in the next election." Moreover, in addition to being employed by the Vatican, Klink's resume "also says he is a member of the Republican National Committee's Catholic Task Force."[39]

Two days after his inauguration, Bush re-imposed the Global Gag Rule restricting foreign non-governmental organizations (NGOs) which receive US Agency for International Development (USAID) family planning funds from using their own or any other funds to provide legal abortion services, lobby their own governments for abortion law reform, or even provide medical counseling or referrals regarding abortion. In part because of Bush's action, by 2008:

> Worldwide, there are 19 million unsafe abortions a year, and they kill 70,000 women (accounting for 13 percent of maternal deaths), mostly in poor countries... More than two million women a year suffer serious complications.... Unsafe abortions cause 4 percent of deaths among pregnant women in Africa, 6 percent in Asia and 12 percent in Latin America and the Caribbean.[40]

Catholic parishes and dioceses continued to build on their connections to the GOP. Under the guise of being "pro-life", anyone interested in promoting the Republican Party could ask the pastor or bishop for permission to distribute political literature in church vestibules or parish centers. In the next four years, Republicans used addresses from parish registries, websites and email lists to distribute information to Catholics for "pro-life" and "sanctity of marriage" positions. Some funding came from businessmen such as Tom Monaghan, who had sold Domino's Pizza to Gov. Mitt Romney's Bain Capital firm for $1 billion. Monaghan set up a political action committee called the Ave Maria List, whose purpose was to "restore the culture of life in our country." According to its literature, "We will target our support with laser-like precision on the most competitive [political] races." During the 2002 election cycle, the PAC funded the Strategic Media Services Inc., which in turn gave 100 percent of its money to Republican campaigns, according to the Center for Public Integrity.[41]

CHAPTER 12

POLITICAL PATRONAGE IN THE GUISE OF CHARITY

Charitable Choice

The neo-Catholic leaders, for all their rhetoric, never pointed out to their followers before the 2000 election that neither the Republican-controlled Congress nor the Supreme Court had delivered on direct aid to Catholic schools or a constitutional amendment banning abortion. They *were* confident, however, that President George W. Bush, although head of the Party which claimed to be against government spending and government funding of social programs, would deliver billions of tax dollars to the administrators of religious and pseudo-religious organizations.

Bush instituted the "Faith-Based Initiative" by executive order. The stream of funding directly to the heads of "faith-based" organizations was the most direct assault on the separation of church and state in the nation's history. GOP leaders were never so naïve as to believe that charitable works do not paint a virtuous veneer on the denomination doling out money and services or that their workers would never use these occasions to proselytize aid recipients on behalf of their religion. In a March 1, 2005, speech, Bush affirmed "those faith-based programs are changing America one soul at a time."

The Bush administration's Faith-Based and Community Initiative was built upon an earlier bipartisan compromise between the Clinton administration and Sen. John Ashcroft, later Bush's first attorney general. The Personal Responsibility and Work Opportunity Reconciliation Act of 1996, otherwise known as the Welfare Reform Act, put in place a five-year time limit on benefits and a work requirement to receive them. An amendment sponsored by Ashcroft was added enabling more religious organizations to receive tax dollars for social services. Prior to this Act, government welfare funds could go to religious groups, but the institutions were required to have separate, secular nonprofit entities to administer the programs. However, the "charitable choice" provision of the 1996 act gave religious charities permission to distribute religious materials on the same premises receiving federal funding.

Bush was the first governor to implement the Charitable Choice clause of the Welfare Reform law. He put together a "Faith-Based Task Force" made up of 16 clergy and volunteer leaders to offer recommendations for the application of Charitable Choice and other faith-based initiatives. He ordered state agencies like the Department of Human Services to remind service providers they were covered by the new federal legislation and no longer had to remove "religious content" from their programs. One department official was quoted as saying that Bush "altered the whole environment of an enormous agency." Bush pushed through other changes including a religion-based program in the state penal system operated by Chuck Colson's Prison Ministries Fellowship.[1]

Almost all of Gov. Bush's recommendations were passed by the 1997 Texas legislature including legislation that allowed faith-based childcare centers and homes to bypass state licensing and regulation by creating a private accreditation system. As noted by the Texas Freedom Network five years later, "positive results have proven impossible to document or measure. Evidence points instead to a system that is unregulated, prone to favoritism and co-mingling of funds, and even dangerous to the very people it is supposed to serve." They also noted that religious groups could already participate in many federal programs by complying with the same rules as other groups.[2]

Faith-Based and Community Initiative

Five days after his inauguration, on January 25, 2001, Bush attended a dinner with Pro-nuncio Archbishop Montalvo in the Washington DC residence of Cardinal Theodore McCarrick. Bush was accompanied by Condoleezza Rice and his "legal adviser," Alberto Gonzalez. Also present were Bishop Joseph Fiorenza, then-president of the USCCB, and several other hierarchs. A Catholic internet news service noted, "Montalvo said the purpose of the dinner was to grow in reciprocal knowledge and understanding." The primary reason for the meeting was to finalize plans for Bush's soon-to-be-announced Faith-Based and Community Initiative. The same article noted, "The initiative has sparked constitutional concerns over 'separation of church and state.' But Bush responded: 'When it is about saving human lives, we must look especially at the efficacy of the programs.'"[3]

Bush created the White House Office of Faith-Based and Community Initiatives (FBCI) by executive order on January 29 and named John J. Dilulio, Jr., a Catholic political scientist and criminologist from the University of Pennsylvania, as head of the department. He promised more than $8 billion during his first year in office to help social service organizations. On January 31, Bush met with a group of 30 Catholic leaders at the White House asking for their help in pushing through his legislation which would support the FBCI. Deal Hudson was asked to set up the meeting. Attendees included Cardinals George of Chicago, Egan of New York, and McCarrick; Archbishop Charles Chaput of Denver; Ken Hacket of Catholic Relief

Services; Tom Monaghan and Fr. David O'Connell, president of the Catholic University of America. "The president and his advisers knew very well that for their faith-based program to work it must establish a full partnership with existing Catholic social service providers. This meeting is the beginning of that partnership," said Hudson after the meeting.[4]

The FBCI was set up according to the model of the USCCB and many diocesan charities. The money flows not to the needy but to the administrators of agencies and organizations which claim to assist them. Like the Catholic systems, there were no provisions for public oversight or accountability to guarantee the money ever reached worthy recipients. While the intentions of those who actually perform the work and donate money to assist others are truly admirable, under both the USCCB and FBCI systems, funds are provided primarily to groups which support the bishops and/or the Republican Party.[5] At the same time, Bush added another administrative layer of funding recipients by directing millions of dollars to newly organized agencies whose only function was to train other groups on how to apply for FBCI funds or to act as a third-party clearing house for further distribution. Here are a few examples:

- It was announced that Food Finders, Inc., a food bank located in Long Beach, California, received $40,000 in FBCI funds distributed by Father Joe's Villages, a faith-based "intermediary" organization.

- The Americans for Community and Faith-Centered Enterprise (ACFE), according to its executives, "was formed to educate policymakers and the public about the faith-based initiative, mobilize support for the initiative among charitable and public policy organizations, and communicate information about the initiative to a diverse and growing coalition of supporters."[6]

- Heritage Community Services in Charleston, South Carolina, was an offshoot of an anti-abortion pregnancy crisis center. Their budget ran about $50,000 per year. After receiving federal grants, "by 2004, Heritage Community Services had become a major player in the booming business of abstinence education. Its budget passed $3 million... supporting programs for students in middle school and high school in South Carolina, Georgia and Kentucky." Many of the newly formed "abstinence only" organizations "are just slush funds for conservative interest groups," according to Bill Smith, vice president of the Sexuality Information and Education Council of the United States.[7]

The USCCB issued a statement on February 12, 2001, applauding the FBCI and the immediate additional financial assistance it provided to Catholic Charities USA, which was already receiving 62 percent, or $1.4 billion, of its annual operating budget from government grants,[8] the Catholic Campaign for Human Development, and the Catholic Health Association representing 2,000 member hospitals. (The Catholic Health Association of America of St. Louis, Missouri, under Fr. Michael Place, had contributed $25,000 to the Bush/Cheney Inaugural Committee.[9])

Not all Catholics were as enthused as their bishops. An article in *Commonweal*, a magazine by and for lay Catholics, noted:

> "Compassionate Conservatism," for those who don't know, is Latin for "If you believe this, I have 300 acres of Florida chads I'd like to sell you." All Bush has to do is to keep mumbling those soothing phrases about the unborn and faith-based initiatives, about "not leaving anyone behind," and how "we must teach our children to be gentle with one another." Apparently that's enough to keep the social consciences of Catholics quiet. In the meantime, Bush has sent to Congress his wholly disingenuous budget proposal in which tax cuts are designed, like Reagan's budgets, to redistribute wealth to the rich rather than the poor.[10]

When an invitation was extended to Bush to give the May 20, 2001, commencement address at the University of Notre Dame, political science professor Peter Walsh remarked, "Commencement is a time to celebrate the values of our university. This is something George W. Bush is incapable of doing." Another faculty member, English professor Valerie Sayers, declared "the Catholic vote is not for sale." At this point, the FBCI was being questioned by some members of Congress for being exactly what it was, the public subsidy of religious (and anyone claiming to be) leaders. Bush used his commencement speech to drum up further support for his FBCI by proposing $1.6 billion in new funds for drug treatment. Outside the hall, protestors held signs stating the "W" in "George W. Bush" stands for "wrong" on labor rights, the environment, tax breaks, the death penalty and other issues.[11]

On May 24, Bush went to Our Lady of the Angels-St. Joseph Center in Cleveland, Ohio, to lay out his legislation proposing a Compassion Capital Fund of $500 million, "to help provide seed money for programs such as these we're witnessing here today." In attendance was Dennis McNulty, Director of Catholic Charities for the Diocese of Cleveland, and Cleveland's Bishop Anthony Pilla. Bush said, "It's a privilege for me to be here with Bishop Pilla, whose reputation at least has preceded him as far as the president goes. I've been looking forward to this opportunity to meet such a fine, noble man, firmly committed to helping the poor."[12] This was before Pilla asked the Vatican for permission to resign within months of being accused of maintaining a "slush fund" and being implicated in a diocesan kickback scheme.

Also present were Ohio's governor, lieutenant governor, and both US senators from Ohio, Mike DeWine and George Voinovich. Voinovich was given an award by Catholic Charities of Cleveland in 2000 after he arranged for the group to testify in the US Senate in opposition to legislation aimed at reducing harmful pollution from coal-burning electric power plants. In recognition of their testimony, the charity was named the clean air "villain of the month" by the nonprofit Clean Air Trust. Frank O'Donnell, executive director of the Clean Air Trust, while noting Catholic Charities' eight-county service area in Northeast Ohio included 185,000 people who suffered from asthma— including 36,000 children—pointed out that the president of Catholic Charities in his congressional testimony cited only statistics provided by the electric power industry's lobbying arm, the Edison Electric Institute. This "creates the unfortunate appearance that Catholic Charities of Cleveland was acting as a front for the electric power industry. It also raises questions about its connections to the electric power industry," per O'Donnell. He further observed the "curious coincidence" that the group's fund-raising arm, the Catholic Diocese of Cleveland Foundation, included on its board of trustees H. Peter Burg, Chairman and CEO of FirstEnergy Corp., sued by the Justice Department for alleged violations of air pollution requirements.[13]

John J. Dilulio became the first senior official to quit the Bush administration, resigning in August 2001. He had aggravated some members of the religious right by directing funds to African-American and Hispanic ministries. Dilulio provided a lengthy description of the Bush administration domestic policy to *Esquire* magazine.

> Dilulio went into the administration with a plan, he said, "but it was sabotaged by White House political operatives more interested in the points they could score with the religious right than getting an inner-city teenager a job...."
>
> "Domestic policy was in the hands of 'Mayberry Machiavellis,'" wrote Dilulio, "staff members who consistently talked and acted as if the height of political sophistication consisted in reducing every issue to its simplest, black-and-white terms for public consumption, then steering legislative initiatives or policy proposals as far right as possible. These folks have their predecessors in previous administrations...but, in the Bush administration, they were particularly unfettered."[14]

Bush then named a more carefully-vetted Catholic, Jim Towey, as the new Director of the Office of Faith-Based and Community Initiatives. Towey had spent ten years as a senior advisor to Republican Sen. Mark Hatfield and Democratic Gov. Lawton Chiles, serving the latter as secretary of Florida's Health and Social Services agency. Towey was also legal counsel for twelve years to Mother Teresa and received the Papal Cross. In his remarks at the announcement of Towey's appointment, Bush welcomed "Your Eminence, Cardinal Bevilacqua; sure good to see you, sir. I've had many a good heart-to-heart visit with His Eminence and I've always come away a better person after having visited with him." Bevilacqua would later be exposed by a Philadelphia Grand Jury for his part in the cover-up of the clerical sexual abuse of children.

In a commencement address at the Catholic University of America on May 14, 2005, Towey modestly asserted, "I'm sure I was chosen for this honor because of my working friendship with a modern day saint: President Bush."

Typically, Towey got his listeners' attention with fear: "A scientist at Stanford University, a Nobel Prize winner no less, who successfully placed human cells in mice, recently announced that he now wants to create mice with entirely human brains. I am not making this up. This should alarm us all."[15] When Towey was invited to speak at the Vatican in 2006, he "blasted critics of his boss, President George W. Bush, who have scored the White House for its reliance on religious rhetoric and faith-based initiatives. Slamming the 'ruthless secularization' of public life, Towey asserted that church-state separation too often robs social programs of their 'spiritual dimension.'"[16]

Faith-based Legislation

The House passed H.R. 7, the Community Solutions Act, in July 2001 which was a major step in funding Bush's FBCI. It would expand the Charitable Choice section of the 1996 Welfare Reform Act and encourage churches and other houses of worship to compete for federal grants in order to operate faith-based social programs. Despite clearing the House in a 233-198 vote, the measure encountered stiffer opposition in the Senate. During the debate over H.R. 7, opponents focused on provisions which would allow religious groups receiving government money to ignore local and state anti-discrimination statutes, and use religion, including sexual orientation, as a criteria in hiring practices.

Neoconservative Sen. Joseph L. Lieberman appeared on the *Fox News Sunday* program July 22, 2001, to announce he was proposing new legislation that would increase the availability of federal funds for religion-based charitable groups. Lieberman said his legislation would compete with H.R. 7. "Right now, this bill (H.R. 7) is framed in a way that seems to have divided us. H.R. 7 would legalize discrimination as we minister to the needs of the poor." However, hiring remained a strong bone of contention. American Atheists questioned whether Lieberman's bill "would allow religious charities to by-pass other regulations that apply to secular groups, such as hiring credentialed professionals in drug and alcohol treatment programs. Religion-based programs like Teen Challenge, often cited as a paradigm in the delivery of rehab services by President Bush, are exempt from having to hire professional psychologists and other therapists, and may instead rely on preachers or untrained Bible-based counselors with little or no academic training."[17]

The USCCB issued a statement in November 2001 supporting passage of legislation similar to H.R. 7 by the Senate. Thus began the most intense effort in USCCB history in support of any specific legislation. Dozens of statements, letters and exhortation to the laity would follow urging them to contact their members of Congress to increase FBCI funding and maintain the ability of Catholic charities and health institutions to use public monies to discriminate in hiring.

Lieberman along with Rick Santorum introduced the Charity Aid, Recovery and Empowerment (CARE) Act, S. 1924 on February 9, 2002. Among the CARE Act's provisions was money for a Compassion Capital fund to provide "technical assistance" to charities. The bill included tax incentives for larger donations to charities. The bill omitted the "charitable choice" hiring provisions questioned by civil rights and civil liberties advocates.

The same month, Bush chose St. Luke's Catholic Church in Washington, DC to announce his welfare reform agenda, proposing spending of more than $17 billion a year on welfare for years 2003 to 2007 including block grants to states. "Under the plan that I'm submitting, up to $300 million a year will be available to *support innovation* and to fund programs which are most effective. (emphasis added) I'm also proposing $135 million for abstinence education programs," Bush told the assembly. The promised tax incentives for charitable donations were omitted as a compromise to include the estate-tax repeal which overwhelmingly benefited the wealthy in the administration's trillion dollar tax cut legislation.

Meanwhile, researchers at the University of Pennsylvania Penn's Center for Research on Religion and Urban Civil Society issued a study in early 2002 showing faith-based programs were not more successful that their secular counterparts. It incorporated 25 previous studies, including one conducted in 2000 by the Milton S. Eisenhower Foundation which examined 81 social-service providers in 27 states over a period of 10 years. The study found "that sound financial management and quality of staff were far more important than religious affiliation in predicting a program's success" and that claims of very high success rates by some faith-based organizations are probably exaggerated. "Closer examination of these accounts of extremely high success rates tends to reveal mere simple summary statistics based on in-house data often compiled by the religious organizations and ministries themselves. What is needed, above all, is accurate and unbiased information that can serve as the basis for an enlightened public discussion." The foreword to the Penn report was written by John J. DiIulio.[18]

On April 11, 2002, Bush invited Senators Santorum and Brownback and "my longtime friend" Cardinal McCarrick, to be present when he promoted the CARE Act. The following day, the USCCB published a letter, signed by McCarrick and Fr. J. Bryan Hehir, president of Catholic Charities USA, to the Chairman of the Senate Finance Committee urging passage of the CARE Act including additional funding for the Social Services Block Grant (SSBG) program. Twice in June, then in July, August, September, October, November and December, the USCCB wrote letters to Congress and issued statements urging Catholics to press their representatives for passage of the CARE Act including retention of the non-itemized charitable deduction and the Compassion Capital Fund.

In December 2002, Bush went to Philadelphia and, with Cardinal Bevilacqua in attendance, announced the creation of FBCI "centers" in USDA (Dept. of Agriculture) and USAID (Agency for International Development) creating additional positions for Bush loyalists in government. He directed FEMA to assist faith-based organizations. The Department of Health and Human Services (HHS) issued regulations implementing the Charitable Choice laws for Substance Abuse and Mental Health Services Administration (SAMHSA), Temporary Assistance for Needy Families (TANF), and Community Services Block Grant (CSBG) "preserving the right of religious groups to maintain their individual identity through hiring." The Department of Education issued final guidance on the eligibility of faith-based organizations for more than $1 billion in after-school programs. The Department of Housing and Urban Development (HUD) was given new regulations covering over $8 billion in grants. "HUD and HHS will revise their regulations to reflect the principle of nondiscrimination," ordered Bush. "Religious groups covered by that executive order are now exempted from past restrictions on employment decisions involving religion." In addition, Bush directed these departments to hire "appropriate staff, administrative support, and other resources to meet its responsibilities."

That same month, a longtime political operative in Rev. Sun Myung Moon front groups, David Caprara, was named as director of the Office of Faith-Based and Community Initiatives for the federal government's Corporation for National and Community Service. That agency runs, among other things, AmeriCorps Vista, which works with community organizations in low-income neighborhoods. Caprara was the former president of the American Family Coalition, a "grassroots leadership alliance" funded by the Washington Times Foundation and founded by Moon.[19] In 2005 HHS, via its Community-Based Abstinence Education Program, awarded a three-year implementation grant of $800,000 to a Moon front group called Free Teens USA headed by Richard Panzer, an alumnus of Moon's Unification Theological Seminary and head of the American Constitution Committee, a political organization affiliated with Moon.[20]

Not usually noted for understatements, the USCCB announced in February 2003, "Both the USCCB and Catholic Charities USA were among the most active supporters of the CARE Act," and urged Catholics to contact their members of Congress to include "new resources... such as the Social Services Block Grant, in this year's faith-based legislation." Letters were sent to Lieberman and Santorum urging them in continue their efforts and another exhortation was delivered to Catholics to support the legislation.

The USCCB congratulated Lieberman, Santorum and themselves when the CARE Act of 2003 passed the Senate on April 9, 2003, restoring $1.3 billion in funding to the Social Services Block Grant (SSBG) program. They expressed regret, however, that there was still no legislative provision allowing hiring discrimination. More USCCB actions followed in May, August and September urging the House and the president to approve SSBG funds.

The Associated Press reported that "faith-based" groups received $1.17 billion in grants from federal agencies in 2003. "That's not enough," said Towey, but he noted that an additional $40 billion in federal money was given out by state governments. The Office of FBCI reported that as of 2003, nineteen governors had faith-based offices as well as 180 mayors including San Diego, Denver, Miami, Philadelphia, and Los Angeles as well as the United States Conference of Mayors

Faith-based Discrimination in Hiring

Successful in their efforts in getting Bush re-elected, the USCCB confidently declared in February 2005, "We expect new bills to be introduced in both Houses this year, and will work to include the full CARE Act and SSBG funding in both bills and in the final product. We also expect to see one or both Houses debate the right of religious organizations to prefer co-religionists in hiring....a major priority for the bishops' conference and other Catholic institutions."

In March and May 2005, Bishop Nicholas DiMarzio, chairman of the bishop's Domestic Policy Committee, along with the heads of Catholic Charities USA and the Catholic Hospital Association, wrote the House urging them to reject any amendment to the Job Training Improvement Act which would bar them from discriminating in hiring. "The Domestic Social Development staff [of the USCCB] also negotiated with Senate and House offices drafting The Second Chance Act to make sure the legislation did not contain language that could be harmful on the hiring issue." In September, DiMarzio urged the House to remove language from the Head Start program which included restrictions on discriminatory hiring, which was adopted. (DiMarzio had to be pressured in 2002 to dismiss an admitted child molester, the Rev. John P. Connor, whom he had allowed to work as a hospital chaplain and live in two parish rectories.[21])

When Towey resigned his position in April 2006, some groups used the occasion to request that the FBCI be shut down. "Jim Towey has waged an unrelenting war against church-state separation," said the Rev. Barry W. Lynn, executive director of Americans United for Separation of Church and State. "He played a key role in using the 'faith-based' initiative for improper partisan purposes, and he did little or nothing to see that Americans get the social-service help they need from their government. That's a sad legacy to leave." Towey had, instead, devoted his efforts to pushing for the right of church-run government programs to discriminate in hiring. In June 2003, Towey's office even issued a 12-page booklet, "Protecting the Civil Rights and Religious Liberty of Faith-Based Organizations: Why Religious Hiring Rights Must Be Preserved."

"When civil rights and civil liberties leaders
criticized the administration's faith-based plan, Towey

would respond with name-calling," said Lynn. "It's a tired, but annoying strategy to defend a constitutionally suspect program." In early 2005 not long after Bush's re-election, Towey vowed before a Washington, D.C., gathering to fight "secular extremists" who oppose the administration's scheme to fund religion and allow government-funded job discrimination. A couple of years earlier, Towey told National Public Radio that legislation containing the administration's faith-based initiative had languished in Congress because debate on it had been "held hostage by some extremist groups that have a view that the public square should be sanitized of all religious influence." He groused to the *Boston Globe* that the faith-based initiative had failed in Congress due to "extremist activity" of groups such as Americans United and the NAACP.[22]

Towey left to become president of St. Vincent's College in Latrobe, Pennsylvania. Bush was invited to give the commencement address on May 12, 2007, causing months of controversy for the small Catholic liberal arts college. Some students, faculty and alumni had argued against the school's invitation based on the Iraq War, torture and other assaults by the Bush/Cheney administration on the lives, health and wellbeing of millions. During the commencement, protesters were directed to a Secret Service-mandated location along a highway off-campus.[23]

On Thursday, at 6:30 p.m., "the kind of timing usually reserved for news the administration wants to bury,"[24] the White House announced on August 19, 2006, Jay F. Hein's appointment as Director of the White House Office of Faith-Based and Community Initiatives and as Deputy Assistant to the president, replacing Towey. The *Associate Press* reported Hein had most recently served as president of the Sagamore Institute for Policy Research, an organization he founded in 2004 which the *AP* described as "a national think tank that specializes in community-based reforms." According to the White House official announcement, Hein would also serve as Executive Vice President and CEO of the Foundation for American Renewal "which provides financial grants and other support to community-based organizations and educates the general public on effective compassion practices."[25]

On June 25, 2007, the US Supreme Court ruled in *Jay Hein, Director, White House Office of Faith-Based and Community Initiatives et al. v. Freedom From Religion Foundation, Inc. et al.* that taxpayers cannot sue the Executive Branch for violating the constitutional separation of church and state since the First Amendment states "*Congress* shall make no law respecting an establishment of religion," [emphasis added] even though these actions are paid for out of general administrative funds.[26] In October 2007, the Justice Department's Office of Justice Programs issued directions to allow programs for drug recovery and mentoring children of prisoners to discriminate in hiring.

Primary Purposes and End Goals

In an article titled, "Grants Flow to Bush Allies on Social Issues" appearing in *The Washington Post* in March 2006, Rep. Mark Edward Souder (R-Ind.), chairman of the Government Reform Subcommittee on criminal justice, drug policy and human resources, admitted the FBCI "has gone political. Quite frankly, part of the reason it went political is because we can't sell it unless we can show Republicans a political advantage to it, because it's not our base," he said, referring to the fact that many of those receiving social services may be Democratic voters. Rep. Chet Edwards (D-Tex.) was more outspoken. "I believe ultimately this will be seen as one of the largest patronage programs in American history," he said.[27]

J. David Kuo, former special assistant to President Bush and deputy director of the Office of Faith-Based and Community Initiatives, wrote a book, *Tempting Faith,* a memoir of his time in Washington working with the religious right. Published in 2006, he described Bush's collaboration between the federal government and religious social services organizations as "political seduction" and a "sad charade to provide political cover to the White House that needed compassion and religion as political tools."[28] He also admitted the Bush administration used "moral values" voters while simultaneously ridiculing their leaders. According to Kuo, Christian National leaders got hugs from White House officials and then behind their backs were disparaged as "ridiculous," "nuts," and just plain "goofy."

Kuo took *60 Minutes* to a convention of evangelical groups and walked around the display booths, looking for any reference to the poor. "You've got homosexuality in your kid's school, and you've got human cloning, and partial birth abortion and divorce and stem cell," Kuo remarked. "Not a mention of the poor. This message has been sent out to Christians for a long time now: that Jesus came primarily for a political agenda, and recently primarily a right-wing political agenda—as if this culture war is a war for God. And it's not a war for God, it's a war for politics. And that's a huge difference."[29]

In summary, the delivery of government social funding through "faith-based" agencies, was intended: 1) to create, reward, and empower a constituency ideologically committed and impassioned by issues unrelated to helping the less fortunate and 2) to create and imbed another government infrastructure which would facilitate the further privatization of government services to the benefit of Bush loyalists. As in all agencies under the Bush executive branch of government, the primary purpose was not to serve the best interests of the American people, but to enrich Republicans.

One example, as reported by Mike Reynolds, is Raymond Ruddy, "a multi-millionaire conservative Catholic," who heads two companies—the non-profit Gerard Health Foundation and Maximus Inc., "the giant services provider that pioneered welfare privatization." Before the 1996 Welfare Reform Act, "Maximus was a 50-million-a-year enterprise." After its passage, "Maximus's earnings jumped to 105 million dollars" and "three years later its revenues tripled." By 2007, Maximus was a "700-million-dollar publicly traded global giant with more than 5,000 employees deployed across the nation and in Canada, Israel, Argentina and Egypt" and had "contracts with state governments to handle child-support collections, implement welfare-to-work and oversee managed care."

> Ruddy has leveraged his generous wallet and insider muscle to push an ultraconservative social agenda, enrich a preferred network of abstinence-only and antiabortion groups, boost profits for his company and line the pockets of his cronies—all with taxpayer dollars.....
>
> One top Bush adviser left [the administration] to take a job at Ruddy's charity, Gerard Health Foundation, and a senior officer at Ruddy's for-profit company, Maximus, left to take a top-level position at the Department of Health and Human Services. Leaders of Christian-right organizations that are Gerard grantees have gained advisory HHS positions—and their organizations have in turn received AIDS and abstinence grants to the tune of at least 25 million dollars. Maximus itself has raked in more than 100 million dollars in federal contracts during the Bush era.[30]

The USCCB and the agencies under their control—Catholic Charities USA, the Catholic Campaign for Human Development, Catholic Relief Services—as well as the Catholic Health Association and National Catholic Partnership on Disability aren't the only groups that hire lobbyists. (Catholic Charities received 65 percent of its 2007 budget from government contracts.[31]) Former President Jimmy Carter observed how individual churches, religious seminaries and other strictly religious organizations now have their own lobbyists in Washington to make sure they get their share of government funds. "As you know, the policy from the White House has been to allocate funds to religious institutions, even those that channel those funds exclusively to their own particular group of believers in a particular religion. Those things in my opinion are quite disturbing," Carter said in May 2007. "As a traditional Baptist, I've always believed in separation of church and state and honored that premise when I was president, and so have all other presidents, I might say, except this one."[32] Other non-Catholic religious leaders had also contested the FBCI. The General Board of Church and Society of the United Methodist Church, the president's own denomination, opposed the initiative because of the employment discrimination issue and the church-state problems.[33]

The FBCI had been enacted by executive order rather than legislative action. New offices and employees had been added to ten Cabinet-level departments with no purpose other than to increase the number of applicants for federal grants. The number of states with their own faith-based offices increased to 35 and efforts continue to grow on the local level in all 50 states. By decentralizing the funding among numerous federal agencies and with the creation of "faith-based" agencies in state and local governments, the FBCI has become embedded in the fabric of this country.

CHAPTER 13

THE SEX ABUSE SCANDAL

In January 2002, the *Boston Globe* ran a series of reports on the sexual abuse of hundreds of Massachusetts children by Catholic priests. Soon, other newspapers ran similar stories showing this travesty had not been limited to the Boston area. As a result, citizens demanded that the government intervene. The following report is just one of several produced from of these investigations.

The Philadelphia Grand Jury Report

On September 21, 2005, a grand jury which had investigated the Archdiocese of Philadelphia for more than three years, issued a scathing report on 63 priests who were known to have sexually abused hundreds of children. Some of the cases uncovered by the grand jury included:

- An 11-year-old girl was repeatedly raped by a priest who took her for an abortion when she became pregnant.

- A fifth grader was molested by her priest inside a confessional.

- A teenage girl was groped by a priest while she lay immobilized in traction in a hospital room.

- A boy was repeatedly molested in his school auditorium where his priest/teacher bent over the boy and rubbed his genitals against the boy until the priest ejaculated.

- A priest, no longer satisfied with mere pederasty, regularly began forcing sex on two boys at once in his bed.

- A boy woke up intoxicated in a priest's bed and found Father sucking on his penis while three other priests watched and masturbated themselves.

- A priest offered money to boys in exchange for sadomasochistic acts of bondage directing them to place him in bondage, to "break" him, to make him their "slave," and to defecate so he could lick the excrement from them.

- A 12-year-old raped and sodomized by a priest, tried to commit suicide and remains in a mental institution as an adult.

- A boy who told his father of the abuse his younger brother was suffering was beaten to the point of unconsciousness. "Priests don't to that" said the father.

- A priest told a 12-year-old boy his mother knew of the assaults and consented to the rape of her son.

Excerpts from the Grand Jury report include:

After reviewing thousands of documents from Archdiocese files and hearing... from over a hundred witnesses, we, the Grand Jurors, were taken aback by the extent of sexual exploitation within the Philadelphia Archdiocese....

Indeed, the evidence arising from the Philadelphia Archdiocese reveals criminality against minors on a widespread scale—sparing no geographic sector, no income level, no ethnic group. We heard testimony about priests molesting and raping children in rectory bedrooms, in church sacristies, in parked cars, in swimming pools, at St. Charles Borromeo Seminary, at the priests' vacation houses in the Poconos and the Jersey shore, in the children's schools and even in their own homes....

Documents clearly established that Cardinal Bevilacqua knew that the priests had admitted abusing minors. They also established that he alone was responsible for subsequently placing or leaving the priests in parishes where they would present a severe danger to children....

Cardinal Bevilacqua had a strict policy, according to his aides, that forbid informing parishioners.... The Cardinal, in fact, encouraged that parishioners be misinformed....

Cardinal Bevilacqua was trained as an attorney.... The Grand Jurors find that in his handling of priests' sexual abuse, Cardinal Bevilacqua was motivated by an intent to keep the record clear of evidence that would implicate him or the Archdiocese. To this end, he continued many of the practices of his predecessor, Cardinal Krol, aimed at avoiding scandal, while also introducing policies that reflected a growing awareness that dioceses and bishops might be held legally responsible for their negligent and knowing actions that abetted known predators....

To protect themselves from negative publicity or expensive lawsuits—while keeping abusive priests active—the cardinals and their aides hid the priests' crimes from parishioners, police and the general public....

In his testimony before the Grand Jury, Cardinal Bevilacqua was still attempting to evade responsibility for placing known sexual offenders in parishes where they had easy access to hundreds of children....

He often suggested he might not have known all the facts and that he delegated the handling of these matters to his Secretary of Clergy. He repeatedly claimed to have no memory of incidents and priests we will never forget....

What makes these actions all the worse, the grand jurors believe, is that the abuses that Cardinal Bevilacqua and his aides allowed children to suffer—the molestations, the rapes, the lifelong shame and despair—did not result from failures or lapses, except of the moral variety....

They were made possible by purposeful decisions, carefully implemented policies and calculated indifference....

In its callous, calculating manner, the archdiocese's "handling" of the abuse scandal was at least as immoral as the abuse itself....

One priest, described as "one of the sickest people I ever knew" by the Archdiocese official in charge of investigations, was allowed by Cardinal Bevilacqua to remain a priest with full access to children until the sex abuse scandal broke in 2002....

One archdiocese official comforted a priest abuser by suggesting that perhaps the priest had been "seduced" by his victim who was 11 years old....

Cardinal Bevilacqua "agreed to harbor a known abuser" from another diocese, after the priest's activities there started becoming known. The practice was known as "bishops helping bishops."[1]

The Philadelphia Grand Jury report followed earlier grand jury reports from Westchester County, New York (June 19, 2002), and Suffolk County, New York (February 10, 2003). There were also Attorney General reports from Manchester, New Hampshire (March 3, 2003), Boston, Massachusetts (July 23, 2003) and Portland, Maine (July 23, 2003)—all just as sickening, all finding similar patterns of abuse and cover-up, and all laying the blame squarely on the Catholic hierarchy for allowing, aiding and hiding these crimes as well as persecution of the victims, their families, and their supporters.

History of the scandal

The sexual abuse of children by priests had been disclosed by the press in several dioceses in the US since at least the 1980's. Jason Berry, writing for the *Times of Acadiana* (Louisiana) in 1985, noted the complicity of prelates in allowing the serial-rapist, Fr. Gilbert Gauthe, to continue his crimes in the article, "Anatomy of a Cover-up." The *National Catholic Reporter* printed a series of investigations into serial predators in the 1990s and other secular newspapers which ignored the threat of being charged with "anti-Catholicism" also carried reports of priests assaulting children. There were flurries of accounts regarding clerical pedophilia from Boston and Worcester County, Massachusetts; San Jose and Orange County, California; Atlanta and Chicago. Peter Steinfels, in a 1992 *New York Times* article noted, "In the past, accused priests were frequently recycled to new assignments without warning to their new parishioners; complaining victims and their parents were often treated by Church officials as potential legal adversaries rather than pastoral responsibilities." However, when a former seminarian recanted his accusations against Cardinal Joseph Bernardin of Chicago, the matter quieted down out of fear that other charges might turn out to be false. During the 1990s, some bishops declared they were instituting programs in their dioceses to review these types of accusation and the majority of Catholics thought the situation had been addressed.

In the February 1996 issue of Fr. Richard John Neuhaus's *First Things* magazine, Philip Jenkins wrote the reason pedophilia had been reported so often in the Catholic Church rather than other religious denominations was because the Church has deeper pockets.[2] Ignoring the fact that lawsuits are decided by independent judges and juries based upon the evidence presented, official Church spokesmen and the neo-Catholic media in the US still continue to cast victims as greedy enemies of the Church and their advocates as having hidden agendas for its destruction.

Prominent members of the Roman Curia have also used this tactic to intimidate victims. After the *Boston Globe's* January 2002 clerical sex abuse series was reported around the world, a Vatican canon lawyer responded in March, "The painful thing is that it's all about money now."[3] Cardinal Dario Castrillon Hoyos, head of the dicastery which supervises the clergy, told the press on March 22 it was important to maintain the perspective that the US Church had already paid millions of dollars to settle suits.[4]

The *Boston Globe* reported:

> Since the mid-1990s, more than 130 people have come forward with horrific childhood tales about how former

priest John J. Geoghan allegedly fondled or raped them during a three-decade spree through a half-dozen Greater Boston parishes. Almost always, his victims were grammar school boys. One was just 4 years old.

Part of the Geoghan story had been reported first in 1996 and Kristen Lombardi of the *Boston Phoenix* had written about him in 2001. What differentiated the *Globe* articles was not only their depth and scope, but also the Pulitzer Prize-winning team of reporters had obtained original documents from the courts. The photographs of these official papers which accompanied the articles showed the signatures of Cardinal Bernard Law and other archdiocesan officials as plain as day. It was the Church's own records which revealed the brutality, defamation and maltreatment of the victims, their families, and anyone who tried to act on their behalf. The articles proved how hundreds of children were assaulted because Law and his predecessors not only failed to stop Geoghan, Fr. Paul Shanley, and other priests, but had moved the offenders from parish to parish and covered their tracks. The documents also revealed the breathtaking hypocrisy of Church leaders, including Law, who for years had blamed the media for sensationalizing and exaggerating what had occurred.

The revelations about the bishops struck at the integrity of the entire Catholic Church. What kind of human being, much less a "moral authority," would aid and abet others in torturing children and then further persecute the victims and their families? Law's inner circle was shown to be handpicked "company men" who could be counted on to put loyalty to the institution before the lives of children. Lay Catholics were more infuriated by the actions of their leaders than the original abuse. Law finally expressed concern for the victims of his criminal conspiracy only after tremendous public pressure. Demands for Law's resignation became a common occurrence. The cardinal went to Rome to discuss his situation with John Paul II who decided resigning was Law's decision to make. Vatican spokesman, Joaquín Navarro-Valls, persuaded Law "to hang on, warning of a 'domino effect' that could bring down other bishops facing similar crises."[5]

Republican and Vatican Responses

After the *Boston Globe,* similar reports followed in the *Dallas Morning News,* the *Cleveland Plain Dealer,* the *New York Times,* the *Washington Post* and others. The reaction of most Catholics in other parts of the country was the same as those in Boston: the utter lack of moral, ethical or legal behavior on the part of the bishops and their staffs and their maltreatment of the victims and their families were more horrifying than the actions of presumed-to-be-mentally-ill child predators. Unfortunately for the vast majority of priests who do not sexually assault children, the caricature of lecherous men in white collars chasing after altar boys became a national joke and the bishop's mitre (pointed hat) became a symbol in editorial cartoons for gross hypocrisy.

Dependent on the Catholic vote in swing states, Republican Party strategists recognized their problem. It was crucial that Church authority and credibility be maintained in order to keep abortion and same-sex marriage as vital issues around which an electoral constituency could be mobilized.

At a March 13, 2002, press conference, President George W. Bush supported the hierarchy.

> A reporter, noting the "growing crisis in the Catholic Church," asked Bush if he thought the Church had acted "swiftly enough to deal with the issue of pedophilia among the ranks of priests." Bush replied, "Well, I know many in the hierarchy of the Catholic Church. I know them to be men of integrity and decency. They're honorable people. I was just with Cardinal Egan today. And I'm confident the Church will clean up its business and do the right thing. As to the timing, I haven't, frankly I'm not exactly aware of the how fast or how not fast they're moving. I just can tell you I trust the leadership of the Church."
>
> The reporter followed up by asking Bush if Law should resign, noting that Bush knows Law personally. "That's up to the Church," Bush replied. "I know Cardinal Law to be a man of integrity. I respect him a lot."[6]

A meeting was arranged between Bush and the pope as quickly as possible allowing for the schedules of two world leaders. In May,

> sources speculated Bush had the important US Catholic vote in mind when he decided to express his view of the scandals. Tuesday morning Bush told reporters, "I will tell the pope I am concerned about the Catholic Church and its standing in the United States." He said the American Catholic Church was "an important part of our great country."[7]

Vatican officials did their best to divert criticism away from the hierarchy. Navarro-Valls addressed the growing scandal during a March 3, 2002, interview. He claimed the victims were mainly teenage boys and therefore homosexuals "just cannot be ordained," although various reports place the number of homosexuals in the priesthood at anywhere from 10 to 50 percent. The *New York Times* reporter conducting the interview noted, "To the extent that others [in the Vatican] are aware of it, many tend to write it off as an American problem."[8]

At a Vatican news conference on March 22, Cardinal Dario Castrillon Hoyos presented a letter purportedly written by John Paul II pledging the Church's support for justice for the victims and calling the "grave scandal" a manifestation of supernatural evil. Castrillon opined, "Concerning the problem of sexual abuse and cases of pedophilia, I have only one answer. In today's culture of pansexualism and libertinism created in this world, several priests, being of this culture, have committed the most serious crime of sexual abuse."[9]

Under pressure from neoconservatives for some damage-control, John Paul II called all the American cardinals to Rome to discuss the crisis. With Secretary of State Cardinal Angelo Sodano at his side, the pope gave a speech on April 23, 2002, to the cardinals with Bishop Wilton D. Gregory of Bellville, Illinois, president of the USCCB, also in attendance. The pontiff excused the US episcopate and pretended this was only an American crisis:

> ....Because of the great harm done by some priests and religious, the Church herself is viewed with distrust, and many are offended at the way in which the Church's leaders are perceived to have acted in this matter. The abuse which has caused this crisis is by every standard wrong and rightly considered a crime by society; it is also an appalling sin in the eyes of God. To the victims and their families, wherever they may be, I express my profound sense of solidarity and concern.
>
> It is true that a generalized lack of knowledge of the nature of the problem and also at times the advice of clinical experts led bishops to make decisions which subsequent events showed to be wrong....
>
> [Regarding the clergy] We cannot forget the power of Christian conversion, that radical decision to turn away from sin and back to God, which reaches to the depths of a person's soul and can work extraordinary change....
>
> The abuse of the young is a grave symptom of a crisis affecting not only the Church but society as a whole. It is a deep-seated crisis of sexual morality, even of human relationships, and its prime victims are the family and the young. In addressing the problem of abuse with clarity and determination, the Church will help society to understand and deal with the crisis in its midst....The Catholic faithful, and the wider community... must know that bishops and priests are totally committed to the fullness of Catholic truth on matters of sexual morality.[10]

Many were dismayed that John Paul II had used the word "perceived" to describe the actions of the bishops and excused their behavior as a "generalized lack of knowledge" based on bad advice from "clinical experts" particularly since the pope and every American bishop had been given a report in 1985, prepared by medical, ecclesial and legal professionals, presenting evidence that priest/offenders had little chance for a cure and were likely to repeat their crimes. A psychiatrist specifically recommended removing those priests from further contact with children.

The 92-page report was initiated by Rev. Thomas Doyle, an American Dominican and Doctor of Canon Law assigned to the Vatican nunciature in Washington DC, in response to the earlier news reports of pedophile priests especially Jason Berry's reporting in the *Times of Acadiana*. It also included advice from an attorney that the survivors should be assisted and not further victimized by diocesan attacks and that the Church should be open with the media. The report warned that massive lawsuits would ensue unless the bishops changed their handling of these cases. Members of the NCCB met behind closed doors at St. John's Abbey the same year to discuss the report,[11] but nothing changed except that Doyle's ecclesial career was over. Still a priest, Doyle became an Air Force chaplain and continued his advocacy for the victims of abuse.

In 1993 when one of the better known treatment centers for pedophile priests was sued directly for releasing its patients to re-assume pastoral assignments, part of the testimony included a warning by Dr. John Salazar, an Albuquerque psychologist, to the clinic and Santa Fe Archbishop James P. Davis that such priests ought not to be released for parish work.[12] Some mental health professionals in charge of "rehabilitating" the rapists later admitted their profits from the lucrative business of operating these clinics (referred to as "retreat centers" by the Church) were dependent on the bishops being provided with favorable prognoses.[13]

Regardless, the bishops' defense of reliance on clinicians does not explain how they could be unaware that sexually abusing children is a crime, or of the fact that their own experience had showed these men were not "cured." It does not explain how, in the name of common decency, they could permit others under their supervision to cause such horrendous pain and suffering to thousands of children. It would later be proved that two-thirds of the American episcopate hadn't even the basic humanity to empathize with this suffering when it would have cost them literally nothing to do so (see John Jay Report below).

Neo-Catholic Response

Neuhaus was among the first to weigh in after the *Globe* articles made national headlines. In the April 2002 issue of *First Things*, Neuhaus began by repeating the charges made by Jenkins in 1996: "Scholars [no citations given] point out that the incidence of abusing children or minors is no greater, and may be less, among priests than among Protestant clergy, teachers, social workers, and similar professions. But, it is noted, Catholic clergy are more attractive targets for lawsuits because the entire diocese or archdiocese can be sued." Neuhaus made no mention that other organizations such as day care centers, social agencies and schools had not only been held accountable for their employees' actions but had also stopped the abuse when it was discovered.

Neuhaus charged the "liberal media" with an "ulterior agenda" of discrediting the Catholic teaching on human sexuality, about which they are genuinely outraged....

We would not know what we do know without the reporting of the *Boston Globe*. It is pointed out that the *Globe*, like its owner the *New York Times*, is no friend of the Church. The suggestion is not that we should kill the messenger, but that we should be keenly aware that the messenger has, on issue after issue, points to score against the teaching and claims of the Catholic Church.

The priests involved in the scandal were primarily ordained in the 1960s and 1970s, wrote Neuhaus, when, "in addition to false compassion and clerical protectiveness, there was in sectors of the Church a wink-and-a-nudge attitude toward what were viewed as sexual peccadilloes especially among clergy involved in social activism."

Disregarding the *Globe's* documentation confirmed by scores of legal proceedings, Neuhaus noted, "What some viewed as embarrassing misbehavior in the 1970s was, by the 1990s, viewed as a heinous crime.... Like most people, bishops did not know, or did not want to know, about rude things that men did together, and sometimes did with little boys." Neuhaus even reverted to the old "the Church is being persecuted":

> The right of religious institutions to govern themselves may be gravely eroded under pressure from lawyers, insurance companies, and the state....In some cases, settlements were agreed to with the guarantee that they would remain forever confidential. In Boston, that guarantee has now been broken by court order. This can be seen as an ominous encroachment by the state on the Church's right to self-governance.

Finally, like the pope, Neuhaus defended the continued placement of predator priests in new assignments. Not to do so would have been, "an erosion of confidence in the possibility of repentance and amendment of life. Such confidence is dismissed as 'naïve' when it comes to priests being given another chance." He concluded by stating, "[Law's] resignation would be a severe loss to the Church in the United States."[14]

Opus Dei's Fr. C. John McCloskey, III, in an article dated April 3, 2002, tied the press reports to Catholic "dissenters" who wanted to discredit the celibate priesthood and force the ordination of women. McCloskey claimed only a very small number of priests were actually involved and he laid the blame squarely on homosexuals by stating the majority of victims were teens and young men who came forward with their grievances for the money to be obtained in redress. In any case, the incidences of assaulting children, he wrote, were mostly confined to the 1970s. The bishops were faulted for depending on psychology instead of recognizing the spiritual dimension of the problem and for allowing homosexuals into the seminaries. Like Navarro-Valls, McCloskey concluded the cure would be to stop ordaining homosexuals.[15]

Articles by George Weigel appeared in the April 10 and 17 editions of *The Catholic Difference*. Weigel admitted it was time for change in the Church but "the deeper reform that we need must begin with a correct identification of the nature of the problem." First is the failure of priests to lead chaste lives. Second is failure of the bishops to "exercise their authority effectively: in terms of sexually misbehaving priests, yes, but also in failing to confront adequately the culture of dissent that has contributed immeasurably to the ecclesiastical atmosphere in which sexual misconduct festers." Third, "It can no longer be denied that the Church has a serious problem of homosexually-oriented clergy....It is not, in the main, a pedophilia crisis....As news reports have made clear [no citations given], however, the great majority of victims of clerical sexual abuse in recent decades have been adolescent boys or young men."

Weigel concluded:

> Finally, it is not a problem of the Church's sexual ethic. A barely concealed subtext of the past three months' debate has been the subtle suggestion, from the press and from the Catholic left [no citations given], 'This is what that repressed Catholic view of sexuality gets you.'

For Weigel the "theologian," the "sin" of course is disobedience.

> [It] is now self-evident from the evidence [none provided] with which we have all been bludgeoned these past three months or so...[that] dissent must be confronted far more vigorously. When seminarians and priests are sent subtle signals that a less-than-enthusiastic acceptance of the Church's teaching on marital ethics [birth control], or on homosexuality, or on the impossibility of ordaining women to the ministerial priesthood can be tolerated, corruption inevitably follows...with lethal results.[16]

Like Weigel, "theologian" Michael Novak, traced the history of priests sexually abusing children to the disobedience which followed the Vatican's 1968 ban on birth control which unleashed the "crisis of sexual morality." He castigated his fellow Catholics for their "sullen, silent rebellion, a separation of the heart from [papal] leadership" and accepting a culture which "has at its heart a teaching of contempt for 'Rome.'" (He attributed his own "dissent" of social activism during the same period, however, to his intellectual and moral integrity!)[17]

Novak wrote that the American bishops' fear of being labeled "conservative" caused them not to assume their "teaching authority" to stop the "rebellious dissent" of the faithful against Church teaching. The uncontrolled disobedience was allowed to grow into a general disregard for all the Church's teaching on sexuality, leading directly to "homosexual rings operating freely in several important seminaries." According to Novak in this June 2002 article, "The really deep secret, then, of the last 40 years is the fear, timidity, and passivity of the American bishops," including an aversion to "antagonizing the secular, liberal press," and not standing firm on Church sexual doctrines including not getting rid of homosexuals from the priesthood.[18]

Weigel got his book, *The Courage to be Catholic*, in print in time to take advantage of interest in the scandal basically repeating the points he had made in his earlier articles. In his review of Weigel's book Novak noted, "As readers of the print media know, but consumers of TV news do not, it was not a 'paedophilia' scandal. There were some awful perpetrators of paedophilia, but the vast majority of victims were teenage males [no citations given] being sexually molested or abused."[19] (Weigel was also quick to capitalize on the death of John Paul II. "Only hours after the pope's death, HarperCollins announced that a new book by Weigel...would come out by year-end and 'examine the death of the pope and the Catholic Church he left behind, while also offering an unparalleled inside account of the election of the next pope.'"[20])

Targeting Boston's Liberal Catholics

In December 2002, 58 pastors of the Boston archdiocese signed a letter asking Law to step down and he resigned days later. Law was a longtime friend of Wojtyla's private secretary and principle gatekeeper, Polish Cardinal Stanislaw Dziwisz. The pope appointed Law archpriest of the Basilica of St. Mary Major, one of Rome's four major churches (the others being St. Peter's, St. John Lateran and St. Paul Outside the Walls). Except for the statute of limitations on child abuse, Law would have gone to prison for his complicity. Instead, he receives the standard Vatican cardinal's salary of $5,800 per month in addition to room, board, and any health expenses. He lives in a two-story apartment which is part of the basilica complex in the heart of historic Rome with his private secretary and a "small community" of nuns from Mexico as domestic servants. Law oversees 25 priest/canons who staff the basilica. He is a member of eight Curia dicasteries, three of which share responsibility for the appointment of all bishops throughout the word, a seat of power shared only by the current Vatican secretary of state and second-in-command to Benedict XVI, Cardinal Tarcisio Bertone. This gives Law a say in the appointment of every bishop, archbishop and cardinal in the US. Novak wrote in all seriousness, "Some in Rome have long seen Law's resignation less as a symbol of disgrace than an act of self-sacrifice."[21]

After Law's resignation, neo-Catholics also rewrote the history of Boston. The point was to discredit Bay State residents who were advocating that Massachusetts become the first state to allow same-sex marriage. In a *National Review* column, Novak blamed Law's departure on "the fierce anti-Catholicism" in modern-day Boston rooted in bigotry against the Irish. According to Novak, it was only natural for the clergy to draw up ranks for an "unusually tribal and mutually protective circling around its own three-generation tradition of moral fault" referring to the generally progressive views of Boston clergy. Next, Novak blamed local colleges for "a 40-year period of massive moral dissent from Catholic moral teaching, especially in regard to sexual and 'gender' questions, in the principal Catholic institutions of learning in Boston." And, "Third is a laity in very large numbers living in open dissent and rebellion, and encouraged in this by many clerical voices—even among their own pastors."[22]

Neuhaus also blamed "bigotry" in today's Boston against the "great unwashed of Irish and Italian immigration" for Law's problems. "Catholic politicians, prosecutors, and judges who want to ingratiate themselves with the establishment seem to vie with one another to prove themselves as anti-Catholic as their betters." And again: "There is no doubt that the Catholic Church has been 'singled out'; that the incidence of sexual abuse in other religious communities, in public schools, and in social services is as high, and possibly higher, [no citations given] than it is in the priesthood. Those institutions, however, are not subjected to a sustained storm of public scandal and outrage." And again: "....the subculture of infidelity that is the source of priestly miscreance in doctrine and life. Why should anyone be surprised that scandals result when priests and teachers of theology make no bones about saying that the Church does not mean what it says about sexuality, celibacy, chastity, and sacred vows, or when they publicly declare that the Church is just wrong in what it teaches?"

Neuhaus concluded that Law did the right thing by stepping down because his ability to lead had been impaired but that his "mistakes and shortcomings...were confusedly entangled with his virtues". Neuhaus also advised Law's successor to "keep that list of fifty-eight [pastors who called for Law to resign] handy."[23] He did. When the Boston archdiocese was forced to close parishes due to the exodus of Catholics and their donations following the scandal, many of these courageous priests were the first to lose their parish assignments.

Pennsylvania's Sen. Rick Santorum joined in. "It is no surprise that Boston, a seat of academic, political, and cultural liberalism in America, lies at the center of the storm" of the clergy sexual abuse scandal. Less than three months before the release of the Philadelphia Grand Jury Report, Santorum refused "to back off on his earlier statements connecting Boston's 'liberalism' with the Roman Catholic Church pedophile scandal, saying that the city's 'sexual license' and 'sexual freedom' nurtured an environment where sexual abuse would occur."[24]

Interestingly, none of the neo-Catholics blamed what they described as the "deep-seated crisis of sexual morality" on the sex-saturated entertainment industry, owned and managed by the same corporate giants which owned their publishers and the talk-shows on which they appeared. In an article appearing in the *New Oxford Review*, the head of a nonprofit which exposes the sources of investment incomes reported that the USCCB along "over 1,000 Catholic dioceses, religious institutes, educational institutions and health care organizations were invested in the very same media conglomerates providing a steady stream of 'adult content' to our television and movie screens and which produce the highly lucrative in-house pornography now available in hotel rooms throughout the world."[25]

The John Jay Report

In June 2002, the USCCB held its regularly scheduled semi-annual meeting in Dallas under the glare of public interest. There were more journalists present than bishops.

> You could see the problem in the televised shots of the audience during the first day of the Dallas conference. After [Bishop Wilton Gregory, president of the USCCB] spoke, a group of abuse survivors got up and told the American bishops their stories, and the faces of the prelates were as implacable as the gargoyles on the Vatican. There was some obvious discomfort, but more than that, somehow, there was an air in the scene of affronted authority, as though listening to this catalog of outrage was simply *infra dignitatem*. Whether he wants it or not, Wilton Gregory's task must be to break through to those blank faces, to point out that, on this issue at least, whatever moral credibility they think accrues to their offices is as dead as St. Peter.[26]

The bishops voted overwhelmingly to approve what became known as the "Dallas Charter." The Charter dealt with the handling of accused priests and the treatment of their victims. No mention was made of the episcopate taking responsibility for, or any consequences that would result from, hierarchical cover-ups nor their continued psychological and legal persecution of the victims who were brave enough to step forward, relate the heinous details of their personal and intimate violation and subject themselves to the smear campaigns being waged against them from the political right. The bishops formed a National Review Board for the Protection of Children and Young People composed of prominent lay Catholics to study the issue and make recommendations. The USCCB commissioned the John Jay College of Criminal Justice to conduct a research study on the extent of the criminal abuse of children by priests.

Former Oklahoma Gov. Frank Keating who, as chairman of the National Review Board tried unsuccessfully to obtain some Church documents, resigned a year later telling the *Los Angeles Times*:

I have seen an underside that I never knew existed. I have not had my faith questioned, but I certainly have concluded that a number of serious officials in my faith have very clay feet. That is disappointing and educational, but it's a fact. To act like La Cosa Nostra and hide and suppress, I think, is very unhealthy. Eventually it will all come out.[27]

The Vatican's reaction was one of exasperation with American prelates for allowing lay persons like Keating to be involved in what they considered to be internal Church affairs.[28]

The John Jay study was based on information provided by the bishops themselves to which they admitted having knowledge. There was no verification as to the validity or completeness of the data. Cases of abuse reported only to a law enforcement or social services agency or a medical practitioner, or incidents the bishops wished to remain secret, were not included. Neither did the report count incidents of sexual abuse of minors which occurred in the hundreds of institutes run by priests and other men (brothers) and women (sisters/nuns) in religious orders (Jesuits, Franciscans, Dominicans, etc.).

Released amid much public interest on February 27, 2004, the report nevertheless counted 10,667 credible incidents of alleged sexual abuse of youths under 18 involving 4,392 diocesan priests and deacons. This meant an estimated four percent of clergy in ministry during the stated time frame of 1950 to 2002 had substantiated allegations made against them. (Another 2,827 new allegations were reported by the bishops,[29] and the number of priests rose to "considerably over 5,000" [30] between the years 2004-2007.)

Table 4.3.1 of the John Jay report stated that 8,499 victims whose gender was indicated were male (80.9 percent) and 2,004 were female (19.1 percent).

Table 4.3.2 noted the age of the victim when the abuse began, but did not break down the following numbers by gender:

- 37 (0.3 percent) of the victims were three and younger.
- 281 (2.5 percent) were ages four through six.
- 951 (10.6 percent) were ages seven through nine.
- 4111 (45.9 percent) were ages ten through thirteen.
- 3576 (39.9 percent) were ages fourteen through seventeen.

The average age of the victims was 12.6 years of age.

Because these numbers have been almost universally misreported, misinterpreted or ignored even by the mainstream media this bears repeating: only 40 percent of the victims were adolescent (aged 14-17) boys *and* girls. The report never mentioned a number or percentage of teenaged male victims which would logically be well below 40 percent, nor did it mention the sexual orientation of the offenders.

Anything But Mea Culpa

Blaming Homosexuals

The neo-Catholics were obviously confident their readers would not read the actual report which was readily accessible on the internet,[31] nor would their supporters know that hetero- and homo-sexuality refer to consensual adult gender attraction or that even adolescents between fourteen and seventeen are considered in most states to be too young for un-coerced assent to an adult.

Deal Hudson, editor of *Crisis* magazine: "[The John Jay report] is absolute confirmation that homosexual predators were the main perpetrators in this scandal."[32]

Weigel: "The [John Jay] report acknowledges the overwhelmingly homosexual nature of the clerical sexual abuse of minors over the past 50 years, without using clinical terms that can serve as evasions—like 'pedophilia'—and in a sober way that cannot be reasonably interpreted as 'scapegoat' or 'gay-bashing.'"[33]

Neuhaus: "A few headlines [no citations given] said that homosexual priests were at the heart of the scandals. There is some expressed unhappiness that the John Jay report uses the category of ages 11 to 17 rather than 13 to 17.... In its report and its February 27 presentation, the John Jay team was manifestly nervous about the homosexuality factor. The woman making the slide presentation at the National Press Club skipped over the data on adolescent males in a nanosecond. A perhaps jaundiced [and unidentified] network reporter remarked afterwards about the downplaying of the homosexuality factor, 'Remember that the John Jay people have to go back and get along in New York City.'"[34]

Robert Geffner, psychologist and editor of the Journal of Child Sexual Abuse, stated that research indicates that homosexuals are no more likely than heterosexuals to violate minors sexually. David Finkelhor, director of Crimes Against Children Research Center at the University of New Hampshire, views sexual attraction to minors as a separate sexual attraction, an opinion also espoused by John Bancroft, physician and director of the Kinsey Institute for Research in Sex, Gender, and Reproduction. Sexual offender researchers Nicholas Groth and Frank Oliveri studied more than 3,000 sex offenders and did not find even one homosexual man who shifted from an attraction to adult men to a desire for minors. Conversely, they found that men who were nonexclusively fixated on children, or who regressed from an attraction to adults to an interest in children, all described themselves as heterosexual and, in addition, usually were homophobic. Similarly, Minneapolis psychologist Peter

Dimock concluded that most minor boys are abused by heterosexual men, some of whom are indifferent to the gender of their victims, choosing either girls or boys based on the minor's availability and vulnerability. Perhaps more sexual predators abuse boys than once was thought but are reluctant to say so and be perceived as homosexuals. The imperative point here is that, for the sexual perpetrators in any one of these groups, *their criminal behaviors stem not from their sexual orientation but rather reflect their psychological immaturity, arrested development, or antisocial, criminal proclivities*, a fact relentlessly presented to the Vatican and just as relentlessly ignored. (emphasis added)[35]

Other than acknowledging that there is a greater proportion of homosexuals in the priesthood than in the general population, Church officials and the right-wing press lied about the causes of the scandal and in defense of the hierarchy. Michael S. Rose, in his book *Goodbye Good Men*, documented what he considered to be the malevolent influence in the American Church by a group of homosexual priests and bishops known to each other who controlled various seminaries and dioceses. He stated that a priest/bishop involved in a homosexual relationship would be more inclined to "look the other way" at another's criminal activities. A. W. Richard Sipe, a former Benedictine monk and psychotherapist who has done extensive studies of the priesthood, responded that sexual orientation is irrelevant. "Priests and bishops who know about each other's sexual affairs with women, too, are bound together by draconian links of sacred silence."[36]

Ten US bishops resigned after revelations that they themselves sexually abused children or vulnerable adults.

After the release of the John Jay report, the mainstream media added credence to the right-wing press by emphasizing that 81 percent of the reported victims were male, sadly dismissing the suffering of thousands of female victims. Even as late as February 2008, the website *beliefnet* had an author posting the following: "The authoritative John Jay College report found that nearly all molesters of youth were gay."[37] What the non-Catholic media could be forgiven for, but not neo-Catholics, is the certain knowledge that an all-male priesthood had greater access to boys, just as the nun's, whose victims weren't counted, had greater access to girls. Every Catholic with the usual upbringing knew that around the parish, the boys—as potential recruits for the priesthood—were invited to hang out with the priests. In addition, there were all-boy choirs, schools, camps, and outings under the direction of the clergy. Boys were invited to sleepovers at the rectory, were taken on trips, were trained to be altar boys.

To a large extent, victim gender selection by priests reflected opportunity. Consider, for example, prison sex, in which heterosexual males with more power and authority within the inmate population select and rape other, less powerful men to achieve sexual release and to impose their power on another person. Boys were much more available to priests than were girls. Parents were thrilled to have a priest single their boy out for attention and encouraged their sons to spend time with Father, even allowing them to travel with the priest.[38]

An American (or Boston) "Problem"

International news agencies reported the clerical sexual abuse of children to be a world-wide occurrence. Twenty-two other countries in addition to the US had reports of bishops covering up for abusers and many more reported just the crime itself. Priest/offenders had not only been shuffled from parish to parish, but from state to state and from country to country in order to hide their criminal records and avoid prosecution. More than a few wound up in Rome.

Prosecutors around the world were stonewalled in their efforts to extradite clergy.

Maricopa County Attorney Rick Romley of Arizona was rebuffed when he asked the Vatican to order two other fugitive priests to surrender. They had fled Phoenix for Mexico and Ireland. The prosecutor's letter to the Vatican secretary of state, Cardinal Angelo Sodano, was sent back resealed, along with a note: 'The item, here enclosed, is returned to the sender because refused by the rightful addressee.'"[39]

More than a hundred priests accused of sexually abusing children fled from the US to Mexico alone.[40] There is no tally of the priests who fled from Mexico—or other Latin American country—to the US, but in countries where the Church is aligned with the government, it has been described to this author that sometimes the father and uncles of abused children took matters into their own hands and the dead priests were reported as victims of "bandits."

As reports of sexual predation by priests and bishops and the cover-up by the pope's hand-picked prelates rolled in from around the world, it became clear John Paul II was as guilty in contributing to the brutalization of children as he was in supporting Latin American death squads and militias and in rallying to the defense of Rwandan clergy and religious accused of genocide. The sex abuse scandal is just further evidence the primary work of his institution is maintaining the privilege, power and immunity of the clerical caste.

Abuse Caused by "Culture of Dissent"

According to Table 3.3.2 of the John Jay study, seventy percent of the accused priests were ordained before 1970, meaning most of their seminary training was completed well before the 1968 encyclical on birth control spawned the so-called "culture of dissent" or unleashed the societal licentiousness attributed to this "rebellion." In addition, since the current global episcopate who protected their priest/predators were selected based on their unquestioning adherence to the pre-Vatican II ideology of John Paul II, if anything, the current scandal should have been attributed to orthodox religiosity.

Neither could it be correctly stated that clerics raping children was endemic only to the US, nor the result of modern "sexual morality," nor moral relativism of the late twentieth century because priests have been sodomizing children throughout Church history. Since the fourth century the Vatican has acknowledged pederasty as both a universal and timeless internal scandal in numerous documents, councils, and admonitions.[41]

Clerical Sexual Abuse is "History"

The data showing that the number of occurrences in the John Jay report spiked in the 1970s may be related to the fact the total number of priests in the US peaked in that period as did the number of American children enrolled in parochial schools and religious education classes.[42] The Baby Boomers are the last generation raised by ethnic-Europeans culturally self-identified by their Catholic religion.

Also, by its nature, the crime of sexually assaulting children is often reported only years—typically decades—later. It takes time for victims to sort through their confusion, fear, and shame. A child is not sure what is happening or how to judge it, especially when, as is most often the case, the abuser is a trusted adult. In addition, the victim may feel somehow guilty if they did not fight against it or tell anyone about it. The introspection and maturity needed to conclude the guilt lies solely with the adult takes many years to develop especially when the victim suppresses the memory of so intimate and unspeakable a violation.

Contributing to the suppression of reporting is the manner in which some victims who "told" were disbelieved or mistreated by their parents, police and/or district attorneys. Some families were ostracized from their parishes if it became known the child accused a priest of such reprehensible conduct.

Sexual crimes, including the sexual violation of children, have the lowest rate of reporting for all crimes. "Only one percent to ten percent of these cases are ever reported. They fall by the way side. And one out of seven victims of all sexual assaults, (against both adults and children) is under age six," according to a veteran of the FBI's Behavioral Sciences unit which dealt with sex offenders.[43] According to Marci Hamilton, a professor at Yeshiva University's Cardozo School of Law and author of *God vs. The Gavel: Religion and the Rule of Law*, 90 percent of child sexual abusers are never prosecuted due to statutes of limitations which restrict the number of years following the crime in which sex abuse may be prosecuted. "Children do not have the maturity or resources to yet decide, on their own, whether to sue or testify (and parents, as we have learned, don't always help them). Moreover, adults who were victims as children need some time to decide whether to go through the additional trauma of suing, or cooperating in a prosecution," according to Hamilton.[44]

The official grand jury and district attorney investigations into child sexual abuse in the Catholic Church noted that statutes of limitations were the greatest hindrance in bringing the perpetrators and their protectors to justice:

- "But for the windfall provided by Pennsylvania's statutes of limitations for serious sexual offences, the priests who sexually and psychologically abused archdiocesan children could be prosecuted for the following serious crimes: rape, statutory sexual assault, involuntary deviate sexual intercourse, indecent assault, endangering welfare of children, corruption of minors. Unfortunately the law stands in the way of justice for victims of childhood sexual abuse." In the Court of Common Pleas First Judicial District of Pennsylvania Criminal Trial Division - In Re: Misc. No. 03-00-239, County Investigating Grand Jury, September 15, 2005

- "New York State Criminal Procedure Law section 30:10 should be amended to eliminate the statute of limitations in cases involving a sexual offense as defined in article one hundred thirty of the penal code committed against a child less than the age of eighteen, use of a child in a sexual performance as defined in section 26305 of the penal law or conspiracy to commit these crimes under New York State Penal Law Article 105." Suffolk County Supreme Court Special Grand Jury, May 6, 2002, Term ID, Grand Jury Report CPL §190.85(1)(C), January 17, 2003

- "The Westchester County April 'E' 2002 believes that legislative action is urgently required to address sexual abuse and misconduct against minors by members of the clergy and their religious institution's improper response to this activity. For this reason, the Grand Jury has recommended that New York's Statute of Limitations be eliminated for crimes of this kind." Report of the April 'E' 2002 Westchester Grand Jury Concerning Complaints Sexual Abuse and Misconduct against Minors by Members of the Clergy, June 19, 2002

In state after state where a bill has been introduced to reform the statute of limitations on child sex abuse, the local (arch)diocese always has funds available to hire attorneys and lobbyists to prevent its passage and Republican state lawmakers can be counted on to vote against the legislation.

Victims Are In This for the Money

"The long-term effects of child sexual abuse may include: post-traumatic-stress-disorder (PTSD), depression and thoughts of suicide, alcohol abuse, drug abuse, self mutilation to mask painful emotions tied to the abuse. Not only the victims, but their family members are affected," according to the US Veteran's Administration.[45] "Known male and female child-sex-abuse-related victims were 2.2 and 2.5 times the general population suicide rate, respectively. Every female, and 80 percent of male child-sex-abuse-related victim suicides, also had a mental disorder," noted an article in the *British Journal of Social Work.*[46]

The last reported tally of US victims of priests known to have committed suicide stood at 144. However, neither the slower deaths from alcohol or drug abuse, eating disorders, poverty and lack of health care, nor the suicides among the victims' parents and/or spouses have been tabulated. When the expense of years of physical and mental health care, under- and unemployment, the harm done by dysfunctional marital and parental patterns caused by the abuse itself, and the additional damage caused by the inhuman measures taken by the bishops, their staffs and brutish lawyers to threaten, harass, demean and defame its victims are considered, it's difficult to say how much money could ever be enough to compensate those who have survived their abuse and their families. One author concluded the attitude of bishops appeared to be: "Your suffering at our hands is negligible, in any case far less important than the damage to our reputation that would accompany a public acknowledgment of the truth."[47]

According to the John Jay report, only 20 percent of the allegations were reported to the Church by lawyers representing victims. The majority (63.5 percent) were reported by the victims or their parents. (The rest came from siblings, police, other employees, etc.) The Church's financial liability in the US—which already exceeds $2 billion—would be a fraction of that amount if these children had been properly cared for from the beginning and their attackers promptly removed from ministry.

Many victims have attested that, while they need the money obtained through settlements for the reasons already stated, what they seek most is the validation that they are no longer "alleged" victims of "alleged" crimes by "alleged" perpetrators. Having already been disbelieved or dismissed, their ability to prove their case in a court of law can be as psychologically healing as years of therapy. We all owe these courageous people a debt of gratitude for their willingness to expose themselves to a court which forces them to reveal in graphic and excruciating details how they have been violated. Not only Catholic children are safer, but due to the notoriety engendered by the scandal, interest has now been extended to protecting all children from sexual abuse.

And Besides, Social Programs Will Suffer

The neo-Catholic press and episcopate have launched a propaganda campaign to persuade Americans that large settlements paid to the victims have already, or would in the future, impair the Church's social programs of caring for the poor or providing health care. However, the majority of social programs run by Catholics are not controlled nor funded by the bishops. Also, a third of the monies paid to victims so far has come from insurers and additional amounts have come from diocesan investments, general revenues and the sale of property. In the largest settlement to date, the Archdiocese of Los Angeles was ordered to pay $660 million to 508 plaintiffs. Allianz SE and Muenchener Rueckversicherungs AG were among more than 10 insurers paying a total of $227 million to cover the claims. The rest would be raised by selling assets, mostly real estate.[48] Several dioceses have claimed bankruptcy, but these actions were taken to preserve assets. Where the USCCB and dioceses have cut back on expenses, it is lay employees who are laid off and local parish and schools shut down. No matter how much has been spent to compensate victims, not a penny has come from a prelate's personal income.

While they have successfully directed their followers' attention to the money paid to the victims, neo-Catholic pundits and prelates are loathe to admit that any financial shortfall has been caused by diminution in income from the third of US Catholics who have left the Church or those remaining who have decided to keep their hands in their pockets. Based upon the previous chapter's examination of the Faith Based and Community Initiative, it is clear that tax dollars are crucial to funding the USCCB, Catholic Charities and Catholic health care providers and this source of funding remains unaffected by, and independent from, legal settlements. Given the lack of oversight and the secrecy of Church finances, it may even be possible government monies are being used to subsidize the high-priced attorneys and lobbyists holding back reform of statutes of limitations.

Targeting Priests While Ignoring Other Professions

The Vatican and neo-Catholics want it both ways. The constant teaching of the Church from at least the middle ages is that a man becomes "ontologically" changed by ordination, that his very essence or nature of being has actually been altered to a higher plane. According to the Church, the priest is specially called by God to act *in persona Christi*—in the person of Christ. John Paul II reminded his ordained that "each priest at his consecration is marked indelibly with Christ's image."[49] "By his ordination and his vow of celibacy, the Catholic priest is set apart from the world for the world's sake," Weigel wrote.[50] Therefore, just by reason of his ordination, a priest is to be given deference and obedience. Yet when referring to criminal behavior by the clergy, the Vatican and the neo-Catholics tell us priests are no different from the rest of us and are not to be held to a higher standard.

The secular press is repeatedly castigated for supposedly persecuting the Church by ignoring the incidence of pedophilia in other professions. The neo-Catholics want us to believe that there is no difference to a child being assaulted by a priest or a nun than by a teacher, coach or Scout leader. But Catholic children were taught that his/her priest and nun are more God-like and to be respected more than even their own parents—that they were to be obeyed because they are holier and incapable of wrongdoing. A sexual attack by a religious figure is therefore something akin to a betrayal by God in the eyes of a child. The harm is not only psychological and physical but spiritual as well. It's bad enough to lose trust in an adult, but to know you have also been abandoned by God is indescribably devastating. To be violated in such a profound manner destroys both the psyche and the soul. When a man or woman dons religious garb meant to set them apart as special, privileged, deserving of trust and deference, a particularly egregious hypocrisy attaches to their moral failures which does not accrue to other professions. To put it simply, they make their living as moral judges and adepts. Other professions do not. To the continuing frustration of these pundits and prelates no statistic on any other profession or religion has approached the grossly underreported 4 percent figured noted in the John Jay report.

But NOT Celibacy

Liberals and secularists were blamed for questioning the role of celibacy as Neuhaus claimed with an "ulterior agenda" of "discrediting the Catholic teaching on human sexuality, about which they are genuinely outraged." They were accused by McCloskey of wanting to change the institution of the priesthood and thereby the whole bureaucratic and hierarchical structure of the Church. It is only natural, however, for the non-ordained to speculate on whether the sheer brutality and cruelty to children could have been sustained for so many centuries by a ruling class which included women and/or men with children of their own.

No one supposes that pedophilia is limited to unmarried adults in the general population, but what serious critics of mandatory celibacy question is whether or not maintaining a group of men who live without the demands of family life or having to support others and who attend school together, recreate and work together to the exclusion of "outsiders," creates an unhealthy attitude of privilege and power among the ordained where they are not to be criticized and a loyalty to the group which supersedes all else. Is there an attitude which engenders a disdain for the laity even to the inclusion of sexual abuse of their children? Does this closed society actually attract men with any number of perversions or sociopathic inclinations they know will be institutionally hidden and protected?

The notion of a married priesthood or the ordination of women is pointless speculation at present since both John Paul II and his successor, Benedict XVI, have made it clear that the Church, at least for the foreseeable future, will continue to ordain only single males to the priesthood and their superiors will continue to demand their loyalty, obedience and dependence unadulterated by love for a spouse and children.

Officially, Homosexuals Are The Scapegoats

Cardinal Joseph Ratzinger, in a 1985 letter to the bishops, took a hard line on homosexuality: "a strong tendency ordered towards an intrinsic moral evil; and thus the inclination itself must be seen as an objective disorder." In 1997, this view was repeated in a Vatican statement issued by Cardinal Dionigi Teltamanzi in "Christian Anthropology and Homosexuality:" "The Church is called, together with every person of good will, to denounce the very grave personal and social risks connected with accepting the so-called 'gay' culture."[51]

The only action (the rest only words) the Vatican has taken in response to the clerical sexual abuse of children was to follow Navarro-Vall's and McCloskey's instruction. The Roman Catholic Church officially prohibited the ordination of homosexuals because, "As regards to deep-seated homosexual tendencies, these are objectively disordered." An exception was made for those with "homosexual tendencies that might only be a manifestation of a transitory problem, as, for example, delayed adolescence. These must be clearly overcome at least three years before diaconal [the last step before priesthood] Ordination." This official decree was signed by "The Supreme Pontiff Benedict XVI," on 31 August 2005, the same man who prissy-slapped ABC News reporter Brian Ross's hand for asking what he considered to be an impertinent question. By declaring homosexuals "objectively disordered," the Church concurred they were responsible for the crisis. Once gay men are barred from the priesthood, so the party-line goes, the pervasive corruption of the clerical ruling class will cease. Yeah.

What Ratzinger really did was throw a bone to his orthodox supporters. The reality is that with a precipitous decline in the number of priests, the Church can't afford to lose such a large number of clergy. It is the Catholic version of "don't ask, don't tell." The unacceptable alternative to fewer priests would be to turn over administrative functions to lay people who have alternative choices for income and retirement benefits outside the Church.

(Any information in this chapter without a specific citation can be verified by the thousands of documents regarding the clerical sex abuse scandal saved on the website bishop-accountability.org.)

CHAPTER 14

THE 2004 PRESIDENTIAL CAMPAIGN

The War in Iraq

Before the Republican Party replaced fear and loathing of communists with fear and loathing of Muslims, William Casey had "supported Islam as a counter to the Soviet Union's atheism, and…sometimes conflated lay Catholic organizations such as Opus Dei with the Muslim Brotherhood, the Egyptian extremist organization, of which Ayman al-Zawahiri, Osama bin Laden's chief lieutenant, was a passionate member."[1] The tragic events of September 11, 2001, made war against Islam a neocon imperative.

Jim Nicholson, George W. Bush's ambassador to the Vatican, related that when he spoke with John Paul II on September 13, 2001,

> The pope told me that he believed the events of September 11 were truly an attack, not only on the United States, but on 'the entire human race,' and that we were justified in taking defensive action. He asked me only to make an appeal to President Bush on his behalf that the United States would hold themselves to the highest standards of justice for which our country is known....
>
> It was at this meeting that the foundations were laid for the support of the Holy See for our campaign against terrorism. It is extraordinary that the pope and the Church wished to help us, and likewise worth noticing that this support continues today.[2]

When Nicholson wrote this in the fall of 2002 that was a less-than-accurate assessment of support from the Vatican for the Bush/Cheney "global war on terror."

Shortly after the 9/11 attacks, John Paul II made a trip to Kazakhstan and Armenia where he made an impassioned plea for peace. Nicholson quickly countered that the US attacks on Afghanistan had the full support of Vatican Secretary of State Cardinal Angelo Sodano, and Vatican foreign minister, Archbishop Jean-Louis Tauran. Joaquin Navarro-Valls added that the Vatican would "understand" the use of force as protection from further threats.[3]

Most Europeans, however—with the important exception of the British Prime Minister, Tony Blair—were listening with trepidation and dismay as the Bush administration revved-up its propaganda to support the eventual invasion of Iraq. For Europeans who had fought two World Wars on their soil, armed conflict is more repugnant than it is to Americans. The continent also had a low opinion of Bush's abilities and intelligence, as did the majority of the Roman Curia. In addition, a US war in the Middle East threatened to destabilize world markets and the capitalist order which included the Vatican Bank. There was a "perception within the Roman Catholic Church hierarchy that a coup d'etat was implemented, one that gave Bush and his leadership near-dictatorial powers to carry out their agenda."[4]

Archbishop Renato Martino, head of the Vatican's UN mission, spoke through the Vatican news agency on September 13:

> What has happened is a reminder that the search for peace is a duty. Every country that has the means to intervene to bring peace must do so. No one can stand and watch. Sooner or later every country must be involved. The United States can no longer be considered invulnerable. Despite the elaborate missile defense program, millions of dollars spent on fighting terrorism, all it took was a couple of penknives to cause a disaster of such proportions. Terrorists are people who are desperate; they feel they have nothing to lose. They see no future so they are ready to kill and to be killed. We must identify the problems at the roots of terrorism and find solutions.[5]

In a radio interview in November 2001, Cardinal Joseph Ratzinger was asked to comment on the US response in Afghanistan: "I'd say for example that among the evangelicals in the United States there are some who fully identify themselves in the words of the Holy Scripture—and if they are truly faithful to the Scriptures, they don't fall into the trap of fanaticism and a religion that becomes violent."[6] The same month, John Paul II, speaking to pilgrims from his study window overlooking St. Peter's Square during his weekly speech (known as the "Angelus" address for the standard opening prayer), expressed his sympathy both for the victims of the terrorist attacks in the US and for Afghans, particularly women, children and old people, forced to abandon their homes because of American bombing.[7]

In his "Message for the Celebration of the World Day of Peace January 1, 2002," John Paul II said that while nations had the responsibility to defend themselves against terrorist attacks,

The guilty must be correctly identified, since criminal culpability is always personal and cannot be extended to the nation, ethnic group or religion to which the terrorists may belong. International cooperation in the fight against terrorist activities must also include a courageous and resolute political, diplomatic and economic commitment to relieving situations of oppression and marginalization which facilitate the designs of terrorists. The recruitment of terrorists in fact is easier in situations where rights are trampled upon and injustices tolerated over a long period of time.[8]

The pope invited leaders from all the worlds' religions, particularly Muslims and Christians, to a Day of Prayer for Peace which took place in Assisi on January 24, 2002. The statement issued by the assembled leaders said, in part: "We commit ourselves to proclaiming our firm conviction that violence and terrorism are incompatible with the authentic spirit of religion, and, as we condemn every recourse to violence and war in the name of God or of religion, we commit ourselves to doing everything possible to eliminate the root causes of terrorism."[9]

In referring to the first anniversary of the 9/11 attacks, the pope stated in September 2002: "The international community can no longer overlook the underlying causes that lead young people especially, to despair of humanity, of life itself, and of the future, and to fall prey to the temptations of violence, hatred and desire for revenge at any cost."[10]

The US Neo-Catholics Tout "Just War" Doctrine

In counterpoint to the drumbeat for war, progressive Catholics referred to the Church's teaching on "just war." According to the *Catechism of the Catholic Church*:

- All citizens and all governments are obliged to work for the avoidance of war. However, as long as the danger of war persists and there is no international authority with the necessary competence and power, governments cannot be denied the right of lawful self-defense, once all peace efforts have failed.
- The strict conditions for legitimate defense by military force require rigorous consideration. The gravity of such a decision makes it subject to rigorous conditions of moral legitimacy. At one and the same time:
    - the damage inflicted by the aggressor on the nation or community of nations must be lasting, grave, and certain;
    - all other means of putting an end to it must have been shown to be impractical or ineffective;

- there must be serious prospects of success;

- the use of arms must not produce evils and disorders graver than the evil to be eliminated.

- These are the traditional elements enumerated in what is called the "just war" doctrine. The evaluation of these conditions for moral legitimacy belongs to the prudential judgment of those who have responsibility for the common good.

The pope and other Vatican officials had been clear as to what type of response they expected from the US. The neo-Catholic pundits now had to explain, as they did with capital punishment, why *they* were not "rebellious dissidents" when they disagreed with the Church and the Catechism to justify Bush's war and counter the pope's call for peace.

In a column dated September 20, 2001, George Weigel wrote: "The just–war tradition needs to be 'stretched,' or developed, to deal with this new reality. In confronting terrorism, 'just cause' cannot be limited to repelling an 'aggression already under way'—as some current Catholic thinking has it. When facing terrorist organizations, pre-emptive military action is not only morally justifiable but morally imperative."[11]

Weigel delivered a lecture at the Catholic University of America in the fall of 2002 later published as an essay in the January 2003 *First Things* which included the usual "weapons of mass destruction" justification for the invasion. As Damon Linker wrote, the essay "provided the Bush administration with this moral and theological go-ahead for unilateral war with Iraq (as well as with any number of other rogue states around the world)." Linker also noted:

In response to writers who concluded that the coming invasion would fall far short of meeting the standards for a just war, Weigel suggested that statesmen reached their final decision for war through the exercise of a "charism of political discernment" enjoyed by all "duly constituted public authorities." This charism—or gift of the Holy Spirit—is "not shared by bishops, stated clerks, rabbis, imams, or ecumenical and interreligious agencies"—all of whom should exercise "a measure of political modesty" in addressing questions of war and peace. (Nowhere did Weigel indicate that modesty was a quality required of politicians and their foreign policy advisors.) It was difficult to read these words without concluding that the theocon message to critics of the administration's foreign policy was to keep their mouths shut and put their faith in the divinely inspired wisdom of the President of the United States.[12]

Fr. Richard John Neuhaus "established himself as the rare priest who would grant interviews to National Public Radio in order to defend the justice of invading Iraq."[13] He wrote that "the time had come to rethink a crucial aspect of the just war tradition. In future conflicts it might become possible to conceive of 'military action in terms not of the last resort but of the best resort.'"[14]

Cardinal Ratzinger responded to the neo-Catholics in an article appearing in *Avvenire,* the official newspaper of the Italian bishops' conference.

> The cardinal does not believe that a unilateral military attack by the United States against Iraq would be morally justifiable, under the current circumstances. "The concept of a 'preventive war' does not appear in the *Catechism of the Catholic Church,*" Ratzinger noted. "One cannot simply say that the catechism does not legitimize the war," he continued. "But it is true that the catechism has developed a doctrine that, on one hand, does not exclude the fact that there are values and peoples that must be defended in some circumstances; on the other hand, it offers a very precise doctrine on the limits of these possibilities."
>
> According to Ratzinger, "It is necessary that the community of nations makes the decision, not a particular power. The United Nations is the [institution] that should make the final decision."[15]

In a remarkably prescient letter, Bishop Wilton D. Gregory, president of the USCCB, wrote a letter to Bush dated September 13, 2002:

> War against Iraq could have unpredictable consequences not only for Iraq but for peace and stability elsewhere in the Middle East. Would preventive or preemptive force succeed in thwarting serious threats or, instead, provoke the very kind of attacks that it is intended to prevent? How would another war in Iraq impact the civilian population, in the short- and long-term? How many more innocent people would suffer and die, or be left without homes, without basic necessities, without work? Would the United States and the international community commit to the arduous, long-term task of ensuring a just peace or would a post-Saddam Iraq continue to be plagued by civil conflict and repression, and continue to serve as a destabilizing force in the region? Would the use of military force lead to wider conflict and instability?
>
> Would war against Iraq detract from our responsibility to help build a just and stable order in Afghanistan and undermine the broader coalition against terrorism?[16]

Two months later, the USCCB issued another statement on Iraq: "Based on the facts that are known to us, we continue to find it difficult to justify the resort to war against Iraq, lacking clear and adequate evidence of an imminent attack of a grave nature. With the Holy See and bishops from the Middle East and around the world, we fear that resort to war, under present circumstances and in light of current public information, would not meet the strict conditions in Catholic teaching for overriding the strong presumption against the use of military force."[17]

During a PBS interview on January 10, 2003, Weigel was asked: "What would you say to Catholics in this country who read and hear what the pope has to say—that attacking Iraq would not be in the "just war" tradition, that it's wrong. He opposes it." Weigel had the temerity to respond:

> Well, in fact, the pope has not said that. The pope has said that he hopes that every possible nonmilitary measure will be used. The US bishops have said that they are not clear in their own minds that this would satisfy the conditions of the "just war" tradition. And to them I would say the *Catechism of the Catholic Church*, in the section on the just war tradition, after listing the traditional criteria says quite explicitly the moral judgment on these matters is left to the prudence of statesmen. It's not the business of Church leaders to make the call. It's the business of Church leaders to clarify the principles, to teach the principles, to make sure that those principles are present in the public debate. But Catholic teaching says that this is a tradition for statesmen and they have to make the call, because they are the only ones with the full information necessary to make the call and they are the ones who have assumed the burden of moral choice here.[18]

(As noted above, the Catechism actually states: "The evaluation of these conditions for moral legitimacy belongs to the prudential judgment of those who have responsibility for the common good," not just government officials.)

Three days later, John Paul II continued to make Iraq "his business" and exercise his "responsibility for the common good" in an address to the diplomatic corps assigned to the Vatican:

> Without needing to repeat what I said to you last year on this occasion, I will simply add today, faced with the constant degeneration of the crisis in the Middle East, that the solution will never be imposed by recourse to terrorism or armed conflict, as if military victories could be the solution. And what are we to say of the threat of a war which could strike the people of Iraq, the land of the

Prophets, a people already sorely tried by more than twelve years of embargo? War is never just another means that one can choose to employ for settling differences between nations....

War is not always inevitable. It is always a defeat for humanity. International law, honest dialogue, solidarity between States, the noble exercise of diplomacy: these are methods worthy of individuals and nations in resolving their differences.

It will always be possible for a leader who acts in accordance with his convictions to reject situations of injustice or of institutional corruption, or to put an end to them. It is precisely in this, I believe, that we rediscover what is today commonly called "good governance." The material and spiritual well-being of humanity, the protection of the freedom and rights of the human person, selfless public service, closeness to concrete conditions: all of these take precedence over every political project and constitute a moral necessity which in itself is the best guarantee of peace within nations and peace between States.[19]

On February 5, 2003, Secretary of State Colin Powell appeared before the UN General Assembly to present the US justification to attack Iraq. Three days later, an official response to Powell's speech appeared in *Civilta Cattolica*, a newspaper published by the Jesuits in Rome in which all of its articles are approved by the Vatican's secretariat of state and reflect official opinion. "The journal attacked the United States' justification for a possible war in Iraq, saying it was motivated by economics and would spark a wave of terrorism and more trouble in the Middle East. The journal suggested that oil was an ulterior motive for a war."[20]

Jim Nicholson asked Michael Novak to fly to Rome to convince the pope and his curia that the Bush invasion of Iraq would be within the parameters of a "just war." While in Rome, Novak was considered a guest of the US State Department and part of its US Speaker and Specialist program. On February 10, 2003, Novak addressed a public audience in Vatican City repeating the charges made by Powell i.e. Saddam Hussein had "weapons of mass destruction" and intended to use them.

In brief, some persons argue today (as I do) that, under the original Catholic doctrine of justum bellum, a limited and carefully conducted war to bring about a change of regime in Iraq is, as a last resort, morally obligatory. For public authorities to fail to conduct such a war would be to put their trust imprudently in the sanity and good will of Saddam Hussein.[21]

Novak convinced no one in Rome and returned to a friendlier forum provided by the *National Review.* In the February 18, 2003 edition, he repeated the lie. "Not that it matters to most people, but the *Catechism of the Catholic Church* lays down as a fundamental principle of its method of thinking about morally obligatory wars that, in the end, the last responsibility for making decisions falls on public authorities - lay persons, not clerics."[22]

The Pope Strives Tirelessly for Peace

Few Americans were aware of the extraordinary efforts on the part of the pope and the Holy See to avert the impending war. As the US rapidly built up its military presence in the Persian Gulf region to within striking range of Iraq, "Vatican officials warned against resolving the Iraqi disarmament problem through war, pointedly rejecting the notion of a 'preventative war' in the case of Iraq." John Paul II "appealed to the United Nations. The pope worked tirelessly to convince leaders of nations on the UN Security Council to oppose Bush's war resolution on Iraq. Vatican sources claim they had not seen the pope more animated and determined since he fell ill to Parkinson's Disease. In the end, the pope did convince the leaders of Mexico, Chile, Cameroon, and Guinea to oppose the US resolution."[23]

- Wojtyla appointed Cardinal Roger Etchegaray as his "Special Envoy to the Iraqi Authorities" on February 10, 2003.

    Cardinal Etchegaray believes that his one-and-a-half hour meeting on Saturday with Saddam Hussein helped to open new possibilities for peace in Iraq....'I am convinced that, at this moment, it is fundamental to restore a climate of trust-basis of all the efforts that are being made. The reconstruction of confidence is a great work, and requires time; it begins with little gestures. Moreover, it is important to have confidence in the work of the United Nations inspectors.'[24]

- John Paul II stated in his Angelus message on February 23:

    For months, the international community has been living in great apprehension of the danger of war, which could unsettle the entire Middle East and aggravate the tensions that unfortunately are already present at the beginning of the third millennium. The believers of all religions must proclaim that we can never be happy if we are in conflict with one another; the future of humanity can never be assured by terrorism and the logic of war. We Christians, in particular, are asked....to keep watch, that our consciences may not give in to the temptations of egoism, deceit, and violence.[25]

- On March 1, Wojtyla sent Cardinal Pio Laghi, a personal friend of his father, to persuade Bush not to start a war.

> The purpose of my visit was to deliver a personal message of the Holy Father to the president regarding the Iraqi crisis, to expound upon the Holy See's position and to report on the various initiatives undertaken by the Holy See to contribute to disarmament and peace in the Middle East... The Holy See maintains that there are still peaceful avenues within the context of the vast patrimony of international law and institutions which exist for that purpose. A decision regarding the use of military force can only be taken within the framework of the United Nations, but always taking into account the grave consequences of such an armed conflict: the suffering of the people of Iraq and those involved in the military operation, a further instability in the region, and a new gulf between Islam and Christianity. I want to emphasize that there is great unity on this grave matter on the part of the Holy See, the Bishops in the United States, and the Church throughout the world.[26]

- John Paul II stated in his Angelus message on March 2:

> Peace, in fact, is a gift of God that must be invoked with humble and insistent trust. Without giving up in the face of difficulties, we must seek out and follow every possible way of avoiding war, which always results in sorrow and grave consequences for all.[27]

- On Ash Wednesday (March 5), the pope declared a day of fasting for the cause of peace, above all in the Middle East. According to his official Vatican biography, "During these weeks, the Pope met numerous authorities and made pressing appeals to avoid the danger of war in Iraq."[28]

- Archbishop Martino stated on March 11:

> "A unilateral attack by the United States on Iraq would be a 'war of aggression.'" Archbishop Martino argued that, contrary to what happened in 1991 with the invasion of Kuwait, on this occasion "there is no aggression and so this preventive war is, in itself, a war of aggression." Martino said terrorism must be combated by addressing "the causes that produce it" and that "evil cannot justify evil."[29]

- On March 13 Martino issued a statement criticizing the US for lobbying UN Security Council members to support military action in Iraq, noting "the pressure that the most powerful nations are exerting in the UN Security Council to influence the votes of the less powerful. Each of the voters should be left free, with no interference. It is not right that the large exert more pressure on the small than their capacity to resist."[30]

- John Paul II stated in his Angelus message on March 16: "In the face of the tremendous consequences that an international military operation would have for the population of Iraq and for the balance of the Middle East region, already sorely tried, and for the extremisms that could stem from it, I say to all: There is still time to negotiate; there is still room for peace, it is never too late to come to an understanding and to continue discussions."

- On March 17 Martino quoted Jesus' words on Vatican Radio: "If a son asks you for bread, you do not give him a stone," and added: "To a people who for 12 years have been begging for bread, preparations are being made to drop 3,000 bombs on them! It is a crime against peace that cries out vengeance before God," the archbishop said. "Let us pray so that the Pharaoh's heart will not be hardened and the biblical plagues of a terrible war will not fall on humanity."[31]

Given the impassioned and urgent efforts of the pope and his men, the resolute dissent of neo-Catholics seems all the more shocking. A week prior to the March 18 invasion, Neuhaus again asserted that war and peace "are matters of prudential judgment beyond the competence of religious authority." He tried to impugn the Holy See's petitions regarding the UN: "The larger and more interesting question is posed by the frequently heard assertion that the UN is the locus of legitimate authority in international affairs. That is asserted but it has not been argued, certainly not in terms of Catholic doctrine regarding legitimate authority." He also belittled the calls for peace from other Vatican officials. "Widespread statements in parts of Europe about American inexperience and 'cowboy' impetuosity would be insulting were they not so adolescent. They are especially unbecoming when made by distinguished prelates associated with the Holy See."[32]

- Part of Bishop Gregory's statement released on March 19, 2003 reads:

We deeply regret that war was not averted. We stand by the statement of the full body of bishops last November. Our conference's moral concerns and questions, as well as the call of the Holy Father to find alternatives to war, are well known and reflect our prudential judgments about the application of traditional Catholic teaching on the use of force in this case....[33]

• In an article written shortly thereafter, Ratzinger concluded: "There were not sufficient reasons to unleash a war against Iraq. To say nothing of the fact that, given the new weapons that make possible destructions that go beyond the combatant groups, today we should be asking ourselves if it is still licit to admit the very existence of a 'just war.'"[34]

Neuhaus responded by stating that he

viewed the many antiwar statements of church leaders, and especially those emanating from the Vatican, with "disappointment, and more than a little embarrassment." As far as Neuhaus was concerned, the lesson to be drawn from the whole sorry episode was obvious: ranking ecclesiastics took the time of US decision-makers, badgering them about whether they had thought of this possible consequence or that....

"Religious leaders should bring more to the discussion than their fears. Nervous hand-wringing is not a moral argument," he wrote.[35]

Even after millions of Iraqi civilians had been killed, wounded, and displaced and much of their country reduced to rubble; after thousands of US troops had also been killed, wounded and permanently maimed at an ongoing cost to US taxpayers in the trillions of dollars, Novak, Weigel and Neuhaus were not about to bite the hands that fed them nor jeopardize their access to the halls of power by admitting their contribution to the slaughter and devastation. Blissfully ignoring his own role in the run-up to the debacle, Neuhaus wrote that "those who condemn the war because soldiers and innocent civilians are killed and maimed are not being serious. This is what happens in war, and is a very good reason for avoiding war."[36]

As he had either not read the John Jay Report or chose to deliberately lie about its findings, so Neuhaus published a mendacious analysis of the final report by Charles Duelfer and the Iraq Study Group which had showed that Saddam Hussein neither possessed weapons of mass destruction nor had any active programs to develop such weapons.

Neuhaus nevertheless claimed that "Saddam had the intention and, if America had dallied or left it to the UN, would have had the weaponry to dominate the Middle East and, in collusion with terrorist networks, inflict massive damage on America and the West" and the belief that Iraq possessed such weapons was thoroughly justified "on the basis of what was known" before the war.

The neo-Catholics "had long ago traded in any intellectual respectability they once possessed on matters of war and peace for the opportunity to serve at the pleasure of the president."[37]

Purging the Vatican Doves

John Paul II's health continued to decline and after 2003 he appeared in public only when seated. In October 2003, Cardinal Christoph Schoenborn broke with traditional Church silence on papal health, acknowledging on Austrian state radio that the pope was "dying."[38] Wojtyla's personal appearances and meetings were further curtailed and official communications delegated to others. As expected, the power struggle among Vatican factions which had begun as much as a decade earlier intensified. Contributions to the Vatican from individual American donors had actually increased in 2002, the year the clerical sex-abuse scandal broke,[39] and increased again in 2003.[40]

Secretary of State Sodano, friend of military dictators and mass murderers, backed by neo-Catholics, took charge. "Virtually every major internal Vatican decision and document landed on Sodano's desk." His suggestion that John Paul II retire was ignored.[41] Now, "Sodano's faithful and shadowy man of action"—Argentine Archbishop Leonardo Sandri—"is the one who makes the wheels turn."[42] In a letter dated June 10, 2003, Sodano had written to Kofi Annan, UN Secretary General, stating he had been directed by John Paul II to express support for the "fundamental role of the United Nations Organization at the present time" in Iraq and calling for a "greater commitment...in order to avoid unilateral actions"[43] but by October, Sodano ordered a halt to "recriminations" over Iraq.

After Archbishop Martino, head of the UN mission, let slip, "if people had listened to the pope, there would not be so many victims weeping now," Sodano replaced him with Archbishop Celestino Migliore. As noted by one reporter, "No more Third World rhetoric and pacifist homilies." Also in October, the Holy See's foreign minister, Cardinal Jean-Louis Tauran, for whom the war in Iraq was a "crime against humanity," was reassigned as "Librarian of the Holy Roman Church." He was replaced by Archbishop Giovanni Lajolo who had been mentored by Sodano's predecessor and P2 member, Cardinal Agostino Casaroli. On October 18, the *Civiltà Cattolica*, the newspaper which had criticized US geopolitics and previously treated Islam with respect, published an article stating, "in all of its history, Islam has shown a warlike and conquering face", that "for almost a thousand years, Europe lived under its constant threat", and that this offensive still continues as proven by the "perpetual discrimination" to which it subjects the Christians in its territories.

L´Osservatore Romano was the last Vatican voice not to be whistling the new tune. During the months before the war, its director, Mario Agnes, had made the newspaper a standard to be raised in the rainbow-colored peace processions, with a front page stamped with huge block type. He continued to thunder against the armed intervention, all the time up until the November 12, [2003, US] attack in Nassiriya, announced on a whole page in words of a haughty coolness. "Cruel Attack," the title screamed. And below: "Another terrible and disquieting expression of the inhuman logic of war has been consummated"....

At the secretariat of state, they swore that this was too much, and Agnes was charged to repair the damage. No sooner said than done. The next day, *L'Osservatore* opened as follows: "The Blood of the Peacemakers." Immediately beneath: "Their blood was shed while carrying out a noble and generous service, directed toward safeguarding and promoting the peace in a territory dramatically marked by the violence of the war and the post-war period."

Avvenire, the organ of the Italian bishops' conference, now gave full support to the occupation of Iraq. The paper was headed by Cardinal Camillo Ruini, president of the conference and an integral part of the diplomatic team of Sodano, Lajolo and Migliore. His chief editor on international politics was Vittorio E. Parsi, a professor at the Catholic University of Milan. In a 2003 interview, Parsi affirmed that "the security of moderate Islam, of Europe, and of the whole world, depends on victory over fundamentalist terrorism in Iraq."[44]

Ruini, who was also Vicar General of the Diocese of Rome, was well-known in the Italian mass media and the usual source for statements on official Vatican positions. He was also grand chancellor of the Lateran University and the Pontifical John Paul II Institute for Studies on Marriage and Family. Parsi, a member of Ruini's "think tank," wrote a book, *The Inevitable Alliance: Europe and the United States beyond Iraq*, extolling the benefits of a trans-Atlantic alliance and in favor of war:

If Europe has the good fortune to live in its "Kantian paradise regulated by laws, and not by force," it is because "someone else is doing the dirty work of maintaining security," Parsi wrote. Europe cannot deceive itself that it can extend peaceful coexistence without the use of force throughout the world, because "in order to promote and defend the good it is necessary to resist evil, sometimes by combat."[45]

Parsi was part of "an orchestrated campaign to galvanize military and financial support for a democratic Iraq among critics of the war such as France and Germany." A front page editorial in *Avvenire*, called for "tens of thousands of NATO troops" to be sent to Iraq to assist the interim government and ensure free elections. "Even the European countries that opposed the American decision to overthrow Saddam Hussein's regime know well that an Iraq in the hands of the worst terrorists and criminals goes against the interests of all," wrote Parsi. According to the British newspaper, *The Telegraph*, "The Vatican's new stance will hearten Mr. Blair and President Bush, whose campaign for re-election has been overshadowed by the crisis."[46]

In December 2003, "the Vatican moved unusually quickly after a cardinal rebuked the United States for treating Saddam Hussein 'like a cow' by showing film of the former dictator having his teeth checked by a US medic after his capture. A senior Vatican official stressed that the cardinal was expressing his personal opinion and not necessarily the view of the pope."[47]

John Paul II's annual messages on January 1, 2004, for the World Day of Peace, and his January 12 address to the diplomatic corps, "both bear the marks of Archbishop Lajolo who in fact cited both of them amply in his first interview as the Holy See's new foreign minister."[48] An interview with Lajolo appeared in the January 15 issue of *National Catholic Reporter*. He defended the right of the US to act unilaterally without "subordination" to the UN and justified the Bush decision for "preventive war."[49]

The Neo-Catholic 2004 Presidential Campaign

The *Boston Globe* reported a July 2003 meeting between leaders of the USCCB and "a group of prominent Catholic business executives, academics, and journalists to discuss the future of the Church in light of the clergy sexual abuse crisis." The meeting took place at the Pope John Paul II Cultural Center in Washington, was hosted by Cardinal Theodore E. McCarrick, archbishop of Washington, and organized by Geoffrey T. Boisi, vice chairman of JPMorganChase and co-CEO of JP Morgan. Participants heard presentations and responses from a number of prominent Catholics including R. Scott Appleby, a professor of history at the University of Notre Dame; Francis J. Butler, president, FADICA (Foundations and Donors Interested in Catholic Activities, Inc.); James D. Davidson Jr., a professor of sociology at Purdue University; Frederick Gluck, former managing director, McKinsey & Co.; Margaret O'Brien Steinfels, editor, *Commonweal* magazine; and Peter Steinfels, who writes a religion column to the *New York Times*.

"A number of laypeople who are very upset about what's been going on in the Church feel they have something to contribute because of their experience in management, and from one perspective, this was a management failure," said one participant, referring to the clergy abuse scandal. "There were a lot of very personal things: People's grandchildren are no longer interested in the Church. These are people who are in their 50s and 60s, who grew up very faithful to the Church, and are worried about where the Church is going."

A spokesman for the bishops' conference, Monsignor Francis J. Maniscalco, said by e-mail, "The meeting was described by those who suggested it as an informal and confidential session for the sharing of some concerns. It was not an organizing or planning meeting. The bishops in attendance were not representing the conference but attended as individuals without any expectation that the meeting would lead to anything beyond the sharing that occurred during its course."[50]

Deal Hudson, still Bush's director of Catholic Outreach, wasn't invited. He was livid.

> This morning, the *Boston Globe* dropped a bombshell of a story.... Reading through the article, the author refers over and over to the 'prominent' Catholics.... Some of them, it turns out, aren't so prominent....I think it's safe to say that the real criterion for involvement was not prominence or influence in the Catholic Church but sympathy with dissenting points of view....
>
> There isn't a single person on the list known for his or her stand in support of faithfulness to the Magisterium, the pope, and the teachings of the Church. If this was a meeting of "prominent Catholics," where are the prominent orthodox representatives? Where are George Weigel, Michael Novak, and Father Neuhaus?
>
> Apparently, those Catholics faithful to the Church don't count. Honestly, can you imagine these bishops holding a conference for a group of prominent conservative Catholics... listening to their concerns...noting their advice? Don't hold your breath. Rest assured that we're going to be following up with this story.[51]

The neo-Catholics demanded a similar meeting, but their focus was on the 2004 election not the sex abuse scandal. Their September gathering was arranged by Hudson and Russell Shaw, former communications director for the USCCB and member of Opus Dei, at the exclusive Cosmos Club "which [USCCB president, Bishop Wilton] Gregory and the other bishops could hardly refuse to attend."[52] Five bishops and three members of their national staff gathered with nearly 40 "faithful" Catholics. Attendees included

Raymond Arroyo, news director of the Eternal World Television Network; William Donohue, president of the Catholic League for Religious and Civil Rights; Atlanta's Frank Hanna, III, one of the founders of Newt Gingrich's GOPAC political operation; Peggy Noonan, commentator and columnist for the *Wall Street Journal*; Robert Novak, commentator with CNN; Kate O'Beirne, senior editor of *National Review*; Kathryn Jean Lopez, associate editor of *National Review;* Bernard Dobranski, dean of Ave Maria School of Law; Fr. Frank Pavone, Priests for Life; Rep. Michael Ferguson (R-NJ); John Klink, former diplomat of the Holy See to the United Nations; Brian Saint-Paul, editor of *Crisis* magazine; Princeton Law Professor Robert George, a member of the President's Council on Bioethics and a leading opponent of stem-cell research; and a slew of less well-known Catholics.[53]

According to George, the meeting was called "to give support to the bishops in their efforts to teach what the Church believes on these issues,"—abortion, gay marriage and stem-cell research. He made it clear the attendees expected the bishops to discipline Catholic politicians who didn't support the Republican agenda.[54] "It doesn't help instruct the faithful when publicly dissenting Catholics are rewarded with positions of participation in official roles in the Church, when they are asked to keynote Catholic dinners and so forth," Hudson told a post-meeting press conference conducted at the Michael J. Novak room at *Crisis* magazine's office.[55] When asked for a comment on the Cosmos Club meeting, the current spokesman for the USCCB, replied, "Bishop Gregory has decided not to comment about either meeting. He's not sure if he could remain as judicious as he should be."[56]

Vice Pres. Dick Cheney visited the Vatican on January 27, 2004, meeting with the pope, Sodano and Lajolo. Cheney spent 13 minutes with the pope and 40 minutes with Sodano and Lajolo. "During a formal exchange of gifts, Cheney... offered the pope a crystal dove, which John Paul stroked appreciatively." Ambassador Nicholson told reporters the pope did not repeat his opposition to the Iraq war, but was "'forward-looking,' focusing on efforts to bring freedom to the country, especially religious freedom."[57] The press release provided by the Vatican after the meeting stated:

> In the course of the discussions there was an exchange of opinions on the international situation, in particular regarding the peace process in the Middle East and the developments in the situation in Iraq. On that occasion, there was also an examination of the moral and religious problems now facing life in the States, especially those involving the defense and promotion of life, the family, solidarity, and religious liberty.[58]

So it was official. Any lingering criticism a US bishop may have harbored against the Iraq War as well as any qualms about Bush being the "pro-life" president, he would keep to himself.

The Attack on John Kerry

By the end of January 2004, Sen. John Kerry had won both the Iowa and New Hampshire Democratic primaries. Kerry, a Roman Catholic, favored keeping abortion legal.

The Missouri primary was scheduled for February 4. In a January 31 television interview, St. Louis Archbishop Raymond Burke declared Kerry would be forbidden to take Communion while campaigning in his archdiocese. Burke claimed that, according to his interpretation of the 1998 amendments to Canon Law (specifically the new Canon 750 and the revised Canon 1371) which had added new penalties for disobedience, Kerry "obstinately persisted in manifest grave sin."[59]

Locally, Burke had raised the ire, not only of Catholics, but community activists by closing parishes and schools in poor neighborhoods and opening new ones in the wealthier suburbs. Florissant Mayor Robert Lowery said that closing four churches in his area which were on the National Registry of Historic Places was "outrageous."[60] St. Louis Mayor Francis Slay met with Burke showing him demographic reports and forecasts in an effort to save some of the inner city parishes and schools, but to no avail. Slay said he was disappointed in the way the archdiocese decided which parishes to close. "The archdiocese is expanding in rich areas and contracting in poor areas," he said. "I think they could have done more to help with their mission, and they chose not to do it."[61]

To deny Communion to a politician by name on the question of abortion was an unprecedented action in both the American and international Church. "In Europe, in effect, the Catholic Church has never addressed or created cases similar to those of Kerry... In recent decades in Europe, bishops, cardinals, and popes have knowingly given Communion to Catholic politicians who advance abortion laws. In 1989, the devoutly Catholic king Baudouin of Belgium temporarily abdicated his throne to avoid signing a law on abortion, but this was an entirely personal gesture: no one in the Church's hierarchy had asked him to do so."[62]

A Vatican reporter listed three current Italian pro-choice politicians who had not been denied the sacrament in Italy's churches, one having received Communion from John Paul II.[63] In 1999, the conference of German bishops had come under fire from the Vatican for supporting counseling centers which issued certificates confirming that pregnant women were in distress, thereby enabling them to obtain legal abortions. At the time, Cardinal Sodano had favored the bishops' compromise whereby the certificates would contain a prohibition against abortion, although it was understood the certificates would be used to secure a termination anyway. Eventually, the bishops were forced to withdraw their support, but no one was denied Communion in the process.[64]

No American priest or prelate had issued the same proscription against pro-choice Republican Catholic politicians such as Arnold

Schwarzenegger during his 2003 gubernatorial campaign (his opponent, Gov. Pete Davis, had signed a law allowing thousands of sex abuse claims against the Church to proceed), nor Rudy Giuliani during his campaigns for mayor or senator, nor Gov. George Pataki of New York, nor had there been any statements specifically naming the Republican Massachusetts Gov. Mitt Romney, a Mormon, or his lieutenant governor for their pro-abortion positions.

In the first extensive interview in which Kerry agreed to discuss his faith, the candidate said,

> "We have a separation of church and state in this country. As John Kennedy said very clearly, I will be a president who happens to be Catholic, not a Catholic president." Kerry, who always made time during his campaign schedule to attend Sunday Mass, described himself as a "believing and practicing Catholic, married to another believing and practicing Catholic," but "I don't tell Church officials what to do and Church officials shouldn't tell American politicians what to do in the context of our public life."[65]

In March 2004, the Center for Applied Research in the Apostolate (CARA) published the results of a national telephone poll of adults who self-identify as Catholic indicating a tight race in the early campaign among Catholics. The 1,001 telephone interviews gave Kerry an edge of 45 percent to 41 percent for Bush among those who said they intended to vote. This difference, however, was within the poll's margin of error for this sub-group of likely voters (±3.5 percentage points).[66]

The same pundits who had insisted on the right of politicians to disobey Church teaching on war and capital punishment, goaded more bishops to "punish" Kerry's "dissent" from Church teaching on abortion. The ensuing "wafer watch"—as comedian Jon Stewart called it—where journalists followed Kerry to church every week to see if he would be denied Communion was one of the stranger episodes in campaign reporting.

Weigel: "What belongs to everyone, since this is a national candidacy, is the responsibility to make clear that when Kerry says the Church's pro-life teaching is a sectarian position which cannot be imposed on a pluralistic society, he is willfully misrepresenting the nature of the Church's position—by suggesting that this is something analogous to the Catholic Church trying to force everyone in the United States to abstain from eating hot dogs on Fridays during Lent [no citation given]."[67]

Novak: "There is a question of a kind of truth in advertising, and it's hidden in the word 'communion.' Communion means communion with the Church; that means with its teaching.... And so the bishops have to say something because the only point of being Catholic is to be faithful to the teachings of Jesus Christ and to the sacraments, and so just a kind of truthfulness requires them to say whether what politicians who do this are doing is right or is it not right."[68]

Neuhaus: The "great move on the part of the bishops... in the case of persistent, unrepentant, public and scandalous defiance of the Church's teaching will range from urging the person not to present himself or herself for Communion to publicly refusing Communion [to that person]."[69]

The financial cost of the sex abuse scandal was growing. The costs of diocesan high-priced attorneys, confidentiality agreements with victims and the shuffling of priests off to very expensive and very private treatment centers was beginning to be exceeded by burgeoning court awards to the victims. A few dioceses had already declared bankruptcy and the process of closing hundreds of parishes and schools had just begun. A poll conducted in December 2004 by Zogby International and the Center of the Study of Church Management at Villanova University, sponsored by Foundations and Donors Interested in Catholic Activities (FADICA), found that 14 percent of Catholics who attended Mass at least once a week or almost once a week, were giving less to their parish and 19 percent were giving less to national Church collections. However, Francis Butler, president of FADICA, said that "on the whole, total donations nationally have not declined because some donors (8 percent locally and 5 percent nationally) have increased their giving."[70] Hierarchs, now more dependent on a few wealthy donors, who hadn't raised an objection to children being sacrificed to the sexual perversions of the ordained or the slaughter of Iraqi children, covered the Catholic media with their devotion to the un-born.

Archbishop Charles Chaput of Denver: "The Church sees abortion as the foundational issue of our time....Candidates who claim to be 'Catholic' but who publicly ignore Catholic teaching about the sanctity of human life are offering a dishonest public witness....And real Catholics should vote accordingly."[71] The Catholic Foundation for the Archdiocese of Denver, listed as a separate, non-profit entity from the rest of the archdiocese, filed a report showing total assets of $96,437,502 as of June 2004, up from $73,490,010 in 2003.

Opus Dei Archbishop John Myers of Newark (where diocesan Catholic schools were subsidized by the William E. Simon Foundation[72]): "On this grave issue [abortion], public officials cannot hold themselves excused from their duties, especially if they claim to be Catholic....I ask and urge that Catholic voters and Catholics in public life carefully consider their position if they find themselves in opposition to Church teaching in these matters."[73]

A Vatican official unabashedly injected himself into US politics:

> Politicians who support abortion must not go to Communion and priests must deny them the sacrament, says Cardinal Francis Arinze, prefect of the Congregation for Divine Worship and the Sacraments....One of the

journalists asked the cardinal if he could give his judgment on the concrete application of this norm in the case of US Democratic presidential candidate John Kerry. 'The norm of the Church is clear,' he said. 'The Catholic Church exists in the USA and there are bishops there. Let them interpret.'"[74]

Bishop Michael Sheridan of Colorado Springs upped the rhetoric by threatening eternal damnation for pro-legalization politicians who "place themselves outside full communion with the Church and so jeopardize their salvation." He continued, "Catholics who vote for candidates who hold these views suffer the same fateful consequences."[75]

Americans United for Separation of Church and State responded by calling on the Internal Revenue Service to investigate electioneering by the Roman Catholic Diocese of Colorado Springs, stating that Sheridan's pronouncement "may have crossed the line into unlawful partisan politicking." "Bishop Sheridan's letter is code language that says, 'Re-elect Bush and vote Republican," Rev. Barry W. Lynn, Americans United executive director, stated. "Everyone knows Bush and Kerry differ on the issue of abortion. Sheridan is using a form of religious blackmail to steer votes toward the GOP." Lynn noted Sheridan's action as part of the larger trend among the Catholic hierarchy to influence Catholic voters in an election year.[76]

However, three US cardinals, Theodore McCarrick of Washington, Roger Mahony of Los Angeles, and Francis George of Chicago, publicly stated their reservations about using Communion as a sanction against politicians. McCarrick wrote in a May column in his diocesan newspaper that he did not want to be involved "in a confrontation at the altar rail with the Sacred Body of Christ the Lord Jesus in my hand. There are apparently those who would welcome such a conflict, for good reasons I am sure, or for political ones, but I would not."[77] The American Life League began a $500,000 print ad campaign targeting bishops who refused to punish Catholic politicians "in a confrontation at the altar rail." The first ad showed Jesus in agony on the cross and asked: "Cardinal McCarrick: Are you comfortable now?"[78]

Meanwhile, Kerry attempted to say as little as possible about the controversy. Kerry did, however, tell the *Los Angeles Times* on May 2, "My oath is to uphold the Constitution of the United States in my public life; my oath privately between me and God was defined in the Catholic Church... which allows for freedom of conscience for Catholics with respect to these choices, and that is exactly where I am."[79] Kerry was referring to the teaching of the Church regarding "primacy of conscience." As articulated by St. Thomas Aquinas, each human being is ultimately accountable only to God and each person is compelled to act according to that which he/she knows to be moral.

In a letter dated May 10, forty-eight Catholic members of Congress, including about a dozen with consistent anti-abortion voting records, wrote a letter to McCarrick who was chairman of a Taskforce on Catholic Bishops and

Catholic Politicians. They addressed the threat from bishops of withholding Communion also arguing for their "primacy of conscience." "We respectfully submit that each of us is in the best position to know the state of our soul and our relationship to God and our Church."[80]

The Vatican intervenes for Bush

Polls continued showing it would be a tight race between Kerry and Bush. The president altered the itinerary of a scheduled trip to Europe so that he could meet with John Paul II before the pontiff left Rome for a trip to Switzerland. While Bush met with John Paul II on June 4, 2004, the streets of Rome were filled with anti-war protesters. Progressive Catholic leaders

> predicted that this meeting was less about President Bush seeking the counsel of Pope John Paul II and more about the upcoming presidential campaign and the important Catholic swing vote. "Bush campaign strategists know full well the value of the well-timed photo-op," said Dave Robinson, national director of a Catholic peace organization. "While video and photographs of Pope John Paul II and President Bush sitting side-by-side will appear in hundreds of news outlets and front pages across the country—and linger in the minds of voters for months to come—the Vatican's harsh criticisms of President Bush's foreign policy will continue to be underreported in the media and, unfortunately, unheard in pulpits across the United States.'"[81]

Which is exactly what happened.

When Bush presented Karol Wojtyla with the US Medal of Freedom, the photo-op created an opportunity for the pope to speak directly in front of the press. As reported widely in Europe, the pontiff scolded Bush. "Your visit to Rome takes place at a moment of great concern for the continuing situation of grave unrest in the Middle East, both in Iraq and in the Holy Land. You are very familiar with the unequivocal position of the Holy See in this regard." John Paul II wanted the situation normalized as quickly as possible "with the active participation of the international community and in particular the United Nations." But the pope did commend Bush's "commitment to the promotion of moral values in American society, particularly with regard to respect for life and the family."[82]

Positive spin verging on outright misrepresentation came from "White House sources and Vatican spokesperson Joaquín Navarro-Valls... [I]t was a cordial encounter that produced a meeting of the minds on Iraq, as well as an appreciation for Bush's stands on life and the family....A senior Vatican diplomat was at pains to emphasize that the meeting between Bush and the pope had been 'very positive,' and that relations with the Americans are 'much closer today than one year ago.'"[83]

According to the John L. Allen Jr. of the *National Catholic Reporter*:

> During his visit, Bush asked the Vatican to push the American Catholic bishops to be more aggressive politically on family and life issues, especially a constitutional amendment that would define marriage as a union between a man and a woman. A Vatican official told *NCR* June 9 that in his meeting with Cardinal Angelo Sodano and other Vatican officials, Bush said, "Not all the American bishops are with me" on the cultural issues. The implication was that he hoped the Vatican would nudge them toward more explicit activism. Other sources in the meeting said that while they could not recall the president's exact words, he did pledge aggressive efforts on the cultural front, especially the battle against gay marriage, and asked for the Vatican's help in encouraging the US bishops to be more outspoken....
>
> Bush supports a constitutional amendment to ban gay marriage and has urged Congress to take swift action. Since polls show that in several battleground states in the fall election a majority of voters is opposed to gay marriage, some Bush analysts think an aggressive push on the issue will help the president's prospects.[84]

Aware of Bush's complaint that "the US bishops were not being vocal enough in supporting him" and his request that the Vatican "push the bishops to become more actively involved" in promoting the Republican social agenda, the USCCB held their semi-annual meeting from June 14 to 19. Usually open to staff members and press, the bishops announced that this meeting would be a closed "retreat." They met at the Inverness Hotel and Conference Center, billed as "one of Denver's finest luxury hotels" with a championship golf course and "five dining and entertainment venues."

Vatican reporter, Sandro Magister, published a copy of a letter Cardinal Ratzinger sent to Cardinal McCarrick and Bishop Gregory on the eve of the meeting. In his preface Magister noted:

> Joseph Cardinal Ratzinger, prefect of the Vatican Congregation for the Doctrine of the Faith, was clear with Theodore Cardinal McCarrick, archbishop of Washington and the head of the "domestic policy" commission of the US Catholic bishops' conference. He was more than clear, he set it down in writing: no Eucharistic Communion for the politicians who campaign for abortion. Read: no communion for the Democratic candidate for the White House, the Catholic John F. Kerry....

But the bishops of the United States made a different decision. After months of discussion, and after days of wrangling at their conference's general assembly in Denver, they published a note entitled "Catholics in Political Life," which leaves to each individual bishop the decision of whether or not to give Communion to pro-abortion Catholic politicians.

The note was passed with 183 voted in favor and 6 against. During the previous weeks, out of 70 bishops who had expressed their opinion to the task force in charge of the matter, those against the idea of withholding Communion had beaten those in favor by a margin of 3 to 1....

Some bishops stated that Communion should be withheld from Kerry. Particularly incendiary anti-Kerry comments came from the bishop of St. Louis, Raymond L. Burke, and of Colorado Springs, Michael J. Sheridan. This provoked a highly spirited discussion, both within and outside of the Catholic Church. The bishops of the United States, who were coming to Rome in groups to meet with the pope for their periodical "ad limina" visits, came under pressure from the Vatican to be severe. But they also faced strong pressures—and justifications— from the other side....But what divides the bishops is what response they should give to "public unworthiness to receive Holy Communion," as Ratzinger writes. The prefect of the Congregation for the Doctrine of the Faith is wholly in favor of refusing the Eucharist to Kerry and other politicians like him. Most of the American bishops are not.

Even many of the bishops and cardinals of "neoconservative" tendency are reluctant to censure publicly the Catholic politicians who are at odds with the Church. One of these is the cardinal and theologian Avery Dulles. In a June 29 interview with *Zenit,* he maintained that by denying them Communion the Church exposes itself to the accusation of wanting to interfere in political life. Another of these is Cardinal Francis E. George, archbishop of Chicago. In an interview with John L. Allen of the *National Catholic Reporter*, he said that the limits that should be placed upon abortion within the realm of politics are "matters of prudential judgment about which there can be many discussions" even within the Church.

Cardinal McCarrick, speaking to the bishops gathered in Denver, made himself the spokesman of the concern "that the sacred nature of the Eucharist might be turned into a partisan political battleground." The real battles, he said, "should be fought not at the Communion rail, but in the public square, in hearts and minds, in our pulpits and public advocacy, in our consciences and communities."[85]

The USCCB issued a statement "Catholics in Political Life" after the meeting backing the moderates' position: "A Catholic moral framework does not easily fit the ideologies of 'right' or 'left,' nor the platforms of any party....The polarizing tendencies of election-year politics can lead to circumstances in which Catholic teaching and sacramental practice can be misused for political ends." Infuriated, the neo-Catholics shifted much of their criticism away from Kerry and towards bullying the bishops who followed the USCCB guideline. They were attacked as cowards or worse.

Neuhaus: "In fact, there are obvious differences between the bishops' statement, 'Catholics in Political Life,' and Cardinal Ratzinger's articulation of 'the doctrine of the Church on this specific issue.' Most notably, what is optional in the former is mandated in the latter. Nonetheless, the June statement is to be welcomed. It acknowledged the worries of the timid while affirming the course decided upon by the likes of Archbishop Burke and Archbishop Myers and emboldening others to follow their example.... There may be substantial reason to believe that a new generation of bishops is prepared to lead."[86]

Novak: "Some [Catholic legislators] have even persuaded themselves that abortion is a perfectly acceptable option for Catholics to support. The silence and indirection of the bishops during the past 20 years convinces them that this is so....Faithful Catholics who know better see that the courage of their bishops is on empty....Bishops seem to be vain flatterers of public passions. If current bishops cannot do the job, better must eventually be found....Since about a decade after *Roe* v. *Wade*...a great many Catholic bishops have been asleep on the watch. The moral tide was rising up their legs, and they did not block it, or try to redirect it, or even raise insistent warnings about its dangerous challenge to the Church. They allowed many Catholic political leaders (of both parties) to drift into accommodation with evil. By being pushovers the bishops have for 30 years allowed them to do so."[87]

Weigel: "The bishops of the United States...have an obligation, by the oaths that they swore on the day of their Episcopal ordination, to preserve the integrity of Catholic teaching and discipline."[88] And, "Every local bishop has a solemn obligation to inform Catholic politicians of the settled nature of the Church's teaching on abortion.... If obstinate resistance continues, each local bishop has other remedies available."[89]

The first hierarch to cave in was Archbishop John F. Donoghue of Atlanta who had put his archdiocese over $100 million in debt building schools in upscale neighborhoods and a plush retirement "village" with apartments for himself and other clergy. Donoghue had also closed two inner-city schools rich in civil-rights historical significance for the City of Atlanta. One of Donoghue's financial supporters was sub-prime credit card (CompuCredit) mogul, Frank Hanna III. The Hannas had converted Georgia's largest health insurer, Blue Cross/Blue Shield of Georgia, from a not-for-profit to a for-profit corporation in 1996. Another Hanna business venture was the Paladin Capital Group (Paladin General Holdings, LLC, Paladin Capital Partners Fund, L.P, Paladin Homeland Security Investors, LLC, Paladin Homeland Security Fund, L.P) set up three months after 9/11 to invest in the soon-to-be burgeoning homeland security industry. Investors include a former CIA director, a former National Security Agency and Defense Intelligence Agency director, as well as former intelligence analysts. A former Defense Advanced Research Projects Agency deputy director is a Paladin adviser.[90] Hanna backed Ralph Reed, former head of the Christian Coalition and tied to Jack Abramoff, when Reed ran for lieutenant governor of Georgia.[91] Hanna was an invited guest, along with Deal Hudson, when the US embassy in Rome organized a conference to celebrate the 20th anniversary of diplomatic relations with the Holy See.[92]

Donoghue issued a statement on August 4, 2004, that Kerry was "not worthy" to receive Communion in North Georgia. The statement was also signed by the bishops of Charlotte, North Carolina and Charleston, South Carolina, suffragens of (supervised by) Donoghue.[93] Other prelates who issued similar statements included Chaput, Archbishop Olmstead of Phoenix and Bishop Paul S. Loverde of Arlington.[94] More than half a dozen other bishops also made sure Catholics in their dioceses knew Kerry was guilty of mortal sin and Bush was not.[95] Yet despite unrelenting pressure from the neo-Catholic press who even floated a bogus story that the Vatican had excommunicated Kerry, the great majority of bishops, archbishops and cardinals did not issue bans against Kerry receiving Communion.

Republican Catholic Outreach

After a strategy session with Catholic GOP leaders on January 22, 2004, Republican National Committee Director of Catholic Outreach, Martin Gillespie, sent a follow-up memo to the attendees reminding them, "We know from existing polling that the outcome of the Catholic vote will be a key determinant in this year's election," reiterating their agreed-upon "to do" list:

- Identify key Catholic leaders and activists throughout the nation.

- Request parish directories and membership lists of Catholic groups and associations.

- Inform the RNC of any Catholic-related events occurring in their area.

- Enlist new Catholic Team Leaders which was "critical for our communications plans."

- Identify individuals willing to serve as Parish Coordinators.

- Catholic Field Coordinators would be paid $2500 per month with $500 for expenses.[96]

"Access to these [parish] directories is critical as it allows us to identify and contact those Catholics who are likely to be supportive of President Bush's compassionate conservative agenda," wrote Gillespie.[97] On April 1, 2004, Bush noted the enactment of the first federally funded school voucher program at the Archbishop Carroll High School in Washington DC, one of the schools which would benefit by the new program. While Democrats said they would try to move the funding for the program back to the District's public schools, Bush announced he would allot $50 million in the next fiscal year to fund vouchers elsewhere in the nation.[98] After the election when Bush was a lame-duck president, the only extension of the program was a temporary one-year fund to aid victims of Hurricane Katrina.

The first National Catholic Prayer Breakfast, held April 28 at the Mayflower Hotel in downtown Washington, was organized by Tom Monaghan, founder of the Ave Maria Fund (investments), the Ave Maria List (which ran a political action committee), the Ave Maria Foundation (a tax exempt organization to promote Catholic "culture"), the Ave Maria Law School and Legatus, a private network open only to top Catholic Republican business executives. Other organizers included Hudson, Neuhaus, Weigel and Fr. William Stetson, who had replaced McCloskey as director of Opus Dei's Catholic Information Center on K Street. Members of the Bush administration, Ave Maria Law School and the Federalist Society were on the advisory council and host committee.

(The purpose of the Ave Maria Law School was to train neocon lawyers for government positions. The Federalist Society, a right-wing lawyers' group which served as "casting couch for the federal judiciary" under Bush, claims Supreme Court neo-Catholic justices Antonin Scalia, Clarence Thomas, John Roberts, and Samuel Alito as members.[99])

According to the organizers, all proceeds after expenses were divided equally between the Sisters of Life, a religious community dedicated to anti-abortion contemplation and activism, and Pope John Paul II "for the support of the activities of the Holy See."[100]

One of the speakers complained about the "attacks on our Church from within and without." Allegiance to the Church's prohibition on abortion is paramount in determining who is a "faithful Catholic," he said. Rep. Walter Jones (R-N.C.) a Catholic convert, urged the 1,000-plus attendees to contact their member of Congress in support of the bill "Houses of Worship Political Speech Protection Act" in order to save the religious tax exemption for overtly-partisan clergy.[101] Even though he had aggressively campaigned for the pro-choice Arlen Specter against the pro-life Patrick Toomey in that same month's Republican primary in Pennsylvania, Sen. Rick Santorum received a standing ovation after stating, "one of the reasons American Catholics are not as fervent is because many in our clergy are not as fervent in teaching the faith,"[102] echoing the constant pressure on priests and bishops to follow the Republican party line.

(Santorum failed to win re-election in 2006. His charity, Operation Good Neighbor Foundation, was shown to be a secret conduit for campaign contributions from donors who wished to remain anonymous and for whom Santorum had granted political favors.[103] A report issued in October 2006 by the minority staff of the Senate Finance Committee noted lobbyist Jack Abramoff, who pled guilty to five criminal felony counts, had also donated to Santorum's Operation Good Neighbor Foundation. The *New York Times* reported that while legal political contributions are limited in amount and the donor's name is public, "the tax-exempt treasuries of willing nonprofits like Americans for Tax Reform, run by the Republican strategist Grover Norquist, became conduits through which funds from lobbyists like Mr. Abramoff and other special interests were transferred to elected officials, their families and their aides in the form of lavish travel, expensive meals, golf outings and tickets to sports and entertainment events."[104] Santorum was then hired by Weigel's Ethics and Public Policy Center.)

Bush was notably absent from the Prayer Breakfast. A White House insider noted, "Word in some Catholic circles is that in-fighting among those who direct Catholic outreach for Republicans may have doomed what could have been a high profile appearance for the president among Catholics just blocks away from the White House."[105]

When Bush met with religious journalists in May, the authority he cited most often was Neuhaus. Bush explained, "He helps me articulate these [religious] things." "A senior administration official confirmed to *TIME* magazine that Neuhaus 'does have a fair amount of under-the-radar influence.'"[106]

A closed-door meeting was held on May 27 by Ed Gillespie and about 100 local Catholic activists at the Omni Parker House in Boston "to build support for President George W. Bush's re-election campaign and for other Republican candidates." Gillespie announced after the meeting Catholics should be more comfortable with Republican policies than with Democratic policies even though Kerry is Catholic and Bush is a Methodist.[107] Catholic Democrats responded to Gillespie's assertion with a report showing Kerry voted most often with previously stated but now largely ignored positions taken by the USCCB among all Catholics in the US Senate. The report, issued by Sen. Richard Durbin (D-Ill.), gave Kerry an overall score of voting with the bishops' former political priorities 61 percent of the time, while Republican Catholic senators all ranked at the bottom of the list. Since abortion and same-sex marriage were now the only issues into which the USCCB poured its attention and resources, positions favoring the Democratic Party no longer mattered. "Abortion rights is the cover for a lot of other cultural grievances," explained David Gibson, author of *The Coming Catholic Church*. "It's the galvanizing issue that allows conservative Catholics to side with Republicans who might be in favor of the war in Iraq, tax cuts for the wealthy, and the death penalty"—all issues rejected by Catholic social teaching.

The polls were showing Kerry with a 50 to 46 percent lead among Catholics when Bush was invited to address the Knights of Columbus national convention held on August 3 in Dallas. While not mentioning the war in Iraq, Bush stressed his support for the Faith Based Community Initiative and "won standing ovations when he reiterated his positions against abortion and same-sex marriage and for keeping 'under God' in the Pledge of Allegiance."[107]

> The president reminded the crowd that his [Catholic convert] brother, Gov. Jeb Bush of Florida, became a Knight a few years ago and that he had reached the rank of third degree....
> "Thank you for restoring moral integrity to the office of president," said Carl A. Anderson, the organization's leader....
> The next day, the Kerry campaign countered that Bush's "compassion" agenda was sloganeering, that his social policies hurt poor American families more than his "faith-based" initiative had helped them ("Bush is opening more soup kitchens and food pantries while keeping families in poverty"), and that he was pandering to Catholics.[108]

Two months before the election, the Republican National Committee launched a website called KerryWrongForCatholics.com. The GOP sent RNC chairman Gillespie and a host of well-known Catholic Republicans on a speaking tour to Catholic groups throughout the swing states. Fr. Frank Pavone posted Bush's speeches on his Priests for Life website and "in a personal capacity" endorsed Bush. Pavone assured his supporters, "Many ask whether one can be a good Catholic or be pro-life and support the war [in Iraq]. The answer is yes...."[109] As they did in 2000, Priests for Life "announced a $1 million campaign, including television commercials, aimed at persuading voters to support candidates who oppose abortion."[110]

Deal Hudson: The "Most Influential" Catholic in Washington

In a November 2003 newsletter, Deal Hudson had written his supporters: "I continue to lead an informal Catholic advisory group to the White House, as well as communicate with various White House personnel almost every day regarding appointments, policy, and events. These efforts have helped to place faithful, informed Catholics in positions of influence." Every Thursday morning, Hudson, together with Karl Rove's assistant, Tim Goeglein, led a conference call to discuss "Catholic" issues: faith-based initiative, education vouchers, judicial nominations, abortion, gay marriage, and stem cell research. In December and January, Hudson attended meetings in the White House and helped launch the Republican National Committee's "Catholic Outreach." On St. Patricks' Day 2004, Bush gave a joint speech with the Irish prime minister. "Immediately after George Bush spoke, the first person he greeted was Deal Hudson," related Ray Flynn, former US ambassador to the Vatican. According to Flynn, "He's probably the most prominent lay Catholic [recognized] by the Bush administration." On May 26, Hudson was one of nine Catholics who met with the president prior to his papal visit.[112]

In a fundraising letter, Hudson promised *Crisis* would take "a close look at some of the bishops who are allowing their local politicians to get away with the 'deception' of calling themselves Catholic while voting for abortion rights." He pressured the USCCB to fire Ono Ekeh, an employee of the Bishops' Secretariat for African American Catholics, because he hosted a "Catholics for Kerry" website. When questioned by the *National Catholic Reporter* if he had any personal regret that Ekeh, a father of three young children, had lost his job, Hudson replied, "If you're going to play in the sandbox then you have to take the consequences of your public utterances and your public actions."[113]

While *NCR* reporter Joe Feuerherd was routinely contacting Hudson's friends and associates for an article he planned to write, some referred to problems in Hudson's past. Feuerherd followed the leads to a lawsuit filed against Hudson by a former 18-year-old freshman enrolled in one of Hudson's classes while he was professor of philosophy at Fordham University. According to the coed, while out one night with a group of students in February 1994 there was a lot of heavy drinking and necking between Hudson and the females present. In her suit, the girl charged that Hudson took advantage of her later that night in his office. The girl reported the incident to university officials and Hudson surrendered his tenure. Hudson was invited to be senior editor of *Crisis* in October 1994. Later, Hudson settled out of court for $30,000.[114]

Predictably, Hudson and the neo-Catholic media accused Feuerherd of invading his privacy in spite of rumors which had surfaced about similar incidents when Hudson taught at Mercer University in Atlanta. When the secular media picked up the story, Hudson was forced to resign his positions with the Republican National Committee and *Crisis* magazine. He became director of the Morley Institute, Inc., supported by the Bradley, Carthage and Olin Foundations. Along with Fr. C. John McCloskey, III, Hudson began writing for the *CatholiCity.com* website.

Vatican Grants Knighthood to Pro-choice Official

In a September 2004 column Weigel wrote: "'Formal cooperation with evil' is a technical phrase, underscoring that the pro-abortion Catholic voter, by embracing the abortion license and furthering it, is thereby cooperating in the death of innocents, which is always gravely evil."[115] Cardinal Sodano, apparently, doesn't read Weigel.

It had been an acute embarrassment for the Holy See when a UN resolution was proposed downgrading its status as a "Non-member State

Permanent Observer." Subsequently, Julian Hunte, a St. Lucia senator serving a one-year term as president of the UN General Assembly, submitted resolution 58/314 titled "Participation of the Holy See in the work of the United Nations" as a presidential text. The general assembly approved the resolution in July 2004 expanding the range and prerogatives of the Holy See as a permanent observer with "privileges"[116] similar to those of member nations. In September 2004, out of gratitude for his services, Cardinal Sodano rewarded Hunte with the prestigious Knight of the Grand Cross Pian Order, the highest papal honor given to a lay person. Before the ceremony took place, a letter written by Human Life St. Lucia president Caroline Flood-Edgar had been sent to the pope and the cardinal informing them that Hunte had voted for pro-abortion legislation.

> "We, as believing and practicing Catholics, are very disturbed and scandalized at the fact that an individual who was pivotal and instrumental in the successful passing of the St. Lucia Criminal Code, which legalized abortion in St. Lucia is now receiving a significant honor from the Catholic church," states Edgar. "Even worse this commendation comes within seven months of him publicly and unapologetically supporting and voting for a law that ignores the teachings of our Church....Even worse, Holy Father, it is issued in your name and presumably with your approval." Edgar went on to note the knighthood was sending a "terrible and disconsolate message" to St. Lucia's Catholics.
>
> His Holiness was even provided with the text of Mr. Hunte's speech in the House. "My own position in the argument on Clause 166 is really simple and very clear," said Hunte at the time. "I think every woman must have a choice. I am a pro-choice man. A woman must be the one who will decide what she wants to do in any given situation."[117]

Countdown to Election Day

By October, 42 percent of white Catholics favored Bush, 29 percent favored Kerry, and 27 percent were undecided according to a Pew Research poll.

Denver Archbishop Chaput discussed the election in 14 of his 28 weekly columns in his diocesan newspaper before the election. His archdiocese organized voter registration drives in more than 40 of the largest parishes and sent voter guides to churches around the state. Many had committees to help turn out voters and distributed applications for absentee ballots. In an October 2004 interview, Chaput said a vote for a Kerry would be a sin which must be confessed before receiving Communion. "If you vote this way, are you cooperating in evil?" he asked rhetorically. "The answer is yes."[118]

Denver Post journalist, John Aloysius Farrell, responding to the attention Chaput was receiving in the media as well as the archbishop's local efforts to sway Colorado voters, pointed out that even though Republicans had controlled both houses of Congress for almost a decade, and all three branches of government for the past two, "ending abortion is just not one of the party's priorities....President Bush has publicly conceded that he won't spend the political capital to try to overturn *Roe*, which he calls the law of the land. It is a position he shares with his mother, Barbara, and wife, Laura. Given an opportunity to challenge *Roe* at last week's debate, Bush sure seemed to be 'cooperating with evil' to me. 'I will pick judges who interpret the Constitution, but I'll have no litmus test,' he said, with a mighty waffle.'"

Breaking with decades of tradition, the Archdiocese of New York did not invite the two presidential candidates to the Alfred E. Smith Memorial Foundation Dinner on October 21. Al Smith was a four-term Democratic New York governor before he became the first Catholic to be nominated for president in 1928. The dinner, held every year since 1960, was one of the most important events in New York politics. Joseph Zwilling, a spokesman for the archdiocese said. "Given that issues in this year's campaign could provoke division and disagreement…, it was felt best to proceed in a different direction, while maintaining all of the ideals and values of the dinner." The 2004 speakers were former President George H.W. Bush and former New York Gov. Hugh L. Carey, a Democrat.[119]

Since the USCCB's official statement for that election year had called not only for an end to abortion but also, in an effort to be seen as bipartisan, asked for compassion for illegal immigrants, the poor, the sick, and the Iraqi populace, a group calling themselves "Catholic Answers" published its own "Voter's Guide for Serious Catholics," urging Catholics to vote based on five "nonnegotiable" issues: abortion, euthanasia, embryonic stem cell research, human cloning and homosexual marriage. Some pastors and bishops distributed "The Voters' Guide for Serious Catholics" which blatantly promoted a Republican agenda instead of the USCCB's "Faithful Citizenship" brochures.[120]

Millions of copies of the "Voter's Guide for Serious Catholics" were distributed in church parking lots and foyers and inserted in parish bulletins. Catholic Answers took out a full-page ad in *USA Today*, and proponents of the nonnegotiables disrupted efforts to promote the bishops' official view of the 2004 election. It was political hardball, with some [diocesan] social action directors subject to e-mail campaigns in which chanceries were flooded with correspondence questioning their orthodoxy and commitment to Church teaching.[121]

The *New York Times* reported, "Many parishes are having free-for-alls over what materials to use in helping Catholics think through their choices."[122]

Pavone urged bishops to disregard the possible loss of their tax exemptions. "Not only are the IRS/FEC restrictions on the Church minimal, but the enforcement policy is even looser. Despite all this, various Church officials will go into all kinds of contortions to protect their assets from legal problems that they think will arise if the Church says that the right to life is primary among all the issues."[123] Pavone had priests from his group going from church to church in swing states giving fellow priests sample homilies for several Sundays before the November 2 election day, inserts for church bulletins and the Catholic Action voter guides. "Father Pavone spoke by telephone from Aberdeen, S.D., where he said he was meeting with dozens of priests and nuns to teach them how to organize transportation to take parishioners to the polls."[124]

"Never before have so many bishops so explicitly warned Catholics so close to an election that to vote a certain way was to commit a sin," noted one Catholic commentator.[125] In addition, the bishops who allowed their surrogates to campaign for Bush and the bishops who remained silent against the more vocal and media-seeking prelates, were just as responsible for the "four more years" of Bush/Cheney death and destruction.

Late in the campaign, progressive Catholics mounted a counterattack, "belatedly and with far fewer resources." In diocesan newspapers in Ohio, Pennsylvania and West Virginia, they bought advertisements with the slogan "Life Does Not End at Birth." Organizers of the campaign say it was supported by 200 Catholic organizations including some orders of nuns and brothers.[126]

Virginia Republican State Sen. Kenneth Thomas Cuccinelli II "said a massive leafletting of cars in church parking lots in 11 battleground states, including Ohio, Missouri, Iowa, Wisconsin and Pennsylvania, by thousands of volunteers on the Sunday before the election helped sway the vote. 'We did 5 million pieces of literature in six hours.'" These voter guides were paid for by state Republican committees.[127]

That same Sunday, the president and Mrs. Bush attended Mass in Miami. Msgr. Jude O'Doherty, pastor of Church of the Epiphany, addressed Bush in front of the congregation. "Mr. President, I want you to know that I admire your faith and your courage to profess it." After O'Doherty listed the Republican positions on "moral values," "the pastor, playing on this year's wave of political ads, said: 'My name is Jude O'Doherty and I approved this message.'" The president received ovations as he arrived and left the church.[128]

Kerry Wins . . .

Like the 2000 presidential election, the 2004 outcome hinged on the results from one state—Ohio. Robert F. Kennedy Jr., in a meticulously-researched exposé illustrated with exclusive documents, sources and charts how "Republicans prevented more than 350,000 voters in Ohio from casting ballots or having their votes counted—enough to have put John Kerry in the White House."

"It was terrible," says Sen. Christopher Dodd, who helped craft reforms in 2002 that were supposed to prevent such electoral abuses. "People waiting in line for twelve hours to cast their ballots, people not being allowed to vote because they were in the wrong precinct—it was an outrage. In Ohio, you had a secretary of state who was determined to guarantee a Republican outcome. I'm terribly disheartened."

Indeed, the extent of the GOP's effort to rig the vote shocked even the most experienced observers of American elections. "Ohio was as dirty an election as America has ever seen," Lou Harris, the father of modern political polling, told me. "You look at the turnout and votes in individual precincts, compared to the historic patterns in those counties, and you can tell where the discrepancies are. They stand out like a sore thumb."

Kennedy also noted irregularities had occurred across the country.

Nearly half of the 6 million American voters living abroad never received their ballots—or received them too late to vote—after the Pentagon unaccountably shut down a state-of-the-art website used to file overseas registrations. A consulting firm called Sproul & Associates, which was hired by the Republican National Committee to register voters in six battleground states, was discovered shredding Democratic registrations. In New Mexico, which was decided by 5,988 votes, malfunctioning machines mysteriously failed to properly register a presidential vote on more than 20,000 ballots. Nationwide, according to the federal commission charged with implementing election reforms, as many as 1 million ballots were spoiled by faulty voting equipment—roughly one for every 100 cast.[129]

Kerry conceded the day after the November 2, 2004, election. It would have been pointless to do otherwise since any recounts or challenges would be subject to the same type of manipulations which had occurred the day before in Ohio and in Florida in 2000. Besides, according to official tabulations, Bush had won the popular vote.

Bush Wins the Catholic Vote

The Catholic vote for Bush was 52 percent with 47 percent for

Kerry. (In Ohio the Catholic vote for Bush was 55 percent.) John Kenneth White, professor of politics at Catholic University in Washington, believed the bishops "helped Bush enormously."[130] Richard N. Ostling of the *Associated Press* reported that based on a poll sponsored by the Pew Forum on Religious and Public Life, Kerry's "failure to capture a majority of Roman Catholics...gave President Bush an important advantage in November's election."[131]

Indeed it had. Bush won the popular vote 62,040,610 to 59,028,111. Based on media-sponsored exit polls, the Republican's Catholic strategy was successful. Bush carried 56 percent (approximately 7.9 million votes) of Catholics who said they attended Mass at least once a week while losing to Kerry among less observant Catholics.[132]

In the year before and after the election, the USCCB reported total operating revenues in 2004 of $90,068,233 of which $40,632,568 (45 percent) came from government grants. In 2005, of the $90,678,918 in operating revenues, $39,221,971 (43 percent) was taxpayer funding.[133]

Neo-Catholics on Torture

A week after the election, Bush nominated his long-time friend, Alberto Gonzales, to succeed John D. Ashcroft as attorney general. The GOP controlled the Senate, so the confirmation was already assured. Nevertheless, numerous groups came forward in protest. Among the first were anti-abortion activists, the American Life League, demonstrating that Bush never had intended to create a "pro-life" administration.

As a member of Texas' highest court, Gonzales ruled with the majority that some teenage girls should not be required to get parental permission for an abortion. In his opinion on the ruling Gonzales wrote, "While the ramifications of such a law may be personally troubling to me as a parent, it is my obligation as a judge to impartially apply the laws of this state without imposing my moral view on the decisions of the legislature." Judie Brown, president of the American Life League, also cited a 2001 interview with the *Los Angeles Times* in which Gonzales was asked whether his personal view of abortion would play a role in his vetting of judges. He responded, "There are no litmus tests for judicial candidates. ... My own personal feelings about (abortion) don't matter. ... The question is, what is the law, what is the precedent, what is binding in rendering your decision. Sometimes, interpreting a statute, you may have to uphold a statute that you may find personally offensive. But as a judge, that's your job."[134]

ACLU Executive Director Anthony Romero issued a statement calling for a confirmation process

"... that scrutinizes Mr. Gonzales' positions on key civil liberties and human rights issues. Particular attention should be devoted to exploring Mr. Gonzales' proposed policies on the constitutionality of the Patriot Act, the

Guantanamo Bay detentions, the designation of United States citizens as enemy combatants and reproductive rights." He also called for Gonzales to be asked about a May 16, 2004, memo, written as counsel to the White House, "which described certain legal protections guaranteed in the Geneva Conventions to persons captured during military hostilities as 'obsolete' and 'quaint.'"[135]

However, the lion's share of protests against Gonzales focused on his avowed support for torture. A dozen high-ranking retired military officers took the unprecedented step of signing a letter to the Senate Judiciary Committee expressing "deep concern" over the nomination. The officers specifically criticized Gonzales for his opinion about whether the US could lawfully ignore portions of the Geneva Conventions and that some forms of torture "may be justified" in the war on terror. "Today, it is clear that these operations have fostered greater animosity toward the United States, undermined our intelligence gathering efforts and added to the risks facing our troops serving around the world," the officers wrote, referring to the Bush administration's detention and interrogation policies.[136]

"We want American service-members who are captured to be protected from torture under international and US laws," said Charles Sheehan-Miles, executive director of Veterans for Common Sense and a 1991 Gulf War veteran. "Under the arguments put forth by Alberto Gonzales, our own service men and women would be subject to torture and we would have no recourse to the Geneva Convention."[137]

Numerous human rights groups, the Society of American Law Teachers, Physicians for Human Rights, and an international organization of survivors of torture condemned the nomination of Alberto Gonzales. Sen. Richard Durbin (D-Ill.) protested the nomination from the Senate floor stating Gonzales "helped to create a permissive environment that made it more likely that abuses would take place' at the Abu Ghraib prison in Iraq and at the Guantanamo Bay detention facility in Cuba." Sen. Edward Kennedy (D-Mass.) discussed the possibility of a filibuster of the nomination, but the Democrats could not guarantee the votes needed to do so. In the end, 35 Democrats voted against the nomination.[138]

Under the leadership of Bush and Gonzales, the United States of America detained over seven hundred persons at Guantanamo Bay, some as young as 13-years-old, subjecting them to cruel, inhuman and degrading treatment without charging them or affording them a trial. The Military Commissions Act was passed denying detainees one of the most basic rights guaranteed by the Constitution, the right to challenge their detention before an independent court (writ of habeas corpus). Against the testimony of intelligence officers and officials that torture or other "alternative interrogation techniques" don't produce reliable information and won't make us safer, the Bush administration refused to eliminate or outlaw these practices. The international community protested against the US practice of "disappearing" suspects into secret CIA prisons as well as "extraordinary renditions" where prisoners are delivered to countries notorious for the use of torture in detention and interrogation.

For at least the last century, popes and bishops have unanimously condemned the use of torture as does the *Catechism of the Catholic Church*. While not opposing the Gonzales nomination directly, Neuhaus responded to the disclosure of the torture and abuse at the American-run Abu Ghraib by noting that although much of the criticism was "motivated by opposition to American policy or generalized America-bashing," he agreed torture was "never morally permissible."

Sen. Sam Brownback (R-Kans.), "a favorite of Catholic conservatives and a 2008 presidential contender, asked no questions about torture during Gonzales's nomination hearing. Sen. Rick Santorum (R-Pa.) voted to confirm Gonzales without expressing a word of concern about his record."[139] Nor did George Weigel, Michael Novak, Deal Hudson, Fr. C. John McCloskey III, or Fr. Frank Pavone. Nor did Archbishops Chaput, Burke, Myers, Donoghue or Olmstead or any of the bishops who campaigned for Bush. Once again, when given the opportunity to demonstrate their adherence to the Catholic faith superseded politics, they were silent.

CHAPTER 15

BENEDICT XVI

The Catholic Church was accustomed to playing a role at the highest level on the global stage. While its interests may coincide with those of dominant secular states whose powers ebb and flow over centuries, its gaze remains firmly fixed on its own best interests and worldview, even where these may contradict those of its ostensible allies.

From "God's Rottweiler" to Opus Dei's Pope

Joseph Alois Ratzinger was born and raised in a small Bavarian village to a devout Catholic family. His brother also became a priest and his sister became his housekeeper. Like his predecessor, he has no married siblings, no nieces or nephews, to provide the pontiff with an adult view of family life from an intimate perspective. Drafted into the Hitler Youth when he was fourteen, after two years he returned to the seminary which he had entered at age twelve. "Having seen fascism in action, Ratzinger today believes that the best antidote to political totalitarianism is ecclesial totalitarianism," according to one of his biographers.[1]

Ratzinger was a theologian and professor at Catholic German universities and was elevated to Archbishop of Munich and Freising in 1977. Pope John Paul II named him head of the Congregation for the Doctrine of the Faith (formerly the Office of the Inquisition) in 1981. Like many other boys from poor or modest means who rise through the ecclesial power structure, he grew accustomed to a life-style of domestic servants, the highest-quality accommodations and accoutrements, and living and working in the almost exclusive company of other clerics and prelates.

As head of the CDF, Ratzinger was ruthless in administering ecclesial punishments to the most noted proponents of liberation theology. Later, his role included the banishment from official positions, including Catholic universities, or the condemnation of the writings, of any progressive theologian/priest who had gained widespread acclaim such as Americans Charles E. Curran and Jesuit Roger Haight, Belgians Dominican Edward Schillebeeckx and Jesuit Jacques Dupuis, Canadian Oblate Andre Guindon, Sri Lankan Oblate Tissa Balasuriya, Indian Jesuit Anthony De Mello, and the Spanish Redemptorist Marciano Vidal. (The non-influential are usually ignored.) Ratzinger earned the epithets "Panzer Kardinal" and "God's Rottweiler," deflecting some of the ire within the Church away from John Paul II although Wojtyla was in total accord with his actions. It has also been widely acknowledged that Ratzinger was the ghost-writer for many of the works attributed to John Paul II.

In part, it was Ratzinger's intellectual rigidity and toughness which made him a long-time favorite of Opus Dei [2] and their choice as the next pontiff. As John Paul II lay dying, Opus Dei Cardinal Julián Herranz, began an active campaign on behalf of Ratzinger by hosting dinners for the electors—114 of the 117 having been appointed by Wojtyla—at the organization's heavily guarded villa outside of Rome or at his own apartment near St. Peter's.[3] The calls of "santo subito" (sainthood now) in St. Peter's Square after the death of John Paul II served to convince the voting cardinals the new pope should be someone who had been close to Wojtyla.[4] One Vatican expert was on record as saying, "Opus Dei is the only group well organized enough working within the power structure of the Roman Curia that can make a difference" in how cardinals vote.[5]

For some, the election of Ratzinger on April 19, 2005, had not been a sure thing since a group of Curial cardinals led by Angelo Sodano along with Giovanni Battista Re and Pio Laghi lobbied against him even as several Italian newspapers reported the two Opus Dei cardinals were supporting him.[6] "If you had wanted to know who was the most likely cardinal to be promoted to pope you shouldn't have relied on the pundits. Nor should you have taken any notice of the Vatican watchers who studied the arcane politics of the Catholic Church. Your best bet would have been...investors in an online futures market. They got it spot on. The Intrade futures market had Cardinal Ratzinger well ahead of the field," wrote the BBC's North America business correspondent.[7] An historian noted that a movement "with adequate liquidity" (read Opus Dei), engaged in "a takeover bid for the papacy itself," had twisted enough arms during the conclave to have Ratzinger elected.[8]

The day following the election, the *New York Times* printed an op-ed piece by "theologian for the neocon clubhouse, the American Enterprise Institute,"[9] Michael Novak:

> Cardinal Ratzinger's selection as pope...has been less heartily welcomed by many commentators in Europe and the United States, who have quickly characterized him as an "authoritarian," a "watchdog" and, most peculiarly, a "neoconservative."

Yet Novak goes on to describe the neoconservative elements of Ratzinger's worldview:

> [H]e worries that democracy, despite its great promise, is exceedingly vulnerable to the tyranny of the

majority, to "the new soft despotism" of the all-mothering state, and to the common belief that liberty means doing whatever you please.

Regarding his "my way or the highway" authoritarianism, Novak wrote, "He may be much more willing to let go of institutions he considers only tepidly Catholic than people expect."[10]

Novak was correct about European commentators. The secularist *Voltaire Network*, "a citizen's initiative financed solely by its readers' support," published an editorial on May 1, 2005, noting:

> Joseph Ratzinger was the organizer of the lobby in the European institutions so that the Bill of Rights and the Constitutional Treaty would not form the European Union on the basis of a political contract between nation-states or between citizens but on the basis of Catholic references. He did not succeed completely, as he admitted in an interview. In the end, the Europeans adopted the Anglo-Saxon point of view and not that of the Holy See. The European Union rejected the political contract between nation-states to adopt that of "common values" but refused to define them as a "Catholic" heritage or in its wider sense as "Christian."....
>
> The international press seems to ignore the prelate's political activities during the years he spent in the Roman Curia. Only the Latin-American media have mentioned his responsibility in the systematic murder of the liberation theologians carried out by the Catholic dictatorships.
>
> In general, the message of the Vatican's communicators [is that] everything must be done to conceal the pope's counterrevolutionary nature [along] with that of the neoconservatives who support him in Washington.... George W. Bush counts on Benedict XVI to add Europe to the "clash of civilizations" although a new "look" must be given to the "Panzer Kardinal."....The new pope is an indispensable element in the Tel Aviv-Washington Axis.[11]

The Heart of the Matter: Money

When John Paul II died, according to one Vatican reporter, he left his successor with a "sumptuous inheritance: a Vatican with balanced books, healthy profits, and trustworthy administrators." [12]

Actually, it is impossible to write definitively about Roman Catholic finance since all disclosures are voluntary and unverifiable. Regardless of the exact figures, the Vatican—comprised of the worldwide administrative body, the Holy See, and a small territory, City of Vatican State—has only two major sources of income, investments and donations. (Efforts to generate other revenue will be covered in a later chapter.) The finances of the Vatican Bank are never revealed. Even though investment income for the Holy See and Vatican City is reported annually, there are various congregations or departments involved in global governance that maintain their own separate and undisclosed portfolios and property such as the five-story papal palace which is never listed as an asset. Some of the donations come from parishes forwarding part of their income to the diocese and the dioceses, sometimes through a national episcopal conference, forwarding part of that income to the Holy See. Other donations come from individuals or groups such as the Knights of Columbus and Opus Dei. The chief financial institution of the Vatican continues to be the Vatican Bank—the Institute for the Works of Religion (IOR). It does not issue loans or checks; its primary function has always been investments.

As the major banking scandal concluded in 1984, "an international commission found the IOR jointly liable for the crash of the Banco Ambrosiano amidst accusations of serious malfeasance."[13] The Italian government ordered that about $600 million be returned to the Vatican's institutional victims, a fraction of the $1.4 billion guaranteed to other banks by the Ambrosiano/IOR partnership which disappeared. An official Vatican statement only said their reparation was made "on the basis of non-culpability" but "in recognition of a moral involvement." After a mysterious deposit to the IOR of $406 million made by Secretary of State Cardinal Agostino Casaroli[14]—for which no other source other than Opus Dei has ever been suggested—the Vatican repaid only $312 million to the Central Bank of Italy. Opus Dei expert Michael Walsh suggested the organization also agreed to pick up 30 percent of the Vatican's annual expenditures.[15]

After Italian magistrates gave up trying to extradite bank officials sequestered inside Vatican City, Pope John Paul II changed the IOR statutes in 1990 so that it would be operated by a supervisory council with an oversight commission of cardinals. A Swiss banker close to Opus Dei selected the council president, an Italian, Angelo Caloia. American Virgil C. Dechant, vice-president of the Knights of Columbus and a heavy contributor to Solidarity, was also named to the council.

Casaroli and his successors, Angelo Sodano and Tarcisio Bertone, have kept their own man as overseer of the IOR on behalf of the Secretariat of State to the present day. Bishop Paul Marcinkus' right-hand-man, Msgr. Donato De Bonis, remained as "prelate" of the Vatican Bank until Caloia had him removed in 1993 for controlling accounts in the name of fictitious foundations. De Bonis was ordained as a bishop and appointed chaplain of the Knights of Malta, a position providing him with diplomatic immunity. Caloia has been reconfirmed every five years and his current appointment expires in 2011.[16]

Regardless of who's in charge, scandal is never far from Roman Catholic finances, always impenetrable and always absent of oversight. US attorneys representing victims of the Catholic-led Ustase/Nazi genocide in Croatia in their suit against the Holy See noted in a press release dated November 23, 2001:

> According to one global source, the Vatican is the main destination for over $55 billion in illegal Italian money laundering and the number 8 destination worldwide for laundered money, ranked well ahead of such offshore havens as the Bahamas, Switzerland, and Liechtenstein.
>
> In a recent report by the *London Telegraph* and the Inside Fraud Bulletin, the Vatican was named as a top "cut out" country along with the offshore banking centers of Nauru, Macao, and Mauritius. A "cut out" country is one whose banking secrecy makes it is all but impossible to trace laundered funds back to their source.
>
> The Vatican Bank is desperately resisting a legal action for an accounting of stolen World War II assets in a San Francisco Federal court (*Alperin v. Vatican Bank*) filed by Serb and Jewish Holocaust survivors. Contrary to the above reports, a declaration filed under penalty of perjury by the Vatican Bank's attorney, Franzo Grande Stevens, states in part that the Vatican Bank's "fundamental purpose is to promote pious acts" and that its depositors "are essentially limited to Vatican state employees, members of the Holy See, religious orders, and persons who deposit money destined, at least in part, for works of piety." Stevens also declared to the court that the pope controls the Vatican Bank and that bank records are not retained after ten years.
>
> It seems that the Vatican Bank, a major illegal money laundering operation, is hiding behind the benign image of John Paul II. Given the Vatican Bank's alleged involvement with Nazi loot and current links to organized crime, a reckoning cannot be far off. The accumulating evidence points to a more piratical than pietical Vatican Bank[17]

The Vatican established the Cayman Islands—an offshore haven for secret bank accounts and previously part of the Diocese of Kingston, Jamaica—as its own diocese in 2000 under the direct jurisdiction of Detroit Cardinal Adam Maida who served on the IOR commission.[18]

Whether in *Zivkovich v. Vatican Bank*, an action similar to *Alperin v. Vatican Bank* noted above, or cases involving sexual abuse by priests including *Doe v. Holy See* in Oregon, *Gomez v. Holy See* in Florida, or *Doe v. Holy See* in Missouri[19] which hold the Vatican responsible for ordering its bishops to contravene civil law, no one has yet cracked the Holy See's immunity as a sovereign nation. A RICO (Racketeer Influenced and Corrupt Organizations) suit, *Dale* v. *Holy See,* was filed in 2005 by the insurance commissioners of Mississippi, Tennessee, Arkansas, Missouri and Oklahoma seeking $600 million in damages. Two former papal nuncios to the US and Cardinal Angelo Sodano were named as defendants because a Vatican Bank account was used as a "cover" by convicted swindler, Martin Frankel, to defraud US life insurance companies. That suit has also failed.

Relations With Other Religions

Benedict XVI enjoyed a "honeymoon" period with his former critics inside the Church who took a wait-and-see attitude towards the new reign. He gave the initial impression of being less stubborn and more open to dialogue than his predecessor. Nevertheless, dialogue quickly changed to monologue and it became clear that neither his position as head of an international organization nor the media spotlight would temper his certitude and Eurocentrism.

In his first three years as pontiff, Joseph Ratzinger managed to undo much of the successes of his predecessor in ecumenical relations. For no apparent reason, the major points made in Ratzinger's paper, *Dominus Iesus,* written in 2000 which disparaged other religions, were reiterated in a document released in July 2007 by his successor as head of the Congregation for the Doctrine of the Faith, Cardinal William Levada. It repeated that only Catholicism can properly be called a true Church (the Orthodox was a Church but suffered from the "wound" of not recognizing the primacy of the pope) and other Christian religions were "defective" and "cannot be called 'Churches' in the proper sense." Religions other than Christianity are "gravely deficient." Their rituals can constitute "an obstacle to salvation" for their followers. In reporting on the 2007 document, several journalists recalled Ratzinger's 1997 interview with *L'Expresse:* "If Buddhism is attractive, it's only because it suggests that by belonging to it you can touch the infinite, and you can have joy without concrete religious obligations," Ratzinger said. "It's spiritually self-indulgent eroticism."

Jews

While the neo-Catholics in the United States found common ground with the neoconservatives in relation to Jewish interests and the Middle East, the Vatican's relations with world Jewry, and indeed the state of Israel, declined. While John Paul II had publicly apologized for the Church's persecution of the Jews in 2000, Ratzinger tried to revive use of the pre-Vatican II Good Friday rite containing the same vocabulary which had incited that persecution. When he lifted the excommunication of the four bishops of the Society of St. Pius X, including the Holocaust denier, Richard Williamson, in early 2009 even some Catholic prelates questioned the pope's judgment.

The friction between the Vatican and Jews is exacerbated by difficult relations with the State of Israel. The Vatican established diplomatic relations in 1993 in the hopes of normalizing the treatment of Catholic institutions and property in Israel especially as it related to taxation and other financial issues which to this day are still not resolved. That Israel makes it difficult for foreign priests and religious workers to obtain work visas is another continuing sore spot. In 2007, tensions rose between the Vatican and Israel when the Holy See's ambassador to Israel initially decided to boycott a Holocaust memorial service because of continuing allegations that Pope Pius XII was silent about the genocide of Jews during World War II.[20]

Muslims

While Benedict's other missteps may be attributed to European chauvinism and triumphalist Catholicism, it would be difficult to attribute his attacks against Islam as merely intellectual parochialism.

When he was first elected, Turkish newspapers worried that the new pope's opposition to Ankara joining the European Union could raise fresh obstacles to its membership. In a 2004 interview with *Le Figaro*, Cardinal Ratzinger had declared that the Muslim but secular Turkey should "seek its future in an association of Islamic nations rather than the EU, which has Christian roots." He added that Turkey had always been "in permanent contrast to Europe" and linking it to Europe would be a mistake.[21]

One of Benedict's first acts as pope was to remove Archbishop Michael Fitzgerald, a leading expert on Islam and Muslim-Christian relations, from his position as president in the Vatican's Council for Interreligious Dialogue. The move was seen as a signal that Ratzinger intended to take a tougher stance against Islam.[22]

The summer after his election, the pope met with Italian journalist, Oriana Fallaci, at Castel Gondolfo. Though an atheist, Fallaci had expressed admiration for Ratzinger's "defense" of European culture against the swelling numbers of Muslim immigrants.[23] Described as a "rabid Islamophobe," the journalist had written phrases such as "Muslims breed like rats" and "the increasing presence of Muslims in Italy and Europe is directly proportional to our loss of freedom." Her 2001 bestseller, *The Force of Reason*, was a "diatribe of invective against Islam." Not all Italians share her views and some of the Italian press criticized the pope for holding the meeting, but the Vatican expressed no regret.[24]

In October 2005, a Danish newspaper published a series of twelve cartoons disrespectful of the Prophet Muhammad setting off a series of riots and protests around the world. With total disregard for—if not an intentional provocation of—a similarly predictable Muslim backlash, Benedict began a September 2006 lecture at the University at Regensburg in Bavaria with a quote from the "erudite" Byzantine emperor Manuel II Paleologos: "Show me just what Muhammad brought that was new and there you will find things only evil and inhuman, such as his command to spread by the sword the faith he preached." Throughout the rest of the address, the pope added nothing to refute the quote nor did he disassociate it from his own views. It was a gratuitous remark, unnecessary to making his conclusions about "Faith and Reason," the topic of his speech.

As a result, churches were burned in the West Bank, demonstrators in Indonesia chanted "Crucify the pope!" and Benedict XVI was burned in effigy in Iraq. Officials in Kashmir confiscated newspapers to avoid possible riots.[25] Christian minorities in Muslim countries, especially in Arab nations and Israeli-occupied Palestinian territories, worried that Benedict had worsened an "antagonistic environment." "Being enthusiastic about one's religion shouldn't lead to judging other peoples' religions. Criticizing others' faith breeds enmity and divisions," Pope Shenouda III, head of the Egypt's Coptic Orthodox Church, told the press. Even Vladimir Putin warned that "religious leaders" should be more careful in their statements.[26]

Though not reversing his opposition to the Iraq invasion, the pontiff's words were said to be "the latest link in the chain of a crusade against Islam started by America's Bush" and "a Catholic stamp to the 'Islam versus the West' justification for the US neoconservative-led 'WWIII on Islam.'"[27] One journalist wondered,

> Why [did] the pope choose to throw a hand grenade into a powder keg, and why [did] he choose to do it at this moment in history? Bush has been trying to portray the war against Islamist militants as a clash of civilizations, one that will last for generations and will determine the future of mankind. Benedict, whether he accepts Bush's view or not, offered an intellectual foundation for Bush's position.[28]

Ratzinger's non-apology was almost as insulting as the quote was offensive. He claimed he was only using the emperor's words as a springboard to further discussion: "At this time, I wish also to add that I am deeply sorry *for the reactions* in some countries to a few passages of my address at the University of Regensburg, which were considered offensive to the sensibility of Muslims. (emphasis added) These in fact were a quotation from a medieval text, which do not in any way express my personal thought."

Turkey's cabinet minister, Mehmet Aydin, commented, "You either have to say 'I'm sorry' in a proper way, or not say it at all; are you sorry for saying such a thing, or because of its consequences?" An Egyptian Muslim scholar told the Arabic al-Jazeera satellite television station that the pope added insult to injury by presuming that Muslims could not comprehend his speech.[29]

The international and influential Islamic political movement, Egypt's Muslim Brotherhood, accepted the pope's apology as "sufficient." Islamic leaders in Indonesia and Malaysia, the largest Islamic countries both of which converted peacefully to Islam, as well as other Muslim clerics around the world, accepted Benedict's explanation realizing there was no benefit to playing into the hands of Christian Zionists who continuously undermine Islamic-Christian understanding.[30]

Former head of the Vatican media, Joaquin Navarro-Valls, gloated, "If I had remained in office, it's quite possible that none of this would have happened. It was a wonderful text, but a few press agencies packaged it in misleading ways. No one in the audience, which included a few Muslims, understood the lecture the way it was characterized later on." George Weigel disagreed. "[Benedict] knew exactly what he was doing. He is saying that irrational violence is displeasing to God. The question Benedict is putting on the table is: 'Does a significant part of Islam have the capacity to be self-critical?'"[31]

A papal trip to Turkey to meet with the Greek Orthodox Patriarch Bartholomew I in late November 2006 had already been scheduled. Turkey's foreign minister, Abdullah Gul, said the visit to his country was still on even though a cancellation was considered. Both Vatican and Turkish diplomats saw it as an opportunity to ease tensions. During the pope's four days in Turkey, no one mentioned the word "Regensburg." Head of religious affairs in Turkey, Ali Bardakoglu, addressing the pope in Ankara, did use the opportunity to set the record straight that "freedom and rational thought" are inherent in Islam. He chastised those who "represent Islam as a religion that brings violence, spread throughout the world by the sword," and stressed that "the Muslim who belongs to a religion that has the word 'peace' at the root of its name feels strongly offended by the accusations made against him."[32] The grand mufti of Istanbul cordially welcomed the pope to the city's famous Blue Mosque where, in one of this pontificate's most famous photo-ops, they prayed together.

Europe as Christendom, and Vice Versa

What Benedict XVI covets the most is the restitution of "Christendom—the deal whereby the Church gains status in society by making itself dependent upon (and useful to) society's governing authorities,"[33] and his first priority has always been Europe. "Joseph Ratzinger was elected pope in part because many cardinals believed that addressing the European crisis [the dwindling number of baptisms and Mass attendees] is the most important challenge facing Catholicism, and the new pope's choice of the name 'Benedict,' with reference to the founder of European monasticism, was a way of signaling where his interests reside."[34] Almost every expression of Benedict's religiosity and ecclesiology reflects an era of Roman Catholic hegemony which had been willing to impose its faith through violence.

While his predecessor recognized the Church as catholic (universal) and enjoyed having African drummers or Aztec dancers at his ceremonies, Ratzinger replaced the papal master of ceremonies (a cleric in charge of "staging" ceremonies) and his personal liturgical staff so that the music heard in St. Peter's would be limited to Gregorian chant and classical European works and the process of replacing modern languages with Latin would begin.

A new haberdasher was hired to dress the pope and hierarchs in even more ostentatious displays of royal silks, satins and fine embroidery and robes with trains were reintroduced. His mitres—the pointy hats restricted by canon law to the ranks of bishop or higher—have become taller and jewel-encrusted. Benedict ordered the restoration of a gilded throne for his use and replaced the silver crozier (shepherd's staff) with a gold one. For his 2008 Palm Sunday Mass, the pope ordered a reproduction of the 30-piece red and gold silk brocaded vestments, embroidered with gold thread and the Medici coat of arms, worn by Leo X for his coronation in 1513. Legend has Leo saying to his brother, "Since God has given us the papacy, let us enjoy it."

However, the more the pope and his Curia pretend to be European nobility, the more they are rejected by the rest of the continent. Representatives to the European Union, with their historic memory of the tragedies of denominational warfare and state-imposed religion, have repeatedly rebuffed efforts by Wojtyla and Ratzinger to exert any influence in that body. The position of the Holy See has been rejected on abortion and stem cell research. The European Parliament passed a motion calling for compulsory recognition of same-sex unions and refused to ratify a Vatican-supported Italian candidate, Rocco Buttiglione, as a commissioner because he supported the Church's current view of homosexuality.[35]

A Singular Status at the UN

With little influence in the EU, the Vatican highly values its unique status in the United Nations. The privileged position held by the Roman Catholic Church in that world body was gained in part by pressure from US Republican Party. When John Paul II began his reign in 1978, the Holy See had full diplomatic ties with only 84 states. The first permanent papal nunciature had been established in the year 1500 in the republic of Venice. The first Protestant nation with ties to the Vatican was Prussia in 1805. The first non-Christian state to establish diplomatic relations with the Holy See was Japan in 1942. Due in part to patronage from, and its insider position with, the Reagan and both Bush administrations, the number has risen to 174 including Israel. The Holy See has special diplomatic relations with the Palestinian Liberation Organization in addition to Russia. Also, the Holy See is now a member of twenty inter-governmental bodies besides the UN, including the African Union and the Organization of American States. It maintains diplomatic relations with the European Union and the Sovereign Military Order of Malta.[36]

One mutual goal of the Holy See and the GOP had been to increase Vatican influence in the UN. The Holy See has been a participant since its founding and the Vatican's relationship with the UN was affirmed in 1957 by Pius XII. In 1964, Paul VI agreed the Holy See could remain as a non-member state with only Permanent Observer status. As such, the Vatican could participate in conferences and give speeches but could not vote.

With the renewed politicization of the Church under John Paul II, the Holy See increasingly inserted itself into UN deliberations, particularly on family planning issues. During the 1994 UN International Conference on Population and Development in Cairo, the relationship between the Vatican and the administration of Bill Clinton was strained when opposition by John Paul II forced the US government to intensify its own campaign in support of the conference.[37]

With backing from the George W. Bush administration, Cardinal Angelo Sodano declared in 2002, "The Holy See is committed to studying the possible forms of its own greater participation in the assembly of the United Nations." When asked, "Could the Holy See become a member state?" the cardinal replied, "If it were useful, I would not exclude it. In that body there were once two permanent observers: Switzerland and ourselves. Now Switzerland has become a member and we are alone. The form of our presence is an open question."[38] (Actually, the PLO was also granted permanent observer status in 1975.) Full membership was denied, but Sodano's partial victory came on July 1, 2004, when the General Assembly gave the Holy See new privileges, among them: the right to participate in the general debate of the General Assembly; the right of reply; the right to have its communications issued and circulated directly as official documents of the Assembly; and the right to co-sponsor draft resolutions and decisions that make reference to the Holy See. The Catholic Church is the only non-member granted such privileges.

This new status came by way of a resolution, "Participation of the Holy See in the work of the United Nations," submitted by Dr. Julian Robert Hunte O.B.E., then president of the UN General Assembly. As previously mentioned, Sodano awarded Hunte the highest honor available to a lay person in the midst of the "wafer watch" against John Kerry in spite of Hunte's pro-choice position in St. Lucia.

One of the challenges to the Holy See's elevated status at the UN came from a consortium of groups favoring legal abortion waging what it called the "See Change" campaign. According to the website, seechange. org, this was "an international effort supported by more than 700 international organizations from 80 countries which believe that the Holy See should participate in the UN in the same way as the world's other religions do—as a nongovernmental organization." Angered by the Church's use of its UN position to obstruct consensus on important documents relating to women's rights and HIV/AIDS prevention, this group tried to have the Holy See expelled from the UN based on what they said was its questionable status as a "state."

> They profess to be interested only in the spiritual, not the temporal, affairs of this Earth. So why do they want to be included in a totally political affiliation of the world's countries? Could it be that the Vatican's agenda is totally political?"

During the same campaign, a group of Dutch officials voted to end the special privileges of the Holy See in the UN. The motion put before their parliament stated:

> Considering that the Catholic Church/the Vatican is the only Church or religious movement that is negotiating with others at Conferences of the United Nations under the condition of "non-member state permanent observer" of the Holy See; being of the opinion that it is undesirable to grant this right only to one Church or religious movement; but that all religions have to be treated in the same way, [members of the Dutch Parliament] request that the government actively urges the Holy See giving up its position of exception.

The issue was settled when the US Republican-led Congress passed a resolution supporting the Vatican threatening that non-passage of Hunte's proposal would "further damage relations between the United States and the United Nations."

Vatican Overtures to Russia and China

Russia and China, stretching to fill the void as US power, wealth and prestige were dissipated by the Bush administration, were thought by Benedict and his foreign policy advisors to provide new opportunities for alliances. They began intensive diplomatic overtures to these other world powers.

The Vatican's foreign minister, Archbishop Giovanni Lajolo, went to Moscow in October 2005 to meet with the Russian foreign minister and separately with the head of the Russian Orthodox Church's foreign relations department. Since the breakup of the Soviet Union in 1991, the Holy See has had a delegate assigned to Moscow and the Kremlin has maintained a mission in the Vatican. In an interview with the Russian press Lajolo said:

> It seems evident to me that the current status of the reciprocal representations in Moscow and the Vatican doesn't correspond to the weight which the Holy See attributes to its relations with the Moscow government, nor in the position which the Holy See—with its 174 apostolic nunciatures and another 20 representatives to international organizations—has in the world. Rather, I think both the parties should work to progress onto full diplomatic relations.[39]

Responding to Lajolo's visit, the head of the Russian Orthodox Church, Patriarch Alexy II, said improved relations would only be possible after the Catholic Church stopped evangelizing for new converts in all prior

Soviet territories and ended discrimination against the Orthodox Church in western Ukraine. This effort had been subsidized since the Cold War by American Catholics with an annual collection. More than $100 million has been sent to the Vatican for the "formidable tasks of restoring church structures and, more importantly, of rebuilding the spiritual centers of their communities" in previously communist-held territories according to Cardinal Justin Rigali, chairman of the USCCB Subcommittee on Aid to the Church in Central and Eastern Europe.[40]

With all religion suppressed by the Soviet government, Russia had witnessed an influx of Christian missionaries from many denominations as soon as the USSR was dissolved. Fighting to maintain its primacy of place in Russia, the Orthodox Church pressured the government to pass a law in 1997 impeding "non-traditional" religions, including Roman Catholicism.

When Vladimir Putin came to power in 2000, he recognized the advantages of having a state religion "to fill the gap left by communism." He protected and promoted the power of the Orthodox Church: "patriotic to the point of being nationalistic—a useful organizing principle for a society suddenly cast adrift, and a valuable source of moral support for the Putin government." Government officials who were atheists under communist rule were now finding it helpful to their careers to attend Russian Orthodox services. When Putin selected Dmitri Medvedev as his successor, Alexy II praised the decision on national television.[41]

The Orthodox Church has received government funding and further intervention in protecting it from potential competitors.[42] Since ninety percent of Russia's Catholic clerics are foreign-born, the government began restricting visas for priests in 2002, even those who had worked in Russia for many years.[43] A leader of the Russian Evangelical Alliance which represents many Protestant denominations said governors appointed by Putin regularly deferred to Russian Orthodox bishops. "Many times officials say to us, 'Please, you must ask the Orthodox bishop about your activity, and if he agrees, then you can work here.'"

According to the BBC, Putin's trip to the Vatican to meet with Benedict in March 2007 could be attributed to his "ambitions for his country as a global power. Russia will encounter many influential Roman Catholics in the globalised world and will not want to have made an enemy of their spiritual leader....It is a tribute to the continuing influence of a Church that claims more than a billion members that President Putin wishes to visit Pope Benedict." Putin told the pontiff he would mediate the difficulties between the Orthodox and Catholic Churches.[44] What Putin did accomplish was allowing Opus Dei to take over two Catholic parishes in Moscow in June 2007.[45]

The Vatican, however, has not yet been able to achieve direct talks with Patriarch Alexy II. When Cardinal Walter Kasper, head of the Pontifical Council for Promoting Christian Unity, announced in June 2008 that a meeting might be arranged soon, a professor at the Moscow Theological Academy responded: "Such commentaries by one of the parties are sometimes a diplomatic move intended to put certain soft pressure on the negotiating parties. It's like they are saying 'We are glad, we are looking forward [to a meeting], why are you avoiding us?'" [46]

In the same month as Lajolo's first trip to Moscow as foreign minister—October 2005—the *London Times* reported the Vatican was ready to break ties with Taiwan in order to establish diplomatic ties with China. "Beijing said that it welcomed better relations but would not tolerate the Vatican meddling in its internal affairs. However, Chinese officials hedged the question of whether Beijing would regard the Vatican appointing Chinese bishops as interference in its internal affairs, saying only that it respected religious freedom."[47]

All religion was outlawed in 1949 following the establishment of the People's Republic of China by the Communist Party. Though only one percent of the population, Roman Catholics suffered great persecution and formed an underground organization supported by multi-national anti-communist groups such as the "Free China" movement headed by Anna Chenault and Clair Booth Luce. Religion thrives under oppression, so having failed to eradicate the Church, Beijing tried to substitute a state-sponsored Catholicism loyal to the Communist Party instead of Rome. In 1957, the government's Religious Affairs Bureau established the Chinese Patriotic Catholic Association to control mainland China's Catholics. The Party appointed bishops independent of the Vatican and each pope has refused to recognize the CPCA as a valid branch of the worldwide Church. Not surprisingly, membership in the underground organization continued to exceed that of the state-run group.

Benedict's desire to extend his influence coincided with China's effort to soften its image before Beijing's 2008 Summer Olympics and significant concessions were arrived at by both parties. Ratzinger has urged both Catholic Churches toward unity through dialogue and joint liturgies. Some recent episcopal ordinations have been carried out with the joint approval of the Vatican and the Communist Party.

"In what may be Rome's strongest public push to normalize relations with China," Benedict sent a 55-page open letter to Chinese Catholics in May 2007 "that essentially lays all the Vatican's diplomatic cards on the table." The pope acknowledged progress had been made on religious freedom but held the right to appoint bishops as non-negotiable. He repeated that the Vatican was ready to move its nunciature from Taiwan to Beijing as soon as this matter was settled. Chinese officials responded by demanding the Holy See first sever ties with Taiwan as a show of good faith. The CPCA refused to distribute the letter to its priests and members. It was reported that the Vatican website, which printed the letter and explanatory text in Chinese, was blocked on the mainland.[48]

There were additional measures to keep the Church's focus on China. John Paul II had assigned the Jesuits to care for the world's migrants and refugees. In January 2008, they were instructed by Benedict to prepare for new missionary efforts in China. Ratzinger urged Chinese Catholics to make a pilgrimage to a Marian shrine located in Shanghai as a show of that community's strength and his ability to mobilize thousands of Chinese. But in the wake of renewed protests surrounding China's occupation of Tibet, the government feared large religious gatherings and restricted access to the shrine.[49] Benedict also announced May 24, 2008, would be a World Day of Prayer for the Church in China and offered a plenary indulgence (total remission of the time a soul spends in purgatory as expiation for his/her sins) to Catholics who offered a novena (nine days of prayers) for this purpose.[50]

Again, in light of international attention being given to the Olympics, Chinese foreign ministry spokesman Qin Gang, told reporters in May 2008 that China was ready to improve its relations with the Vatican and had made "efforts in this regard....We are ready to conduct further dialogue on the basis of fundamental principles and make progress in normalization of bilateral relations."[51] Once the Olympics ended, no further conciliatory statements have come from the Chinese and neither side has budged on the essential issues.

(The third emergent economic powerhouse, India, was never officially atheist as was the former Soviet Union and China. There is no religious void to be filled by Roman Catholicism which has had a presence on the subcontinent since the time of the Portuguese explorers yet claims less than two percent of the population. Because India's major exposure to Christianity was from Portuguese and English imperialists, Mahatma Gandhi expressed the same view as many of his countrymen with his famous quote: "Oh, I don't reject your Christ. I love your Christ. It's just that so many of you Christians are so unlike your Christ.")

The Church's Relation With Italy

The first and foremost secular government with which the Catholic Church must retain good relations is Italy. Italian financiers "maintain a close relationship with the Vatican hierarchies, with the Catholic associations and with the prelature of the Opus Dei. In an Italy where politics counts less than finance, the Church wields more power in the bank business now than in the period in which the country was mainly run by the Christian Democratic Party."[52]

Structurally separate from the Vatican, the Italian Catholic Church receives huge amounts of funding from the government based on the 1929 Lateran Treaty with adjustments (some would say punishments) made in 1984 to settle the Vatican Bank scandal. Eight euros for each 1000 euros of earned income is withheld from Italian taxpayers for charitable purposes. They may choose that their taxes be given to the Italian government, the Catholic Church or one of five other recognized religions including the Lutheran Church, Jewish Community, and Adventists. Only 40 percent of Italians make that designation. Taxes collected from the remaining 60 percent of Italians are divided in the same proportion as the specified selections of the 40 percent. The result is that 90 percent of the entire tax is given to the Italian Episcopal Conference (CEI), "almost one billion euros a year, 991 million euros in 2007."[53]

While the CEI receives payments in advance of the next year, other religions have to wait three years and then have to beg for their share—something to keep in mind when Benedict et al complain about any unequal treatment their institution receives in other countries. In addition to the 8x1000, the government also gives the CEI stipends for priests and "650 million euros to pay religion teachers, 700 million euros for Catholic schools and health facilities (which don't provide all the services the State schools or hospitals provide to non-Catholic citizens) and 250 million euros to defray the costs of large events" in recognition that these occasions draw tourists who benefit the general economy. The CEI reports that it uses 20 percent of its income for charities, 35 percent for salaries and the remaining part, "for not very well specified 'cult necessities,' 'catechesis' and for 'real estate administration expenses.'"[54]

As pointed out in a recent Italian radio broadcast sponsored jointly by the Fondazione Critica Liberale Fondazione Critica Liberale (a foundation promoting the thought and practice of liberalism) and the Confederazione Generale Italiana del Lavoro (one of the three most important labor unions in Italy):

> Most of the historical real estate in downtown Rome belongs to the Vatican. Those buildings used by the Catholic Church when the pope ran central Italy before 1860 remained in the ownership of the Vatican. Only important people connected with the Vatican can get an apartment in one of these historical buildings. Yet the Italian State spends the taxpayers' money to restore those buildings: for example the "Propaganda Fide" palace in Piazza di Spagna was restored using 6 million euros of the taxpayer's money.
>
> While all basilicas and all Catholic landmarks are being restored at the taxpayer's expense to allow the Vatican to make money from the tourism organized by the "Opera Romana Pellegrinaggi," [the Vatican's own travel agency for tourists] the restoration of other public tourist landmarks like the Colosseum or the walls of ancient Rome are being almost completely ignored and sometimes made with private money. The shuttle bus "Roma Cristiana" (Christian Rome) run by the Vatican connecting all the Basilicas of Rome is mostly made at the expense of the City of Rome....
>
> "Black financing" includes the ability of the IOR to operate without any respect of international law and get money and transfer money of their "well connected friends" all over the world. Most of the money sent to Africa or to other underdeveloped regions all over the world is not spent for charity but mostly for propaganda purposes, for recruitment and for political reasons. This money has allowed the Vatican to enter the Italian political

scene and support only those members of the Italian Parliament who follow the directives of the Vatican....

Proposals were made for initiatives to be taken in the near future in order to eliminate the privileges of the Vatican. The hope is that the European authorities will intervene to order the Italian government not to allow the Vatican to run businesses in unfair competition with the other normal private business.[55]

The European Commission, part of the EU, demanded Italy explain the tax benefits provided to the Catholic Church on income from properties which "now amount to an estimated €1 billion" in view of its interference in Italian government affairs.

At the end of 2005 Silvio Berlusconi, then the centre-right prime minister, extended the Church's tax exemptions to include buildings used by the Church for businesses such as hostels or health clinics. Mr. Berlusconi's move was regarded by the Left as a blatant attempt to court the Catholic vote on the eve of the 2006 elections, which he narrowly lost to Romano Prodi and the centre Left.

The Prodi Government amended the tax breaks last year, saying that only Church activities "which are not exclusively commercial" were exempt. However, the word "exclusively" left a loophole allowing properties with even a minor form of religious activity to benefit.

The Church owns 100,000 properties in Italy, 2,000 of them used as hospitals, clinics or rest homes. In Rome alone the Church owns 65 rest homes, 250 schools, 580 institutes, convents and monasteries and 18 hospitals.

Maurizio Gasparri, of the right-wing Alleanza Nazionale, charged the EU with siding with the "anti-Catholic Left" in Europe. But Paolo Cento, the Deputy Economics Minister and a Green, said that there was "a need to end this form of privilege for the Church." Monsignor Angelo Bagnasco, the head of the Italian Bishops Conference, said the issue was a pretext for attacks on the Church and that the tax breaks enabled it to "benefit society."[56]

Bush-ally Silvio Berlusconi, an experienced politician not embarrassed by hair implants and cosmetic surgery, is the richest man in Italy and a media mogul. He provides the Vatican viewpoint through all his broadcast outlets and his media companies work on Opus Dei productions. On Berlusconi's TV stations only the Catholic Church can air public service announcements asking Italians to designate the CEI as the recipient of their 8x1000 "as a magnificent opportunity to help the derelicts of the earth. There appear children of the poor countries, hungry and miserable. To have those emaciated faces smile again is easy: just a signature on the tax form and a quota of your 'Irpef' (the personal earned yearly income) will be delivered to them."[57]

Center-left Prime Minister Romano Prodi took office after defeating Berlusconi in a close election in April 2006. In addition to changing some tax exemptions, Prodi planned to fight the Vatican's effort for more restrictive abortion legislation (legal in Italy in the first trimester), make divorce easier, and proposed recognizing unmarried partnerships, including gays. "You'll see. They [the Church] will provoke a Prodi government crisis," predicted an Italian cleric to journalist, Curzio Maltese. The prime minister was "hit by a volume of fire unchained every day against the Prodi government by the ecclesiastical hierarchies, cassocks going back and forth to public and private TV news programs....The Catholic hierarchies use the ethical issues to mask very important economic interests."[58]

The Vatican elevated a minor incident into a national brouhaha in order to "provoke a Prodi government crisis." The rector of Rome's La Sapienza University invited the pope to speak to a thousand hand-picked guests in the main lecture hall in January 2008. Sixty-seven science professors and lecturers at La Sapienza signed a letter protesting the invitation based, in part, on Ratzinger's 1990 statement: "At the time of Galileo the Church remained much more faithful to reason than Galileo himself. The process against Galileo was reasonable and just." A hundred students staged a sit-in in the rector's office demanding the pope's visit be canceled. Some students erected banners on campus and said they would greet the pope with loud rock music because Ratzinger had referred to it as "the devil's work." Some said they would organize a gay and lesbian parade.[59]

No violence was suggested and the rector said students would have a designated area where they could protest. Yet the Vatican announced the pope was canceling his speech based on advice of "authorities" who could not guarantee his safety. This charge was repeated by several hierarchs to the media. The government issued a strong denial with assurances the pope had always, and would continue, to receive their protection. But the Italian Church has access to more media outlets than a center-left government and the damage was done.[60]

The story that Benedict was a victim of censorship from intolerant left-wing radicals (and by implication, Prodi supporters) was carried by the right-wing press around the world and eventually picked up by the mainstream media. CNN's Rome bureau chief confirmed it was quite extraordinary for the pope to cancel the visit just because of the objections of some students and professors.[61] Prodi urged the pontiff to change his mind. "No voice must go silent in our country, let alone that of the pope," he said in an official statement. But Benedict refused to go and sent a copy of his intended speech to the university and the press resulting in it being more widely read than if he had delivered it in person.

Though his government had provided economic growth and reduced unemployment, the prime minister lost popular support. The fatal blow came when Justice Minister Clemente Mastella, head of the UDEUR, the Roman Catholic party (the Christian Democrats disappeared in the mid 1990s from widespread corruption), withdrew his support from the Prodi coalition. Mastella and his wife were being investigated for corruption and Mastella stated he wasn't getting enough political support from the Prodi government.[62] Some on the Left accused the Vatican of persuading Mastella to sabotage Prodi.[63] By the end of January, Prodi resigned leading the way for Berlusconi's return to power.

Once back in office, Berlusconi was granted a private audience with Benedict. His office reported that Berlusconi told the pope "the values of liberty and tolerance, and the sacredness of human life and the family" are priorities of his government. The Vatican reported, "Attention also turned to certain matters associated with the implementation of the current agreements between the Holy See and Italy."[64] Berlusconi was interviewed by phone on a morning talk show on Canale 5, "the flagship station of his three-network TV empire," before his papal audience and he said "the pope and his Church cannot help but be pleased by the actions of this government." At the public part of their meeting, Berlusconi gave the pope a gold cross worn on the chest, inlaid with diamonds and topaz.[65]

CHAPTER 16

BENEDICT XVI VISITS THE US

US Donations to the Vatican

Donations are an important source of Vatican revenue and in 2006 comprised more than a third of its reported income with the US being the largest national donor.[1]

In 2005 it was noted, "American Catholics usually supply about 25 percent of the [Vatican's] annual operating budget," although they comprise only 6 percent of the world's 1.1 billion Roman Catholics.[2] When Cardinal Sergio Sebastiani, president of the Prefecture for the Economic Affairs of the Holy See, gave a breakdown of donors by nationality in July 2006, he stated that of the $93.3 million received in donations in 2005, a third came from dioceses, groups and individuals in the US. Contributions to the 2005 Peter's Pence collection totaled $59.4 million of which 29 percent was from the US.[3] (The next largest contributors are Italy and Germany—the kirchensteuer still being in effect since the 1933 concordat was signed with Hitler.) In a separate annual collection for foreign missions, the US is "by far" the largest contributor.[4] The last time (July 2007) Vatican finances were reported before Pope Benedict's trip to the US, the nationality of the primary donors was omitted.[5]

When Pope Benedict XVI came to the US April 15-20, 2008, every Catholic official in Rome and Washington insisted the timing had nothing to do with American politics nor the fact that this was a presidential election year. No one mentioned whether the trip was also in the best interests of the Holy See. The Church's influence, and therefore its ability to merit US donations, is diminished every time a candidate backed by the hierarchy loses an election. Besides, after being rebuffed by the EU, Russia and China, the US was still Benedict's most powerful friend.

Navigating the Diplomatic Thicket

There was much at stake for the Holy See and the Republicans in Benedict's visit—and it was made even more diplomatically complex by the perils of linking the Vatican with the increasingly despised Bush administration and its neo-Catholic advocates. Benedict was caught between a rock and a hard place. When the pope bolsters the Republicans from whence comes much of his support, he risks losing more stature in the international community. With a solution which would benefit both the Vatican and the GOP, it was reported that Benedict was considering a trip to the US to address the United Nations General Assembly, possibly at the beginning of its next term starting in September 2007. [6] The pope would have the prestige of addressing the world body and the Americans could tout Benedict's trip as an endorsement for the Republican Party.

Within days after UN Secretary General Ban Ki-moon's audience with Benedict in April 2007, the Vatican announced a firm invitation had been extended for the pope to address the UN. At the time, "there is no date or program" for the pope's trip, according to Fr. Federico Lombardi, director of the Vatican press office.[7] Officials in Rome and the US insisted the trip had nothing to do with American politics. But the papal visit, originally tentatively scheduled for September 2007, would take place during a presidential election year after all. The first public response from an American prelate came when Cardinal Sean P. O'Malley, OFM Cap (a Franciscan and Bernard Law's replacement) invited the pope to include Boston on his itinerary "saying a visit to the city that was at the heart of the clergy abuse scandal would send a positive message to Catholics."[8]

Next, the president met with Benedict at the Vatican on June 9, 2007, during his trip to Europe to attend the G-8 meeting in Germany. While Bush was in Rome, extensive protests closed much of the city. He met privately with the pope "for more than half an hour", meaning less than an hour. The Holy See press office listed the subjects covered as: the Israeli-Palestinian conflict, Catholic communities in Lebanon and Iraq, Africa and the Darfur crisis, Latin America, human rights and religious freedom, the defense and promotion of life, marriage and the family, the education of the young and sustainable development. The US Ambassador to the Holy See, Francis Rooney, reported they spoke about the environment, immigration, terrorism, fundamentalism, the fight against AIDS, Lebanon, and aid to Africa.[9]

The first tentative itinerary for the pope's trip was released in September 2007. The visit, scheduled for April 15-20, 2008, would begin in Washington DC where the pope would meet the president, would possibly include a stop in Baltimore which was celebrating its bicentennial as the first metropolitan archdiocese in the US, while in New York the pope would also visit Ground Zero in addition to the UN, and the last stop would be Boston.[10] The final itinerary for the pope's trip was confirmed by the papal nuncio appointed to the US by Benedict, Archbishop Pietro Sambi, in November through an announcement issued by the US Conference of Catholic Bishops. Boston and Baltimore which had only pastoral significance were dropped while the politically important Washington DC was retained. In their notice, the USCCB stated, "the visit could mark a rebirth of the Church in the United States after the trauma of the sexual abuse crisis."[11]

A new PR team of "progressive papal aides" headed by Archbishop

Claudio Maria Celli, director of the Vatican's Department of Social Communications which supervises its television and media operations, was assigned to the pope. "Celli, whose amiable face hides one of the sharpest minds in the Vatican, seized at once on the dangers of the Church being seen as 'fundamentalist.'" Prof. Mary Ann Glendon, a neo-Catholic token female and new US Ambassador to the Holy See, said America would find Ratzinger had made "a smooth transition from scholar to universal pastor."[12]

(Glendon sits on most of the same boards as Novak, Weigel and Neuhaus. In 1995, she headed the 22-member delegation of the Holy See to the Fourth United Nations' Women's Conference in Beijing. Glendon was awarded the $250,000 Lynde and Harry Bradley Foundation Prize in 2003.[13] She once referred to the invasion of Iraq as a "humanitarian intervention" although admitting "that wasn't the precise issue."[14])

When the sex abuse scandal broke in 2002, Ratzinger had accused the US media of "a planned campaign" of exaggerating the crisis to discredit the Church. With new handlers in place, Benedict was ready to admit there was a problem and in January 2008 he instructed "all dioceses, parishes, monasteries, convents and seminaries to organize continuous daily prayers to express penitence and to purify the clergy [no mention of the hierarchy]." Vatican officials explained the prayers were in addition to the code adopted by the Church in 2005 to ensure that men "with deep-seated homosexual tendencies" do not enter seminaries, still the only action taken in Rome to address the worldwide scandal. Cardinal Cláudio Hummes, head of the Vatican Congregation for the Clergy, now admitted the scandal was exceptionally serious although it was probably caused, he said, by "no more than 1 percent" of the 400,000 Catholic priests around the world.[15] Since the US bishops' had themselves reported the percentage to be at least 4 percent, the Vatican was implying, once again, this was mainly an "American" problem.

To make amends to the Protestant-majority in the US offended by Ratzinger's pronouncement that their denominations are not "proper" Churches and suffered from "defects," the press was notified the first week in March the pope was ready to admit Martin Luther "did not intend to split Christianity but only to purge the Church of corrupt practices."

> Cardinal Kasper said: "We have much to learn from Luther, beginning with the importance he attached to the word of God." It was time for a "more positive" view of Luther, whose reforms had aroused papal ire at the time but could now be seen as having "anticipated aspects of reform which the Church has adopted over time."

The Vatican also announced plans to erect a statue of Galileo in 2009 to honor the 400th anniversary of his discovery of the telescope.[16]

Muslim scholars were invited to meet with the Pontifical Council for Inter-Religious Dialogue in Rome to begin laying the groundwork for a meeting between the pope and leading Muslims.[17] The Vatican announced the pope would pray for the redemption of Islamic terrorists "consumed by hate" when he visits Ground Zero—described as what would be the "emotional highpoint" of his trip—asking God to "put them on the path of love" instead. The Vatican hastened to add this was not a call for the conversion of Islamic extremists to Christianity. The Vatican also reassured Muslims that the pope's very public and widely reported baptism of a Muslim convert at Easter was not part of "a new crusade" against Islam.[18]

Concerned about the discord between the pope and Jews, the USCCB planned two private meetings for Benedict with rabbis and other Jewish leaders in Washington and New York. The Vatican expressed its "respect and esteem" for Jews and Judaism "before Pope Benedict XVI's forthcoming tour of the United States."

> The statement said that the Holy See was "confident that changes made to certain expressions [in the Good Friday liturgy] did not have as their intention, in any way whatsoever, to show a change in the Catholic Church's attitude towards the Jews." It added that the Vatican "repeats its strong desire that the progress made in mutual comprehension and respect between Jews and Christians over recent years will grow further."[19]

In February 2008, the Pew Forum on Religion & Public Life released a study showing the number of Americans (16.1 percent) unaffiliated with any religion was increasing.

> Catholicism experienced the greatest net losses.... While nearly one-in-three Americans (31 percent) were raised in the Catholic faith, today fewer than one-in-four (24 percent) describe themselves as Catholic. This means that roughly 10 percent of all Americans are former Catholics.... Latinos, who already account for roughly one-in-three adult Catholics, account for nearly half of all Catholics ages 18-29 (45 percent).

Speaking in English to pilgrims in St. Peter's Square the Sunday before he left Rome, Ratzinger received applause from priests on the plaza waving American flags: "Dear brothers and sisters, I ask you all to pray for the success of my visit, so that it may be a time of spiritual renewal for all Americans."

Preparations were under way on this side of the Atlantic and US taxpayers were paying the bulk of expenses, including security, surrounding the papal tour. The local governments justified their expenditures by anticipating revenues to be generated by tourist spending. Part of the costs would be paid by the archdioceses of Washington and New York.[20]

Washington's Archbishop Donald W. Wuerl said parish and diocesan money would not be used and he raised more than $3 million from undisclosed wealthy donors. The spokesman for New York's Cardinal Edward Egan said they would also seek support from wealthy donors but the cardinal was unconcerned about using parish donations despite the archdiocese's other financial needs. "People in the archdiocese welcome an opportunity to help support a tremendous moment in the history of the archdiocese."[21]

The news media, especially cable news networks which planned to provide round-the-clock live coverage, lined up their commentators, reporters and equipment to capture every minute of the scheduled public events. "The visit is a news event that also serves as a kind of running infomercial for the Vatican: theologians and priests recruited to provide their expertise about the papal mission also relish the opportunity to move beyond scandals and advance the Church's message," explained the *New York Times*.[22] Both DC and New York police departments set up barricades to create penned-in areas for protesters, including the victims of clerical sex abuse and their supporters, out of sight of the pope and the TV cameras.

Hosting the Vicar of Christ

The president, Mrs. Bush and their daughter, Jenna, drove out to Andrews Air Force Base to personally greet Ratzinger, an honor not bestowed on any other dignitary before or since. (Bush had also been the only sitting president to attend a pope's funeral.) There was a military honor guard, a receiving line of officials including a slew of American hierarchs and about 800 invitation-only guests.

Benedict XVI, Vicar of Christ on Earth, traveled with a 30-man entourage of Roman Curia officials, liturgical advisers, doctors, media experts and security personnel.[23] The Roman monarch received an official greeting on the South Lawn of the White House including a 21-gun-salute and the playing of both national anthems. An estimated 13,500 persons, the largest crowd of the Bush presidency, were present to greet His Holiness. Catholic members of Congress, 146 in all, were present but the neo-Catholic Supreme Court justices were in session and unable to attend. The best seats in the audience were reserved for Catholic prelates.

Bush's speechwriters relied heavily on Roman Catholic sources.

- "Americans believe that the measure of a free society is *how we treat the weakest and most vulnerable* among us." (Catholic social justice)

- "Here in America you'll find a nation that welcomes the role of faith in *the public square*," from Fr. Neuhaus's book, *The Naked Public Square,* denouncing the absence of religion in civic life and adopted by the religious right as a blueprint to impose their morality on the entire nation.

- "When our Founders declared our nation's independence, they rested their case on an appeal to the *'laws of nature, and of nature's God.'* We believe in *religious liberty*. We also believe that a love for freedom and a *common moral law are written into every human heart.*" A book by Fr. John Courtney Murray S.J., *We Hold These Truths: Catholic Reflections on the American Proposition*, posited that the Declaration of Independence—self-evident truths, man is endowed by his Creator with certain unalienable rights—was an expression of the Catholic doctrine of Natural Law, defined as "a common moral law written into every human heart." Murray's work was also the basis of the Vatican II document on religious liberty reversing the centuries-old Vatican position that Catholicism should be a state-sponsored religion imposed by a civic government obedient to the pope.

- "We need your message to reject this *'dictatorship of relativism,'*" a phrase invented and often used by Benedict which, when distilled to its basic message, means that any position opposing his has been imposed on and accepted by the intellectually weak, easily swayed by relativistic (and transitory) ideas.

Predictably, the pre-selected guests burst into applause when Bush told the pope that Americans "need your message that all life is sacred," a shared code that only unborn life matters.

On Fox News, Shepard Smith underlined the religious congeniality between President Bush and the pope, whom he described as an "honorary Republican." And Msgr. James Lisante, a Fox News contributor, told Mr. Smith that he detected a political message buried in the pope's speech. "If Senator Obama or Hillary Clinton are listening to the speech and want the Catholic vote, and they clearly do, then they have to know what the Holy Father is saying: 'The sanctity of life is very important to us,'" he said. And if they do not pay attention, Monsignor Lisante warned, "then we can't take you seriously either." Actually, it was Mr. Bush who said "all human life is sacred." At the White House, Benedict did not mention the church's position on abortion or birth control.[24]

The pontiff and president had a short, private meeting in the Oval Office, after which the Vatican and White House press office issued a joint statement listing the same impossibly long list of topics as purportedly discussed during Bush's audience at the Vatican the preceding July.

Benedict was driven to the nunciature for a private luncheon with US cardinals, the presidium of the USCCB and his Roman entourage. They dined on china hand-painted with the papal insignia and made in Italy especially for the occasion. The table linens were also specially designed.

There were "baroque-style goblets of red, blue and green—flown in from Florence—at each setting and beautiful bouquets of white, yellow, pink and peach roses sitting on the runner." As the restaurateur hired to prepare the meal described it, "There was a feeling of power in the room." At the end, a four foot by three foot cake decorated with a replica of St. Peter's Square and the pope's image was wheeled in as the guests sang "Happy Birthday."[25]

A rare State Dinner was held to honor the pope. Michael Novak was looking forward to attending: "There's going to be Catholic leaders in town from all over the country for the pope's visit, and by and large these people have been very strong supporters of President Bush. It was too good a political opportunity to miss."[26] About 250 guests were invited to the Bavarian-themed menu including the 2008 Republican candidate for president, Sen. John McCain, (a televised debate with Democratic contenders was held the same evening), Speaker of the House Nancy Pelosi, Chief Justice John Roberts and Justices Antonin Scalia, Anthony Kennedy, Clarence Thomas and Samuel Alito; also House Minority Leader John Boehner, Carl Anderson, Supreme Knight of the Knights of Columbus, George Weigel, and more than 20 members of the Catholic clergy from around the country.[27] Benedict declined to attend even though there were no competing events on his schedule. (A prayer-service was scheduled with the US episcopate early in evening which could have been moved-up to an earlier time.) Vatican officials attributed his refusal to the pontiff's advanced age and need for rest.

The few non-officials allowed to meet the pope while he was in the US were as carefully pre-selected and screened as his encounters with the press. Before leaving Washington, the US bishops gave the pope a check for $870,000 for his personal use.[28]

When Benedict moved on to New York,

> A fleet of US military helicopters was arrayed near the papal plane parking slot [at Kennedy Airport], prepared to fly Pope Benedict, his entourage and some members of the media to the Wall Street heliport. From the heliport, the papal motorcade had just over a mile of Manhattan streets to travel to reach the United Nations for the pope's first appointment in the city.[29]

Just as George W. Bush admonished other countries for their failings in maintaining "democracy and freedom," Benedict spoke to the assembled diplomats at the UN about human rights, human dignity, and religious freedom although less than a year earlier, one hundred Catholic German theologians signed a letter challenging Benedict to allow theologians more freedom. The letter's content was originally written as an article by a retired professor of the University of Tübingen who wrote that the Congregation for the Doctrine of the Faith was still organized in much the same way as when it was known as the Holy Inquisition, as a body for exercising censorship.[30] Within a month after Ratzinger's UN address, the Vatican issued a ban on the US tour of Australian Bishop Geoffrey Robinson, invited by lay Catholics to discuss his new book, *Confronting Power and Sex in the Catholic Church: Reclaiming the Spirit of Jesus*. As instructed, the US hierarchy barred the retired bishop from speaking to his American audiences on Church property.

Benedicts's address to the UN General Assembly was commonly described as "densely-packed." He usually speaks and writes in convoluted "Vaticanese" which requires careful reading to understand. His meaning was clear, however, when he had addressed the US episcopate at Washington's Shrine of the Immaculate Conception two days before:

> Any tendency to treat religion as a private matter must be resisted....Far from a Catholic approach to "thinking with the Church," each person [erroneously] believes he or she has a right to pick and choose.

In his homily at New York's Yankee Stadium, Ratzinger advocated

> authority ... obedience. To be frank, these are not easy words to speak nowadays. Words like these represent a "stumbling stone" for many of our contemporaries....

Benedict's impact at the UN—if any—was short-lived. On June 4, 2008, the General Assembly elected by acclamation a Catholic priest, Miguel d'Escoto Brockman, as president of the upcoming session beginning in September. A proponent of the liberation theology despised by Ratzinger, d'Escoto had served as Nicaraguan foreign minister. Ordained as a Maryknoll priest before assuming his post in the Sandinista government, d'Escoto once called Reagan "the butcher of my people" and George W. Bush his "spiritual heir."[31]

The selection of a Central American politician opposed to Vatican-supported right-wing governments may have been a backlash against an action taken in May by the Holy See's UN mission. The mission awarded its 2008 Path to Peace Award to Salvadoran President Elias Antonio Saca Gonzales. Saca is a member of the Nationalist Republican Alliance (ARENA) Party, founded in 1982 by the late Roberto D'Aubuisson who was judged by a UN war crimes commission to be responsible for thousands of death squad murders and as the "intellectual author" of the assassination of Archbishop Oscar Romero.

Benedict met briefly with Muslim, Buddhist, Hindu and Jain religious leaders while he was in Washington and a short ecumenical prayer service was held with other Christian denominations at St. Joseph's Church in Manhattan where he expressed "my sincere appreciation for the invaluable work of all those engaged in ecumenism."

His major fence-mending was directed at American Jews. In

addition to a private meeting in the nation's capital with Jewish leaders, the pope briefly visited a New York Synagogue after his UN address. Among the invited guests were Lloyd C. Blankfein, chairman and chief executive at Goldman Sachs; former Mayor Edward I. Koch; Ronald Lauder, the businessman and philanthropist who is president of the World Jewish Congress; Jerome Lauren, senior vice president of Ralph Lauren; Stephen A. Schwarzman, chief executive of the Blackstone Group, a major private equity firm; Asaf Shariv, Israel's consul general in New York; and James D. Wolfensohn, a former chairman of the World Bank. "He was very sincere in expressing his wish for improved relations between our faiths," said Philip Weisberg, a finance executive. "This is someone who represents a huge group of people, so this is historic."[32]

Historic or not, Rabbi James Rudin wrote in the *New York Times*: "In Washington, [the pope] ...delivered only a small portion of his prepared remarks. The symbolism was rich; the substance was not. In New York City...the pope again spoke very briefly and failed to mention his Church's vigorous condemnation of anti-Semitism or the Vatican commitment for Catholics to reverently remember and teach about the Holocaust."[33]

Addressing Sex Abuse and Immigration

Being advised the subject of the sex abuse scandal could not be avoided, Benedict prepared statements for several occasions. On board the flight from Rome, he gave scripted responses to selected written questions submitted in advance: "I am ashamed and we will do everything possible to ensure that this does not happen in future." During his address to the US hierarchy at the National Shrine of the Immaculate Conception, his sermon given at the Mass at Nationals Stadium and a sermon at the Mass held in New York's St. Patrick's Cathedral for clergy and religious, Benedict remained consistent with all his other remarks during the first four years of his reign regarding the sexual abuse of children—only priests were at fault, prelates bear no responsibility, the clergy are suffering due to the acts of a few, and nothing more than conciliatory speeches should be expected from the Vatican. The US episcopate had been given the green light to continue pouring all their resources into concealing, obfuscating and denying justice to their victims.

Described as the high point of his six-day visit, Benedict met with five survivors of clerical sex abuse who had been pre-screened and pre-interviewed. The event had not been listed on the official itinerary and— given that he and his predecessors have shunned all contact with their victims—it was a surprising moment. Boston's Cardinal O'Malley, one of the few prelates who understands the depth of the revulsion caused by the scandal, had strenuously lobbied for these 25 minutes out of a six-day tour. (Papal press secretary, Fr. Lombardi, told the press the pope had requested the meeting.)[34] O'Malley presented Benedict with a large book with the names of 1500 boys and girls written in calligraphy, victims from the Boston archdiocese alone. It was reported Benedict was genuinely touched by the gesture.

Afterwards, several of the victims described the pope as being sincerely moved by their meeting as did the family members of some of those who were killed on September 11, 2001, after they met with Benedict at Ground Zero. When he spoke, the phrase "Islamic terrorists consumed by hate" was omitted and instead Benedict prayed for "peace in the hearts of all men and women [asking God to] turn to your way of love those whose hearts and minds are consumed with hatred."

The second most frequently mentioned subject in the pope's US addresses after the brutalization of Catholic children, was immigration. Benedict spoke several times of the need to protect family unity threatened by deportations and about the need to protect immigrants' human rights. During the huge spectacles at both Nationals and Yankee Stadiums some of the Bible passages were read in Spanish and the pope spoke briefly in that language. "Accusing the pope of 'faith-based marketing,' [Rep. Tom Tancredo (R-Colo.)] said Benedict's comments welcoming immigrants 'may have less to do with spreading the Gospel than they do about recruiting new members of the Church.'"[35]

Assessments of Benedict's Visit

The American press used the Pew study's reported exodus of native-born Americans from the Catholic Church as background for Benedict's tour. Two April 14 front-page headlines read: "Pope's US visit seen as pivotal" (*Chicago Tribune*) and "In US, a Pained and Uncertain Church Awaits the Pope" (*New York Times*). A *TIME* magazine article also dated April 14 put the challenge more bluntly: "Benedict's arrival in the US is being seen as a make-or-break moment for Rome to regain the trust of its American flock."[36]

The mainstream media held to that story line during the trip. The Pew Forum on Religion & Public Life and the Project for Excellence in Journalism studied the news coverage afforded Benedict April 14-20. The major findings were:

- The pope's visit accounted for 16 percent of the overall "newshole," the time or space available in an outlet for news content. In the first four months of 2008, the only stories that received more coverage during a single week were the presidential campaign, the US economy and the Eliot Spitzer sex scandal.

- Out of all the newshole dedicated to the pope's visit, more than half (54 percent) was comprised of stories that focused on the impact of the clergy sex abuse scandal and/or the relationship between the pope and American Catholics.

Media coverage largely ignored the pope's relationships with other groups. Just one percent focused on the pope's meeting with other religious leaders, and only three percent focused on the pope's relation with the Bush administration or the pope and American politics. Only two percent of the coverage made any reference to the presidential campaign.[37]

Benedict successfully mitigated much of the antagonism generated by the sex abuse scandal in the general public including uninformed Catholics. Polls conducted following his visit showed the same immediate upsurge in Catholic self-identity and Mass attendance as follows a World Youth Day event. A survey conducted by the Knights of Columbus the week following Benedict's visit (between April 22-29, 2008), stated 54 percent of Catholics were "more in touch with their spiritual values as a result of the pope's visit, and 41 percent said they were more likely to vote in the November elections,"[38] thus fulfilling the underlying political purpose of the pope's visit.

Not only Catholics but all Americans were the intended audience. The display of affection and admiration between the pontiff, held in generally high regard by Americans, and the president was meant to, at least subliminally, bolster the image of Bush and, by extension, all Republican politicians. As Michael Novak wrote,

> The warmth of feeling for the pope was tangible, and so was the good chemistry between the pope and President George Bush. The warm feeling was very powerful. Both president and pope looked very happy....
>
> [Bush] has done his best to soak up Catholic wisdom and Catholic ways of thinking about things. I don't think we are ever going to get a more Catholic president. Even the *Washington Post* said the other day that he is the "first Catholic president."[39]

Richard Mouw, president of Fuller Theological Seminary and a supporter of Evangelicals and Catholics Together (ECT), used the occasion to write of the closeness evangelicals have with the pope. "He was a big hit, not only with grassroots Catholics, but also with the larger American population, even with the non-religious. He was firm in his basic convictions without coming across as cranky. This won over many who were not sure what to expect."[40]

For Benedict, it was in his own best interest to be gracious to the only world leader who supported his positions on abortion, stem-cell research and same-sex marriage and the nominal leader of his largest bloc of donors. As news accounts repeatedly pointed out, the pontiff and president had disagreed over the Iraq War but the pope made no direct mention of their differences on the subject while he was in the US. As journalist Francis X. Rocca noted: "It would be uncharacteristically undiplomatic of any pope to let past differences get in the way of constructive collaboration with a world superpower." Fr. Thomas J. Reese S.J., a senior fellow at Georgetown University's Woodstock Theological Center, and author of *Inside the Vatican* concurred: "The Vatican knows how to agree and disagree with heads of state and work with them anyway. It's got a big agenda." Neo-Catholic Fr. Joseph Fessio S.J., head of Ignatius Press, Benedict's principal English-language publisher, explained: "In terms of authentic, normative Catholic teaching, I don't see any area in which the pope and President Bush disagree. Iraq is not a matter of Catholic social teaching. That was a prudential decision on whether or not the use of force was justified. The pope would be the first to tell you that good Catholics can disagree on that."[41]

It was left to progressive lay Catholics to note that, like John Paul II, Benedict's papal "culture of life" blessings had been extended to those who care nothing for the living.

> Can the pope possibly be so suffused with his peculiar brand of theology that he is oblivious to what happened when he was a young man during the Third Reich. Is it possible that papal advisers forgot to tell him that the post-WWII Nuremberg Tribunal described an unprovoked war of aggression, of the kind that the Third Reich and George W. Bush launched, as the "supreme international crime, differing from other war crimes only in that it contains the accumulated evil of the whole?" Could they have failed to tell the pope he would be hobnobbing with war criminals, torturers and the enabling cowards in Congress who refuse to remove them from office? For this Catholic, it was a profoundly sad spectacle—profoundly sad.[42]

Some Catholics [43] were also aghast at Benedict's placing full blame on the priests while failing to acknowledge the bishops' criminal conspiracy in the "raping, sodomizing and sexual terrorizing of thousands of boys and girls."

> Overall, the coverage of the visitor once known as "God's Rottweiler" was clearly aimed at bringing us a redeemed Pope Benedict—a "really nice guy," "humble," "sweet," "kindly," "shy," and "a good listener who loves dialogue."
>
> Given that, kudos go to the newscasters who provided some historical context. ABC Evening News deserves credit for Dan Harris's reminder of Benedict's original public reaction when the sex abuse scandals broke in 2002, when the most comfort he could offer was to say: "Always temptations of human beings are present. Also for the priests, so always we have to accept that." And credit goes to Good Morning America's Brian Ross for a

report on the 19 bishops and cardinals accused of abuse or cover-up of abuse who had neither lost their titles nor been prosecuted; his prime example was the cushy fate of former Palm Beach, Florida, Bishop Anthony J. O'Connell, who admitted to sexually abusing a teenage seminary student and is now comfortably ensconced in a lovely Trappist Abbey.[44]

In Italy, the state media network, RAI, hosted a panel discussion on the pope's US trip. Present were Cardinal Pio Laghi, the former pro-nuncio to the US; Gian Maria Vian, director of *L'Osservatore Romano*, the Vatican newspaper; Greg Burke of the Fox News Channel and John L. Allen Jr. of the *National Catholic Reporter*. During the program, they responded to listener phone calls and e-mails.

> Why, host Massimo Franco and the listeners wanted to know, didn't Benedict XVI make more of an issue out of the difference between the United States, particularly the Bush administration, and the Catholic Church on the issue of capital punishment?....For Italians, it seems equally shocking that Benedict came to the United States, one of just six nations which account for the bulk of annual executions worldwide, and didn't bring up capital punishment.
> For many Italian Catholics, and perhaps Catholics in other European countries as well, the death penalty is what abortion is for many Catholics in the United States—the defining moral issue of the time....
> After the failure of a Vatican-backed referendum to overturn the Italian law [allowing abortion] in 1981, many Italian Catholics have made their peace with the situation. Despite periodic rumors of moves to amend the abortion statute, the Church has generally not invested tremendous social capital in those efforts. Instead, it has concentrated its political muscle elsewhere, for example in a successful campaign in 2005 to invalidate a referendum that would have liberalized in vitro fertilization....
> For American Catholics, this focus on the death penalty rather than abortion can often seem terribly imbalanced. According to Amnesty International, there were 1,591 executions worldwide in 2006, while the estimated number of abortions around the world each year is on the order of 45 million....
> For Italian Catholics, on the other hand, the moral gravity of the death penalty often looms larger because in this case the state is not merely tolerating an act of killing,

but actually performing it. It's one thing, they argue, for women in painful circumstances to make a tragic choice; it's another for a state, which purports to embody the values of civilized society, to put someone to death while espousing the values of justice and due process of law. From that point of view, it's not so much the numbers involved, as the statement capital punishment makes about the moral fabric of the state itself that jars the conscience.[45]

The meeting with the victims and Benedict's repeated request that they be treated with compassion did, in fact, help change the tenor of the neo-Catholic American press. There was a diminution in the constant portrayal of the survivors as greedy vultures out to destroy the Church and instead, articles appeared which acknowledged their suffering. Even Russell Shaw, former spokesman for the USCCB and the Knights of Columbus and member of Opus Dei who described himself as the ultimate "company man" for right-wing Catholicism, wrote a book, *Nothing To Hide: Secrecy, Communication, and Communion in the Catholic Church* in which he discussed "the abuse of secrecy in the Church, the scandals it has caused and the serious problem of mistrust that exists in the credibility of the Church."

But nothing changed for the pope and his prelates. Benedict's words encouraging bishops to care for the abused were for public consumption only. US nuncio, Archbishop Pietro Sambi, in a post-visit interview, stated Benedict responded to the "rumor" that bishops "who handled cases badly" were never disciplined by the Church without offering one example that this had ever happened. Nor, according to Sambi, would any such action become necessary in the future since the bishops guilty of any wrongdoing were already replaced. "The bishops of today are really honest and engaged in solving this problem," he lied.[46]

Sambi referred to the pre-approved script read at the pope's meeting with his prelates in Washington which had included the tepid admission that the situation was "sometimes very badly handled by the bishops." This statement was read by Cardinal Francis George, president of the USCCB, and the archbishop of Chicago who had rejected the advice of his own review board to remove Fr. Daniel McCormick from ministry thereby allowing him to sexually abuse more children in 2005.

Regarding Benedict meeting with victims, Sambi couldn't have been more offensive: "We're helping these people who really need help—not those who are trying to gain money...."[47] After Benedict's meeting with George and the other bishops, one victim spoke for millions: "We were hoping for a reprimand. He was looking into the faces of the men who were directly responsible, and instead of a reprimand, he praised them."[48]

In fact, Benedict continues to reward men willing to overlook the sexual perversions of priests and religious or who are themselves guilty of molesting minors. Ratzinger named Cardinal William J. Levada as his replacement as head of the Congregation for the Doctrine of the Faith which, in addition to censorship, is the body responsible for judging priests accused of sexual abuse. Prior to his appointment in Rome, Levada was Archbishop of San Francisco. The founding chairman of the board he appointed to review allegations of clerical sex abuse resigned in 2004 accusing diocesan leaders, including Levada, of "deception, manipulation and control." The chairman said Levada blocked the release of their findings on allegations involving 40 priests.[49] Benedict also promoted Bishop Gerhard Ludwig Müller of Regensburg to the Congregation for the Doctrine of the Faith after Müller had reassigned a parish priest who was already convicted in 2000 and later re-arrested for suspected sexual abuse of children committed between 2003 and 2006.[50] Benedict named Philadelphia's Cardinal Justin Rigali to the powerful Congregation for Bishops (the department in charge of selecting prelates worldwide) in spite of Rigali's official response to the Philadelphia Grand Jury Report: "[W]e cannot accept the inference that there was any intentional unlawful or criminal behavior on the part of officials of the archdiocese."[51] The pope sent a handwritten anniversary congratulations to Polish Archbishop Juliusz Paetz who resigned after it was disclosed he sexually molested seminarians. Benedict thanked him for his "saving work for the good of the Church" and the prelate has had several recent audiences with the pontiff.[52]

Immediately on his return to Rome, Benedict promoted to archbishop Baltimore's Bishop Edwin O'Brien, the former head of US military chaplains who had fired victims' advocate and Air Force chaplain, Fr. Thomas Doyle, J.C.D., C.A.D.C., just before he was eligible for retirement. The pope also promptly promoted St. Louis Archbishop Raymond Burke, the first US hierarch to deny communion to John Kerry, as head of the Apostolic Signatura, the Church's "Supreme Court," although for the past several years Burke had invited dozens of proven, admitted, and/or credibly accused priests from around the country to live cost-free at his Church-run facilities without adequate supervision and allowing some to work in parishes.[53]

> With Burke's appointment, three important Vatican offices are now led by Americans....That's a clear sign of appreciation for the American Church, a sentiment especially strong in Rome these days in the wake of what was considered a remarkably successful visit to America by Benedict XVI in April.
>
> Broadly speaking, many senior Vatican officials are deeply pessimistic about the direction of the European Union, which they see as in the grip of a radical form of secularism. In that context, Vatican officials increasingly see the United States as their most natural conversation partner in global affairs—a major world power shaped by the Christian heritage, home to the fourth largest Catholic community in the world, with a civil society in

which Churches are taken seriously and faith is afforded a vibrant public voice. The appointment of another American is confirmation of a tendency to look across the Atlantic for leadership.[54]

CHAPTER 17

THE 2008 PRESIDENTIAL CAMPAIGN

More than any election in the past generation, the security and welfare of the United States of America was at stake in the 2008 Presidential Election. The majority of voters were horrified at what had been wrought by the "religious" right during the past eight years.

Summation of the Bush Presidency

Iraq

The number of deaths attributable to the US invasion stood at 4,274 Americans, 318 coalition troops, 139 journalists and 1264 contractors. Over 30,000 US troops were wounded.[1] The number of ensuing suicides among Iraq veterans has been extraordinarily high and is only now beginning to be quantified. The impact on the spouses, children and extended family members of the killed and physically and mentally wounded is inestimable.

More than 100,000 Iraqis have died from violence since the 2003 invasion.[2] This is a minimal estimate since thousands of Iraqis are still missing and civilians were buried without official records. Indirect deaths due to destruction of the Iraqi infrastructure (water, electricity, etc.) health care and stress are also not included.[3] Also not counted is the displacement of millions of Iraqis into refugee camps in bordering countries and the subsequent deaths occurring outside the country.

Torture and Deaths of Detainees

More than 750 people had been detained at Guantánamo Bay, most rounded up by US-paid bounty hunters. Thousands of detainees remained in US custody in Iraq and Afghanistan (the number peaked at 26,000 in 2007), and the US government held an unknown number of detainees in secret custody in unknown locations and unknown conditions in other countries.[4]

About 100 detainees died while in US custody. "Of these, 34 are suspected or confirmed homicides. People were beaten to death at Bagram Airbase and Abu Ghraib using techniques authorized by the

Bush administration."[5] At least three dozen who were held in foreign CIA prisons were missing. "Efforts by human rights organizations to track their whereabouts have been unsuccessful, and no foreign governments have acknowledged holding them."[6]

Not every death was a foreign national. American soldier Alyssa Peterson, an Arab-speaking interrogator assigned to the prison at a US airbase in Iraq, committed suicide on September 15, 2003, after refusing to take part in torture. "She said that she did not know how to be two people; she...could not be one person in the cage and another outside the wire."[7]

Deaths on the Border

The number of southern border-crossing deaths more than doubled between 1995 and 2005 with the percentage of female decedents more than doubling according to an August 2006 report by the Government Accounting Office (GAO). The annual number of deaths increased from 241 in 1999 to 472 deaths recorded in 2005. This increase in deaths occurred despite the fact there had been a decreasing number of illegal entries. While the estimated number of undocumented entries fell 15.9 percent between 1998 and 2004, the number of border-crossing deaths per year increased by 29.1 percent.[8]

The rise in deaths was "the direct result of more agents, more fencing and more equipment" the Rev. Robin Hoover, founder of the Tucson-based Humane Borders, told the *Associated Press*. "The migrants are walking in more treacherous terrain for longer periods of time, and you should expect more deaths."

The New Poverty

Legislation enacted under the Bush administration had made the distribution of income more unequal as shown in data from the Congressional Budget Office (CBO). "Because high-income households received by far the largest tax cuts—not only in dollar terms but also as a percentage of income—the tax cuts have increased the concentration of after-tax income at the top of the spectrum. In 2006, after-tax incomes rose by more than twice the rate among the top 1 percent of households than among any other income group. The average household in the top 1 percent had an income of $1.2 million, up $63,000 just from the prior year. This $63,000 gain is nearly two times the *total* income of the average middle-income household. By 2006, top incomes were 23.0 times higher than those of the middle fifth of American households. This income amounts to approximately $61 billion in additional income for the top 1 percent."[9]

A world-wide economic crisis unknown since the Great Depression, caused in large part by lack of government regulation and oversight, began in 2008. Poverty results in not only a decrease in health care but an increase in stress, crime and domestic violence. Does a decrease in the quality of air, food (The most recent salmonella outbreak involving peanut butter sickened nearly 500 people and killed 10. Others involved baby formula, spinach, jalapenos, cooked ham, etc.[10]), water and recreation, obstruction of worker and product safety (Each year about 28,000 deaths and over 33 million injuries are associated with consumer products.[11]) and the lack of affordable health care have a cumulative effect? Of 225 countries listed in the *CIA World Factbook,* 45 had lower Infant Mortality Rates than the US. From the same source, the overall death rate (number of deaths divided by population) in the US was higher than both the world average and 117 other countries, meaning millions of US babies, children and adults would still be alive if they had had the good fortune to have been born in one of the other countries listed, many of them Muslim or socialist.

Abortions

There were approximately 9,856,900 abortions during George W. Bush's two terms according to estimates by the National Right to Life[12] even with billions of dollars pumped into Republican agencies for abstinence education, pregnancy counseling and legal and political challenges to the right of women to have an abortion. Since 89 per cent of US abortions occur in the first 12 weeks of pregnancy, those who agree with the ambiguity of traditional Christianity as do the majority of European nations, including Italy, would posit the vast majority of abortions involved no "person" other than a pregnant woman. Some small number of the remaining 11 percent would be due to women exercising the same right to self-defense the Catholic Church reserves to males or serious abnormalities resulting in death of the fetus or certain death of the newborn. They would also point out the solid correlation between poverty and abortion since the abortion rate among women living below the federal poverty level is more than four times that of wealthy women.[13]

Some anti-abortionists sincerely accept as true that a human being is created at the moment of conception and act on their belief by offering care to pregnant women and babies, even to adopting children themselves. What separates a Republican "pro-lifer" from a Democrat or Independent is that while they claim a zygote, embryo or fetus has a right to life, for Republicans that right is extinguished as soon as a baby draws its first breath. From that point on, the death of all human beings becomes "negotiable" or can be justified by political expediency, greed and neglect. It is the silence of so-called "moral" leaders on post-partum death and suffering, or their defense of those who cause misery and destruction, which makes words like *hypocrisy* and *sinful* inadequate.

The Campaign Begins

Among the leading Republican presidential candidates, former Gov. Mitt Romney, a Mormon, represented the big-money wing of the GOP and had the support of most neo-Catholics. Sen. Sam Brownback, although a Catholic, wasn't sufficiently pliable nor was he as well known. As a pro-choice Catholic, former New York Mayor Rudy Giuliani, was unacceptable.

Former Baptist minister and governor of Arkansas, Mike Huckabee, was clearly the evangelical favorite. But Romney and Huckabee split the religious right and Sen. John McCain won the Republican primaries. When Karl Rove was asked if McCain matched George W. Bush's appeal to "faith-based" voters, he replied, "He does not."[14] Paul Weyrich, progenitor of the religious right, stated early in the campaign he would vote for a third-party candidate before he would vote for McCain probably because the senator had written in his book, *Worth the Fighting For*.

> Weyrich possesses the attributes of a Dickensian villain. Corpulent and dyspeptic, his mouth set in a perpetual sneer as if life in general were an unpleasant experience, he is the embodiment of the caricature often used to unfairly malign all religious conservatives. I like to think I know a pompous, self-serving son of a bitch when I see one.[15]

Regardless of Weyrich's personal feelings, as expected in early March "100 prominent Catholics nationwide have come together to support John McCain for President" because they would back the GOP presidential candidate no matter who it was. (If Giuliani had won the nominee he would have become a "pro-lifer" just as Romney had done.) The National Catholics for McCain Committee was co-chaired by Brownback and former Oklahoma Gov. Frank Keating. In addition to former Secretary of State Alexander Haig, of the other nine members comprising the Leadership Committee, four were current or former elected officials from Ohio and three were Cuban-Americans from Florida including Sen. Mel Martinez. It was Martinez aide and legal counsel, Brian H. Darling, who admitted writing the memo spelling out the political advantages for Republicans to intervene in the case of Terri Schiavo.[16]

Familiar names on the National Catholics for McCain Steering Committee included Princeton Law Professor Robert P. George; Martin Gillespie, former director of Catholic Outreach for the Republican National Committee; Frank Hanna III from Atlanta; Deal Hudson; John Klink, former Vatican diplomat; Thomas Melady, former US Ambassador to the Holy See; Tom Monaghan, founder of the Ave Maria groups and schools; Cathy Ruse, former chief pro-life spokesperson for the US Conference of Catholic Bishops; and high ranking officials from the Ave Maria School of Law, Catholic University of America Columbus School of Law and the Franciscan University of Steubenville. Of the ten members of the Catholic Students For McCain Leadership Committee, six were from these three schools.[17]

"These are the usual suspects," said Chris Korzen, executive director of the progressive Catholics United. "In general terms, these are folks who have a history of putting partisan politics ahead of the teachings of their faith. It is more of the same, and if they were serious about being engaged Catholics they would be challenging McCain on the war and torture where McCain is not on the side of Catholic theology."[18]

Catholics United was one of several groups of progressive Catholics who had learned an important lesson in the 2004 election and this time were ready to counter the neo-Catholic noise machine early on. When Hudson wrote some articles praising McCain, Catholics United issued a public letter to the senator: "Deal Hudson is not the type of Catholic leader you want publicly associated with your campaign," referring to the well publicized lawsuit Hudson settled with the 18-year-old coed from Fordham University.[19] After losing his position as editor of *Crisis* magazine due to the public disgrace, Hudson formed his own website, InsideCatholic.com, to peddle such items as his 5-CD set. Hudson claimed it would provide purchasers with "every fact" they "need to expose and refute the Left's attacks on Christians in politics" because "an attack on the religious right is actually an attack" on faithful Catholics.[20]

There was a real threat, however, that with McCain as the party's standard-bearer, evangelicals might decide to sit this one out. To make his candidacy more attractive to this faction, the McCain campaign heavily courted John Hagee for his endorsement. Hagee was pastor of the Cornerstone Church in San Antonio, Texas, a non-denominational evangelical community with more than 18,000 members. As president and CEO of John Hagee Ministries, the preacher reached a television and radio audience of 99 million homes.

Hagee was also leader and founder of the politically powerful group, Christians United for Israel (CUFI) whose main focus is winning a war against Islam. "If a line has to be drawn, draw it around Christians and Jews. We are united," Hagee had declared. "It is time for America to...consider a military preemptive strike against Iran to prevent a nuclear holocaust in Israel and a nuclear attack in America," exhorted the preacher.[21]

Religious conservatives had been put off by tales of McCain's temper, and by his ungallant termination of his first marriage. They remembered how he had lashed out against their own in 2000, condemning Pat Robertson and Jerry Falwell as "agents of intolerance," and likening them to Louis Farrakhan and the Reverend Al Sharpton. "I am convinced Senator McCain is not a conservative, and, in fact, has gone out of his way to stick his thumb in the eyes of those who are," the evangelical leader James Dobson said in a statement read to a national radio audience on Super Tuesday. "I cannot and I will not vote for Senator John McCain, as a matter of conscience."

That week, religious conservatives helped deliver six states to the former Baptist minister Mike Huckabee. When Hagee's endorsement came three weeks later, McCain hoped that it might begin to repair his relationship with the religious right.[22]

McCain succeeded in getting Hagee to agree to a joint appearance and at the media event arranged by his campaign, the senator and pastor exchanged a hug and the usual mutual praise and pleasantries. The press asked McCain some standard campaign questions. When someone asked McCain what he thought about Hagee's views on the end of the world McCain was baffled and could only reply, "All I can tell you is that I'm very proud to have Pastor John Hagee's support. He has support and respect throughout the nation, and, uh, I've continued to appreciate his support and his advocacy for the freedom and independence of the state of Israel."[23]

The campaign, however, had failed to look deeper into Hagee's background before soliciting his endorsement. When reports of the meeting included examples of Hagee's inflammatory rhetoric such as calling the Roman Catholic Church "the Great Whore of Babylon" and accusing the Church of supporting Adolf Hitler, McCain at first repeated, "I'm very proud to have Pastor John Hagee's support," and then added defensively, "I don't have to agree with everyone that endorses my candidacy."[24]

The Catholic League's Bill Donohue complained about McCain seeking the approval of "the biggest anti-Catholic bigot in the evangelical community."

Former head of the Christian Coalition, Ralph Reed, suggested that Hagee contact Deal Hudson for damage control and Hudson instructed Hagee to write a letter of apology to Donohue and to meet with him. Hudson also arranged for Hagee to meet with 22 Catholic Republicans, after which Hagee issued the statement: "Out of a desire to advance greater unity among Catholics and Evangelicals in promoting the common good, I want to express my deep regret for any comments that Catholics have found hurtful. After engaging in constructive dialogue with Catholic friends and leaders, I now have an improved understanding of the Catholic Church, its relation to the Jewish faith, and the history of anti-Catholicism."[25]

In May, an article quoted a sermon by Hagee stating the Holocaust was part of God's plan to bring the Jews back to Palestine before the apocalypse. McCain renounced Hagee's endorsement calling the pastor's end-time views "crazy and unacceptable." At the same time, McCain also rejected the endorsement he had received from Pastor Rod Paisley, another warmonger for Israel.

Friends of Hagee say that he was deeply pained by McCain's actions, and other evangelical leaders began to feel that their mistrust of McCain had been warranted. Hudson feared that McCain had wrecked Rove's religious machine....

Acting on his own, Hudson sent feelers to some evangelical leaders to gauge the possibility of their working together, independently of the McCain campaign, to defeat Obama. "No way," one evangelical told Hudson, declining the offer. "It might help John McCain."[26]

The 2008 National Catholic Prayer Breakfast was held during Pope Benedict's visit in April. A good turnout was assured with so many neo-Catholics already in Washington DC. Sitting on the board of directors for the event were:

Joseph Cella, treasurer of Fidelis, (Fidelis Political Action, a PAC; Fidelis Media Fund, a 527 "public-education" entity; and its legal arm, Fidelis Center for Law and Policy) a group of Catholic "advocacy organizations defending life, faith and family" whose political action committee gave exclusively to Republican candidates in 2006, primarily Sen. Rick Santorum.

Austin Ruse, president of the Culture of Life Foundation and Institute. Ruse told the *New York Times* after the 2004 election: "Those 25 percent of voters who said moral values were the animating issues in this election, that is us. We understand that President Bush is a very loyal guy, and we believe that President Bush will be loyal to those who put him there."

Jacqueline Halbig, Bush appointee to the Department of Labor's Center for Faith and Community Based Initiatives, and former employee of both the Christian Coalition and the Family Research Council.

Leonard Leo, former Republican National Committee Catholic Outreach Director and vice president of the Federalist Society. Leo also served on the Bush-Cheney campaign's Catholic Working Group.

Bill Saunders, counsel for the Family Research Council of Human Rights, and Federalist Society Vice Chair for Religious Liberty.[27]

Having skipped the first breakfast in 2004, Bush's attendance at the 2008 prayer event was his fourth in as many years. He addressed his friend, Opus Dei Archbishop José Gomez of San Antonio, as "tejano" (Spanish for "Texan"; archaic spelling Texano) and thanked Chief Justice of the Supreme Court, John Roberts, for his presence. Bush announced a White House Summit on Inner-City Children and Faith-Based Schools which would expand voucher programs. He stated he shared Pope Benedict's "concern for Christians in the Middle East, and his desire to see a peaceful and independent Lebanon," without saying what he planned to do about it. Bush also reminded his audience which included other hierarchs, "I don't know if you really realize this, but in 2006, 3,000 direct federal grants totaling more than $2 billion were made to faith-based organizations—including many Catholic organizations."

Before the event, Catholics United had asked keynote speaker Archbishop Donald Wuerl "to use his remarks to dispel any attempt by political operatives to suggest his participation indicates a close alliance between the Church and the Republican Party," which he didn't.

Bush Visits Benedict—Again

When Bush visited Benedict in Rome during his ignominious "farewell tour" of Europe in June, this would be his sixth meeting with a pope and his third with Benedict in a little over a year.

> Never in US history has a president consulted so often with the leader of the Catholic Church. Carl Anderson, a former Reagan aide who now heads the Knights of Columbus, calls it "remarkable." "Less than 50 years ago," he said, "it was a question as to whether a Catholic should even be able to run for president."
> Bush has emphasized his admiration for the papacy, and in particular for Benedict, whom he has called a "very smart, loving man." Less obvious is how the pope views the president.[28]

It was no secret this pope and his Curia held Bush in the same low regard as other Europeans. Without waiting for the usual joint announcement, the White House Press Office informed the media Bush would visit Benedict before the Vatican had even confirmed the meeting would occur. One Vatican official close to the pontiff told *Reuters*: "The pope is doing this because he is a gentleman. That's the long and short of it."[29]

Bush met with Silvio Berlusconi two days before visiting the pope as thousands demonstrated outside the US Embassy in Rome. Bush urged a stronger Italian presence in Afghanistan and Berlusconi expressed his desire to be involved in the discussions about Iran's nuclear program.[30]

The usual location for an audience with heads-of-state is the pope's library in the Vatican Palace but a spokesman said Benedict wanted to reward Bush for the "warmth" of his reception at the White House. The two men spoke for half an hour in the twelfth-century Tower of St John, a private area in the Vatican gardens. Bush was overheard whispering: "What an honor, what an honor, what an honor!" as he climbed the steps to the tower. Several Italian newspapers cited Vatican sources who suggested that Bush would follow his brother Jeb and Tony Blair and convert to Catholicism. One of those sources agreed that Bush was the most "Catholic-minded" president since John F Kennedy. "George William Rutler, a New York-based priest who is close to the president, was quoted by the *Washington Post* earlier this year saying that Mr. Bush 'is not unaware of how evangelism, by comparison with Catholicism, may seem more limited both theologically and historically.'"[31]

Reports that Bush would convert to Catholicism have dated as far back as 2003 when Michael Novak wrote, "Never have Catholics had so solicitous a friend in the White House. So pro-Catholic are the president's ideas and sentiments that there are persistent rumors that, like his brother Jeb, the governor of Florida, G.W. might also become a Catholic."[32]

Both Bush and Dick Cheney are United Methodists. Considering the moral integrity demonstrated by leaders of his own denomination in rejecting his more egregious policies as compared to the US Catholic hierarchy, it is little wonder Bush would favor those who favored him. Writing about Benedict's US visit, journalist Ray McGovern noted, "Bush has refused, time and time again, to meet with his Methodist bishops. And now he has the imprimatur of the pope."[33]

In November 2005, 109 United Methodist bishops from every region of the US as well as Europe, Africa, and Asia had released a joint Statement of Conscience entitled, "A Call to Repentance and Peace with Justice."

> We repent of our complicity in what we believe to be the unjust and immoral invasion and occupation of Iraq. In the face of the United States Administration's rush toward military action based on misleading information, too many of us were silent. We confess our preoccupation with institutional enhancement and limited agendas while American men and women are sent to Iraq to kill and be killed, while thousands of Iraqi people needlessly suffer and die....[34]

Immediately after their 2005 statement, the Methodist bishops were assailed by the Institute on Religion & Democracy (IRD).

> A few days after the bishops' Statement of Conscience was made public, the [neoconservative] *Weekly Standard* published an IRD response. (Fred Barnes is the executive editor of *Weekly Standard* and a board member at IRD.)....
>
> It accused the bishops of "flogging the President." Its graphic denunciation of the bishops followed the neoconservative party line, condemning the bishops for being out-of-touch "liberal elites" who promote "anti-Americanism" and have "hostility to capitalism" (Tooley, 2005a).
>
> This was followed by a Christmas fundraising appeal from IRD dated December 22, 2005, in which it smeared the bishops a second time. IRD claimed that the bishops' Statement of Conscience is "insulting" to the "brave young men and women" who are serving in Iraq (Tooley, 2005b). Never mind that family members of the bishops have been and are serving in Iraq. IRD sneers at the bishops' call for peace, justice, and reconciliation in Iraq as sounding "like warmed-over 1960s utopianism" and proceeds to mock them as "flower children and chronic demonstrators who never really grew up and faced the real, sinful world" (Tooley, 2005b).

The IRD declared: "No doubt, if transported back in history, these bishops likewise would have impartially lamented the continued warfare between Allied and German forces in Normandy in 1944, while blaming the plight of millions of victims of fascist aggression on the United States." (Tooley, 2005b). This malicious accusation, typical of IRD, is made despite the fact that among the bishops are decorated World War II and Korean Era combat veterans.

IRD is not above using explicit hate language to attack mainline Protestant leaders. Eight days after President Bush's famous "mission accomplished" declaration, Dave Berg, a "segment producer" for the "Tonight Show with Jay Leno" wrote a commentary for IRD, posted on its website on May 9, 2003 (Berg, 2003). After Berg announced that "the war in Iraq is coming to a victorious close," he attacked "the godless army of America's mainstream Protestant leaders" who "worship at the altar of the United Nations" and "gave aid and comfort" to our enemies. He named Jim Winker, General Secretary of the United Methodist General Board of Church and Society, Bishop Clifton Ives of West Virginia, and Bishop William Dew of Arizona, among his targets. He then directed toward these United Methodist leaders, baseless accusations. He said these respected men of God have "hatred for President Bush and for America itself." (Berg, 2003).

In the past year [2005-2006], IRD has published a series of particularly demeaning attacks questioning the faithfulness and integrity of the United Church of Christ (UCC) and its elected leadership (IRD in the Media, 2006; Rempe, 2006). One article mocked the UCC by calling it the "Church of Sponge Bob" (Tooley, 2005c). The United Church of Christ comes out of the deepest roots of American religious liberty. It is the direct heir of the Pilgrim fathers and mothers, making the UCC the oldest church in the United States of America. When Rev. John H. Thomas, President of the UCC, challenged IRD over its repeated baseless attacks against his communion... IRD spokesperson Steve Rempe said: "In Thomas's case, I'm seeing an advancing case of paranoia" (Banerjee, 2006).

IRD has assaulted the integrity of myriad honorable Protestant and Jewish leaders including Archbishop Desmond Tutu; Rev. Jim Wallis of the Sojourners community; Rabbi Michael Lerner of Tikkun; Baptist Dr. Tony Campolo; Archbishop of Canterbury Rowan

Williams; Bishop Mark Hanson, Presiding Bishop of the Evangelical Lutheran Church in America; Rev. Gardner C. Taylor, past president of the Progressive National Baptist Convention; Rabbi David Gelfand at The Jewish Center of the Hamptons; the Most Rev. Frank Griswold, presiding Bishop of the Episcopal Church ; and Rev. Welton Gaddy of The Interfaith Alliance (Faith and Freedom, 2006; United Methodists Affirming Christ's Teachings in our Nation, 2006; IRD in the Media, 2006; Neuhaus, 1997). This is an incomplete list of those attacked.

Dr. Randall Balmer is an evangelical Christian, editor-at-large of the conservative *Christianity Today* magazine, and Professor of American Religion at Columbia University. He conducted research on the IRD for his new volume entitled *Thy Kingdom Come: How the Religious Right Distorts the Faith and Threatens America.* Balmer made these observations about IRD: "What has really impressed me in the course of writing this book is the kind of infrastructure that the neo-cons have built over the past decades. IRD is an important element in that infrastructure. I don't think it's overstated to say it's a conspiracy" (Balmer, 2006).

What is unique about IRD is that it is a *Catholic-directed* attack on *Protestant* churches [emphasis added— Robert George, Richard John Neuhaus and Michael Novak sit on the Board of Directors]....We believe that the sustained attempt by one segment of the leadership of the Catholic Church to undermine the leadership of mainstream Protestantism is a unique breach of ecumenical relations. How other Catholic leaders deal with the debates internal to the Catholic Church introduced by its neocons is a matter with which Protestants have no business interfering. But Protestants have the right to expect that those Roman Catholic leaders who wish to maintain ecumenical relations with Protestants will publicly disown and reject the activities of the IRD.[35]

(No Catholic leader has yet denounced the IRD.)

Communion-Denial Strikes Again

In reporting about a symposium held mid-April 2008 at a Jesuit university, "Faithful Citizenship: Principles and Strategies to Serve the Common Good," the *National Catholic Reporter* noted that in the latest document issued by the US Conference of Catholic Bishops to direct Catholic voters, the word "evil" is used sixteen times, the phrase "intrinsic evil" or "intrinsically evil" is directly applied to only five issues - abortion, euthanasia, human cloning, destructive research on human embryos, and racism - the latter being a feeble attempt at the appearance of bipartisanship.

> At one point in the symposium, a nontenured academic sitting in the audience engaged in a heated debate with Teresa Collett, whose paper defended the Church's position on abortion....At the end of the session, the nontenured academic refused to give his name to the *NCR*. Even in the open academic environment, arguing about the abortion issue, especially making the case that it should remain legal, proved intimidating....
>
> David J. O'Brien, professor emeritus of history at Holy Cross College in Worcester, Mass., said in his presentation that though Church officials have taken "strong stands" on such issues as war, poverty and immigration, "they are rarely spoken of in church and are clearly not considered definitive for Catholics." And Jesuit Fr. David Hollenbach cautioned that the issues of abortion and stem-cell research have hijacked other critical issues such as torture, unjust wars and economic disparity....
>
> Hollenbach, who holds the chair in Human Rights and International Justice at Boston College, concluded, "Lists of evils, intrinsic or otherwise, and condemnations of actions or persons, are just what we do not need from the Church and its leaders if we are to inspire action for the common good."[36]

Like their pontiffs, entire libraries could be filled with the current US episcopate's empty rhetoric about human rights and peace and economic justice. Appointed by Opus Dei Popes John Paul II and Benedict XVI, the bishops have carried water for the Republican Party since the 1990s and their actions speak louder than their words. These prelates sought media attention and banned Catholics from receiving Communion about only one issue in the 2008 election—abortion. The bishops also continued to lead political opposition to same-sex marriage rather than address the real issues threatening families such as poverty, health care and housing. They declared that embryonic stem-cell research to alleviate disease and save lives debased the American moral fiber more than Republican hatred of Muslims and immigrants. Until just before election day, if there was any active (non-retired) American prelate who thought otherwise, his silence was deafening.

As soon as the pro-choice Catholic governor of Kansas, Kathleen Sebelius, was mentioned as a possible running mate for Barack Obama in August, Archbishop Joseph Naumann of Kansas City boldly warned the Democratic presidential candidate, "I think it would be a bad judgment on Senator Obama's part to select someone who was in conflict with the Church....[37]

Naumann's suffragen bishops, Ronald Gilmore of Dodge City, Paul Coakley of Salina, and Michael Jackels of Wichita—dropping the pretense that racism is an "intrinsic evil"—signed a letter stating "[I]t is a correct judgment of conscience that we would commit moral evil if we were to vote for a candidate who takes a permissive stand on those actions that are intrinsically evil—elective abortion, euthanasia, physician-assisted suicide, the destruction of embryonic human beings in stem cell research, human cloning, and same-sex 'marriage'—when there is a morally-acceptable alternative."[38] Archbishop Raymond Burke joined the chorus from his new position in Rome, stating: "Not only politicians but also anyone who supports legal abortion should not receive Communion and everyone who administers Communion should take responsibility for denying it to them."[39] Burke also gave an interview in the Italian bishops' newspaper, *Avvenire,* calling the Democrats the "Party of Death."[40] Archbishop Charles Chaput of Denver addressing the group, Roman Catholics for Obama, warned them that they "need a compelling proportionate reason to justify [their support for Obama.] What is a 'proportionate' reason when it comes to the abortion issue? It's the kind of reason we will be able to explain, with a clean heart, to the victims of abortion when we meet them face to face in the next life."[41] Chaput didn't mention what his own conversation would be with babies lost through war and poverty.

> The registered Republican Archbishop [Naumann] of Kansas City revived the use of Holy Communion as a political weapon to take [Sebelius] down. He publicly called on her to stop taking Communion with her Catholic community because of her widely-known opposition to the use of criminal law in dealing with abortion....In her most recent veto message, Gov. Sebelius offered a detailed description of the lengths to which she had gone to address the abortion issue constructively, and lauded the success her administration had achieved in decreasing its incidence.
>
> Coincidentally, a California law school professor and constitutional scholar, Douglas Kmiec, who is one of the country's most outspoken opponents of abortion, found himself denied Communion because of his public support for Senator Obama. Prof. Kmiec was attending a Mass prior to giving a speech to [Monaghan's Legatus] group of Catholic businessmen, and reported on the website *CatholicOnline* that he was singled out because of his prominence as an Obama supporter.
>
> The common thread in these two stories is that individual Catholic authorities took it upon themselves to judge that an association with a Democratic presidential

candidate was sufficient cause for a subtle form of excommunication from the Catholic community.[42]

Kmiec had worked in the Office of Legal Counsel under Reagan. When George W. Bush was elected, he became dean of Catholic University of America's Columbus School of Law "spending time with fellow Federalist Society members such as Antonin Scalia and Samuel Alito."[43] "Kmiec was recruited by the Mitt Romney campaign to give pro-life bona fides to the once pro-choice governor of Massachusetts." When McCain won, Kmiec found it impossible to work for the Republican ticket.

"Let me put this as kindly as I can," he said. "Senator McCain was not the most generous of heart, or honest of disposition, toward his primary opponents. I always want to concede his integrity, because I can't ever envision myself surviving a POW experience of the kind that he survived, and I admire those years of his life —but that admirable contribution to American history was greatly dimmed by seeing him up close and personal in the primaries."

Kmiec considered the candidacy of Barack Obama.

"His insights [on abortion] were not only significantly different from the Democrats of the past," Kmiec says, "but they were significantly better than either the Democrats or the Republicans of the past, in the sense that he argued that religion shouldn't be a wedge issue, and that we should stop demonizing each other on that basis."....
A week after Romney withdrew from the race, Kmiec wrote about his Obama reflections in an article for the online magazine *Slate*....He mused that, while abortion was still of paramount importance to Catholics, years of Republican rule had not significantly reduced its occurrence.
Kmiec's conservative Catholic friends were aghast, and several of them, including Deal Hudson, rebuked [reviled would be closer to the truth] him in Catholic publications, some even suggesting that he was motivated by ambition. Kmiec thought the response heavy-handed, and observed that if this was an example of Republican religious outreach, then John McCain's campaign was in trouble. "It was a brick through the window with a note attached, and the note said, 'Obey, or else.' I never quite figured out what the 'or else' was. I'm a tenured old professor not looking to go anywhere....What is it they're going to dangle in front of me?"[44]

One of Obama's campaign workers asked Kmiec if he would consider a more formal support for the Democratic candidate. Kmiec expressed his reservations about Obama's position on abortion. Kmiec was assured that, although Obama was pro-choice, he was not pro-abortion. At a meeting with Obama, with the evangelist Franklin Graham also present, the candidate explained to Kmiec that he intended to reduce the number of abortions by helping women continue their pregnancies to full term. Kmiec endorsed Obama on March 23, Easter Sunday.

In an interview with the *New York Times*, Kmiec stated,

> [T]he better question is how could a Catholic not support Barack Obama? Senator Obama's articulated concerns with the payment of a living wage, access to health care, stabilizing the market for shelter, special attention to the needs of the disadvantaged and the importance of community are all part of the Church's social justice mission. Applying this to the issue of abortion, the senator has repeatedly indicated that he is not pro-abortion, that he understands the serious moral question it presents, and, most significantly, that he wants to move us beyond the 35 years of acrimony that have done next to nothing to reduce the unwanted pregnancies that give rise to abortions....
>
> In my view, Obama and Biden seek to fulfill the call by Pope John Paul II in the encyclical "Evangelium Vitae," to "ensure proper support for families and motherhood." It cannot possibly contravene Catholic doctrine to improve the respect for life by paying better attention to the social and economic conditions of women which correlate strongly with the number of abortions.[45]

When asked to comment on being barred from the sacrament, he responded,

> To be the subject of an angry homily at Mass last April 18 and excoriated as giving scandal for endorsing Senator Obama and then to be denied Communion for that "offense" was the most humiliating experience in my faith life....
>
> I remain deeply troubled that other Church leaders not fall into similar traps. That would do untold damage to the Church within the context of American democracy. There are clearly partisan forces that want nothing more than to manufacture or stir up faith-based opposition to their political opponents.[46]

Kmiec's words went unheeded. As soon as Obama did choose a

pro-choice Catholic, Sen. Joe Biden, as his running mate, one could sense the huffing and puffing in episcopal mansions across the country. Within hours of the announcement on August 23, a website called Catholics Against Joe Biden appeared and Archbishop Chaput declared that Biden should not receive Communion—thereby kicking off a new "wafer watch."[47] No bishop refuted that Brian Burch, president of the Fidelis PAC, was speaking for them when he issued a statement also on August 23: "Now everywhere Biden campaigns, we'll have this question of whether a pro-abortion Catholic can receive Communion." Burch added, "Barack Obama has re-opened a wound among American Catholics by picking a pro-abortion Catholic politician…a slap in the face to Catholic voters."[48]

Bob Krebs, the communications director for Biden's home Diocese of Wilmington "confirmed that Biden's bishop will not permit the senator even if elected Vice President of the United States of America to speak at Catholic schools." Never explaining why this announcement was not made during all the years Biden was a senator, Krebs added, "[I]t would apply to Senator Biden whether he was a Senator or the Vice President or any type of public figure."[49] George Weigel also announced on August 23. "I don't think it's a happy day for Catholics when a man who is literally dead wrong on *what the Catholic leadership of the United States has said for over three decades is the most important issue of social justice in our country* [emphasis added] is named to a national ticket and attempts to present himself as an intellectually serious and coherent Catholic."

Some were hoping Biden would carry out his threat as quoted in the *Cincinnati Enquirer.* "The next Republican that tells me I'm not religious, I'm going to shove my rosary beads down their throat."[50]

Putting Abortion Back On Center Stage

If the selection of Biden raised their blood pressure, Speaker of the House Nancy Pelosi caused hierarchical apoplexy. McCain and Obama made their first joint appearance since winning the primaries at an event hosted by the Rev. Rick Warren on Saturday, August 16. During the televised interview, the pastor asked both presidential candidates, "At what point does a baby get human rights?" McCain answered, "At the moment of conception." Obama's response to the same question was more nuanced. "I think that whether you are looking at it from a theological perspective or a scientific perspective, answering that question with specificity, you know, is above my pay grade." He added that he supports *Roe vs. Wade* but said the issue has "moral and ethical content" and stressed his commitment to reducing the number of abortions.

Appearing afterwards on "This Week with George Stephanopoulos," Obama was asked whether his response—"above my pay grade"—was "too flip." The senator told Stephanopoulos, "Probably. Yes. All I meant to communicate was that I don't presume to be able to answer these kinds of theological questions. What I do know is that abortion is a moral issue…

and that in wrestling with those issues, I don't think that the government criminalizing the choices that families make is the best answer for reducing abortions."

The day after the Biden announcement, even before the full press of bishops and neo-Catholic propagandists could launch a full-scale attack, the Sunday, August 24th edition of "Meet the Press" included the following exchange between host, Tom Brokaw, and Pelosi:

BROKAW: Senator Obama [said] the question of when life begins is above his pay grade, whether you're looking at it scientifically or theologically. If he were to come to you and say, "Help me out here, Madame Speaker. When does life begin?" what would you tell him?

PELOSI: I would say that as an ardent, practicing Catholic, this is an issue that I have studied for a long time. And what I know is, over the centuries, the Doctors of the Church have not been able to make that definition. And St. Augustine said at three months. We don't know. The point is, is that it shouldn't have an impact on the woman's right to choose. *Roe v. Wade* talks about very clear definitions of when the child—first trimester, certain considerations; second trimester; not so third trimester. There's very clear distinctions. This isn't about abortion on demand, it's about a careful, careful consideration of all factors that a woman has to make with her doctor and her god. And so I don't think anybody can tell you when life begins, human life begins. As I say, the Catholic Church for centuries has been discussing this, and there are those who've decided...

BROKAW: The Catholic Church at the moment feels very strongly that it...

PELOSI: I understand that.

BROKAW: ...begins at the point of conception.

PELOSI: I understand. And this is like maybe 50 years or something like that. [See Chapter 4] So again, over the history of the Church, this is an issue of controversy. But it is, it is also true that God has given us, each of us, a free will and a responsibility to answer for our actions. And we want abortions to be safe, rare, and reduce the number of abortions. That's why we have this fight in Congress over contraception. My Republican colleagues do not support contraception. If you want to reduce the number of abortions, and we all do, we must—it would behoove you to support family planning and, and contraception...

Faithful to their benefactors, the hierarchs began pummeling Pelosi with lies. The next day, the USCCB issued a statement that Pelosi "misrepresented the history and nature of the authentic teaching of the Catholic Church against abortion," while never challenging Weigel for having also stated that abortion had been given primacy by the US Catholic leadership for only "over three decades." Though Pelosi never claimed to be speaking for anyone other than herself nor had she claimed to be a theologian, Archbishop Donald Wuerl, Archbishop Chaput and his auxiliary, Bishop Conley, Cardinal Edward Egan and Pittsburgh Bishop David Zubik accused her of claiming to be both a theologian and spokesperson for the Catholic Church. [51] Within a week, the prelates of Chicago, Colorado Springs, Dallas, Fargo, St. Paul/Minneapolis, San Francisco and Rockville Centre, New York, also provided statements to the press denouncing Pelosi.

On the Tuesday morning following her interview with Brokaw, a spokesperson for Pelosi issued the following statement:

> The Speaker is the mother of five children and seven grandchildren and fully appreciates the sanctity of family. She was raised in a devout Catholic family who often disagreed with her pro-choice views.
>
> After she was elected to Congress, and the choice issue became more public as she would have to vote on it, she studied the matter more closely. Her views on when life begins were informed by the views of Saint Augustine, who said: "...the law does not provide that the act [abortion] pertains to homicide, for there cannot yet be said to be a live soul in a body that lacks sensation..." (Saint Augustine, On Exodus 21.22)
>
> While Catholic teaching is clear that life begins at conception, many Catholics do not ascribe to that view. The Speaker agrees with the Church that we should reduce the number of abortions. She believes that can be done by making family planning more available, as well as by increasing the number of comprehensive age-appropriate sex education and caring adoption programs.
>
> The Speaker has a long, proud record of working with the Catholic Church on many issues, including alleviating poverty and promoting social justice and peace.[52]

A week after Pelosi's interview, Biden appeared on the same program and was asked the same question:

BROKAW: If Senator Obama comes to you and says, "When does life begin? Help me out here, Joe," as a Roman Catholic, what would you say to him?

BIDEN: I'd say, "Look, I know when it begins for me." It's a personal and private issue. For me, as a Roman Catholic, I'm prepared to accept the teachings of my Church. But let me tell you. There are an awful lot of people of great confessional faiths - Protestants, Jews, Muslims and others - who have a different view. They believe in God as strongly as I do. They're intensely as religious as I am religious. They believe in their faith and they believe in human life, and they have differing views as to when life [begins]....

BROKAW: But if you, you believe that life begins at conception, and you've also voted for abortion rights....

BIDEN: No, what I voted against was curtailing the right, criminalizing abortion. I voted against telling everyone else in the country that they have to accept my religiously based view that it's the moment of conception. There is a debate in our Church, as Cardinal Egan would acknowledge, that's existed. Back in "Summa Theologia," when Thomas Aquinas wrote "Summa Theologia," he said there was no—it didn't occur until quickening, 40 days after conception. How am I going out and tell you, you or anyone else that you must insist upon my view that is based on a matter of faith? And that's the reason I haven't.

Bishop Robert Morlino of Madison, Wisconsin, at the 11 a.m. Mass immediately following the program announced he would not be giving his prepared sermon in order to comment on the Biden interview. Feigning magnanimity, Morlino allowed that Pelosi and Biden were "confused" due to the education they received after the Second Vatican Council when "even priests and bishops" taught erroneous doctrine. In referring to Pelosi's education, Morlino stated, "After all, it was in San Francisco and we know how that can be." (Pelosi's father was a US congressman from Maryland and mayor of Baltimore where she was raised. She graduated from Trinity College in Washington DC in 1962, before the end of the council and didn't move to San Francisco until 1969. Biden's education post Vatican II was non-religious, a J.D. from Syracuse University College of Law.)

Since his sermon was off-the-cuff ("You can see I'm worked up about this," Morlino said at one point) with no time for careful spin, Morlino blurted, "They're stepping on the pope's turf and mine." He concluded by asserting that only the pope and bishops are "guided by the Holy Spirit," and therefore only they have the authority to hold a public opinion on Catholic matters.[53]

The following morning, Chaput castigated Pelosi and Biden for "flawed moral reasoning," charging Biden had "compounded the problem."[54]

In an interview with *Religion News Service*, Archbishop Chaput was asked why he has not also denounced the conflict between John McCain's support for embryonic stem-cell research and his statement that life begins at conception. Chaput responded by denying that McCain held that position. When reminded by the interviewer that McCain has made public statements of support for embryonic stem-cell research on numerous occasions, Chaput switched gears, arguing that he would only have reason to express criticism if McCain had vocal Catholic support, "if a group came out [named] 'Catholics for McCain.'" There is in fact a "Catholics for McCain" organization.[55]

Two days after Biden's appearance on Meet the Press, the USCCB issued another official denunciation of both Pelosi and Biden on behalf of the American Church. "We point out the connectedness between the evil of abortion and political support for abortion"[56] And again, although Biden had not claimed to be speaking for anyone other than himself, the anxious Archbishop Wuerl sent a letter to his priests stating—as if they weren't already aware of this views—"the interpretation of the Catholic faith is the responsibility of the bishops."[57] The prelates of both Kansas Cities, Archbishop Naumann in Kansas and Bishop Robert Finn in Missouri, issued a joint statement with the, by now, standard falsehoods: "It is particularly disturbing to witness the spectacle of Catholics in public life vocally upset with the Church for teaching what it has always taught on these moral issues for 2,000 years."[58]

The Knights of Columbus Supreme Knight, Carl Anderson, wrote an open letter to Biden as a full-page advertisement in several major US newspapers. The letter attacked Biden's Catholicism and "compared the vice presidential candidate's views on abortion to those of pre-Civil War advocates of slavery."

Catholic Democrats, a state-based network of groups, responded by noting that Anderson "grossly mischaracterized Sen. Biden as an advocate of abortion while carelessly ignoring the racial overtones of invoking slavery in attacking the running mate of history's first black presidential nominee.... The letter ignores Sen. Biden's strong commitment to Catholic social teaching, reflected in legislation he was instrumental in passing, including: the United States Commission on Civil Rights Act of 1983, the Global Climate Change Act in 1987, Stopping Genocide in Bosnia, Kosovo and Darfur in 1993 and 2004 respectively, and the Kids 2000 Act among many others during his 25 years of service as US senator."[59]

Cardinal Francis George, president of the USCCB, ordered that his letter denouncing and "correcting" Pelosi and Biden be read in every church at every Mass in the Archdiocese of Chicago the following weekend. "The cardinal's letter might as well have carried a John McCain-Sarah Palin letterhead on behalf of the Republicans in this presidential race," noted a Chicago *Sun-Times* columnist.[60]

Chaput had issued a directive prohibiting his clergy from "endorsing or contributing money in partisan elections" but telling them they had an "obligation to speak out on important moral issues such as abortion or immigration." *The Coloradoan* newspaper did a search of the Federal Election Commission records and noted that through June about 100 contributors to federal candidates or political parties in the 2007-08 election cycle listed their occupation as a Catholic priest or deacon. The reporters found that the majority of contributions were to Republican groups and candidates, "particularly outspoken opponents of abortion," and not proponents of immigration reform.[61]

While the media may have tried to keep an eye on Catholic "nonpartisanship," after eight years of Bush appointments to the executive and judicial branches, the Catholic hierarchy no longer feared loss of their tax exemptions. Copies of Chaput's invective against Pelosi and Biden were distributed at Catholic churches as far away as Macon, Georgia.[62]

The National Conventions

During the Democratic National Convention held in Denver the last week in August, the *Washington Times* noted Chaput's "headline-grabbing criticism of party bigwigs and his decision to schedule major events this week during the convention's prime-time speeches." On the first night of the convention,

> Archbishop Chaput led a pro-life rally and prayer march outside a Planned Parenthood office in north Denver that started at 7:30 MST, about the same time as Michelle Obama, wife of presumptive Democratic presidential nominee Barack Obama, was speaking to the convention....
>
> Wednesday night, Archbishop Chaput drew hundreds to a signing of his newest book, *Render Unto Caesar: Serving the Nation by Living Our Catholic Beliefs in Political Life*, at a bookstore about 15 miles from the Pepsi Center. The signing began at the same time the Democratic National Convention launched a line-up of speakers that included former President Bill Clinton and vice-presidential pick Sen. Joseph R. Biden Jr.[63]

Howard Dean, chairman of the Democratic National Committee, stated at the convention, "We in the Democratic Party don't believe that you have to change your values to cater to people of faith. We have been people of faith for a long time, but we haven't known how to talk about it." In part, to make up for the snub to then-governor of Pennsylvania, Bob Casey, who was denied a speaking role at the party's 1992 convention, Bob Casey Jr. was invited to address the convention. The anti-abortion senator had defeated Rick Santorum in 2006.

The convention opened with an interfaith gathering on Sunday with remarks from Colorado's Catholic governor, Bill Ritter. The CEO of the Democratic National Convention Committee told attendees, "We didn't move to bring faith to the party. Faith has always been here." Doug Kmiec participated in a panel on Thursday as part of a series of Faith Caucus meetings, a first for Democrats. Obama, during his acceptance speech before more than 80,000 at Denver's Invesco Field, said while people may disagree on whether abortion should remain legal or not, "surely we can agree on reducing the number of unwanted pregnancies in this country."[64] The Democratic Party platform addressed ways to provide support to pregnant women who want to continue their pregnancies to term. The platform promised accessible pre- and post-natal health care, help with parenting skills, income support and adoption programs. On the third day of the convention, Catholics in Alliance for the Common Good issued a report showing that providing social and economic supports for women and family contributed to a significant reduction in abortions.[65]

When the Republican National Convention was held the following week in St. Paul, Twin Cities Archbishop John Nienstedt, "a staunch conservative and rising star in the US Church," offered Mass in his cathedral for convention delegates on Sunday and hosted a reception afterwards in the church courtyard. Present at the gathering was Teresa Collett, the law school professor mentioned in the previously quoted *NCR* article, who had been an expert witness for the State of Alaska when the Republican vice-presidential nominee, Gov. Sarah Palin, supported an abortion parental notification law—later struck down by Alaska's highest court. Collett was an invited guest at the convention and planned on using the RNC "as an opportunity to connect party leaders with local Church leaders who care about abortion." Rep. Chris Smith (R-N.J.) told the same reporter, "Even nominal Catholics need to…realize that this man (Obama) wants to be the abortion president."[66]

With the start of the Republican Convention delayed one day due to Hurricane Ike, on Labor Day, September 1, McCain flew to Philadelphia on his private jet. With the lead-in, "McCain's in town, mum on schedule," the *Philadelphia Inquirer* reported the senator's motorcade drove directly to a private meeting at the residence of Cardinal Justin Rigali, chair of the USCCB's Committee for Pro-Life Activities.[67] Former Gov. Frank Keating, co-chair of Catholics for McCain, acknowledged that McCain had also visited with Chaput shortly before the Democratic convention but said "the meetings McCain has held with bishops around the country were 'strictly ceremonial.'" When asked about the prelates' responses to Pelosi and Biden, "Keating welcomed their comments as 'statements of affectionate support' for McCain."[68]

Also on Labor Day, Biden received a "hero's welcome" in his hometown of Scranton, Pennsylvania, where local Bishop Joseph Martino had made it clear Biden would be denied Communion.[69] In case anyone may have missed his earlier efforts to sway Pennsylvania voters, Martino repeated his proscription against Biden in a two-page letter with orders that it both be read at all Masses and additionally placed in the parish bulletins.[70] "I think you'd have to have been living in a cave for the last five years not to know that this letter is intended to promote John McCain's candidacy," said Rob Boston, a spokesman for Americans United for Separation of Church and State.[71] In response to Martino, a group of lay Catholics ran an advertisement in the Scranton paper the same weekend as Martino's letter in which they reminded Catholics the Church also considers racism a sin and that it was, indeed, permissible to vote for Obama.

At the Cathedral of St. Peter in Wilmington, Delaware, where Biden lives, Fidelis was given permission to promote its video that abortion and same-sex marriage trump the Gospel message to love our neighbor at every Mass. Many other Catholic parishes advertised the video on their websites and bulletins

On September 3, Catholics for McCain held a reception in St. Paul during the Republican convention. The event was titled, "Render Unto Caesar," in order to promote sales of Chaput's new book[72] Also during the GOP convention, Cardinal Rigali wrote an article for his archdiocesan newspaper comparing abortion to the Holocaust and Republicans to Pope Pius XII as the defenders of humanity.[73] Since Republicans had done as much to stop abortions as the pope did to stop the Holocaust, at least that part of the analogy was unintentionally applicable. When a parish priest in Missouri also linked the Democratic Party with Hitler, a representative of the AFL-CIO walked out of Mass.[74]

A line from the GOP platform draft which urged a reduction in abortions was replaced with the demand that abortion should be eliminated entirely with no exceptions for rape, incest or the health of the mother. The article as adopted repeated the 2004 platform. "The Republican Party stands courageously for the protection of innocent life," said Deirdre McQuade, assistant director for policy and communications in the USCCB's Office of Pro-Life Activities.[75] Bishop Thomas Wenski of Orlando led the delegates in prayer the last night of the convention

Sarah Palin

Going into the convention, McCain still needed more enthusiastic support from the evangelicals. The biggest bombshell of the 2008 campaign came the day after the Democratic National Convention ended with the announcement of Sarah Palin as John McCain's running mate. The news successfully drove media coverage about Obama's electrifying speech at the Invesco Stadium from the headlines. Sarah Palin, former mayor of the Alaskan town of Wasilla, population 6,000, and governor of the state, population 670,000, was presented as the person most qualified to be President of the United States of America should anything happen to the health of a 72-year-old who already had had several bouts with melanoma and refused to have his medical records released for thorough scrutiny.

Alaska's culture and economy is unlike any other state. More than four-fifths of Alaska's revenue comes from oil creating so much wealth that the state mails a dividend check each year to every citizen. In 2008, the amount was $3,269 per capita.[76] However, the 44-year-old mother of five and former "Miss Alaska" contestant who attended five colleges in six years before getting a bachelors degree was anti-abortion, anti-gay, pro-war and liked to shoot animals. The Republican base went wild with enthusiasm.

In addition to reflecting McCain's further surrender of his judgment and personal principles to his ambition, Palin's selection was the culmination of everything the neo-Catholics could hope for in a candidate for national office—a figure with star power but no personal base, intellectually and ethically deficient, who would, they assumed, think, do and speak as instructed. It would soon become evident Palin wasn't vetted any more carefully than Hagee.

Palin had already demonstrated her commitment to neoconservative principles by trashing through false innuendo the reputation of a former Wasilla City Council member who had been her instructor and guide.

> According to some political observers in Alaska, this pattern—exploiting "old-boy" mentors and then turning against them for her own advantage—defines Sarah Palin's rise to power. Again and again, Palin has charmed powerful political patrons, and then rejected them when it suited her purposes. She has crafted a public image as a clean politics reformer, but in truth, she has only blown the whistle on political corruption when it was expedient for her to do so. Above all, Palin is a dynamo of ambition, shrewdly maneuvering her way through the notoriously compromised world of Alaska politics, making and breaking alliances along the way.[77]

Palin ran unsuccessfully for lieutenant governor in 2002, chaired the Alaska Oil and Gas Conservation Commission beginning in 2003 and quit in 2004, and was elected governor in November 2006. She officiated as mayor and governor according to Republican values. Experienced and dedicated civil servants were replaced with inept friends and supporters; the "haves" were given additional tax breaks and the sales tax was increased disproportionately burdening the "have-nots." She left the city of Wasilla in debt. She was charged with using the state treasury as her personal ATM. The state's natural resources were to be depleted for the benefit of the wealthy. When a bipartisan group of Alaskan legislators agreed to investigate whether Palin dismissed the state's Public Service Commissioner for his failure to fire a state trooper—Palin's ex-brother-in-law—as directed by the governor's family and staff, Palin's maneuvering to stonewall the investigation shocked Alaskans. Once Palin was added to the national ticket, the McCain campaign sank to new lows, even by GOP standards, with racist innuendo, distortions and falsehoods.[78]

    As governor, Palin declared a Christian Heritage Week, a religious right movement promoting official recognition of the US as a Christian nation. Quotes from the Founding Fathers are used out of context or falsified to misleadingly imply the patriots wanted to create a Christian nation and to promote the unity of church and state.[79]

A Baptist minister in Palmer, Wasilla's twin town in the borough of Matanuska-Susitna, had experience with Palin since the time she was a Wasilla City Council member in the 1990s. Rev. Howard Bess wrote a book, *Pastor, I Am Gay*, which Palin tried to have removed from the Wasilla Public Library along with others. Bess agreed to an interview within a couple of weeks of her vice-presidential nomination.

> "At this point, people in this country don't grasp what this person is all about. The key to understanding Sarah Palin is understanding her radical theology," Bess said. Speaking of the Mat-Su Valley, "Things got very intense around here in the '90s—the culture war was very hot here," Bess said. "The evangelicals were trying to take over the valley. They took over the school board, the community hospital board, even the local electric utility. And Sarah Palin was in the direct center of all these culture battles, along with the churches she belonged to."....
>
> In 1996, evangelical churches mounted a vigorous campaign to take over the local hospital's community board and ban abortion from the valley. When they succeeded, Bess and Dr. Susan Lemagie, a Palmer OB-GYN, fought back, filing suit on behalf of a local woman who had been forced to travel to Seattle for an abortion. The case was finally decided by the Alaska Supreme Court, which ruled that the hospital must provide valley women with the abortion option....
>
> Another valley activist, Philip Munger, says that Palin also helped push the evangelical drive to take over the Mat-Su Borough school board. "She wanted to get people who believed in creationism on the board," said Munger, a music composer and teacher. "I bumped into her once after my band played at a graduation ceremony at [Palin's church] the Assembly of God. I said, 'Sarah, how can you believe in creationism—your father's a science teacher.' And she said, 'We don't have to agree on everything.' I pushed her on the earth's creation, whether it was really less than 7,000 years old and whether dinosaurs and humans walked the earth at the same time. And she said yes, she'd seen images somewhere of dinosaur fossils with human footprints in them."

Munger also asked Palin if she truly believed in the End of Days, the doomsday scenario when the Messiah will return. "She looked in my eyes and said, 'Yes, I think I will see Jesus come back to earth in my lifetime.'"[80]

It was the End Times ideology embraced by Palin which worried those who study the evangelicals mobilizing their congregations for a soon-to-come "holy war." It cast a frightening pall over Palin's fitness to be a heartbeat away from control of America's armed forces and nuclear arsenal.

While it is very true that Palin's churches may officially still retain mention of the Rapture in some form, there is absolutely nothing in these sermons, associations and activities to indicate that they are waiting around to be snatched from the earth. Conversely, they are intent on taking control of society and government in the here and now.

Ed Kalnins of Wasilla Assembly of God is actively preaching and teaching theology which comes directly from the leadership of the New Apostolic Reformation/Third Wave....Kalnins is quite open and blatant about the need for his church to take control for the Kingdom, starting with Wasilla and Alaska.[81]

As opposed to other Christians who strive to bring the Kingdom of God to the world through kindness and good deeds, the New Apostolic Reformation/Third Wave dominionists plan on ruling the "Kingdom" after winning their holy war.

As one of Palin's supporters wrote:

When McCain announced that he had chosen Palin as his running mate, I was reminded of the biblical story of Deborah, the Old Testament prophet who rallied God's people to victory at a time when ancient Israel was being terrorized by foreign invaders. Deborah's gender didn't stop her from amassing an army; she inspired the people in a way no man could.[82]

Baptized as a Catholic while an infant, Palin was re-baptized into the Wasilla Assembly of God when she was twelve. She remained a member until she ran for lieutenant governor in 2002 when she joined the Wasilla Bible Church, another nondenominational congregation. In recent years, Palin also attended Wasilla's Church on the Rock.[83] When she was in the state capital, Palin attended the Juneau Christian Center. The JCC scheduled an event for March 2009 organized by Christians United for Israel which was later removed from CUFI's web page.

The pastor of the JCC, asked his congregation in a July 28, 2007 sermon:

> Do you believe we're in the last days? After listening to Newt Gingrich and the prime minister of Israel and a number of others at our gathering, I became convinced, and I have been convinced for some time. We are living in the last days.[84]

Palin, however, always maintained her closest religious ties to the Wasilla Assembly of God. For the twenty months she had been governor before McCain's announcement, Palin continued to reside in Wasilla roughly half the time.[85] It was at the Wasilla Assembly of God where Palin gave her often-quoted remarks in June 2008, "I think God's will has to be done in unifying people and companies to get that gas pipeline built. So pray for that...that I can do my job there in developing my [sic] natural resources." At the end of Palin's speech, Kalnins spoke of his belief that "Alaska is one of the refuge states in the last days," a reference to when a remnant community has to defend Christianity before their final victory.

> Kalnins has preached that the 9/11 attacks and the invasion of Iraq were part of a "world war" over the Christian faith, one in which Jesus Christ had called upon believers to be willing to sacrifice their lives. "What you see in a terrorist—that's called the invisible enemy. There has always been an invisible enemy. What you see in Iraq, basically, is a manifestation of what's going on in this unseen world called the spirit world....We need to think like Jesus thinks. We are in a time and a season of war, and we need to think like that. We need to develop that instinct. We need to develop as believers the instinct that we are at war, and that war is contending for your faith.....
> "Jesus called us to die. You're worried about getting hurt? He's called us to die. Listen, you know we can't even follow him unless you are willing to give up your life....I believe that Jesus himself operated from that position of war mode. Everyone say 'war mode.' Now you say, wait a minute Ed, he's like the good shepherd, he's loving all the time and he's kind all the time. Oh yes he is—but I also believe that he had a part of his thoughts that knew that he was in a war."....
> [The JCC] maintains very close relations with John Hagee's "Christians United For Israel." Hagee was one of two "Joel's Army"-connected pastors [Joel's Army will be the youngest warriors] McCain formerly used as "spiritual

advisors" in an attempt to curry favor with the dominionist wing of the GOP. And this relationship is troubling, to say the least.....

At least three of four of Palin's churches are involved with major organizations and leaders of this movement. The Third Wave is based on the idea that in the end times there will be an outpouring of supernatural powers on a group of Christians that will take authority over the existing church and the world.[86]

Palin spoke at the Wasilla Assembly of God's Master's Commission graduation ceremony in June 2008. The Master's Commission is a three-year post high school religious study program costing $8,000 per year. Prior to being congratulated by the governor, Wasilla's Master's Commission students flew from Alaska in April 2008 to participate in a prophecy conference led by Rick Joyner and Steve Thompson at their Morningstar Ministries in North Carolina. During a session at Morningstar recorded the second week of August 2008, Thompson told his audience:

See, Jesus is waiting—seated at the right hand of the Father, having all authority on Heaven and on Earth, having commissioned and empowered and deployed his disciples to go out to enforce the victory and the judgment that he won over the enemy and waiting until his people rise up and demonstrate their glory and those enemies are put under the feet of the body of Christ.[87]

Joyner had written as far back as 1996:

Then I turned and saw the army of the Lord standing behind me. There were thousands of soldiers, but they were still greatly outnumbered. I was shocked and disheartened as it seemed that there were actually many more Christians being used by the evil one than there were in the army of the Lord. I also knew that the battle that was about to begin was going to be viewed as The Great Christian Civil War because very few would understand the powers that were behind the impending conflict. (*The Final Quest*, Whitaker House, New Kensington, PA, 1996, p. 22)[88]

Baptist minister, Rev. Howard Bess, addressed the prospects of Palin being a heartbeat away from the Oval Office.

It's truly frightening that someone like Sarah has risen to the national level," Bess said. "Like all religious fundamentalists—Christian, Jewish, Muslim—she is a dualist. They view life as an ongoing struggle to the finish between good and evil. Their mind-set is that you do not do business with evil—you destroy it. Talking with the enemy is not part of their plan. That puts someone like Obama on the side of evil.

The real disturbing thing about Sarah is her mind-set. It's her underlying belief system that will influence how she responds in an international crisis, if she's ever in that position, and has the full might of the US military in her hands. She gave some indication of that thinking in her ABC interview, when she suggested how willing she would be to go to war with Russia.

This person's election would be a disaster for the country and the world."[89]

According to the McCain campaign, any unfavorable reporting about Sarah Palin was proof the media is anti-Christian. Referring to articles and news accounts which questioned her experience and grasp of the issues, McCain's campaign manager Rick Davis, appearing on conservative Hugh Hewitt's radio program, claimed, "You know, I would say beyond that, there's something going on in the media right now, and I've seen it on television in the last couple of nights, and that's literally an attack on Christianity itself."[90]

The irony was that in Sarah Palin, the country now had a national candidate belonging to a sect ready to wage a real, shooting "holy war" against Catholics as much as any other Christians who challenged their power. Towards the end of the campaign, Palin was working harder to promote her own 2012 presidential aspirations than for the election of John McCain.[91] Given the history of American assassinations, the concern for Barack Obama's safety is quite justified, but if elected, it would have been John McCain who needed food-tasters.

Christian National Initiatives

As they had done in previous elections, the GOP strategy was to get as many anti-gay, anti-abortion and anti-immigration proposals on the ballot as possible to drive "moral values" voters to the polls where they would also select the Republican candidate.

In California, Catholics for the Common Good, the California Catholic Conference and other groups formed CatholicsForProtectMarriage.com to recruit volunteers and contributors for Proposition 8 which would overturn the state Supreme Court's ruling that same-sex couples have the right to designate their unions as marriages. The Knights of Columbus contributed more than $1 million.[92]

Arizona's two Catholic bishops urged Church members to vote for Proposition 102, a constitutional ban on gay marriage.[93]

Florida's Ballot Initiative 7 sought to repeal a provision of the state constitution which prohibited spending public funds on religious institutions. Ballot Initiative 9 proposed changing a section of the constitution to explicitly allow the public funding of scholarships, including those to religious and other private schools.[94]

Anti-abortion initiatives included:

- California—Requiring a doctor to notify parents before giving abortions to minors.
- South Dakota—Directly outlawing abortion except for the health of the mother, rape and incest.
- Colorado and Montana—Embryos from the moment of conception have legal rights.

In total, 45 states considered nearly 450 measures related to abortion in 2008, a 12 percent increase over the previous year.[95]

The Post-Convention Campaign

With Palin on the ticket and the increasing likelihood that an Obama victory might actually be possible, the religious right had no choice but to pitch in and work for McCain. Paul Weyrich and James Dobson finally came around to endorsing McCain as did other Christian Nationalist leaders.

The neo-Catholics began another "anti-Obama" offensive. Deal Hudson originated the smear that Obama was pro-infanticide because as an Illinois state senator, Obama voted against The Born Alive Infant Protection Act. Obama would not support the legislation because protections were already in place should an extremely rare late-term abortion result in a live birth. The American Medical Association held the same position. In addition,

> The first two iterations of the Illinois bill did not contain language that explicitly re-affirmed abortion rights granted under *Roe v. Wade* [and] the Illinois legislation was bundled together with a measure that threatened doctors with criminal prosecution if they incorrectly applied the Born Alive bill.[96]

The National Right to Life Committee picked up the ball and ran with it, misrepresenting both the legislation and Obama's role. Raymond Ruddy, one of the hundreds of new "faith-based" multi-millionaires, paid for BornAliveTruth.org to air television advertisements in battleground states accusing Obama of infanticide.[97]

By mid-September, Obama/Biden had been denounced by 55 bishops and the candidates were "being trashed across every state of the union by Catholic newspapers, TV and radio stations, and blogs. It is a tsunami of rejection."[98] In response to this one-sided media blitz, another anti-abortion Catholic leader, Nicholas P. Cafardi, backed Obama. Cafardi is a civil and canon lawyer and a professor and former dean at Duquesne University School of Law in Pittsburgh. "Obama's support for abortion rights has led some to the conclusion that no Catholic can vote for him. That's a mistake. While I have never swayed in my conviction that abortion is an unspeakable evil, I believe that we have lost the abortion battle—permanently. A vote for Sen. John McCain does not guarantee the end of abortion in America. Not even close."[99]

At the time of his pro-Obama statement, Cafardi was a member of the board of trustees at the Franciscan University of Steubenville. The university's spokesman announced, "Our president spoke with Dr. Cafardi and let him know that this was causing concern among our constituents... His letter of resignation arrived a few days after that conversation."[100]

The Alliance Defense Fund (ADF) recruited evangelical pastors across the country to begin endorsing McCain from the pulpit beginning Sunday, September 28.

The ADF was founded in 1994 by religious right leaders such as D. James Kennedy and James Dobson to counter the American Civil Liberties Union (ACLU). Funded by several right-wing foundations,[101] the ADL "spends more than $20 million a year to underwrite legal battles and train lawyers to push the country in socially conservative directions." The group had challenged same-sex marriage initiatives, stem-cell research funding, rules limiting the distance between protesters and abortion patients, had helped the Boy Scouts ban gay Scout leaders and fought the contrived "war on Christmas."[102]

Calling a press conference to announce the initiative, ADF attorney Erik Stanley declared that clergy have a constitutional right to support candidates as part of their religious services. The legal consortium hoped that in the six remaining Sundays before Election Day, McCain would receive the largest number of endorsements with the greatest capability to turn out voters at no cost to his campaign or the GOP.[103]

The first Sunday in October is designated by the USCCB as "Pro-Life Sunday." Bishops and priests throughout the US used the occasion to exhort Catholics, for the sake of their immortal souls, to vote in favor of maintaining the wealth and power of the bishops and their benefactors.[104] That Sunday, New Jersey Bishop Arthur J. Serratelli compared Obama to Herod, the New Testament ruler who ordered the killing of all infant males under the age of two.[105]

On October 30, a countrywide demonstration by Catholics who opposed Obama "because of his radical support of child-killing" was endorsed by at least a dozen prelates but primarily promoted by Operation Rescue founder, Randall Terry.[106]

In 1999, the pastor of Terry's Binghamton, New York, Christian church had expelled him from the congregation for abandoning his wife and children and engaging in "sinful" relationships with other women.[107] Joining the Charismatic Episcopal Church during the interim, Terry became a Roman Catholic in 2006.[108] (Newt Gingrich, also accused of abandoning his first wife and children, joined the Catholic Church in March 2009, the same religion as his third wife with whom he had carried on an adulterous affair while still married to his second wife.)

Terry unsuccessfully (he received 7 percent of the vote) ran for Congress in Upstate New York as a third-party candidate in 1998.[109] When he campaigned for the Florida State Senate in 2006, Terry used robo-calls with a professional impersonator of Bill Clinton (with a brief disclaimer) endorsing his Republican primary opponent.[110]

Terry's second wife, together with a graduate of the Franciscan University in Steubenville, distributed anti-Giuliani flyer's ahead of the 2008 Florida Republican presidential primary at a St. Petersburg Catholic church featuring a "fictitious candidate named Smith who espouses owning blacks. Halfway through the six-page flyer the reader learns the racist slant of the flier was a joke."[111]

A pamphlet, written by Terry and styled to be mistaken for the USCCB's own "Faithful Citizenship" brochure, was used in Catholic parishes. Terry also sent an open letter to all US bishops advising them they had no choice but to advise their flocks that a Catholic in good conscience could not vote for Obama. One published response reads as follows:

> Dear Randall,
> I have…read the Open Letter to the US Bishops and the brochure "Faithful Catholic Citizenship."
> You have done an excellent job of presenting the authentic teaching of the Catholic Church and applying it to the candidacy of Barack Hussein Obama.
> I encourage you to disseminate the two documents as widely as possible. More and more bishops are speaking up in the way you desire.…
> Blessings!
> +Rene Henry Gracida
> Bishop Emeritus of Corpus Christi[112]

In Scranton, Pennsylvania, a local October forum on the election at St John's Catholic Church was discussing the pastoral letter, "Faithful Citizenship," which the USCCB adopted at its 2007 meeting to guide Catholic voters. The forum was interrupted by Scranton's bishop, Joseph Martino, who thundered: "No USCCB document is relevant in this diocese. The USCCB doesn't speak for me." The bishop took particular issue with the claim that voters could consider topics other than abortion.

Finally, the day before the election, Bishop Joseph Finn of Kansas City, Missouri, was asked in a radio interview: "There are Catholics listening right now who are thinking strongly or are convinced that they will vote for Barack Obama. What would you say to them?" The bishop replied: "I would say, give consideration to your eternal salvation." Bishop Finn, who is a member of Opus Dei, had earlier compared the 2008 election to the naval Battle of Lepanto, when a papal fleet turned back Muslim invaders in 1571.[113]

To their enormous credit, two prelates allowed national press exposure of their agreement that Catholicism was about more than one issue - Latino Bishop Gabino Zavala, an auxiliary in the Los Angeles Archdiocese, and African-American Bishop Terry Steib of the Diocese of Memphis.[114]

The Catholic Vote Proves To Be Elusive

Karl Rove was correct in that the evangelical vote was a given although Obama had increased the Democratic vote among evangelicals from 21 to 25 percent. However, unlike the 2004 election, the majority of Catholics (54 percent) voted for the Democrat. Latinos made up most of the difference, although 49 percent of white Catholics voted for Obama, up from 43 percent who had voted for Kerry.[115]

Some posited that the increase in "religious" voters who voted for a Democrat was due to Obama's ability to talk about his own faith when the need arose. While Palin appealed to fundamentalists, Biden had shown an easy comfort with his cultural Catholicism.[116] There was also a new coalition which could show "God-speak" was not the exclusive domain of the Republican Party. These new "Religious Left" groups—Catholics United, Catholics in Alliance for the Common Good, Faith in Public Life, Network of Spiritual Aggressives, and Red Letter Christians—emphasized that the teachings of Jesus Christ superseded the admonitions of Christian Nationalist leaders and their narrow focus on wedge issues.

The Matthew 25 Network, named for the Gospel chapter in which Jesus calls on his followers to "care for the least of these," was formed by evangelical, Roman Catholic, mainline Protestant, and Pentecostal Christians. Its purpose was to broaden the public discourse on "values" to include non-violence and caring for the poor, and also to counter falsehoods or smears targeting Obama. The PAC sponsored radio and television advertisements aimed specifically at Christians, mostly on Christian radio in key swing states. They placed ads in religious publications as well. As for appealing to Catholics, "Obama says he found his Christian faith while working as a community organizer among low-income people in a Catholic-sponsored program," Sharon Daly, former vice president of Catholic Charities, emphasized. She believed that as "Catholics reflect on this and get to know more about him," their support will grow.[117]

In May 2008, a group of centrist evangelical leaders urged their followers not to be "useful idiots," exploited for Republican votes. Their statement titled an "Evangelical Manifesto" encouraged their co-religionists to think outside the box.[118]

Bill Berkowitz, a longtime observer of the neoconservative movement and a frequent writer for *Media Transparency* wrote in September 2007:

Prior to the 2006 election, the GOP's multi-year organizing effort to woo Catholic voters paid off in part because, working hand-in-glove with conservative philanthropy, it sought out, found and funded a number of Catholic neoconservatives who would essentially become spokespersons for the Republican Party....

Berkowitz goes on to specifically name Michael Novak and Ralph McInerny, founders of *Crisis* magazine, Deal Hudson, its subsequent editor, and Rev. Richard John Neuhaus, editor-in-chief of *First Things*.

The 2006 mid-term election brought about another shift amongst Catholic voters as they began drifting back to the Democratic Party. During the campaign, Democratic candidates appeared to be more comfortable talking about their religious beliefs, they attempted to broaden the "values" debate to include poverty, health care, the environment, and care for those with AIDS, and they devoted significant resources to the election organizing effort.

Catholic voters were clearly disturbed by the Bush/Cheney quagmire in Iraq; disgusted by the administration's horrifyingly slow response to Hurricane Katrina; appalled by the epidemic of corruption and cronyism within the administration; dismayed by the Bush administration's disregard for the constitution; and distrustful of the growing power of conservative Christian evangelicals.[119]

The "growing power of conservative Christian evangelicals" was reflected by the fact that, by 2007, the percentage of Americans identifying themselves as evangelical (26.3) exceeded Catholics (23.9) according to the Pew Forum on Religion and Public Life.[120] However, while "polling indicates evangelicals voted in full force, and that Republicans came away with a healthy 70 percent of their votes, down only 8 percentage points from what they gave President Bush in 2004,"[121] the 2006 election proved to some that Catholics were still the largest bloc of "swing voters." Catholics voted Democratic in the 2006 election by a 55 percent to 45 percent margin per the National Election Pool exit polls.

Noting that Catholics make up about a third of voters in the battleground states of Michigan, Missouri, Ohio and Pennsylvania, G. Terry Madonna, a political scientist at Franklin & Marshall College in Lancaster, Pennsylvania stated, "Whoever wins the Catholic vote will generally win our state and, most of the time, the nation."[122] So the microscopic examination of Catholic voters continued through the 2008 cycle.

A poll commissioned by Catholics for Choice conducted in the beginning of July, showed among white Catholics, McCain led 47 to 37; among Hispanics (one in six Catholic voters) Obama led 61 to 23. Obama also led among Catholics aged 18-34 and women under 45.[123] Polling conducted by Pew in early August showed Obama with a 47-42 percent lead among Catholic voters with white Catholics favoring McCain 45-44. Evangelicals polled 68-24 for McCain.[124] The poll also showed that Democrats had made progress in changing their image and 38 percent of respondents said the party is "friendly toward religion," up from 26 percent two years earlier. Even so, considerably more—52 percent—viewed the Republican Party as religion-friendly.[125]

By the end of August, Steven Waldman, co-founder, CEO, and Editor-in-Chief of *Beliefnet.com*, was getting nearer the truth. In an article titled "The Crucial Catholic Vote: Does It Exist?" Waldman wrote:

> It is true that since 1960, the party that won the Catholic vote, won the overall popular vote—yet Catholic political views seem to be relatively detached from Catholic Church teachings. Most American Catholics support abortions being legal contrary to clear Church teaching. Most use birth control, contrary to teaching. Most supported the Iraq war, despite warnings from then-Pope John Paul II and later Pope Benedict XVI.
>
> For the most part, Catholics simply switch around like the population as a whole, voting whatever the big issue of the day is—the war, terrorism, the economy, the candidate's character. There doesn't seem to be anything all that Catholic about the Catholic vote.[126]

The Pew Forum on Religion and Public Life poll supported this view. When questioned as to whether or not abortion should be legal, Americans responded as follows:

Religious affiliation	Legal in all cases	Legal in most cases	Illegal in most cases	Illegal in all cases	Don't know/ Refused
Nat'l total	18%	33%	27%	16%	6%
Catholics	16%	32%	27%	18%	7%
Evangelical	9%	24%	36%	25%	6%

Perhaps the generally accepted perception of Catholics as a bellwether of the electorate was due to the fact they were more demographically representative of the nation as a whole than other religious affiliations. They are geographically dispersed—29 percent in the Northeast, 24 in the Midwest, 24 in the South and 23 in the West— and ethnically/

racially mixed (as much as any US religion)— 65 percent white, 29 percent Hispanic and the remaining 6 percent evenly distributed among Black, Asian and Other.[127]

Except among older, blue-collar ethnics who still accepted guidance from their Church, it was becoming evident by 2008 a "Catholic" vote did not exist—only voters who happened to be Catholic. Because of the earlier GOP "Southern strategy" of veiled racism and appeal to social conservatives who considered themselves disrespected by an "elite" media and intelligentsia, Republicans had erased the earlier twentieth-century division between Democrats as the party of the working man and Republicans as the party of the rich. However, by the early twenty-first century, Midwest factory workers shared the same concerns regardless of their religious affiliation; voters in the South and rural areas still exhibited more parochialism than open-mindedness; Westerners were rugged libertarians; and urbanites still reflected a tolerance engendered by day-to-day multi-cultural contacts.

What had changed was the politics of the US Catholic episcopate so that right-wing Catholics received from their religious leaders the same permission for bigotry, hatred and love of war as their evangelical brethren. In 2004, neo-Catholics had persuaded enough of their co-religionists on an emotional rather than rational level that John Kerry was a "bad" Catholic and an affront to their religious identity. The 2004 presidential election was the first after 9/11 but occurred before the worst fighting had commenced in Iraq. Unassimilated Latinos were more receptive to their Catholic clergy's instructions and the deportations of illegal immigrants and stricter enforcement of the border hadn't yet reached crisis proportions. But by 2008, the economy was the most important issue for most voters regardless of their professed religion, ethnicity, or race.

CHAPTER 18

EPILOGUE

Mission Accomplished

The United States experienced the greatest redistribution of wealth in US history during the George W. Bush administration. His tax cuts alone left $1.8 trillion in the pockets of the rich and out of the US Treasury.[1] For the first time since the Great Depression, President Bill Clinton had left the federal government with a budget surplus compared to a projected Bush deficit of $500 billion. From 2000 to 2008, the first seven years of which were claimed to be a time of economic growth by the Republican Party, the national debt more than doubled from $5.5 to over $11 trillion—more than $36,000 for every man, woman and child in the US.

As of 2006, according to the *Wall Street Journal*, "in the most recently reported five years, the share of income reported by the very wealthy has risen faster than the group's share of income taxes."[2]

In 1997 over 144,000 tax returns were filed with adjusted gross incomes of $1 million or more. The number rose to 240,000 in 2004. How much additional income came from tax shelters, shady deals, illicit foreign investments, offshore accounts, etc., or how much came from the vast "privatization" of government services which took pay checks away from middle class public employees and provided a windfall to "connected" contractors, is anybody's guess.

When wealth is looked at separately from income, the top one percent own between 40 to 50 percent of the nation's wealth, more than the combined assets of the bottom 95 percent. In March 2006 *Forbes* reported 793 billionaires in the US with combined net worth of $2.6 trillion. In March 2007 *Forbes* reported 946 billionaires in the US with combined net worth of $3.5 trillion—a one-year increase of 19 percent in the number of billionaires and an increase of 35 percent in their net worth while severe poverty was at its highest point in three decades.[3]

Americans spend twice as much per capita for healthcare than the average of other industrialized countries[4] the excess going to health insurers, pharmaceutical companies and hospital administrators, even though the US death rate exceeds the world's average.

Bill Moyers noted on his PBS broadcast in the spring of 2008:

> Since George W. Bush has been in office 5 million
> Americans have slipped into poverty, 8 million have lost
> their health insurance and 3 million have lost their pensions.
> Yes, in the last seven years median household income
> for working-age Americans has declined by $2,500. Yes,
> our country, for the first time since the Great Depression,
> now has a zero personal savings rate and, all across the
> nation, emergency food shelves are being flooded with
> working families whose inadequate wages prevent them
> from feeding their families."

In the thirty years since the mysterious death of Pope John Paul I, the neo-Catholics had succeeded—at least for a few decades—in establishing an American national religion which could galvanize its followers into right-wing political activism. In 1978, religious denominations in the US had had their own distinct theologies. But through unlimited financing of think tanks and media, and the purchase of religious leaders from Rome to Kalamazoo, some Americans were persuaded to abandon their own denominations, most of which were founded by European settlers escaping church/state oppression, to join together in a belief system whose core had been designed in accord with the Republican Party platform.

In polling done in 1990 and 2001 for the American Religious Identification Survey conducted by the Graduate Center of the City University of New York, Baptists and Methodists decreased in number over that period. Those who called themselves "Protestant" without specifying a denomination fell by 73 percent while those who referred to themselves as "Christian" grew by 76 percent. The "born-agains" decreased also by 73 percent while the "evangelical" label gained 326 percent. Christians who described themselves as "nondenominational" grew by 1,176 percent. Catholics increased by 11 percent due to the influx of Latino immigrants while the number of native-born decreased. By 2007, those identifying themselves as traditional Protestants were only 18.1 percent of the US population according to the Pew Forum on Religion and Public Life.

The neo-Catholics succeeded in assimilating right-wing Americans into a common religious discourse, political sympathy and sense of priorities. Non-Catholic Christian Nationalists now preach about "natural law" and parrot papal phrases such as the "culture of life" and the "tyranny of relativism." They adopted the neo-Catholic position that abortion trumps all other issues in deciding elections and that stem-cell research and same-sex marriage actually pose a threat.

The Catholic right abandoned the teachings of the Roman Catholic Church in order to reject evolution (although the Church views all valid science as an explication of God's creation) as more dangerous to their children than violence and pornography. The public school prayer and Bible readings once denounced by Catholics as an infringement on the separation of church and state and a form of discrimination against practitioners of other religions is now back on the agenda as a bedrock of national morality. A cheery "Happy Holidays," a catchall greeting for the period between Thanksgiving and New Year's, has become heresy on their lips. Orthodox Catholics who as children enjoyed "trick or treating" dressed as pirates or princesses have joined other cultural conservatives in banning their children's participation in "pagan" Halloween festivities.

By changing the religious landscape, the neo-Catholics and their Protestant surrogates had placed the Republican Party in control of the White House, Congress or both for 26 of the 28 years between 1980 and 2008. Persuaded by the prospect of control over domestic morals and mores as well as US world domination, until 2006 roughly 40 percent of Americans had turned their backs on the separation of church and state and flocked to neoconservative congregations or the right-wing of the Catholic Church. The remaining 10+1 percent needed to constitute a Republican majority were those laughing all the way to the bank.

Christian National Failures

The tenets of the national religion and its purposes were summarized in 1998 as follows:

> Scapegoating of immigrants, the homeless, the unemployed, racial and ethnic minorities and other targeted sectors in order to obscure the immoral system causing the suffering and deaths of hundreds of thousands [as] absolutely necessary [for] the multinational capitalist entities to be able to pursue and increase the accumulation of profits and wealth.[5]

In addition to the tragedy of millions of premature deaths, illness and widespread poverty, Christian Nationalists taught us that truth doesn't matter. In 1988, the neocons floated the story that Massachusetts Gov. Michael Dukakis had psychiatric treatment. In 1992, they accused Arkansas Gov. Bill Clinton of having worked for the KGB. In 2000, Vice President Al Gore was "delusional." In 2004, they "swift-boated" Massachusetts Sen. John Kerry. These lies

> would reverberate through the right-wing echo chamber and often into the mainstream press. Usually, the charges spotlighted a purported flaw so severe—such as mental instability or treason—that the Democrat would be disqualified in the eyes of many voters.
>
> Also, since it's difficult to prove a negative, mainstream news outlets often would treat the charges as

a point of legitimate dispute, forcing the Democrat to issue a denial or refuse to comment. Sometimes, TV pundits would add insult to the injury by critiquing how poorly the smeared Democrat countered the attack.[6]

In 2008, the charge that Sen. Barack Obama was a Muslim educated in a "madrassa" school never died.

Rupert Murdoch's Fox News and *New York Post* further spread the stories that Obama was a Muslim militant. Talk show host Rush Limbaugh repeated over and over "Osama, Obama" and right-wing pundits insisted on using Obama's middle name—Hussein—in order to connect him to both Osama Bin Laden and Saddam Hussein, although Hussein is a common and respected name in the Muslim world.[7]

In June, the first attack book repeating that same and other lies, *The Case Against Barack Obama,* written by David Freddoso who worked as a political reporter for Robert Novak, was distributed by another of the war-mongering Fr. McCloskey-converts, Alfred Regnery's publishing company and publicized by the same firm which had worked on Regnery's Swift Boat Veterans for Truth book, *Unfit for Command.* [8]

Every GOP official understood the mission. Sen. John McCain ran TV ads suggesting Obama was the anti-Christ. Gov. Sarah Palin told crowds Obama was "pallin' around with terrorists." In Virginia, a Republican Party official charged his volunteers to keep making the Obama-Osama connection. The chairman of the Colorado Republican Party, in describing his function to produce fallacious press releases during the Democratic Convention, told the *Denver Post,* "Just consider this the Ministry of Truth." As those who've read George Orwell's *1984* already know, "The Ministry of Peace concerns itself with war, the Ministry of Truth with lies, the Ministry of Love with torture and the Ministry of Plenty with starvation." Orwell wrote: "These contradictions are not accidental, nor do they result from ordinary hypocrisy; they are deliberate exercises in doublethink."[9]

More shocking was the corruption of those who had once been considered moral exemplars. While the clerical sex abuse scandal taught us that Catholic prelates would lie to save their bank accounts, now they lied just to prop up the GOP.

After losing the 2008 election, the USCCB launched a nationwide campaign against a non-existent supposedly Democrat-supported Freedom of (Abortion) Choice Act.

When Obama asked for a review of Bush's Provider Refusal Bill, a broadening of three laws already in place which protect health care workers' right to refuse to participate in abortions, sterilizations or providing birth control, USCCB president Cardinal George issued a statement,

[W]e are deeply concerned that such an action on the government's part would be the first step in moving our country from democracy to despotism. Respect for personal conscience and freedom of religion as such ensures our basic freedom from government oppression.

And the USCCB issued a News Release: "Message Spread on Web Sites, You Tube—Don't Move From 'Democracy to Despotism,' Cardinal Francis George Warns"[10]

Bush's regulation, enacted two days before he left office, would enable anyone—physicians, nurses, operating-room staff, medical office workers, pharmacists—to deny any service, information or advice to patients—blood transfusions, vaccines, family planning, HIV/AIDS treatment, end-of-life services—based solely on their personal interpretation of morality. For example, the rule would protect "a biblical fundamentalist nurse who refuses to give anesthesia to a woman in labor on the grounds that the Bible condemns all women to suffer in childbirth."[11]

Obama expressed concern that the Bush regulation was overly broad and not one bishop explained why, since our freedom from government oppression and freedom of religion depended on it, they had never requested this regulation before nor had they condemned Bush for waiting eight years before implementing it.

Along with Obama's announcement that he was reversing Bush's prohibition on federal funding for stem-cell research within very stringent guidelines, the White House provided a copy of the proposed guidelines. Funding was approved for research only using human embryonic stem cells from embryos created solely for reproductive purposes by in vitro fertilization. The embryos would have to no longer be needed for reproduction, scientists must obtain written consent from embryo donors and only voluntary donation would be allowed, without pressure or financial incentives. Funding would not be allowed for stem cells obtained from other sources, including cloning; for in vitro fertilization embryos created specifically for research purposes; nor for parthenogenesis, the development of an unfertilized egg.

In response, the USCCB news release stated: "Proposed NIH guidelines divorce stem cell research from ethical foundation—Innocent humans treated as commodities for body parts."[12]

In March, Fr. John Jenkins, president of Notre Dame University, invited Obama to speak at that year's commencement and to receive an honorary degree. The announcement noted, "Barack Obama will be the ninth US president to be awarded an honorary degree by the University of Notre Dame and the sixth to be the Commencement speaker," one of them being George W. Bush. Jenkins was charged by 80 US prelates with, among other things, devaluing human life, betraying his Catholic faith, ignorance of the Catholic religion, sucking up to the powerful, intellectual vanity, advancing personal goals, attempting to "confuse" Catholics, cowardice, and capitulating to fear of seeming to be "out of touch."[13] Archbishop Chaput accused him of "prostituting our Catholic identity"[14] and Opus Dei Bishop Robert W. Finn declared, "We are at war!" against Catholics who supported Jenkins.[15]

At the time that Archbishop Donald Wuerl of Washington DC wrote the following listing his objections, the Provider Refusal Rule was still under review and a viable Freedom of Choice Act was still only a figment of his imagination:

> [T]his administration is moving us to a point where people who conscientiously object to taking human life might lose their jobs in clinics and hospitals as a result. That's a fear expressed by opponents of the Freedom of Choice Act, which would eliminate restrictions on abortion and might... force pro-life heath care workers to choose between their jobs and their beliefs....
>
> In his circles of Hell, Dante places... at the core those who sinned against the truth.[16]

A New US/Vatican Relationship

Other than one retired bishop who noted that the integrity of higher education should be maintained (like Ratzinger's invitation to speak at La Sapienza), not a single prelate defended Jenkins. However, much to the embarrassment of the neo-Catholics, support came from the Vatican's daily newspaper, *L'Osservatore Romano,* which lauded Obama's Notre Dame speech for finding common ground with the Catholic Church on reducing the number of abortions. Actually, the paper had already printed a series of admiring articles about the new US president's desire for cooperation in foreign relations, peace in the Middle East, the elimination of nuclear arms (which could destroy all humanity), and his interest in economic justice.

In the run-up to the first meeting between Pope Benedict and Obama to take place while the president was attending a G-8 summit in July, 2009, "an influential Swiss cardinal and Vatican advisor" favorably associated Obama's efforts to reduce abortions with "the thinking of St. Thomas Aquinas and early Christian tradition about framing laws in a pluralistic society." This authentic theologian compared Obama's Notre Dame address to Pope Paul VI's encyclical *Ecclesiam Suam* in its accent on dialogue and common ground, and to the document *Dignitatis Humanae* of the Second Vatican Council (1962-65) on conducting the search for truth in a pluralistic society.[17]

How is the Vatican able to shift gears so effortlessly? As stated previously, the Holy See acts first on its own behalf and the staff of its Secretariat of State are masters of realpolitik. Even when their favored party loses an election, the US is still the world's greatest power and its officials merit being courted.

What about funding from the US right-wing? In July 2008, the

Vatican reported a deficit in 2007 due mainly to "the brusque and very accentuated" drop in the value of the US dollar and partly to the poor performance of the stock market, meaning Bush's economic failures were also bad for the Roman Catholic Church. In 2007, US diocesan contributions had fallen to second place behind Germany and "$14.3 million came from a single anonymous donor."[18] The Vatican also posted a loss for 2008 with Americans remaining first only in contributions to the pope's private and personal fund.

After being elected, Ratzinger had set about making the Vatican more financially self-sufficient by cutting personnel costs and increasing other sources of revenue. Along with the formation of its own travel agency which books tours to international pilgrimage destinations, the Vatican began charging copyright fees on the use of its vast library of papal and other documents, making tourism inside Vatican City more profitable and accepting advertisements in its publications and broadcast media.

The Poisoning of US Religion

As much as they debased political discourse and praxis, neo-Catholics desecrated religion even more, their spokesmen having preached the antithesis of Gospel values.

Sixteen- to thirty-year-olds (called the Millennial generation), too young to remember a time before the Republican "culture wars," exhibit a greater degree of criticism toward Christianity than did previous generations when they were at the same stage of life, according to a 2007 book, *unChristian: What a New Generation Really Thinks About Christianity ... and Why It Matters,* by David Kinnaman. The results of his study conducted with Gabe Lyons showed that half of the young persons polled perceived Christianity to be judgmental, hypocritical, and too political. One-third said it was old-fashioned and out of touch with reality. Kinnaman noted their perceptions were not rooted in misinformation, but were based on their own personal interaction with Christians and in churches.

Those findings were similar to the Pew Forum on Religion and Public Life study conducted in 2007 which found the number of Americans who said they are unaffiliated with any particular faith (16.1 percent) was more than double the number who said they were not affiliated with any particular religion as children. Among Americans aged 18-29, one-in-four said they were not currently affiliated with any religion. A poll conducted in August 2008 by the same organization found a majority (52 percent) of Americans agreed with the position that churches and other houses of worship should keep out of political matters. This number was up from 43 percent in 1996.[19]

The Southern Baptists, the second largest US denomination behind Roman Catholics, noted a steady decline in their numbers in their annual report released in April 2008 by LifeWay Christian Resources, the publishing arm of the Southern Baptist Convention. This religion, which measures its success by the number of persons baptized each year, reported the number of baptisms had fallen since reaching a peak in 1972. While acknowledging the national trend away from mainline Protestantism to nondenominational congregations, the convention's president, Rev. Frank Page, said part of the blame can be placed on a perception that Baptists were "mean-spirited, hurtful and angry people" and that the denomination had been known too much in recent years for "what we're against" than "what we're for." Page noted,

> Our culture is increasingly antagonistic and sometimes adverse to a conversation about a faith in Christ. Sometimes that's our fault because we have not always presented a winsome Christian life that would engender trust and a desire on the part of many people to engage in a conversation on the Gospel. All Southern Baptists should recommit to a life of loving people and ministering to people without strings attached so people will be more open to hearing the Gospel message.[20]

Even among evangelicals, the Millennials were breaking ranks with their elders. While 40 percent still identified as Republicans in 2007, that number was down 15 percent just since 2005. A pastor of a more liberal congregation noted the effect the nomination of Sarah Palin had on his group.

> Doug Pagitt, pastor of Solomon's Porch in Minneapolis, said young evangelicals in his circle feared that Palin's ascendancy signaled a return to "old-school divide and conquer politics" and a narrow focus on abortion politics. "On blogs and social networking sites that connect more center-left young evangelicals" the choice of Sarah Palin as McCain's running mate was seen as a "a cynical political ploy, a depressing return to the culture wars and damaging to efforts to broaden the evangelical dialogue."[21]

It is appropriate that the denomination which served as both model and leader for the establishment of Christian Nationalism should suffer the greatest loss in the number of adherents. As mentioned in a previous chapter, while nearly a third of Americans adults polled in 2007 say they were raised Catholic, less than a fourth still identify themselves as such, meaning almost ten percent of the US population now describe themselves as former Catholics. According to another Pew study conducted in 2009, Catholics as a percentage of the US population drops to 20 percent of those aged 18-29[22] and half of those are Latino. But the USCCB should find even less comfort in those numbers since the percentage of Latinos who are Catholic is also dropping.[23] And of those who still self-identify as

Catholics, fewer are attending Mass[24] and fewer are obedient to their priests and bishops.[25] Seventy percent of US dioceses have had to down-size by closing parishes and/or merging others.[26]

The Opus Dei popes have had the same effect on the global Church and Islam can now claim to be the world's largest religion. "In many parts of the world, Catholic seminaries are nearly empty, parochial schools are closing, churches are locked during the day, and rectories, convents, and novitiates are vacant. Ideologues, representing no one but themselves, fight over the ruins," sociologist Fr. Andrew Greeley noted in 2008.[27] Even with counting infant baptisms rather than adult affirmations, the number of Catholics worldwide is increasing below the rate of the general population. This is true on every continent except some of the poorest areas of Asia and Africa. While the spectacle of doddering, mostly white, old men dressed in opulent costumes in baroque settings may continue to draw millions of worldwide television viewers to staged papal events, fewer are stepping up to pay for it. As Thomas Merton, famous author and Trappist monk, put it:

> Authority has simply been abused too long in the Catholic Church and for many people it just becomes utterly stupid and intolerable to have to put up with the kind of jackassing around that is posed in God's name. It is an insult to God Himself and in the end it can only discredit all idea of authority and obedience. There comes a point where they simply forfeit the right to be listened to.[28]

The Future

As a wise friend, Sam D'Orio, pointed out to me, a pendulum never stops in the middle. If US politics runs on a forty-year cycle as some like political consultant, James Carville, have proposed, then 2008 was the point when the pendulum began its sweep back towards the left. In 1928, the US was heading into the Great Depression bringing with it Franklin D. Roosevelt and the New Deal. In 1968, Richard M. Nixon was elected based on fear the country was falling into anarchy. By 2008, the country was in shambles due to unregulated greed and power.

As usual, the impetus for change comes from a new generation. The original neoconservative vision of Irving Kristol and Paul Weyrich—a compliant American populace under the direction of an authoritative religion combined with US hegemony in the rest of the world—failed due to changing demographics as much as by its own corruption. For their purposes, only enough white Christians were needed in addition to the rich to create Dick Cheney's famous "50 percent plus one." But as time went by, the percentage of minorities—African-Americans, Hispanics and Asians—grew, as did the number of whites with a higher education. According to the US Census Bureau, by 2042 European-Americans will be the minority.

Not surprisingly, polls showed the same political disparity between the more racially diverse 18 to 30-year-olds who supported Obama by a large majority and older white adults just as other surveys had reported differences in religious affiliations between the Millenials and their elders.

A survey conducted by Faith in Public Life in 2008 showed,

> "Younger Americans, including younger Americans of faith, are not the culture war generation."....They are "bridging the divides that entrenched their elders and ushering in an era of consensus in which the common good trumps the clash of ideologies."
>
> The director of communications strategy at Faith in Public Life said, "Expect to see the dividing lines of the culture wars continue to fade."[29]

In an interview about his 2008 book, *The Way We'll Be*, pollster John Zogby stated,

> "The results of my polling tell me that the coalition of angry Christians is in sharp retreat. People want more from their president than a perfect attendance record at the local prayer breakfast." They want "a competent manager," a military commander and someone who "can promote the image of the US abroad." Zogby attributed much of this shift to the First Globals, a label he applied to the Millennial generation.
>
> He suggests that tomorrow's American majority will be less materialistic, less tolerant of baloney, more practical and more closely linked to the rest of the world. "At long last, cynicism bottoms out," he predicted....
>
> Zogby decries the current age of "grinding political meanness;" a change like that "would be little short of revolutionary."[30]

Whatever generalization may be made of each generation does not negate the fundamentals of George Lakoff's "strict-father" and "nurturing parent" description of voters (or however one wishes to label the left and right positions on a bell-curve of political worldviews.) The recognition, however, that most people fall in the middle was the fundamental strategy of the Obama campaign. While Christians who attended church every Sunday continued to favor McCain, and those who seldom or never go favored Obama, the shift in this election was among Americans who attend services occasionally. In 2004, they favored Bush over Kerry by a slight margin and in 2008 sixty percent supported Obama.[31]

However, the fusion of right-wing extremism to religion will be with us for the foreseeable future. Christian Nationalism still satisfies those of every age who seek authority and certitude. At the Cologne World Youth Day event, a 21-year-old from Bitteroot Valley, Montana, was excited about the leadership of Benedict XVI.

"As Joseph Cardinal Ratzinger, he was like the church's bulldog," said the youth. "He was puttin' the smack-down on heresy....There was a lot of slightly misguided teachings that I grew up with. Knowing that there's somebody up there who's made his entire cardinal's career out of straightening out those heresies and defending the true, solid teachings of the Church is something I am very, very excited about for the youth."[32]

Conservative Catholic and evangelical Millennials still flock to the abortion issue as their black and white, line-drawn-in-the-sand, "with us or against us" issue, as did their elders. And like their elders, it is not about "love of neighbor (babies)" but a reaction against "attacks" by "liberals." T-shirts sold at Rock for Life concerts read, "You will not silence our message. You will not mock our God. You will stop killing our generation."[33]

Some blame religion for the right-wing's devotion to mendacious discourse, conflict and violence. But it is not the source, only a unifying banner. The tragedies in Northern Ireland and the Balkans were not over differences in religious doctrines but over political and socio-economic interests and grievances. Fundamentalists will always find the certainty of sectarian or racial superiority as an attractive "hook" on which to hang their fear and hatred. Claims of superiority of any kind have always had their draw.

Is religion in the US permanently disfigured by neocon ideology with so many denominations seemingly split along political lines much as what happened when congregations separated into Northern and Southern divisions during the Civil War era? Will abortion and same-sex marriage become as much non-issues in the future as slavery is today? Will Americans of the same denomination be able to worship together again within their own faith traditions based upon their shared creedal beliefs rather than their political party?

Contrary to Christian Nationalism, religion need not be a means to manipulate others. A sense or belief that there is an "other" which is "holy" is innate to the human race and in itself can be both liberating and energizing. All societies have communal expressions of worship. Parents still want their children raised in a religious tradition even if only to have their own moral precepts reinforced by a community.

Many Catholics have left their traditional parishes to form new congregations either in public settings or private homes headed by married and/or women priests or with no ordained leaders where all are invited to share Communion, a trend documented in the book, *American Catholics Today: New Realities of Their Faith and Their Church*, co-authored by William V. D'Antonio, James D. Davidson, Dean R. Hoge and Mary L. Gautier. The book noted that Millennials who participate in these types of communities have an attendance rate of 90 percent and serving the poor was a core belief of 91 percent. In addition, "statistics show that evangelicals are increasingly fleeing from Sunday worship to 'house churches' in their living rooms, creating what *Time* magazine described in a March 2006 article as a flight by disgruntled evangelicals from megachurches to 'minichurches.'"[34]

What shape organized religion will take as the Millennials assume leadership positions is unknown but if history is a guide, we will be safe from a fundamentalist national majority for the next four decades.

ENDNOTES

Chapter 1: Neoconservatism Begins

1   http://www.heritage.org/research/nationalsecurity/cda04-11.cfm

2   http://en.wikipedia.org/wiki/Vietnam_War

3   "What Is the Military-Industrial Complex?" *TIME Magazine*, April 11, 1969 http://www.time.com/time/magazine/article/0,9171,900729,00.html

4   Ibid

5   Robert Parry, "Who Should Concede? The Secret History of Modern U.S. Politics" *consortiumnews.com* November 13, 2000 http://www.consortiumnews.com/2000/111300a.html

6   George Packer, "The Fall of Conservatism" *The New Yorker* May 26, 2008 http://www.truthout.org/article/the-fall-conservatism

7   Shadia Drury, "Saving America: Leo Strauss and the Neoconservatives" *The Evatt Foundation 2001-2002* http://www.informationclearinghouse.info/article6750.htm

8   Dale Vree, "Editorial: What is a Neoconservative? – & Does It Matter?" *New Oxford Review* December 2005 http://www.newoxfordreview.org/article.jsp?did=1205-editorial

9   http://en.wikipedia.org/wiki/Commentary_Magazine

10   "Stephen Spender Quits Encounter" *The New York Times* May 8, 1967 and Thomas W. Braden, "I'm glad the CIA is 'immoral'" *The Saturday Evening Post* May 20, 1967 Provided by http://en.wikipedia.org/wiki/Encounter_(magazine)

11   "Leo Strauss" *SourceWatch* http://www.sourcewatch.org/index.php?title=Leo_Strauss

12   Stephen Eric Bronner, "Constructing Neo-Conservatism" *Logos* Spring 2004http://www.logosjournal.com/bronner_neocon.htm

13   Shadia Drury, "Leo Strauss and the Grand Inquisitor" *Free Inquiry Magazine* Volume 24, Number 4 http://www.secularhumanism.org/index.php?section=library&page=drury_24_4

14   Thom Hartmann's "Independent Thinker" Book of the Month Review of *Leo Strauss and the American Right* by Shadia B. Drury *buzz flash.com* August 4, 2005 http://www.buzzflash.com/hartmann/05/08/har05008.html

15   Alec R. Vidler, *The Church in an Age of Revolution* (London: Penguin Books Ltd, 1961) 19

16   Seamus Breathnach, *Irish Criminology* Universal Publishers 2005 http://www.irishcriminology.com

Chapter 2: Catholicism: The Neoconservative Religion of Choice

1   John Spivak "Socioeconomic and Political Context of the Plot" excerpted from *A Man in His Time* (New York: Horizon 1967) 294-298 http://coat.ncf.ca/our_magazine/links/53/spivak-excerpt.html

2   Penny Lernoux, "Who's Who? Knights of Malta Know" *National Catholic Reporter* May 5, 1989 http://www.mosquitonet.com/~prewett/ncrmay890910.html and http://www.mosquitonet.com/~prewett/ncrmay891113.html

3   http://www.heraldica.org/topics/orders/ordmalta.htm

4   Martin A. Lee, "Their Will Be Done" *Mother Jones* July/August 1983 Issue http://www.motherjones.com/news/feature/1983/07/willbedone.html

5   "Italians still seek truth about Masonic terror bombing 27 years ago" *Aftermath News* August 5, 2007 http://aftermathnews.wordpress.com/2007/08/05/italians-still-seek-truth-about-masonic-terror-bombing-27-years-ago/

6   Allen Douglas, "Italy's Black Prince: Terror War Against the Nation-State" a review of *The Black Prince and the Sea Devils: The Story of Valerio Borghese and the Elite Units of the Decima Mas* by Jack Green and Alessandro Massignani (Cambridge, Mass.: Da Capo Press 2004) *Executive Intelligence Review* February 4, 2005 Issue http://www.larouchepub.com/other/2005/3205_italy_black_prince.html*)*

7   Lee, supra note 4.

8   http://www.odan.org/tw_escriva_name_changes.htm

9   "The Real Power of OPUS" *Tempo* January 21, 2002 - Issue No. 1029 http://www.mgr.org/TempoODS_pg15.html

10   John Follain, *City of Secrets: The Truth Behind the Murders at the Vatican* (New York: William Morrow, 2003) 106

11   Lee, supra note 4.

12   "Special: Nazis, the Vatican, and CIA" Covert Action Information Bulletin Winter 1986 No. 25 Pages 27-38 http://www.mosquitonet.com/~prewett/caqsmom25.1.html

13   The Real Power of OPUS," supra note 9.

14   Greg Grandin, "Milton Friedman and the Economics of Empire: The Road from Serfdom" *Counter Punch* November 17, 2006 http://www.counterpunch.org/grandin11172006.html

15   Lernoux, supra note 2.

16   "Special: Nazis, the Vatican, and CIA," supra note 12.

17   John Swomley, "The Secret World of Opus Dei," *The Human Quest* May/June 2000 http://www.findarticles.com/p/articles/mi_qa3861/is_200005/ai_n8889207

18   Arthur Jones, "Their Kingdom Come: Inside the Secret World of Opus Dei" *National Catholic Reporter* October 23, 1998 Provided by FindArticles (Gale, Cengage Learning) http://findarticles.com/p/articles/mi_m1141/is_n1_v35/ai_21278964/pg_1?tag=content;col1

19   Paul L. Williams, *The Vatican Exposed: Money, Murder and the Mafia.* (Amherst NY: Prometheus Books 2003) 51

20   Peter J. Wosh review of *Money and the Rise of the Modern Papacy: Financing the Vatican 1850-1950* by John F. Pollard (Cambridge University Press, 2005) http://www.hbs.edu/bhr/archives/bookreviews/79/pwosh2.pdf

21   David Yallop, *In God's Name - An Investigation into the Murder of Pope John Paul I* (New York: Carroll & Graf, 1984) 94,95

22   Ibid 98

23   Allen Douglas, "Italy's Black Prince: Terror War Against the Nation-State" a review of *The Black Prince and the Sea Devils: The Story of Valerio Borghese and the Elite Units of the Decima Mas by* Jack Green and Alessandro Assigning (Cambridge Mass.: Da Capo Press, 2004) *Executive Intelligence Review* February 4, 2005 Issue http://www.larouchepub.com/other/2005/3205_italy_black_prince.html

24   Lernoux, supra note 2.

25   Williams, supra note 20 at 74, 75.

26   Lee, supra note 4.

27   Yallop, supra note 22 at 108.

28   Douglas, supra note 24.

29   Peter Stoler with Jonathan Beaty and Barry Kalb, "The Great Vatican Bank Mystery" *Time Magazine* September 13, 1982 http://www.time.com/time/magazine/article/0,9171,951806-1,00.html

30   Wosh, supra note 21.

31   Richard N. Gardner, *Mission Italy: On the Front Lines of the Cold War* (Lanham, Maryland: Rowman & Littlefield Publishers, Inc. 2005) 11, 36

32   Ibid

33   John Francis Pollard, *Money and the Rise of the Modern Papacy: Financing the Vatican, 1850-1950* (Cambridge University Press, 2005) 200 Google Books

34   Lee, supra note 4.

35   Williams, supra note 20 at 97.

36   Lee, supra note 4.
37   Christine M. Roussel, "A very blunt critique of the Pontificate of Pope Benedict XVI..." *ARCC Light* http://www.catholica.com.au/gc2/cr/002_cr_150308.php
38   Andrew Nagorski, "John Paul II and Communism" *Newsweek* April 2, 2005 http://www.msnbc.msn.com/id/3276657/
39   "The Papacy of John Paul" *Our Sunday Visitor* http://www.osv.com/OSV4MeNav/MyCatholicFaithOnlineResources/ThePapacyofJohnPaulII/tabid/182/Default.aspx
40   Darris McNeely review *Man of the Century, The Life and Times of Pope John Paul II* by Jonathan Kwitney (New York: Henry Holt & Co,.1997) *World News and Prophesy* http://www.ucgstp.org/bureau/wnp/wnp0003/book.htm
41   http://cnnstudentnews.cnn.com/SPECIAL/2005pope/stories/bio2
42   David Yallop, *The Power and the Glory: Inside the Dark Heart of John Paul II's Vatican* (New York: Carroll & Graf Publishers, 2007) 13
43   Jane Barnes and Helen Whitney, "John Paul II: His Life and Papacy" *PBS Frontline* http://www.pbs.org/wgbh/pages/frontline/shows/pope/etc/bio.html
44   Lee, supra note 4.
45   Yallop, supra note 43 at 19.
46   Jesús López Sáez, *El Dia de la Cuenta: Juan Pablo II a Examen,* (Asociacion Comunidad de Ayala 2002) http://www.comayala.es/Libros/ddc/
47   Lee, supra note 4.

Chapter 3: Hawks and Neocons Align

1   Paul Westman "Ronald Reagan 1911- 2004: An Evaluation - The Kitchen Cabinet - Part of a Series" *National Vanguard - History* August 28, 2004 http://72.14.205.104/search?q=cache:2HbkIr6nHncJ:www.nationalvanguard.org/printer.php%3Fid%3D3666+%22henry+salvatori%22%2Bcatholic&hl=en&ct=clnk&cd=27&gl=us
2   *CorpWatch : General Electric* http://www.corpwatch.org/article.php?list=type&type=16
3   *Military Industrial-Complex Contract Values Per Company* http://www.militaryindustrialcomplex.com/totals.asp?thisContractor=General%20Electric%20Company
4   Don D. Moldea, "The Corruption of Ronald Reagan" *Moldea.com and Investigative-Jounalism.com* July 15, 1999 http://www.moldea.com/ReaganRedux.html
5   Sam Donaldson, a review of *Dark Victory: Ronald Reagan, MCA and the Mob* by Dan Moldea, (New York: Viking 1986) *Washington Monthly* October 1986 http://findarticles.com/p/articles/mi_m1316/is_v18/ai_4473387
6   Rick Perlstein, "General Electric Kool-Aid, The Untold Story of Ronald Reagan's Political Conversion" *The New Republic Online* January 4, 2007 http://www.tnr.com/doc.mhtml?i=w070101&s=perlstein010407
7   Michael Schaller, *Reckoning with Reagan* (New York: Oxford University Press 1992) 13
8   William F. Buckley, Jr. "Henry Salvatori, RIP - Businessman - Obiturary" *National Review* August 11, 1997 http://findarticles.com/p/articles/mi_m1282/is_n15_v49/ai_19674154
9   Paul Westman "Ronald Reagan 1911- 2004: An Evaluation - The Kitchen Cabinet - Part of a Series" *National Vanguard - History* August 28, 2004 http://72.14.205.104/search?q=cache:2HbkIr6nHncJ:www.nationalvanguard.org/printer.php%3Fid%3D3666+%22henry+salvatori%22%2Bcatholic&hl=en&ct=clnk&cd=27&gl=us
10   "Neocon 101" *Christian Science Monitor* (2004) http://www.csmonitor.com/specials/neocon/neocon101.html
11   Sidney Blumenthal, "Dick Cheney was never a 'grown-up'" *Salon.com* April 14, 2008 http://www.salon.com/books/excerpt/2008/04/14/cheney/print.html
12   Ibid
13   "Zionist infiltration of the US Government" http://www.zionismexplained.org/infiltration/infiltration.html
14   Blumenthal, supra note 11.
15   Blumenthal, supra note 11.
16   Blumenthal, supra note 11.
17   Blumenthal, supra note 11.

18   *Source watch : Joseph Coors* http://www.sourcewatch.org/index.php?title=Joseph_Coors

19   Paul M. Weyrich, "The most important legacy of Joe Coors" March 24, 2003 http://www.enterstageright.com/archive/articles/0303/0303coors.txt

20   "The Heritage Foundation: Power Elites: The Merger of Right and Left" http://www.watch.pair.com/heritage.html

21   "Paul Weyrich" *Right Web Profile* http://rightweb.irc-online.org/profile/1384.html

22   "The Heritage Foundation," supra note 20.

23   "The Heritage Foundation," supra note 20.

24   "The Heritage Foundation," supra note 20.

25   Robert Parry, "Mysterious Republican Money" *Consortiumnews.com* September 7, 2004 http://www.consortiumnews.com/2004/090704.html

26   Ibid

27   "Jeffrey H. Coors" *Source Watch* http://www.sourcewatch.org/index.php?title=Jeffrey_H._Coors

28   "The Heritage Foundation," supra note 20.

29   Bob Burton, "Battle Tanks: How Think Tanks Shaped the Public Agenda" *PR Watch Newsletter, Center for Media and Democracy PR Watch.org* Fourth Quarter 2005, Vol. 12, No. 4 http://www.prwatch.org/prwissues/2005Q4/battletanks

Chapter 4: Formation of the Religious Right

1   Penny Lernoux, "Who's Who? Knights of Malta Know" *National Catholic Reporter* May 5, 1989 http://www.mosquitonet.com/~prewett/ncrmay890910.html and http://www.mosquitonet.com/~prewett/ncrmay891113.html

2   Frank Cocozelli, "The Catholic Right" *Talk to Action - Reclaiming Citizenship History and Faith* May 8, 2006 http://www.talk2action.org/story/2006/5/8/72320/82268

3   George Lakoff, "Metaphor, Morality and Politics" Social Research (Volume 62, no. 2) (Graduate Faculty of the New School for Social Research, 1995) *The Institute for Cultural Democracy* 1995 http://www.wwcd.org/issues/Lakoff.html

4   "The New Right Takes Aim" *TIME* August 20, 1979 http://www.time.com/time/magazine/article/0,9171,947346,00.html

5   "The Heritage Foundation: Power Elites: The Merger of Right and Left" http://www.watch.pair.com/heritage.html

6   98 percent of American Catholics belong to the Latin Rite of the Roman Catholic Church. Weyrich was a deacon in the Melkite Church, one of numerous Eastern Rites all with relatively few members but all in full communion with the Church of Rome. Few inside or outside the neoconservative movement noted the distinction including Weyrich himself.

7   "Moral Majority" *Wikipedia* http://en.wikipedia.org/wiki/Moral_Majority

8   Patricia Zapor, "Rev. Falwell's Moral Majority: How it changed politics and religion" *Catholic News Service* May18, 2007 http://www.catholicnews.com/data/stories/cns/0702860.htm

9   "The New Right Takes Aim," supra note 4.

10   "The Heritage Foundation," supra note 5.

11   Robert Parry, "Dark Side of Rev. Moon: Buying the Right" *The Consortium* 1997 http://www.consortiumnews.com/archive/moon3.html

12   David Molpus, "Televangelist, Christian Leader Jerry Falwell Dies" *NPR All Things Considered* May 15, 2007 http://www.npr.org/templates/story/story.php?storyId=10188427

13   "The New Right Takes Aim," supra note 4.

14   "Richard Viguerie" *Source Watch* http://www.sourcewatch.org/index.php?title=Richard_Viguerie

15   Frank Rich, "Just How Gay Is the Right" *New York Times* May 15, 2005 http://www.nytimes.com/2005/05/15/opinion/15rich.html?pagewanted=2&_r=1

16   Michael Isikoff, "Church Spends Millions On Its Image" *Washington Post* September 17, 1984 http://www.washingtonpost.com/wp-srv/national/longterm/cult/unification/image.htm

17   "The New Right Takes Aim," supra note 4.

18   Isikoff, supra note 16.

19   Jerry Meldon, "US Shields Japan's WWII Denials" *Consortiumnews.com* February 24, 2007 http://www.consortiumnews.com/2007/022407b.html and "World Anti-Communist League" http://rightweb.irc-online.org/gw/2815.html

20   "The New Right Takes Aim," supra note 4.

21   The Council for National Policy, Past/Present Officers & Prominent Member Profiles Part III ~ N - Z http://watch.pair.com/database2.html

22   "American Society for the Defense of Tradition, Family and Property" *Wikipedia* http://en.wikipedia.org/wiki/American_Society_for_the_Defense_of_Tradition,_Family_and_Property and http://www.pfaw.org/pfaw/general/default.aspx?oid=23350

23   John Conway book review *The Theocons: Secular American under Siege* by Damon Linker (New York: Doubleday 2006) *Association of Contemporary Church Historians* (Arbeitsgemeinschaf t kirchliche Zeitgeschichtler) Newsletter - June 2007 - Vol. XIII, No. 6

24   Frank Cocozzelli, "The Catholic Right, Part IV: William Donohue And The Politics Of The Catholic League" *Talk to Action - Reclaiming Citizenship, History and Faith* June 4, 2006 http://www.talk2action.org/story/2006/5/23/82935/0830

25   Lakoff, supra note 3.

26   Declaration on Procured Abortions http://www.vatican.va/roman_curia/congregations/cfaith/documents/rc_con_cfaith_doc_19741118_declaration-abortion_en.html

27   Dr. David L. Perry, "Abortion and Personhood: Historical and Comparative Notes"http://home.earthlink.net/~davidlperry/abortion.htm

28   Timothy P. Weber, *On the Road to Armageddon: How evangelicals became Israel's best friend* copyright 2004 Baker Academic, a division of Baker Publishing Group, Adapted with permission http://www.beliefnet.com/story/151/story_15165_1.html

29   Peter J. Boyer, "Party Faithful" *The New Yorker* September 8, 2008 http://www.newyorker.com/reporting/2008/09/08/080908fa_fact_boyer?currentPage=all

30   Patton Dodd, "The End is Nigh? Is Middle East turmoil a fulfillment of biblical prophecy?" *belief net.com* http://www.beliefnet.com/story/196/story_19667_1.html

31   Weber, supra note 28.

Chapter 5: Two Popes Named John Paul

1   David A. Yallop, *In God's Name - An Investigation into the Murder of Pope John Paul I* (New York: Carroll & Graf 1984) 21

2   Ibid 36

3   Ibid 37

4   Ibid 162

5   Ibid 86-88

6   Ibid 208-209

7   Chuck Goudie, "FBI files show MLK faced opposition from Chicago church leader" *abc7chicago.com* January 15, 2007 http://abclocal.go.com/wls/story?section=news&id=4938716

8   Yallop, supra note 1 at 210-211.

9   David Yallop, *The Power and the Glory - Inside the Dark Heart of John Paul II's Vatican* (New York: Carroll & Graf, 2007) 3

10   John Cornwell, *A Thief in the Night: the Mysterious Death of Pope John Paul I* (New York: Simon and Shuster 1989) 109

11   http://jesuswouldbefurious.org/murderedpope

12   Andrzej M. Salski, "Polish Community in San Francisco and the Bay Area Helped to Reopen Old Slavic Church" *The Summit Times*, Vol. 4, No. 14-15/1996 http://users.rcn.com/salski/No14-15Folder/PoloniaReopenedChurch.htm

13   Tad Szulc, "The Making of the Pope" *Newsweek Society, MSNBC.com* April 1, 2005 http://www.msnbc.msn.com/id/7351202/site/newsweek/

14   Andrew Greeley, "Politics, piety mix during convention-like conclave" *Chicago Sun-Times* April 4, 2005 http://findarticles.com/p/articles/mi_qn4155/is_20050404/ai_n13615006

15   Cornwell, supra note 10 at 93.

16   Szulc, supra note 13.

17   Patricia Zapor, "Bridgeport's Bishop Egan named as Cardinal John O'Connor's Successor" *Catholic News Service* 2000 http://www.catholicherald.com/articles/00articles/eganny.htm

18   Szulc, supra note 13.

19   John Follain, *City of Secrets, The Truth Behind the Murders at the Vatican* (New York: Wm Morrow 2003) 109

20   Jesús López Sáez, *El Dia de la Cuenta: Juan Pablo II a Examen*, (Asociacion Comunidad de Ayala 2002) http://www.comayala.es/Libros/ddc/

21   Gunther Simmermacher, "The Conclave of October 1978: How John Paul II Became Pope." *Southern Cross*, October 15-21, 2003 http://www.mail-archive.com/pope-john-paul-ii@yahoogroups.com/msg00008.html

22   John L. Allen Jr., "How a Pope is Elected" *National Catholic Reporter Special Edition* April 2005 http://www.nationalcatholicreporter.org/update/conclave/how_to.htm

23   Kenneth L. Woodward with Loren Jenkins, Elaine Sciolino and Paul Martin, "A Pope from Poland." *Newsweek*, October 30, 1978   http://www.msnbc.msn.com/id/7350902/site/newsweek/

24   Simmermacher, supra note 21.

25   Woodward, supra note 23.

26   López Sáez, supra note 20.

27   Woodward, supra note 23.

28   Carl Bernstein and Mark Politi, *His Holiness: John Paul II and the Hidden History of Our Time* (New York: Doubleday 1996) 179

29   Woodward, supra note 23.

30   Andrew Greeley, *The Making of the Popes 1978: The Politics of Intrigue in the Vatican* (Chicago: Andrews McMeel 1979) 40

31   Jonathan Kitney, *Man of the Century, The Life and Times of Pope John Paul II* New York: Henry Holt and Co., 1997 http://www.amazon.com/gp/reader/0805026886/ref=sib_fs_bod/002-7985625-0375200?ie=UTF8&p=S00O&checkSum=gPpWY6vQbbyd9RToKiVh%2BkDSOleYh9xf4hPfsFFWFCA%3D#reader-link(Kwitney 10

32   Ibid

33   López Sáez, supra note 20.

34   George Weigel, *Witness to Hope: The Biography of Pope John Paul II* (New York: Harper Collins, 2005) 251 Google Books

35   Michelle Laque Johnson, "What the Pope taught us" *Catholic Standard and Times* April 7, 2005 http://www.archphila.org/cst_archives/050407/third.html

36   Yallop, supra note 1 at 264

37   Yallop, supra note 1 at 268

38   http://en.wikipedia.org/wiki/Aldo_Moro

39   Yallop, supra note 1 at 272

40   Yallop, supra note 1 at 278

41   Yallop, supra note 1 at 296

42   Yalop, supra note 1 at 297

43   Yallop, supra note 1 at 324

44   Sandro Magister, "The Pope's Banker Speaks: 'Here's How I Saved the IOR'" *www.chiesa* June 18, 2004 http://chiesa.espresso.repubblica.it/dettaglio.jsp?id=7048&eng=y

45   Yallop, supra note 1 at 310

46   Yallop, supra note 1 at 310

47   John Cornwell, *Breaking Faith: The Pope, the People and the Fate of Catholicism* (New York:Viking Compass 2001) 289

48   Gordon Urquhart "Opus Dei: the Pope's Right Arm in Europe" *The Center for Research on Population and Security* http://www.population-security.org/cffc-97-01.htm

49   Yallop, supra note 1 at 324.

50   Magister, supra note 45.

51   David Montero "Cracking the Silent Citadel: On the Trail of God's Bankers" *El Andar*

Summer 2002 Issue   http://elandar.com/back/summer02/stories/story_montero.html

Chapter 6: John Paul II and Latin America

1   David A. Yallop, *In God's Name - An Investigation into the Murder of John Paul I* (New York: Carroll & Graf 1984) 313

2   Penny Lernoux, "Prophets of Change in Latin America, Catholic Bishops Challenge Military," *The Nation,* 1976   http://www.aliciapatterson.org/APF001976/Lernoux/Lernoux02/Lernoux02.html

3   Jonathan Marshall, Peter Dale Scott, Jane Hunter "Growth of Reagan's Contra Commitment" Paper excerpted from the book *The Iran-Contra Connection: Secret Teams and Covert Operations in the Reagan Era* (South End Press 1987) http://www.thirdworldtraveler.com/Ronald_Reagan/ReaganContraCommit_TICC.html

4   Special: Nazis, The Vatican, and CIA" *Covert Action Information Bulletin* Winter 1986 No. 25 http://www.mosquitonet.com/~prewett/caqsmom25.2.html

5   Lernoux, supra note 2.

6   Lernoux, supra note 2.

7   Martin A. Lee, "Their Will be Done" *Mother Jones* July/August issue 1983 http://www.motherjones.com/news/feature/1983/07/willbedone.html

8   "Special", supra note 4.

9   Lernoux, supra note 2.

10   Lernoux, supra note 2.

11   Lernoux, supra note 2.

12   John L. Allen Jr. "These Paths Lead to Rome" *National Catholic Reporter* June 2, 2000 http://www.natcath.com/NCR_Online/archives/060200/060200a.htm

13   Gianni Cardinate, "First stop, Puebla" *30DAYS*, Issue No. 1 - 2004 http://www.30giorni.it/us/articolo.asp?id=2858

14   Allen, supra note 12.

15   Excerpts taken from: John Eagleson & Philip Scharper, Ed, PUEBLA AND BEYOND, (Orbis Books, Maryknoll NY (c) 1979) Provided Courtesy of: Eternal Word Television Network, 5817 Old Leeds Road, Irondale, AL 35210 www.ewtn.com

16   Penny Lernoux, Feature article for the *National Catholic Reporter* April 28, 1989 excerpt from *The People of God: The Struggle for World Catholicism.* (New York: Viking 1989) http://www.mosquitonet.com/~prewett/ncrapr89pg1014.html

17   Institute of Religion and Democracy, *Right Web Profile International Relations Center* http://rightweb.irc-online.org/profile/1496

18   Ibid

19   Lee, supra note 7.

20   http://www.infoplease.com/ce6/sci/A0857412.html

21   http://en.wikipedia.org/wiki/Crack_epidemic

22   Robert Reed, "Juan Perón and Cocaine Politics" *The Consortium* November 12, 1999 http://www.consortiumnews.com/1999/111299a.html

23   Yallop, supra note 1 at 262.

24   "Searching for Life: The Grandmothers of the Plaza de Mayo and the Disappeared Children of Argentina" http://www.usfca.edu/fac-staff/webberm/plaza.htm#ch7

25   Marie Trigona "Clergyman to Stand Trial for 'Dirty War' Crimes in Argentina" Americas Program, Center for International Policy (C.I.P.) August 12, 2007 http://www.worldpress.org/Americas/2895.cfm

26   "Searching for Life", supra note 24.

27   Allen, supra note 12.

28   Chuck Goudie, "Four indicted over 1982 murder with links to Chicago archdiocese" *ABC7Chicago.com*, abclocal.go.com/wls/news/041805_ns_gods_banker.html

29   Marshall, Scott and Hunter, supra note 3.

30   Robert A. Hutchinson, *Their Kindom Come: Inside the Secret World of Opus Dei* (New York : St. Martin's Press 1999) 213-214 Google Books

31   Goudie, supra note 28.

32   Marshall, Scott and Hunter, supra note 3.

33   Robert Parry, "Contra-Cocaine: Evidence of Premeditation" *The Consortium* June 1, 1998 http://www.consortiumnews.com/archive/crack12.html

34   Lee, supra note 7.

35   Lee, supra note 7.

36   Robert Parry and Tamar Jacoby, "A symbol of opposition to Sandinista rule: Cardinal Obando y Bravo" *Newsweek* June 15, 1987 http://www.mosquitonet.com/~prewett/contrascardinal.html

37   Ibid

38   Lernoux, supra note 16.

39   "Group Watch: Knights of Malta" *Interhemispheric Resource Center* http://www.voxfux.com/features/knights_of_malta_facts.html

40   "Drugs, Law Enforcement and Foreign Policy" United States Government Printing Office, Provided by *Wikipedia* http://en.wikipedia.org/wiki/Manuel_Noriega

41   Rachel Donadio, "Pio Laghi, Papal Envoy, Dies at 86" *New York Times* January 12, 2009 http://www.nytimes.com/2009/01/13/world/europe/13laghi.html?n=Top/Reference/Times%20Topics/Subjects/C/Cardinals%20(Roman%20Catholic%20Prelates

42   Stephen Engleberg with Jeff Gerth, "Bush and Noriega: Examination of Their Ties" Special to the *New York Times* September 28, 1988 http://query.nytimes.com/gst/fullpage.html?res=940DE1DA1F30F93BA1575AC0A96E948260

43   Michael Schaller, *Reckoning with Reagan* (New York: Oxford University Press 1992) 150

44   Ronald H. Cole, *Operation Just Cause: The Planning and Execution of Joint Operations in Panama 1988 - 1990* Joint History Office, Office of the Chairman of the Joint Chiefs of Staff, Washington D.C. 1995 Google Books

45   Editorial, "Why El Salvador matters" *National Catholic Reporter* June 27, 2008http://ncronline3.org/drupal/?q=node/1306

46   Lee, supra note 7.

47   Msgr. Ricardo Urios, from a talk in Westminster, Roehampton and Aylesford, "Archbishop Romero - a saint for the 21st century" *Independent Catholic News* May 22, 2007

48   Ibid

49   Chris Kraul and Henry Chu writing for the *Los Angeles Times*, "Latin American Catholics' problem with Pope John Paul II" *The Seattle Times* April 11, 2005 http://seattletimes.nwsource.com/html/nationworld/2002237743_popelatam11.html

50   "Group Watch," supra 39.

51   "Special", supra note 4.

52   "Special", supra note 4.

53   "El Salvador: Papal Appointment of a Conservative as Archbishop of San Salvador Stirs Debate" *NotiSur*, May 5, 1995 http://retanet.unm.edu/LADB-articles/21856.html

54   Editorial, supra note 45.

55   Will Weissert and Juan Carlos Llorca, "Guatemalan Files Renew Hope of Justice" *Associated Press* January 6, 2007 http://www.washingtonpost.com/wp-dyn/content/article/2007/01/06/AR2007010600444.html

56   John Swomley, "The Secret World of Opus Dei" *Human Quest* May/June 2000 http://findarticles.com/p/articles/mi_qa3861/is_200005/ai_n8889207/pg_1

57   "Guatemala: Catholic Church and Rightist Parties Exchange Accusations About Mixing Politics and Religion" August 31, 1999 Basic data from Cerigua weekly briefs, 08/13-19/90 http://retanet.unm.edu/LADB-articles/9012.html

58   "150 Guatemalans Seize Cathedral in Protest" *Associated Press* November 1, 1985 http://query.nytimes.com/gst/fullpage.html?res=9B00E4DD1438F932A35752C1A963948260&n=Top%2fReference%2fTimes%20Topics%2fOrganizations%2fR%2fRoman%20Catholic%20Church%20

59   "Group Watch", supra 39.

60   "Priest charged again in bishop's death - Bishop Juan Gerardi of Guatemala allegedly killed by Mario Orantes - Brief Article" *Christian Century* April 12, 2000 http://findarticles.com/p/articles/mi_m1058/is_12_117/ai_61793346

Chapter 7: Making Movie Actor Reagan "God's Man"

1   Margalit Fox, "Edward E. McAteer, 78; Empowered Christian Right" *New York Times* October 10, 2004 http://query.nytimes.com/gst/fullpage.html?res=9F03EFDC133B F933A25753C1A9629C8B63

2   Robert Marus and Greg Warner, "Ronald Reagan's ascent to office paralleled rise of Religious Right" *Associated Baptist Press* June 8, 2004 http://www.abpnews.com/2034.article

3   Michael Schaller, *Reckoning with Reagan* (New York: Oxford University Press 1992) 13

4   Jonathan Marshall, Peter Dale Scott, Jane Hunter, "Growth of Reagan's Contra Commitment" excerpted from the book *The Iran-Contra Connection*, (South End Press, 1987) paper www.thirdworldtraveler.com/Ronald_Reagan/ReaganContra-Commit_TICC.html

5   Robert Reed, "Juan Perón and Cocaine Politics" *The Consortium* November 12, 1999 http://www.consortiumnews.com/1999/111299a.html

6   Marshall, Scott and Hunter, supra note 4.

7   Robert Parry, "October Surprise X-files (Part 7): Bush & a CIA Power Play" *The Consortium* http://www.consortiumnews.com/archive/xfile7.html

8   David A. Yallop, *In God's Name - An Investigation into the Murder of Pope John Paul I* (New York: Carroll & Graf 1984) 315

9   "William J. Casey" *Answers.com* http://www.answers.com/topic/william-j-casey

10   "International Rescue Committee" *International Relations Committee - Right Web* http://rightweb.irc-online.org/gw/2801

11   "Creating a Task Force to Investigate the Holding of Americans as Hostages by Iran in 1980" (House of Representatives - February 5, 1992) *Congressional Record* http://www.fas.org/irp/congress/1992_cr/h920205-october-clips.htm

12   Marshall, Scott and Hunter, supra note 4.

13   Marshall, Scott and Hunter, supra note 4.

14   http://www.dkosopedia.com/wiki/Heritage_Foundation

15   http://www.dkosopedia.com/wiki/Joseph_Coors

16   Sarah Posner, "Secret Society" *AlterNet* March 1, 2005 http://www.alternet.org/story/21372/

17   Right Web/ Profile/ Council for National Policy http://rightweb.irc-online.org/pro-file/1462.html

18   Ibid

19   David D. Kirkpatrick, "The 2004 Campaign: The Conservatives; Club of the Most Powerful Gathers in Strictest Privacy" *New York Times* August 28, 2004 http://query.nytimes.com/gst/fullpage.html?res=9C0CE3DA1E3EF93BA1575BC0A9629C8B63

20   Thomas J. Reese, S.J., *Archbishop: Inside the Power Structure of the American Catholic Church* (San Francisco: Harper & Row 1989) http://woodstock.georgetown.edu/church_studies/reese/archbishop/ab-chap1.htm

21   Sandro Magister, "The U.S. Ambassador to the Vatican: 'After September 11, the Pope Said to Me...'" *www.chiesa* http://chiesa.espresso.repubblica.it/dettaglio.jsp?id=6886&eng=y

22   Reese, supra note 20.

23   Magister, supra note 21.

24   Carl Bernstein and Marco Politi, *His Holiness: John Paul II and the Hidden History of Our Time* (Doubleday,1996)

25   http://en.wikipedia.org/wiki/Zbigniew_Brzezinski

26   Jonathan Kwitney, *Man of the Century: The Life and Times of Pope John Paul II* (New York: Henry Holt and Co. 1997) http://www.nytimes.com/books/first/k/kwitny-century.html?_r=1&oref=slogin

27   Martin A. Lee, "Their Will Be Done" *Mother Jones* July/August issue 1983 http://www.motherjones.com/news/feature/1983/07/willbedone.html?welcome=true

28   Penny Lernoux, Excerpt from *People of God: The Struggle for World Catholicism* (Viking 1989) *National Catholic Reporter* April 28, 1989 http://www.mosquitonet.com/~prewett/ncrapr89pg1014.html

29   Ibid
30   Paul Kengor, "Reagan's Catholic Connections" *Catholic Exchange* June 11, 2004
      http://www.catholiceducation.org/articles/catholic_stories/cs0080.html
31   Carl Bernstein, "The Holy Alliance" (1 of 2 Special Reports) *Time Magazine* February
      24, 1992 http://www.time.com/time/magazine/article/0,9171,974931-1,00.html
32   Kengor, supra note 30.
33   Bernstein, supra note 31.
34   Bernstein, supra note 31.
35   Kengor, supra note 30.
36   Marius Heuser and Peter Schwarz, "Pope John Paul II: a political obituary" *World
      Socialist Web Site* April 6, 2005 http://www.wsws.org/articles/2005/apr2005/pope-
      a06.shtml
37   Magister, supra note 21.
38   Reese, supra note 20.
39   Lernoux, supra note 28.
40   Thomas J. Reese, S.J., "Three Years Later: U.S. Relations with the Holy See"
      America Magazine January 17, 1987 woodstock.georgetown.edu/church_studies/
      reese/america/a-wilson.htm
41   Lernoux, supra note 28.
42   Carl Bernstein, "The US and the Vatican on Birth Control" *Time Magazine* February
      24, 1992 http://www.population-security.org/15-CH7.html
43   John M. Swomley, "Political Power of Roman Catholic Bishops" *The Human Quest*
      May-June 1992 http://www.population-security.org/swom-92-05.htm
44   Reese, supra note 40.
45   Ibid
46   Lernoux, supra note 28.
47   Reese, supra note 40.
48   Lernoux, supra note 28.
49   Reese, supra note 40.
50   Lernoux, supra note 28.
51   http://www.phillyburbs.com/pointsofinterest/shrine/Guests.htm
52   Schaller, supra note 3 at 125.

Chapter 8: John Paul II and the Media

1   Jeff Israely, "And in His 82nd Year, He Rested" *TIME Magazine* March 31, 2002
      http://www.time.com/time/magazine/article/0,9171,221092,00.html
2   "Pope Used Media to His Advantage: Media-Savvy John Paul II Got His Message
      Out Via Media and Technology" *ABC News* April 2, 2005 http://abcnews.go.com/
      Health/Pope/Story?id=635184&page=1
3   "Even in Death, a Media Superstar" *ZENIT.org* April 16, 2005 ZE05041603
4   Hermann Haering, "Due Respect for the Man, Due Resistance However to His Mes-
      sage - The Catholic Church and the Media" Essay translated by Natalie K. Watson
5   "Pope Used Media to His Advantage", supra note 2.
6   Haering, supra note 4.
7   Deborah Caldwell, "Bush's Catholic Courtship Strategy" *beliefnet* http://www.belief-
      net.com/story/146/story_14691_1.html
8   Kathryn Jean Lopez, "A Great Communicator" *National Review Online* April 20,
      2005 http://www.nationalreview.com/lopez/lopez200504200802.asp
9   Ibid
10   *L.A. Weekly* issue date February 20, 1987, quoted by Jim Naureckas "Media
      Monopoly: Long History, Short Memories. ABC Was Born Out of Fear of Media
      Consolidation" *fair.org* November/December 1995 http://www.fair.org/index.
      php?page=1332Extra!
11   "What Happened to Fairness" *NOW with David Brancaccio* http://www.pbs.org/now/
      politics/fairness.html
12   "News" *Los Angeles Lay Catholic Mission* February 1998 http://www.losangelesmis-
      sion.com/ed/news/0298news.htm

13   "Parents' Group Warns Against 4 Fox Shows" *Associated Press* October 19, 2005 http://www.parentstv.org/PTC/news/2005/toptenlist_ap.htm

14   Lopez, supra note 8.

15   "Pope Used Media to His Advantage", supra note 2.

16   John M. Swomley, "The Threat of Theocracy" *Christian Ethics Today* Issue 036 Volume 7 No 5 October 2001 http://www.christianethicstoday.com/Issue/036/The%20 Threat%20of%20Theocracy%20-%20By%20John%20M%20Swomley_036_20_. htm

17   Joe Feuerherd, "Financially Strapped Archdiocese Subsidizes Troubled Center" *National Catholic Report* February 10, 2006 http://natcath.org/NCR_Online/ archives2/2006a/021006/021006h.php

18   Ibid

19   Jonathan Petre, "Third Secret is revealed...but mystery still haunts the faithful" http://members.fortunecity.com/templarser/fatima.html

20   Douglass K. Daniel "Reagan Adviser Michael Deaver Dies" *Associated Press* August 18, 2007 http://www.ajc.com/news/content/shared-gen/ap/US_President_ And_White_House_Advisers/Obit_Deaver.html

21   Haering, supra note 4.

22   John L. Allen Jr., "All Things Catholic" *National Catholic Reporter* August 4, 2006 http://www.nationalcatholicreporter.org/word/word080406.htm#seven

23   "Knights of Columbus presents pope with check for $2.5 million" *Catholic News Service* October 9, 2003

24   Michael Rezendes and Thomas Farragher, "Archdiocese mortgages Law's home to pay debt" *Boston Globe* September 28, 2002 http://www.boston.com/globe/spotlight/ abuse/stories3/092802_mortgage.htm

25   "Bertone condemns abuse lawyers" *The Tablet* August 18, 2007 http://www.thetablet. co.uk/articles/10226

26   "Knights Info" South Attleboro Knights of Columbus - Council 5876 http://kofc5876. com/id9.html

27   *Knights of Columbus News Release*, April 2, 2005

28   David Remnick, "The Pope in Crisis" *The New Yorker*, October 17, 1994 quoted by Gordon Urquhart "Opus Dei: the Pope's Right Arm in Europe" *The Center for Research on Population and Security* http://www.population-security.org/cffc-97-01. htm

29   Nick Pisa, "Vatican Hid Pope's Parkinson Disease Diagnosis for 12 Years" *Telegraph.co.uk* March 19, 2006 http://www.telegraph.co.uk/news/main.jhtml?xml=/ news/2006/03/19/wpope19.xml

30   John Follain, *City Of Secrets, The Truth Behind The Murders At The Vatican* (New York: HarperCollins, 2003) 107

31   "Vatican death update" *CNN* May 5, 1998 http://edition.cnn.com/WORLD/europe/9805/05/vatican.death.update/index.html

32   Mark Fellows, "The Smell of Death" *Catholic Family News* November 3, 2003 http://209.85.165.104/search?q=cache:L5xJ8fQrYRQJ:www.odan.org/media_ smell_of_death.rtf+fellows%2Bsmell+of+death&hl=en&ct=clnk&cd=1&gl=us

Chapter 9: The Neo-Catholic Church

1   Penny Lernoux, Excerpts from *People of God: The Struggle for World Catholicism*. (New York: Viking 1989) *National Catholic Reporter* April 28, 1989 http://www. mosquitonet.com/~prewett/ncrapr89pg1014.html

2   Jason Berry and Gerald Renner, *Vows of Silence: the Abuse of Power in the Papacy of John Paul II* (Free Press: 2004) 87

3   Thomas J. Reese, S.J. *Archbishop: Inside the Power Structure of the American Catholic Church* (San Francisco: Harper & Row 1989) http://woodstock.georgetown. edu/church_studies/reese/archbishop/ab-chap1.htm

4   Dr. [Phd.] Stephen Mumford *American Democracy & The Vatican: Population Growth & National Security* (Amherst, NY: Humanist Press 1984) http://www.mosquitonet. com/~prewett/amdem203.html

5   Lernoux, supra note 1.
6   Lernoux, supra note 1.
7   http://www.seattlecatholic.com/misc_20040105.html
8   Joseph Sobran "Bishop in the Doghouse - Raymond Hunthausen" *National Review* December 19, 1986 http://findarticles.com/p/articles/mi_m1282/is_v38/ai_4580932/print
9   Tran Chung Ngoc, Ph.D., "Dialogue with Pope John Paul II: Crossing the Threshold of Ignorance" *Giao Diem* http://giaodiem.com/FotoNews/tcn-dialogue.htm
10   Lernoux, supra note 1.
11   Sobran, supra note 8.
12   Sobran, supra note 8.
13   Sobran, supra note 8.
14   Sobran, supra note 8.
15   Richard N. Ostling, "'Unreservedly' Loyal to the Pope U.S. Bishops Reluctantly Back Rome Against a Liberal Colleague" *TIME Magazine* November 24, 1986 http://www.time.com/time/magazine/article/0,9171,962894-1,00.html
16   Ibid
17   Lernoux, supra note 1.
18   Decree on the Bishops' Pastoral Office in the Church, #38
19   Ostling, supra note 15.
20   Lernoux, supra note 1.
21   "The Ultimate Test of America's Greatness" Remarks at Conclusion of 1987 Pastoral Visit to the United States: The farewell message on Saturday evening, September 19, 1987, in the presence of Vice-President George Bush and other dignitaries. http://www.vatican.va/holy_father/john_paul_ii/speeches/1987/september/documents/hf_jp-ii_spe_19870919_congedo-stati-uniti_en.html
22   http://www.ncbi.nlm.nih.gov/pubmed/10561657
23   http://web.archive.org/web/20070814095925/http://www.epm.org/articles/doctors.html
24   Thierry Meyssan, "The Opus Dei Sets Out to Conquer the World" *Voltair Network* January 25, 1996 http://www.voltairenet.org/article136480.html?var_recherche=Vatican?var_recherche=Vatican
25   Thomas C. Fox, "After 30 years, bishops, politicians, voters vexed by abortion" *National Catholic Reporter* September 11, 2008 http://ncronline3.org/drupal/?q=node/1792
26   http://www.usccb.org/prolife/tdocs/index.shtml
27   Vincent J. Genovesi, *In Pursuit of Love-Catholic Morality and Human Sexuality* (Collegeville, Minnesota: "A Michael Glazier Book" 1996) 299 quoting Gallagher, ed. *Homosexuality and the Magisterium*, 928   Ibid 301 quoting "Homosexuality, The New Vatican Statement"," 271
29   John M. Swomley, "One Nation Under God...National Council of Catholic Bishops Seeks to Influence Policy" *Gale Group* 1998   http://findarticles.com/p/articles/mi_m1374/is_n3_v58/ai_20770505/print
30   Gretchen Keiser, "U.S. Bishops Affirm Need To Support Catholic Schools' Mission" *Georgia Bulletin* December 5, 2002 http://www.georgiabulletin.org/local/2002/12/05/j/
31   David Gonzalez, "Frustration Over a $25,000 Catholic School" *New York Times* September 29, 2007 .http://select.nytimes.com/mem/tnt.html?_r=2&tntget=2007/09/29/nyregion/29academy.html&tntemail1=y&oref=slogin&emc=tnt&pagewanted=all&oref=slogin
32   Joseph Claude Harris, "Bishops' Schools Plan Flawed from the Start" *National Catholic Reporter* March 27, 1998 http://findarticles.com/p/articles/mi_m1141/is_n21_v34/ai_20449166/pg_4
33   John M. Swomley, "The Vatican connection: how the Catholic Church influences the Republican party" *Humanist* Nov-Dec, 1996 http://findarticles.com/p/articles/mi_m1374/is_n6_v56/ai_18844575/print
34   Ibid
35   Gill Donovan, "Ambition, Defense of Institutional Church Drove Cardinal's Career" *National Catholic Reporter* December 27, 2002 http://ncronline.org/NCR_Online/

archives/122702/122702f.htm

36   Ibid

37   Swomley, supra note 29.

38   Arthur Jones, "Texas sues Bishop Gracida; he sues back - Corpus Christi Bishop Rene H. Gracida is accused of conflict of interest in the administration of a charitable fund" *National Catholic Reporter* May 24, 1996 http://findarticles.com/p/articles/mi_m1141/is_n30_v32/ai_18341631

39   Swomley, supra note 33.

40   Editorial "Three Meetings, Three Faces of U.S. Catholicism - Call to Action, Catholic Campaign for America, and the U.S. Catholic Bishops" *National Catholic Reporter* December 15, 1995 http://findarticles.com/p/articles/mi_m1141/is_n8_v32/ai_17917966

41   Swomley, supra note 33.

42   Swomley, supra note 33.

43   Robert Parry, "Henry Hyde: Mr. Cover-up" *Consortiumnews.com* November 30, 2007 http://www.consortiumnews.com/2007/113007.html

44   Luis E. Lugo, "The Catholic Campaign for America" *The Center for Public Justice* March-April, 1996 http://www.cpjustice.org/stories/storyReader$869

45   Editorial "By any other name, it was an endorsement - Cardinal John J. O'Connor appears in a photo-op with presidential candidate Bob Dole" *National Catholic Reporter* July 12, 1996 http://findarticles.com/p/articles/mi_m1141/is_n34_v32/ai_18480020

46   Gustav Niebuhr, "Cardinals Condemn Clinton Abortion Veto" *New York Times*, April 17, 1996 http://query.nytimes.com/gst/fullpage.html?res=9E04E6DD1E39F934A25757C0A960958260&sec=&spon=&pagewanted=all

47   Swomley, supra note 33.

48   Editorial, supra note 45.

49   John M. Swomley, "The Vatican connection: how the Catholic Church influences the Republican party" from *Christian Ethics Today* April 1997 *The Center for Research on Population and Security* http://www.population-security.org/swom-97-04.htm

50   Ibid

51   Ibid

52   Ibid

53   Penny Lernoux, Excerpt from *People of God: The Struggle for World Catholicism* (New York: Penguin Books) 1990 http://www.cephas-library.com/church_n_state/church_and_state_new_christian_right.html

Chapter 10: Neo-Catholic Protagonists

1   Dale Vree, Editorial "Your Voice of Orthodox Catholicism, Without Any Strings Attached" *New Oxford Review* September 2005 http://www.newoxfordreview.org/article.jsp?did=0905-editorial

2   John F. Quinn, "America: Not So Great After All, The Neoconservative Catholics' Dramatic Change of Direction" *New Oxford Review* October 1998 http://www.newoxfordreview.org/article.jsp?did=1098-quinn

3   http://rightweb.irc-online.org/profile/1310

4   Robert A. Sungenis, "Politics, Religion, Israel and the Seduction of the Catholic Voter" *Catholic Apologetics International* http://www.catholicintl.com/catholicissues/politics2.htm

5   Rev. Andrew J. Weaver, Ph.D., "Neocon Catholics target mainline Protestants" *Media Transparency* August 11, 2006 http://www.mediatransparency.org/storyprinterfriendly.php?storyID=142

6   http://en.wikipedia.org/wiki/American_Enterprise_Institute

7   http://www.newamericancentury.org/iraqclintonletter.htm

8   Michael Novak "A Layman's Dissent" *Times Magazine* November 8, 1982 http://www.time.com/time/magazine/article/0,9171,925820-1,00.html

9   Joe Feuerherd, *National Catholic Reporter* August 19, 2004 quoted by Bill Berkowitz, "Neocon Catholic leaders nurtured by GOP and Conservative Philanthropy on their

heels" *Media Transparency* September 23, 2007 http://www.mediatransparency.org/story.php?storyID=212

10   Ibid

11   Todd David Whitmore, "The Loyal Dissent of Neo-Conservative Economics, Part I" October 2, 1998 http://www.nd.edu/~cstprog/19981002.htm

12   Michael Novak "John Paul the Great" April 11, 2005 http://www.michaelnovak.net/Module/Article/ArticleView.aspx?id=123

13   Quinn, supra note 2.

14   Zwick and Zwick, 1999 quoted by Weaver, supra note 5.

15   Joel Connelly, "In the Northwest: Catholic Scholar Still Seeking Real Tolerance" *seattlepi.com* October 14, 2002 http://seattlepi.nwsource.com/connelly/91022_joel14.shtml

16   http://www.eppc.org/scholars/scholarID.46/scholar.asp

17   http://www.mediatransparency.org/search_results/info_on_any_recipient.php?recipientID=103

18   Weaver, supra note 5.

19   Quinn, supra note 2.

20   Bob Abernethy's interview with George Weigel *Religion & Ethics Newsweekly* May 10, 2002 Episode no. 536 http://www.pbs.org/wnet/religionandethics/week536/gweigel.html

21   Jonathan Luxmoore and Jolanta Babiuch "Unpublished Work by John Paul II Sparks Debate" *The Sunday Herald*, October 1, 2006 http://www.sundayherald.com/58242

22   Vree, supra note 1.

23   Weaver, supra note 5.

24   Mary Arnold, "Richard John Neuhaus interviewed" *AD2000* Vol 4 No 5 (June 1991) http://www.ad2000.com.au/articles/1991/jun1991p10_706.html

25   Quinn, supra note 2.

26   George Weigel, "John Paul II and the Crisis of Humanism" *First Things* December 1999 http://sandbox.firstthings.com/article.php3?id_article=3251&var_recherche=humanae

27   http://www.mediatransparency.org/search_results/info_on_any_recipient.php?175

28   "Documentation: A New American Compact: Caring About Women, Caring for the Unborn," *First Things*, November 1992

29   Richard John Neuhaus, "The Church on the Rocks" *First Things* August/September 2000 http://www.firstthings.com/article.php3?id_article=2645

30   http://www.firstthings.com/article.php3?id_article=4454&var_recherché

31   Bill Berkowitz, "Campaign to court Catholics" *WorkingForChange* July 31, 2001

32   Quinn, supra note 2.

33   Weaver, supra note 5.

34   Zwick and Zwick, 1999 quoted by Weaver, supra note 5.

35   Weaver, supra note 5.

36   Father John McCloskey, A book review of *The Clash of Civilizations and the Remaking of World Order* by Samuel P. Huntington (Simon and Schuster, 1996) Originally appeared in *L'Osservatore Romano* (English Edition) in the July 23, 1997, edition (No. 30) http://www.catholicity.com/mccloskey/clash.html

37   Michael J. Matt, "A Return to Chartres" *The Remnant* 2006 http://www.remnant-newspaper.com/Archives/archive-2006-a_return_to_chartres.htm

38   Father John McCloskey "2030: Looking Backwards" First appeared in *Catholic World Report* in the May 2000 issue. http://www.catholicity.com/mccloskey/2030.html

39   Charles P. Pierce, "The Crusaders" *Boston Globe* November 2, 2003 http://www.boston.com/news/globe/magazine/articles/2003/11/02/the_crusaders/

40   Father John McCloskey book review of H.W. Crocker III *Triumph: The Power and the Glory of the Catholic Church, a 2000-Year History* (Prima Communications: 2001) http://www.catholicity.com/mccloskey/triumph.html

41   Joe Conasan, "Was Hanssen a Spy for the Right Wing, Too? *New York Observer*, August 6, 2001 http://www.observer.com/node/44794

42   Walter Pincus and Mike Allen "Leak of Agent's Name Causes Exposure of CIA Front

Firm" *Washington Post* October 4, 2003 http://www.washingtonpost.com/ac2/wp-dyn/A40012-2003Oct3?language=printer

43   Jason Leopold, "Valerie Plame Still Wants to Know..." *t r u t h o u t | Report* November 13, 2007 http://www.truthout.org/docs_2006/111307J.shtml)

44   Amy Sullivan, "Bob in Paradise: How Novak Created His Own Ethics-free Zone" *Washington Monthly* December 2004 http://www.washingtonmonthly.com/features/2004/0412.sullivan.html

45   Ibid

46   http://www.rhrealitycheck.org/right/priests-for-life

47   "Faithless Politics: Priests for Life defies Constitution and Conscience" Opposition Notes *Catholics for Choice* www.catholicsforchoice.org/pubs/documents/OppNotes_Priests_Web.pdf

48   Ibid

49   http://www.priestsforlife.org/frpavonebio.html.

50   "Faithless Politics", supra note 47.

51   "Faithless Politics", supra note 47.

52   http://www.priestsforlife.org/frpavonebio.html

53   John L. Allen Jr., "Opus Dei Prestige on Display at Centenary Event" *National Catholic Reporter* January 18, 2002 http://www.natcath.com/NCR_Online/archives/011802/011802f.htm

54   Ibid

55   Will Bunch "Sen. Rick Santorum (R-Opus Dei): Cracking a GOP senator's 'Da Vinci code'" *attytood.com* http://www.attytood.com/archives/001764.html

56   "Sour Charity" *The American Project* February 21, 2006 http://www.gather.com/viewArticle.jsp?articleId=281474976731591

57   Ibid

58   Ibid

59   "Santorum Charity at Center of Republican Culture of Corruption" *Democratic Party* March 7, 2006 http://www.democrats.org/a/2006/03/santorum_charit.php

60   Will Bunch "With A Little Help From His Friends" *The American Prospect* February 20, 2006 http://www.prospect.org/cs/articles?articleId=11174

61   Joe Feuerherd, "Senate rolls over for Negroponte; Prayer breakfast brings 'faithful Catholics' together" *National Catholic Reporter* April 28, 2004, http://www.nationalcatholicreporter.org/washington/wnb042804.htm

Chapter 11: The 2000 Presidential Campaign

1   "Catholic Bishops Called on to Repudiate Republican Claim that GOP Positions are 'Closest' to Catholic Church's" April 13, 2000 *Catholics for Choice* http://www.cath4choice.org/news/pr/pressrelease04-13-2000.asp

2   Max Blumental quoted by Rev. Andrew J. Weaver, Ph.D., "Neocon Catholics target mainline Protestants" *Media Transparency* August 11, 2006http://www.mediatransparency.org/storyprinterfriendly.php?storyID=142

3   Peter J. Boyer, "Party Faithful" *The New Yorker* September 8, 2008 http://www.newyorker.com/reporting/2008/09/08/080908fa_fact_boyer?currentPage=all

4   Patricia Miller, "Conservative Catholics and the GOP - National Affairs" *USA Today (Society for the Advancement of Education)*, November 2002 http://findarticles.com/p/articles/mi_m1272/is_2690_131/ai_94384315/pg_1

5   http://en.wikipedia.org/wiki/Karl_Rove

6   William V. D'Antonio, Jacqueline Scherer, "Research challenges bold GOP boast - Republicans represent Catholic teaching best" *National Catholic Reporter*, August 11, 2000 http://findarticles.com/p/articles/mi_m1141/is_36_36/ai_64697539

7   Lawn Griffiths, "Author coached White House on Catholic issues" *East Valley Tribune* May 2, 2008 http://www.eastvalleytribune.com/story/115389

8   Frances Kissling, "Is God a Republican" *Religion News Service* http://www.beliefnet.com/story/21/story_2166.html

9   Editorial, "Like Father, Like Son" *iF* Magazine *consortium news.com* October 18, 1999 http://www.consortiumnews.com/1999/101899a.html

10   http://en.wikipedia.org/wiki/Karl_Rove

11   Francis X. Clines, "The Nation: Cross Purposes; Mixing God and Politics And Getting Burned" *New York Times* March 5, 2000 http://query.nytimes.com/gst/fullpage.html?res=9A03E4D81738F936A35750C0A9669C8B63&sec=&spon=&pagewanted=1

12   Frank Bruni with Nicholas D. Kristof "The 2000 Campaign: The Texas Governor; Bush Rues Failure to Attack Bigotry in Visit to College" *New York Times* February 28, 2000 http://query.nytimes.com/gst/fullpage.html?res=9802E1DE1539F93BA15751C0A9669C8B63&sec=&spon=&pagewanted=1

13   Kissling, supra note 8.

14   Raymond A. Schroth, "Stopping the press.(case of the Philadelphia Inquirer, Ralph Cipriano, and the Philadelphia archdiocese)(Statistical Data Included)" *National Catholic Reporter* March 2, 2001 http://www.encyclopedia.com/doc/1G1-71763367.html

15   Kate O'Beirne "The Catholic Factor: Which Way Will They Swing?" *National Review* August 28, 2000 http://findarticles.com/p/articles/mi_m1282/is_16_52/ai_64341394/pg_2

16   Frank Bruni and Alison Mitchell, "The 2000 Campaign: The Texas Governor; Bush Says Integrity Makes Him Right for Job" *New York Times* November 5, 2000 http://query.nytimes.com/gst/fullpage.html?res=9F00E7DB1539F936A35752C1A9669C8B63&sec=&spon=&pagewanted=all

17   "Bush Tries to Resurrect Flagging Faith-Based Initiative, Enlist Catholic Church at Notre Dame Speech" *Flashline* American Atheists, May 23, 2001 http://www.atheists.org/flash.line/faith19.htm

18   Miller, supra note 4.

19   http://www.catholicsforchoice.org/pubs/documents/OppNotes_Priests_Web.pdf

20   Jennifer Gonnerman, "Father Frank's Crusade: A Staten Island Priest Leads a Costly and Well-Organized Campaign Against Abortion" *Village Voice* May 23 - 29, 2001 http://www.villagevoice.com/news/0121,gonnerman,24947,1.html

21   http://www.priestsforlife.org/newsletters/v10n4julaug00.htm

22   Richard John Neuhaus, "The Church on the Rocks" *First Things* August/September 2000 http://www.firstthings.com/article.php3?id_article=2645

23   E.J. Dionne, Jr. "There is No 'Catholic Vote.' And Yet, it Matters" *Washington Post* June 18, 2000 http://www.qev.com/washpostdionnejune182000.htm

24   "The Power Behind the Nominee: Marvin Olasky, Faith-Based 'Partnerships,' and the Threat to State-Church Separation," *Flashline* American Atheists August 4, 2000 http://www.atheists.org/flash.line/elec10.htm

25   Richard Cohen, "Death Penalty: Al With His Finger in the Wind" *Washington Post* June 13, 2000 http://www.commondreams.org/views/061300-102.htm

26   Wayne Madsen, "Bush's 'Christian' Blood Cult. Concerns Raised by the Vatican" *CounterPunch* April 22, 2003 reprinted with permission from the author http://www.counterpunch.org/madsen04222003.html

27   "A Memorial to Karla Faye Tucker Brown" quoted from the *Houston Chronicle*, August 11, 1999 http://www.geocities.com/rainforest/canopy/2525/karlamain.html

28   http://www.usccb.org/sdwp/national/criminal/appeal.shtml

29   Ralph McInerny, "End Notes: Home Thoughts From Abroad" *Crisis* June 9, 2003 http://www.crisismagazine.com/june2003/endnotes.htm

30   Michael Novak "Just Tragic? The Justice in Saddam Hussein's Execution" *An NRO Symposium* January 1, 2007 http://www.declaration.net/news.asp?docID=5589&y=2007

31   James Nuechterlein, "Forgiveness & the Death Penalty" *First Things* April 2000 http://www.firstthings.com/article.php3?id_article=2590

32   Evelyn Pringle, "Ted Olson - Bush Administration Preemption Gang - Part I" *LawyersandSettlements.com* March 3, 2008 http://www.lawyersandsettlements.com/articles/10095/preemption-medtronic.html

33   http://cara.georgetown.edu/Press112204.pdf

34   Richard Parker, "The Politics of God" *Kennedy School Bulletin* Autumn 2004 http://www.ksg.harvard.edu/ksgpress/bulletin/autumn2004/features/god.htm

35   Thomas B. Edsall, *Building Red America: The New Conservative Coalition and the*

Drive for Permanent Power (Basic Books 2006) p 91 Google Books

36   John L. Allen Jr., "Political factors increase embassy's stature" *National Catholic Reporter* March 22, 2002 http://natcath.org/NCR_Online/archives2/2002a/032202/032202i. htm

37   Carl Raschke, "Catholics as 'Value Voters'" *Guernica* October 2004 Issue http:// www.guernicamag.com/features/7/catholics_as_values_voters/

38   William A. Galston, "The Catholic Vote in the 2008 Democratic Primary Campaign" The Brookings Institution May 5, 2008 http://www.brookings.edu/speeches/2008/0505_catholic_galston.aspx

39   John M. Swomley, "The Threat of Theocracy?" *St. Paul School of Theology* Issue 036 Volume 7 No 5 October 2001 http://www.christianethicstoday.com/Issue/036/The%20Threat%20of%20Theocracy%20-%20By%20John%20M%20Swomley_036_20_.htm

40   Denise Grady, "The Deadly Toll of Abortion by Amateurs" *New York Times* June 1, 2009 http://www.nytimes.com/2009/06/02/health/02abort.html?hp

41   Deborah Caldwell, "Bush's Catholic Courtship Strategy" *beliefnet* 2006 http://www. beliefnet.com/story/146/story_14691_1.html

Chapter 12: Political Patronage in the Guise of Charity

1   http://www.tfn.org/files/fck/TFN%20CC%20REPORT-FINAL.pdf

2   Ibid

3   "So Far, Sympathetic Signals From President Bush" *Zenit.org* January 28, 2001 http://zenit.org/article-415?l=english

4   "30 U.S. Catholic Leaders to Meet With Bush" *Zenit.org* January 30, 2001 http:// zenit.org/article-438?l=english

5   Thomas B. Edsall, "Grants Flow to Bush Allies on Social Issues" *Washington Post* March 22, 2006 http://www.truthout.org/docs_2006/032206C.shtml

6   http://www.mediatransparency.org/pdastory.php?storyID=44

7   Edsall, supra note 5.

8   "Faith-Based Debate" *NewsHour with Jim Lehrer* July 19, 2001http://www.pbs.org/newshour/bb/congress/july-dec01/faith_7-19.html

9   http://www.opensecrets.org/2000elect/other/bush/inaugural.asp

10   Rodger Van Allen, "Et Cetera - Catholics and Politics" *Commonweal* May 4, 2001 FindArticles.com. 27 Dec. 2007. http://findarticles.com/p/articles/mi_m1252/is_9_128/ai_75445671

11   "Bush Tries to Resurrect Flagging Faith-Based Initiative, Enlist Catholic Church at Notre Dame Speech" *Flashline American Atheists* May 23, 2001 http://www.atheists. org/flash.line/faith19.htm

12   http://www.whitehouse.gov/news/releases/2001/05/20010524-1.html

13   http://www.cleanairtrust.org/villain.0602.html

14   "'Compassionate Conservatism' just words" Editorial *National Catholic Reporter* December 13, 2002 http://www.encyclopedia.com/doc/1G1-95631995.html

15   CUA, under direct supervision of the bishops, is a "neo-Catholic" institution. A CUA law professor, Clifford S. Fishman, in testimony before the US Senate in 2002, argued why it was constitutional for police to spy on US citizens based on "reasonable suspicion" rather than the more stringent proof of "probable cause." (Statement and Memorandum of Clifford S. Fishman, Professor of Law The Catholic University of America Concerning S 2586 and S 2659 July 31, 2002, Proposals to Amend the Foreign Intelligence Surveillance Act31 July 2002 -- Senate Intelligence Committee) CUA received $347,660 in grants from the Department of Defense in fiscal year 2005. (Jeff Severns Guntzel, "Catholic colleges, universities soak up Pentagon dollars" *National Catholic Reporter* March 9, 2007)

16   "'Faith Czar' attacks church-state separation in Vatican speech" *Church & State* March 1, 2006 Americans United for Separation of Church and State http://www. highbeam.com/doc/1G1-143580526.html

17   "Lieberman crafting revised faith-based funding bill: A coming liberal sellout on the religion tax in America?" *American Atheist*, #937, 23 July 2001 http://www.hartford-

hwp.com/archives/45/199.html

18   "Bush Promotes Support For 'All Religions Under The Almighty God'" *Church & State People & Events* May 2002 Americans United for Separation of Church and State http://www.au.org/site/News2?abbr=cs_&page=NewsArticle&id=5584&security=1001&news_iv_ctrl=1075

19   Don Lattin, "Moonies knee-deep in faith-based funding" *San Francisco Chronicle* October 3, 2004 http://www.rickross.com/reference/unif/unif239.html

20   Jeremy Leaming, "Loss Of Faith: White House Faith Czar Towey Departs, As Doubts About Bush 'Faith-Based' Initiative Continue To Grow" *American United for Separation of Church and State* June 2006 http://www.au.org/site/News2?page=NewsArticle&id=8251&abbr=cs_

21   http://www.bishop-accountability.org/resources/resource-files/databases/Dallas-MorningNewsBishops.htm

22   "Americans United Applauds 'Faith Czar' Towey's Departure From White House" April 18, 2006 http://www.au.org/site/News2?abbr=pr&page=NewsArticle&id=8141

23   Dan Majors, "After months of controversy, Bush's St. Vincent speech praised" Pittsburgh Post-Gazette May 12, 2007 http://www.post-gazette.com/pg/07132/785510-85.stm

24   Alan Cooperman, "New Chief Oversees a Less Visible Faith Office" *Washington Post* August 25, 2006 http://www.washingtonpost.com/wp-dyn/content/article/2006/08/24/AR2006082401371.html

25   Bill Berkowitz, "Bush Names New Faith-based Czar" *Media Transparency* August 19, 2006 http://www.mediatransparency.org/story.php?storyID=143

26   Don Byrd, "Is Bush's Faith-Based Initiative on the Decline?" *Talk to Action* January 10, 2008 http://www.talk2action.org/story/2008/1/10/17272/5609

27   Edsall, supra note 5.

28   Lawn Griffiths, "Author coached White House on Catholic Issues" *East Valley Tribune* May 2, 2008 http://www.eastvalleytribune.com/story/115389

29   "David Kuo on 60 Minutes: 'The Name of God is being Destroyed in the Name of Politics" *SilentPatriot* October 15, 2006 http://www.crooksandliars.com/2006/10/15/david-kuo-on-60-minutes-the-name-of-god-is-being-destroyed-in-the-name-of-politics/)

30   Mike Reynolds, "The Abstinence Gluttons" *The Nation* June 18, 2007 Issuehttp://www.thenation.com/doc/20070618/reynolds

31   Rocco Palmo, "In Virginia, 'Botched' and Brutta All Over" *Whispers in the Loggia* June 18, 2008 http://whispersintheloggia.blogspot.com/

32   "Jimmy Carter Criticizes President Bush and Faith-Based Initiative" A compilation of news stories by the *Roundtable on Religion and Social Welfare Policy*, May 22, 2007 http://www.jewsonfirst.org/faithbased.php

33   "Americans United Applauds 'Faith Czar' Towey's Departure From White House" April 18, 2006 http://www.au.org/site/News2?abbr=pr&page=NewsArticle&id=8141

Chapter 13: The Sex Abuse Scandal

1   "'A Continuous, Concerted Campaign of Cover-Up' Excerpts from the Grand Jury's Report" *Philadelphia Inquirer* September 22, 2005 *BishopAccountability.org*http://www.bishop-accountability.org/news/2005_09_22_PhiladelphiaInquirer_AContinuous.htm from Nancy Phillips and David O'Reilly "An 'Immoral' Cover-up" *Philadelphia Inquirer* September 22, 2005 *BishopAccountability.org* http://www.bishop-accountability.org/news/2005_09_22_Phillips_AnImmoral.htm

2   Philip Jenkins, "The Uses of Clerical Scandal" *First Things* February 1996 *BishopAccountability.org* http://www.bishop-accountability.org/news/1996_02_Jenkins_TheUses.htm

3   Melinda Hennenberger, "Vatican Weighs Reaction to Accusations of Molesting by Clergy" *New York Times* March 3, 2002 *BishopAccountability.org* http://www.bishop-accountability.org/resources/resource-files/timeline/2002-03-03-Hennenberger-NavarroValls.htm

4   Alessio Vinci, "Pope responds to sex abuse cases" CNN.com March 22, 2002 http://

archives.cnn.com/2002/WORLD/europe/03/21/vatican.sex.abuse/

5   John L. Allen Jr., "After the Fall" *National Catholic Reporter,* January 25, 2008http://www.ncronline.org/NCR_Online/archives2/2008a/012508/012508a.htm

6   "Bush Backs Embattled Catholic Hierarchy As Pedophilia Crisis Grows" Church & State People & Events *Americans United for Separation of Church and State* May 2002 http://www.au.org/site/News2?abbr=cs_&page=NewsArticle&id=5584&security=1001&news_iv_ctrl=1075

7   UPI, "Bush and Pope Discuss Abuse Scandal, Mideast, Russia," *NewsMax.com Wires,* May 29, 2002http://www.newsmax.com/archives/articles/2002/5/28/153409.shtml

8   Hennenberger, supra note 3.

9   "Bush Backs Embattled Catholic Hierarchy", supra note 6.

10   *Boston Globe* April 24, 2002 http://www.boston.com/globe/spotlight/abuse/stories/042402_pope_text.htm

11   Patrick J. Wall, "The Crafty Perpetrators Remain" January 30, 2008 http://patrickjwall.wordpress.com/2008/01/30/the-crafty-perpetrators-remain/

12   Demetria Martinez, "Priests' treatment facility rocked by suits - at issue: returning abusers to ministry" *National Catholic Reporter* February 26, 1993   http://www.encyclopedia.com/doc/1G1-13540799.html

13   Ron Russell, "Camp Ped" *Los Angeles New Times* August 15, 2002http://bcsd.freeservers.com/C/sex/081802_cardinal_roger_mahony.htm

14   Richard John Neuhaus, "Scandal Time" *First Things* April 2002 http://www.firstthings.com/ftissues/ft0204/public.html

15   Father John McCloskey "La Iglesia de E.U. Sacudida por los Casos de Pederastia de Sacerdotes" *Aceprensa* April 3, 2002   http://www.catholicity.com/mccloskey/pederastia.html

16   George Weigel, "From Scandal to Reform: (Parts 1 and 2) The Imperative of Orthodoxy" *Catholic Difference* April 10 and 17, 2002 http://www.eppc.org/news/newsID.1244/news_detail.asp and http://www.eppc.org/news/newsID.1245/news_detail.asp

17   Michael Novak, "The Culture of 'Dissent'" *Catholic Education Resource Center* reprinted with permission from *National Review* March 29, 2002 http://www.catholiceducation.org/articles/religion/re0541.html

18   Michael Novak, "Bishops Ignore Elephant — and Camel" *NationalReviewOnline* June 18, 2002 http://www.nationalreview.com/novak/novak061802.asp

19   Michael Novak, "Review of *The Courage to be Catholic,* by George Weigel" *AD2000* Vol 15 No 9 October 2002   http://www.ad2000.com.au/articles/2002/oct2002p16_1166.html

20   "Even in Death, a Media Superstar" *ZENIT.org* April 16, 2005 ZE05041603

21   Novak, supra note 19

22   Michael Novak, "The Boston Disease – What remains after Cardinal Law" *National Review Online* December 13, 2002 http://www.magisterium.net/disease1.htm

23   Richard John Neuhaus "Boston and Other Bishops" *First Things* February 2003 http://www.magisterium.net/neuhaus.htm

24   Susan Milligan, "Santorum resolute on Boston rebuke" *Boston Globe* July 13, 2005 http://www.boston.com/news/local/articles/2005/07/13/santorum_resolute_on_boston_rebuke/

25   Thomas Strobhar, "Holy Porn" *New Oxford Review* February 2008 http://www.newoxfordreview.org/article.jsp?did=0208-strobhar

26   Charles P. Pierce, "The Bishop's Quandary" *Boston Globe* July 21, 2002 http://boston.com/globe/spotlight/abuse/stories2/072102_magazine_5.htm

27   Timothy Noah, "Free Frank Keating" *Slate Magazine* June 16, 2003 http://www.slate.com/id/2084446/

28   Sandro Magister, "Operation Courage. George Weigel´s Recipe for Healing the Church" *www.chiesa* June 9, 2002 http://chiesa.espresso.repubblica.it/articolo/6882?eng=y

29   "Annual abuse audit and survey find soaring costs, fewer allegations" *Catholic News Service* March 7, 2008 http://www.catholicnews.com/data/briefs/cns/20080307.htm

30 "US Catholic church paid 615 mln dlrs for abuse cases in 2007: report" *AFP* March 7, 2008 http://afp.google.com/article/ALeqM5iJGuPlThz-KZlr8Us0Fr6by_nVtA

31 http://www.usccb.org/nrb/johnjaystudy/incident3.

32 Kevin Cullen, "More than 80 percent of victims since 1950 were male, report says," *Boston Globe*, Feb. 28, 2004, http://www.boston.com/globe/spotlight/abuse/stories5/022804_victims.htm

33 "Framed Within a Genuinely Catholic and Ecclesial Sensibility" *ZENIT News Agency* March 1, 2004 Code: ZE04030122

34 "The Catholic Reform," *First Things* May 2004 http://firstthings.com/ftissues/ft0405/public.html#reform

35 Mary Gail Frawley-O'Dea "Experts on Sex Offenders Have News for Vatican: Abusers' Behavior Does Not Stem from Orientation, Studies Show" *National Catholic Reporter* December 9, 2005 http://www.bishop-accountability.org/news2005_07_12/2005_12_09_ODea_ExpertsOn.htm

36 "View from the Eye of the Storm" Keynote Address, LINKUP National Conference, Louisville, Kentucky, February 23, 2003 http://www.richardsipe.com/Lectures/linkup_national_conference.htm

37 Ron Dreher, "The Gay Priest Problem" *beliefnet* February 6, 2008 http://blog.beliefnet.com/crunchycon/2008/02/the-gay-priest-problem-1.html

38 Mary Gail Frawley-O'Dea, supra note 35.

39 Brooks Egerton and Reese Dunklin, "Special Reports: Catholic Bishops and Sex Abuse" *Dallas News 2002* http://www.dallasnews.com/cgi-bin/bi/dallas/2002/priests.cgi

40 Kay Ebeling "SNAP Mexico City challenge unique: find protection and safe haven for victims before going to the police" *CityofAngels4: Epimeno* February 1, 2008http://cityofangels4.blogspot.com/2008/02/snap-mexico-citys-challenge-unique-find.html

41 Thomas P. Doyle, A. W. R. Sipe, and Patrick J. Wall *Sex, Priests, and Secret Codes: The Catholic Church's 2,000-Year Paper Trail of Sexual Abuse* (Santa Monica, Calif.:Bonus Books) 2006

42 http://cara.georgetown.edu/bulletin/index.htm

43 John Karas, "Retired Detective Now Stalks the Mind of a Predator" *East Hartford Gazette* January 24, 2008 http://www.zwire.com/site/news.cfm?newsid=19230175&BRD=1642&PAG=461&dept_id=10299&rfi=6

44 Marci Hamilton, "Will State Legislatures Stand Up to the Catholic Church, and Pass Strong Anti-Child Abuse Laws?" *Findlaw.com* February 24, 2003 http://writ.news.findlaw.com/hamilton/20030224.html and Bill Frogameni, "Uncovering Child Sex Abuse: A Stand-Off with the Catholic Church" *Ms. Magazine* August 9, 2007 http://www.alternet.org/rights/58365/

45 http://www.ncptsd.va.gov/ncmain/index.jsp

46 http://bjsw.oxfordjournals.org/cgi/content/abstract/34/2/181

47 R. Scott Appleby, "Behind a Bodyguard of Lies," *The Boston Globe Book Review*, March 14, 2004 http://www.boston.com/globe/spotlight/abuse/print5/031404_review.htm

48 Maria Sheehan "Allianz, Munich Re among insurers to pay for US priest abuse settlement" *Thomson Financial* http://www.hemscott.com/news/latest-news/item.do?newsId=46868830739546

49 "The Priesthood: John Paul II's Holy Thursday Letter Sets Guidelines" *AD2000* March 23, 2000 http://www.ad2000.com.au/articles/2000/may2000p7_54.html

50 George Weigel, "The Importance of the Priest in Sanctifying the Church" *zenit.org* May 17, 2003

51 Thomas B. Edsall, *Building Red America: The New Conservative Coalition and the Drive for Permanent Power* (Basic Books 2006) 90 Google Books

Chapter 14: The 2004 Presidential Campaign

1 *Ghost Wars: The Secret History of the CIA, Afghanistan and bin Laden, from the Soviet Invasion to 10 September 2001* by Steve Coll, (New York: Penguin, 2004) quoted by Chalmers Johnson, "Abolish the CIA!" *TomDispatch.com* November 5,

2004 (This piece is adapted from and printed thanks to the permission of the London Review of Books where, in slightly altered form, it appeared on 21 October 2004, pp. 25-28.)

2   Sandro Magister, "The U.S. Ambassador to the Vatican: 'After September 11, the Pope Said to Me...'" *www.chiesa* November 13, 2002 http://chiesa.espresso.repubblica.it/articolo/6886?&eng=y

3   John L. Allen, Jr., "New American ambassador says U.S. has Vatican support" *National Catholic Reporter* October 26, 2001, http://www.highbeam.com/doc/1G1-79965734.html

4   Wayne Madsen, "Bush's 'Christian' Blood Cult" *CounterPunch* April 22, 2003 Reprinted with permission from the author. http://www.fromthewilderness.com/free/ww3/042803_vatican.html

5   Interview: "The Search for Peace Is a Duty" *zenit.org* September 13, 2001 http://www.zenit.org/article-2361?l=english

6   "Cardinal Ratzinger, After the 9/11 Attacks" *zenit.org* April 27, 2005 http://www.zenit.org/article-12865?l=english

7   David Willey, " Pope calls Assisi peace meeting" *BBC News* November, 18 2001, http://news.bbc.co.uk/2/hi/europe/1663138.stm

8   http://www.vatican.va/holy_father/john_paul_ii/messages/peace/documents/hf_jp-ii_mes_20011211_xxxv-world-day-for-peace_en.html

9   http://www.vatican.va/holy_father/john_paul_ii/letters/2002/documents/hf_jp-ii_let_20020304_capi-stato_en.html

10   "To Fight Terrorism, Go to Its Root Causes, Says John Paul II" *zenit.org* September 8, 2002 http://zenit.org/article-5276?l=english

11   George Weigel, "Reality of terrorism calls for fresh look at just-war tradition" *The Catholic Difference* September 20, 2001 #http://www.eppc.org/news/newsID.585/news_detail.asp

12   Damon Linker, "How Jesus Endorsed Bush's Invasion of Iraq" *IkhwanWeb* October 29, 2006 http://www.ikhwanweb.com/Article.asp?ID=3165&SectionID=142

13   Damon Linker, "How Jesus Endorsed Bush's Invasion of Iraq" Excerpted with permission from *The Theocons: Secular America Under Siege, AlterNet* October 28, 2006 http://www.alternet.org/waroniraq/43576/?page=entire

14   Ibid, supra note 4.

15   "Cardinal Ratzinger Says Unilateral Attack on Iraq Not Justified" *zenit.org* September 22, 2002 http://www.zenit.org/article-5398?l=english

16   http://www.usccb.org/sdwp/international/bush902.shtml

17   http://www.usccb.org/bishops/iraq.shtml

18   Bob Abernethy, "Interview: George Weigel" *Religion & Ethics Newsweekly* January 10, 2003 http://www.pbs.org/wnet/religionandethics/week619/weigel.html

19   http://www.vatican.va/holy_father/john_paul_ii/speeches/2003/january/documents/hf_jp-ii_spe_20030113_diplomatic-corps_en.html

20   Vatican journal: oil drives war plan - Church Notes" *Catholic New Times* February 9, 2003 http://findarticles.com/p/articles/mi_m0MKY/is_3_27/ai_111012295

21   "'Asymmetrical Warfare' & Just War" *National Review Online* February 10, 2003 http://www.nationalreview.com/novak/novak021003.asp

22   Michael Novak, "Civilian Casualties & Turmoil" *National Review Online* February 18, 2003 http://www.nationalreview.com/novak/novak021803.asp

23   Madsen, supra note 4.

24   "Saddam Has the Will to Avoid the War, Says Papal Envoy" *zenit.org* February 16, 2003 http://www.zenit.org/article-6557?l=english

25   Sandro Magister, "War in the Gulf. What the Pope Really Said" *www.chiesa* March 20, 2003 http://chiesa.espresso.repubblica.it/articolo/6928?eng=y

26   "Cardinal Laghi's Statement Following Meeting with Bush" *zenit.org* March 6, 2003 http://www.zenit.org/article-6721?l=english

27   Magister, supra note 25.

28   http://www.vatican.va/news_services/press/documentazione/documents/santopadre_biografie/giovanni_paolo_ii_biografia_pontificato_en.html

29   "Unilateral Attack Would Be 'War of Aggression,' Says Vatican Official" *zenit.org*

March 11, 2003 http://www.zenit.org/article-6753?l=english

30   "Vatican Official Criticizes Pressures Exerted in U.N. Security Council" *zenit.org* March 13, 2003 http://www.zenit.org/article-6772?l=english

31   "Military Intervention in Iraq Would Be a Crime, Says Vatican Official" *zenit.org* March 17, 2003 http://www.zenit.org/article-6804?l=english

32   "Father Richard Neuhaus on the Iraqi Crisis" *Catholic Education Resource Center* March 10, 2003 Reprinted with permission from Zenit - News from Rome. http://catholiceducation.org/articles/religion/re0627.html

33   http://www.usccb.org/sdwp/peace/stm31903.shtml

34   "Cardinal Ratzinger on the Abridged Version of Catechism" *zenit.org* May 2, 2003 http://zenit.org/article-7161?l=english

35   Linker, supra note 12.

36   Linker, supra note 12.

37   Linker, supra note 12.

38   "Pope nearing death - Cardinal" *BBC News* October 2, 2003 http://news.bbc.co.uk/1/hi/world/europe/3159714.stm

39   Victor L. Simpson, "Vatican Reports Deficit for Third Year" *Associated Press* July 7, 2004 *BishopAccountability.org* http://www.bishop-accountability.org/news2004_07_12/2004_07_07_Simpson_VaticanReports.htm

40   Gregory Viscusi, "Holy See in the Red" *theage.com.au* April 7, 2005http://www.theage.com.au/news/Business/Holy-See-in-the-red/2005/04/06/1112489559959.html

41   Vicente Navarro, "Opus Dei and John Paul II A Profoundly Rightwing Pope" *Counterpunch.org* April 8, 2005 http://www.counterpunch.org/navarro04082005.html

42   Sandro Magister, "Lent in the Vatican: The Pope, the Curia, and the Conclave" *www.chiesa* February 11, 2005 http://chiesa.espresso.repubblica.it/articolo/22533?&eng=y

43   http://www.vatican.va/roman_curia/secretariat_state/2003/documents/rc_seg-st_20030620_sodano-annan_en.html

44   Sandro Magister, "Iraq: The Church Goes on a Mission of Peace" *www.chiesa* November 11, 2003 http://chiesa.espresso.repubblica.it/articolo/6997?eng=y

45   Sandro Magister, "A Reminder for the Vatican: There´s No Way Out of Alliance with America" *www.chiesa* October 27, 2003 http://chiesa.espresso.repubblica.it/articolo/6987?eng=y

46   Julian Coman and Bruce Johnston, "Vatican buries the hatchet with Blair and Bush over Iraq" *The Telegraph* September 10, 2004   http://www.telegraph.co.uk/news/main.jhtml?xml=/news/2004/10/10/wirq10.xml&sSheet=/portal/2004/10/10/ixportal.html

47   "Cheney meets pope, rallies U.S. troops" *Associate Press* January 27, 2004 http://www.msnbc.msn.com/id/4027404

48   Sandro Magister, "Dick Cheney Meets with the Pope. The Lajolo Doctrine on the New World Order" *www.chiesa* February 4, 2004 http://chiesa.espresso.repubblica.it/articolo/7017?&eng=y

49   John L. Allen, Jr., "Interview with Archbishop Giovanni Lajolo" *National Catholic Reporter* January 15, 2004 http://ncronline.org/mainpage/specialdocuments/lajolo.htm

50   Michael Paulson, "Bishops seek out opinions, in private" *Boston Globe* July 11,2003 http://boston.com/globe/spotlight/abuse/stories4/071103_opinions.htm

51   Deal Hudson, "The Dissenters' Secret Meeting" *CatholiCity.com* http://www.catholicity.com/commentary/hudson/secretmeeting.html

52   Charles P. Pierce, "The Crusaders" *Boston Globe* November 2, 2003 http://www.boston.com/news/globe/magazine/articles/2003/11/02/the_crusaders/

53   Joe Feuerherd, "Meeting of the Minds" *National Catholic Reporter* September 9, 2003 http://www.nationalcatholicreporter.org/todaystake/tt090903.htm

54   Pierce, supra note 52.

55   Feuerherd, supra note 53.

56   Pierce, supra note 54.

57   John L. Allen, Jr., "Pope to Cheney: world needs peace" *National Catholic Reporter* February 6, 2004 http://www.encyclopedia.com/doc/1G1-113338217.html

58   Magister, supra note 48.
59   Barbara Kralis, "A Primer on Canon 915" *Catholic Online* February 5, 2004 http://www.catholic.org/featured/headline.php?ID=691
60   Tim O'Neil, "Catholic parishes fight draft closure list" *St. Louis Post-Dispatch* November 7, 2004
61   Tim Townsend, "As parishes wither, others bloom" *St. Louis Post-Dispatch* June 25, 2005
62   Sandro Magister, "Obama's Pick for Vice President Is Catholic. But the Bishops Deny Him Communion" *www.chiesa* August 27, 2008 http://chiesa.espresso.repubblica.it/articolo/206336?eng=y
63   Sandro Magister, "The Kerry Affair: What Ratzinger Wanted from the American Bishops" *www.chiesa* July 3, 2004 http://www.chiesa.espressonline.it/dettaglio.jsp?id=7055&eng=y
64   *National Catholic Reporter* October 8, 1999 and *The Tablet* April 28, 2001
65   Karen Tumulty and Perry Bacon Jr., "A Test of Kerry's Faith" *TIME.com* Apr. 05, 2004http://www.time.com/time/election2004/article/0,18471,605436,00.html
66   "Sixty-three Percent of Catholics Voted in the 2004 Presidential Election" Center for Applied Research in the Apostolate, Georgetown University November 22, 2004 http://209.85.165.104/search?q=cache:ED-DLj4XfFoJ:cara.georgetown.edu/Press112204.pdf+catholic+voter+turnout%2B2004+election&hl=en&ct=clnk&cd=1&gl=us
67   Phil Brennan, "Pope's Biographer: Kerry Distorting Catholic Doctrine" *NewsMax.com* April 16, 2004 http://archive.newsmax.com/archives/articles/2004/4/15/215724.shtml
68   Interview with Jeffrey Brown, "Bishops and Ballots" *PBS News Hour*, June 14, 2004http://www.pbs.org/newshour/bb/religion/jan-june04/cath_6-17.html
69   Jerry Filteau, "Seminar examines merits of denying Communion to dissident politicians" *Catholic News Service* September 17, 2004 http://www.catholicnews.com/data/stories/cns/0405132.htm
70   Dennis Coday, "Laity wonders where the money goes" *The National Catholic Reporter* January 28, 2005 http://ncronline.org/NCR_Online/archives2/2005a/012805/012805k.htm
71   Archbishop Charles Chaput, "How to tell a Duck from a Fox" *Denver Catholic Register* April 14, 2004 http://www.archden.org/dcr/news.php?e=75&s=2&a=1835
72   Ken Thorbourne, "Catholic schools get grant dollars" *The Jersey Journal* December 26, 2005
73   Liz Willen, "Koslowski's Crime Pays at Alma Mater, Where Name Stays on Hall" *Bloomberg.com* July 20, 2005 http://www.bloomberg.com/apps/news?pid=100001 03&sid=aViu1Vf.0HVA&refer=us
74   "No Communion for Pro-Abortion Politicians, Says Cardinal Arinze," *zenit.org* April 23, 2004 http://www.zenit.org/article-9912?l=english
75   Andrew Walsh "Kerry Eucharistes" *Religion in the News* Summer 2004, Vol. 7, No. 2http://www.trincoll.edu/depts/csrpl/RINVOL7No2/KerryEucharistes.htm
76   "IRS Should Investigate Electioneering By Colorado Springs Catholic Diocese, Says Americans United" May 26, 2004 http://www.au.org/site/News2?page=NewsArticle&id=6675&news_iv_ctrl=0&abbr=pr&JServSessionIdr004=1u0bay19f3.app1b
77   Walsh, supra note 76.
78   Alan Cooperman, "Ad Assailes D.C. Cardinal" *The Washington Post* May 7, 2004 http://www.highbeam.com/doc/1P2-168468.html
79   Walsh, supra note 76.
80   http://www.ncronline.org/mainpage/specialdocuments/catholic_congress.pdf
81   "Pope's Criticism of President Bush should not be Obscured by Media Photo-op" *Common Dreams* June 4, 2004 http://www.commondreams.org/news2004/0606-11.htm
82   "Pope chides Bush over Iraq woes" *BBC News* June 4, 2004 http://news.bbc.co.uk/2/hi/europe/3773545.stm
83   John L. Allen Jr., "The Vatican and America" *National Catholic Reporter* June 11, 2004 http://www.nationalcatholicreporter.org/word/word061104.htm
84   Ibid

85   Sandro Magister, "The Kerry Affair: What Ratzinger Wanted from the American Bishops" www.chiesa July 3, 2004 http://www.chiesa.espressonline.it/dettaglio.jsp?id=7055&eng=y

86   John Richard Neuhaus "Bishops at a Turning Point" First Things October 2004 http://www.firstthings.com/article.php3?id_article=379&var_recherche=john+kerry

87   Michael Novak, "In and Out of Communion" National Review Online, June 15, 2004 http://www.michaelnovak.net/Module/Article/ArticleView.aspx?id=90

88   George Weigel, "The Body Politic and the Body of Christ: Candidates, Communion and the Catholic Church" Pew Forum on Religion & Public Life June 23, 2004 http://pewforum.org/events/index.php?EventID=58

89   George Weigel, "A primer on the Holy Communion controversy" The Catholic Difference July 12, 2004 http://www.eppc.org/publications/pubID.2161/pub_detail.asp

90   M. Asif Ismail, "The Sincerest Form of Flattery" The Center for Public Integrity, Outsourcing the Pentagon November 18, 2004

91   Stephanie Ramage, "Cowboys and Indians" The Sunday Paper October 24, 2005

92   PST by Nyer December 5, 2004 http://www.freerepublic.com/focus/f-news/1294810/posts

93   http://www.archatl.com/archbishops/donoghue/20040804.html

94   "Pre-Election Letter to the People of Arlington" Special to the Catholic Herald (From the issue of 10/28/04) October 31, 2004 http://www.catholicherald.com/loverde/2004homilies/election1028.htm

95   http://64.233.169.104/search?q=cache:vG7lFUnJw1cJ:www.nkyrtl.org/2004sep.pdf+winski%2Borlando%2Bvoting&hl=en&ct=clnk&cd=2&gl=us

96   Martin J. Gillespie, RNC Director of Catholic Outreach, January 22, 2004 http://www.ncronline.org/mainpage/specialdocuments/rnc_document.pdf

97   Joe Feuerherd, "Catholic League targets Kerry outreach" National Catholic Reporter August 11, 2004 http://www.nationalcatholicreporter.org/washington/wnb081104.htm

98   Kelly Amis Stewart, "Bush Hails DC Vouchers at Catholic School" School Reform News The Heartland Institute April 1, 2004 http://www.heartland.org/Article.cfm?artId=14654

99   Daniel Schulman, "Bush's Shadow Justice Department: Did the Federalist Society Have a Hand in Attorney Firings?" Mother Jones June 7, 2007 http://www.motherjones.com/politics/2007/06/bushs-shadow-justice-department-did-federalist-society-have-hand-attorney-firings

100   http://209.157.64.201/focus/f-news/1122906/posts?page=3

101   "Catholic right holds first prayer breakfast" Christian Century, May 18, 2004 COPYRIGHT 2004 The Christian Century Foundation, COPYRIGHT 2004 Gale Group http://findarticles.com/p/articles/mi_m1058/is_10_121/ai_n6159159

102   Joe Feuerherd, "Senate rolls over for Negroponte; Prayer breakfast brings 'faithful Catholics' together" National Catholic Reporter April 28, 2004 http://www.nationalcatholicreporter.org/washington/wnb042804.htm

103   "How Santorum Got $8.5 Million for His Charity's Largest Donor" Philadelphia Daily News March 1, 2006 http://www.truthout.org/docs_2006/030206K.shtml

104   Frances R. Hill, "Congress's Charity Cases (Sen. Santorum?)" New York Times October 17, 2006 http://www.nytimes.com/2006/10/17/opinion/17Hill.html

105   "Guess Who Didn't Come to Breakfast" Washington Prowler The American Spectator April 28, 2004 http://www.spectator.org/dsp_article.asp?art_id=6494

106   Rev. Andrew J. Weaver, Ph.D. "Neocon Catholics target mainline Protestants" Media Transparency August 11, 2006 http://www.mediatransparency.org/storyprinterfriendly.php?storyID=142

107   Eric Convey "GOP recruiting Catholics to help defeat Democrats" Boston Herald May 27, 2004 carolmckinley.blogspot.com/2004_05_23_carolmckinley_archive.html

108   Richard Benedetto, "Bush courts Catholics at Knights of Columbus confab" USA TODAY August 3, 2004 http://www.usatoday.com/news/politicselections/nation/president/2004-08-03-bush-fundraiser_x.htm

109   Elisabeth Bumiller, "Bush Talks to an Appreciative Catholic Crowd" New York Times August 4, 2004http://www.nytimes.com/2004/08/04/politics/campaign/04bush.html?ei=5090&en=72a3b19570ee5a8d&ex=1249272000&partner=rssuserland&pagew

anted=all&position=

110 http://www.catholicsforchoice.org/pubs/documents/OppNotes_Priests_Web.pdf.

111 Bill Berkowitz, "Neocon Catholic leaders nurtured by GOP and Conservative Philanthropy on their heels" *Media Transparency* September 23, 2007http://www.mediatransparency.org/pdastory.php?storyID=212

112 Joe Feuerherd, "The Real Deal" *National Catholic Reporter* August 19, 2004 http://www.nationalcatholicreporter.org/update/bn081904.htm

113 Ibid

114 Ibid

115 George Weigel, "Cardinal Ratzinger and the Conscience of Catholic Voters" *The Catholic Difference* September 29, 2004 http://www.eppc.org/publications/pubID.2177/pub_detail.asp

116 In the context of the 40th anniversary of the Holy See's Permanent Observer Mission to the UN, on 1 July 2004, the General Assembly adopted a Resolution, by acclamation, confirming and strengthening the rights of the Holy See as a Permanent Observer in the UN. The Holy See now enjoys, among other things, the right to participate in the general debate of the General Assembly; the right of reply; the right to have its communications issued and circulated directly as official documents of the Assembly; and the right to co-sponsor draft resolutions and decisions that make reference to the Holy See. http://www.holyseemission.org/index2.html

117 Nicole McDonald "Anti-abortion sisters petition Pope Stop Hunte Award" *The Star Online* September 17, 2004 http://www.stluciastar.com/weekend/friSept17-04/lead.htm also see http://www.cardinalrating.com/cardinal_106__article_924.htm

118 David D. Kirkpatrick and Laurie Goodstein, "Group of Bishops Using Influence to Oppose Kerry" *New York Times* October 12, 2004 http://www.nytimes.com/2004/10/12/politics/campaign/12catholics.html?pagewanted=1&ei=5070&en=aa0c895712b321fe&ex=1113019200

119 Karina Saltman, "Bush, Kerry not invited to charity dinner" *CNN* September 17, 2004http://www.cnn.com/2004/ALLPOLITICS/09/17/smith.dinner/index.html

120 Joe Feuerherd, "Bishops' 'Faithful Citizenship' undermined by conservative groups", *The National Catholic Report*, February 17, 2005 http://www.nationalcatholicreporter.org/washington/wnb021705.htm

121 Ibid

122 David D. Kirkpatrick and Laurie Goodstein, "Group of Bishops Using Influence to Oppose Kerry" *New York Times* October12, 2004 http://www.nytimes.com/2004/10/12/politics/campaign/12catholics.html?pagewanted=1&ei=5070&en=aa0c895712b31fe&ex=1113019200

123 Fr. Frank Pavone, "Distorted Citizenship" *Priests for Life* Http://priestsforlife.org/articles/distortedcitizenship.htm

124 Kirkpatrick and Goodstein, supra note 123.

125 Kirkpatrick and Goodstein, supra note 123.

126 Kirkpatrick and Goodstein, supra note 123.

127 Julia Duin, "GOP tells of success wooing Catholic vote", *The Washington Times* November 4, 2004 http://www.washtimes.com/national/20041104-113015-7468r.htm

128 Bennett Roth and Julie Mason, "Monsignor Jude O'Doherty and President Bush" *Houston Chronicle* October 31, 2004 http://www.freerepublic.com/focus/religion/1265031/posts?page=1

129 Robert F. Kennedy Jr. "Was the 2004 Election Stolen?" *Rolling Stone* June 1, 2004 http://www.rollingstone.com/news/story/10432334/was_the_2004_election_stolen

130 Jim Remsen, "Bush got majority of Catholic vote in U.S., but not state", *Detroit Free Press www.freep.com*, November 8, 2004 http://www.edisonreaserch.com/home/archives/DetroitFreePress11-08-04.pdf

131 Richard N. Ostling, "A faith-based look at '04 vote" *Associated Press* February 4, 2005 http://www.religionheadlines.org/heads_050204.php

132 "Sixty-three Percent of Catholics Voted in the 2004 Presidential Election" *Center for Applied Research in the Apostolate*, Georgetown University, November 22, 2004 http://209.85.165.104/search?q=cache:ED-DLj4XfFoJ:cara.georgetown.edu/

Press112204.pdf+catholic+voter+turnout%2B2004+election&hl=en&ct=clnk&cd=1 &gl=us

133   http://www.usccb.org/finance/financialstatements2006.PDF

134   *CNN*, November 11, 2004 http://www.cnn.com/2004/ALLPOLITICS/11/11/bush. cabinet/index.html

135   Ibid

136   Dan Eggen, "Gonzales Nomination Draws Military Criticism" *Washington Post* January 4, 2005 http://www.washingtonpost.com/wp-dyn/articles/A45727-2005Jan3.html

137   "EPIC Joins Military Veterans in Questioning Gonzales Nomination" http://www. epic-usa.org/Default.aspx?tabid=468

138   Zachary Coile, "Senate OKs Gonzales as Attorney General" *San Francisco Chronicle* February 4, 2005 http://www.commondreams.org/headlines05/0204-24.htm

139   J. Peter Nixon, "Catholic Politicians" *Commonweal* February 25, 2005 / Volume CXXXII, Number 4   Kirkpatrick and Goodstein, supra note 123.

Chapter 15: Benedict XVI

1   John L. Allen Jr., *Cardinal Ratzinger: The Vatican's Enforcer of the Faith* (New York: Continuum, 2000) Quoted by Christine Roussel, "A very blunt critique of the Pontificate of Pope Benedict XVI..." *ARCC Light* http://www.arcc-catholic-rights.net/

2   Thierry Meyssan, "Opus Dei Sets Out to Conquer the World" *Voltaire Network* January 25, 1996 http://www.voltairenet.org/article136480.html?var_recherche=Vatican?var_recherche=Vatican

3   Sandro Magister, "Lent in the Vatican: The Pope, the Curia, and the Conclave" *www. chiesa* February 11, 2005 http://chiesa.espresso.repubblica.it/articolo/22533?&eng=y

4   Christine Roussel, "A very blunt critique of the Pontificate of Pope Benedict XVI..." *ARCC Light* http://www.arcc-catholic-rights.net/

5   Dr. Clive Gillis, "Papabile: Deep currents flow within Rome as the next Conclave looms" *EIPS* March 31, 2003 http://www.ianpaisley.org/article.asp?ArtKey=papabile

6   Larry B. Stammer and Tracy Wilkinson, "Selecting a New Pope" *Los Angeles Times* April 19, 2005 http://www.findarticles.com/p/articles/mi_m1141/is_28_37/ai_75021417

7   http://clericalwhispers.blogspot.com/2007_03_01_archive.html

8   Sandro Magister, "Vatican Storylines: Those Who Are Resisting Benedict XVI" *www. chiesa* January 19, 2006 http://chiesa.espresso.repubblica.it/articolo/44944?&eng=y and Paul Elie, "The Year of two Popes: How Joseph Ratzinger stepped into the shoes of John Paul II - and what it means for the Catholic Church" *The Atlantic Monthly* January/February 2006 http://www.theatlantic.com/doc/200601/ratzinger

9   David Olive, "End of the Neo-Cons" *The Toronto Star* November 5, 2006

10   Michael Novak, "Rome's Radical Conservative" *New York Times* April 20, 2005http:// www.nytimes.com/2005/04/20/opinion/20novak.html

11   "The Image of Benedict XVI" May 1, 2005 *Voltaire Network* http://www.voltairenet. org/article30120.html?var_recherche=Vatican?var_recherche=Vatican

12   Sandro Magister, "The Pope's Banker Speaks: 'Here's How I Saved the IOR'" *www.chiesa* June 18, 2004 http://chiesa.espresso.repubblica.it/dettaglio. jsp?id=7048&eng=y

13   John Cornwell, *Breaking Faith: The Pope, the People and the Fate of Catholicism* (New York: Viking Compass 2001) 289

14   Magister, supra note 12.

15   Gordon Urquhart "Opus Dei: the Pope's Right Arm in Europe" *The Center for Research on Population and Security* http://www.population-security.org/cffc-97-01. htm

16   Sandro Magister, "All the Denarii of Peter. Vices and Virtues of the Vatican Bank" *www.chiesa.espressonline.it* June 15, 2009 http://chiesa.espresso.repubblica.it/ articolo/1338861?eng=y

17   http://www.vaticanbankclaims.com/vatpr.html

18   Ibid

19   John L. Allen Jr. "Vatican asks Condoleezza Rice to help stop a sex abuse lawsuit"

National Catholic Reporter March 3, 2005 http://nationalcatholicreporter.org/update/bn030305.htm

20 Dr. Robert Moynihan, "Pope's Nuncio to Give Major Address in Washington on September 26 2008" An *Inside the Vatican* Magazine Newsflash www.insidethevatican.com

21 "New Pope's Views on Turkey/EU Stir Unease in Ankara" *Reuters* April 20, 2005 http://www.freerepublic.com/focus/f-news/1387459/posts

22 Gerard O'Connell, "Naming of new cardinals seen key indicator of pope's curial reform" *UCANews* February 21, 2006 http://www.catholic.org/international/international_story.php?id=18785

23 "Why Oriana Fallaci Received a Papal Audience" *Zenit.org* September 6, 2005 http://zenit.org/article-13907?l=english

24 Madeleine Bunting, "A man with little sympathy for other faiths" The Guardian September 19, 2006http://www.guardian.co.uk/world/2006/sep/19/catholicism.religion

25 Alexander Smoltczyk, "How the Pope Angered the Muslim World" *SPIEGEL Magazine* November 24, 2006 http://www.spiegel.de/international/spiegel/0,1518,450456,00.html

26 *Associated Press* September 17, 2006, quoted by Nicola Nasser, "A Catholic Stamp to a US War" *OpEdNews* September 21, 2006 http://www.opednews.com/articles/1/opedne_nicola_n_060921_a_catholic_stamp_to_.htm

27 "WWIII on Islam" is a term used by the former Republican Speaker of the House of Representatives Newt Gingrich in a recent speech at the American Enterprise Institute (AEI); he was quoted by Jim Lobe, *Asia Times* on September 14, 2006 according to Nasser.

28 George Friedman, *www.stratfor.com* September 19, 2006, quoted by Nasser

29 Ibid

30 Ibid

31 Jon Meacham with Edward Pentin, "A Pope's Holy War" *Newsweek* September 25, 2006 Issue http://www.msnbc.msn.com/id/14866559/site/newsweek/

32 Sandro Magister, "The Lecture in Regensburg Continues to Weigh on the Islamic Question" *www.chiesa* December 4, 2006 http://chiesa.espresso.repubblica.it/articolo/101884?eng=y

33 Simon Barrow, "Christendom remains the Pope's real fallibility" *Ekklesia* September 20, 2006 http://www.ekklesia.co.uk/content/barrow/article_060920papal.shtml

34 Editorial: "The Image of Benedict XVI" *voltairenet.org* May 1, 2005 http://www.voltairenet.org/article30120.html?var_recherche=Vatican?var_recherche=Vatican

35 http://en.wikipedia.org/wiki/The_European_Union_and_the_Catholic_Church

36 "God's Ambassadors" *The Economist* July 19, 2007 http://www.economist.com/world/international/displaystory.cfm?story_id=9516461#top and Sandro Magister, "Mission Impossible: Eject the Holy See from the United Nations" *www.chiesa* August 21, 2007 http://chiesa.espresso.repubblica.it/articolo/162301?&eng=y

37 Sandro Magister "The U.S. Ambassador to the Vatican: After September 11, the Pope Said to Me..." *www.chiesa* November 13, 2002 http://chiesa.espresso.repubblica.it/dettaglio.jsp?id=6886&eng=y

38 Sandro Magister, "Sodano Isn´t Leaving the Vatican - Nor the 'Glass Palace'" *www.chiesa* November 26, 2002 http://chiesa.espresso.repubblica.it/articolo/6891?&eng=y

39 Nicole Winfield, "Vatican Seeks Diplomatic Ties With Russia" *Associated Press* October 27, 2005 http://www.newsday.com/news/nationworld/world/wire/sns-ap-vatican-russia,0,2535834,print.story?coll=sns-ap-world-headlines

40 "US Catholics Aid Post-Communist Lands" *Zenit.org* August 1, 2008 http://www.zenit.org/article-21635?l=english

41 Clifford J. Levy, "At Expense of All Others, Putin Picks a Church" *New York Times* April 24, 2008 http://www.nytimes.com/2008/04/24/world/europe/24church.html?_r=1&th=&emc=th&pagewanted=all

42 Robert Pigott, "Putin seeks fresh start with Pope" *BBC NEWS* March 13, 2007 http://news.bbc.co.uk/2/hi/europe/6442333.stm

43 "Russian Visa System Leaves Priests Scrambling" *Zenit.org* April 29, 2008 http://

www.zenit.org/article-22453?l=english

44   Pigott, supra note 42.

45   Miriam Díez i Bosch, "Opus Dei Marks 1 Year in Russia" *Zenit.org* July 24, 2008 http://www.zenit.org/article-23327?l=english

46   "Statements on upcoming meeting between pope, patriarch may be diplomatic move" *Interfax-Religion* June 3, 2008 http://www.interfax-religion.com/?act=news&div=4753

47   Richard Owen, "Vatican ready to end its 50-year feud with China" *The Times* October 29, 2005

48   Jeff Israely, "The Pope Reaches Out to China" *TIME* July 3, 2007 http://www.time.com/time/world/article/0,8599,1639679,00.html

49   "China moves to limit access to Catholic shrine in Shanghai" *Associated Press* April 24, 2008 http://www.azstarnet.com/allheadlines/235730

50   "Pope authorizes indulgences for Hong Kong Catholics praying for China" *Catholic News Service* May 13, 2008 http://www.catholicnews.com/data/briefs/cns/20080513.htm

51   "China ready for further dialogue with the Vatican" *The Hindu News Update Service* May 8, 2008 http://www.hindu.com/thehindu/holnus/003200805081923.htm

52   Ibid

53   Matteo Tonelli, "Costi, omertà e pedofilia - L'altro lato della tonaca" *la Repubblica.it* May 26, 2008 http://www.repubblica.it/2008/05/sezioni/spettacoli_e_cultura/libro-chiesa/libro-chiesa/libro-chiesa.html AndCurzio Maltese, "I conti in tasca alla Chiesa" *La Repubblica* May 15, 2008 from an investigation entitled "La questua" andRaphael Zanotti, "8x1000, più soldi al Molise che al Terzo Mondo" *La Stampa* August 4, 2008 http://www.lastampa.it/redazione/cmsSezioni/economia/200808a rticoli/35394girata.asp#

54   Ibid

55   Mario Staderini "Lauto finanziamento. La Chiesa cattolica e le tasse degli italiani" (Auto financing. The Catholic Church and the Italian taxpayer) *www.radioradicale.it* February12, 2008 http://www.radioradicale.it/scheda/247121/lauto-finanziamento-la-chiesa-cattolica-e-le-tasse-degli-italiani

56   Richard Owen, "Vatican faces EU inquisition on tax" *Times Online* August 31, 2007 http://www.timesonline.co.uk/tol/news/world/europe/article2357980.ece

57   Zanotti, supra note 53.

58   Maltese, supra note 53.

59   Richard Owen, "Pope cancels university visit after protests" *Times Online* January 15, 2008 http://www.timesonline.co.uk/tol/comment/faith/article3192376.ece

60   John Hooper, "The long arm of the Vatican?" *The Guardian* January 22, 2008 http://commentisfree.guardian.co.uk/john_hooper/2008/01/the_long_arm_of_the_vatican.html

61   "Galileo protest halts pope's visit" *CNN.com/Europe* January 15, 2008 http://edition.cnn.com/2008/WORLD/europe/01/15/pope.protest/

62   Simon Montlake, "Italian government nears collapse after key Prodi ally defects" *Christian Science Monitor* January 22, 2008 http://www.csmonitor.com/2008/0122/p99s01-duts.html

63   Richard Owen, "Romano Prodi resigns after losing confidence vote" *The Times* January 25, 2008 http://www.timesonline.co.uk/tol/news/world/europe/article3248017.ece

64   "Pope and Italian Premier Discuss Sacredness of Life" *Zenit.org* June 6, 2008 http://www.zenit.org/article-22823?l=english

65   "Berlusconi meets with pope" *ANSA.it* June 6, 2008 http://www.ansa.it/site/notizie/awnplus/english/news/2008-06-06_106219551.html

Chapter 16: Benedict XVI Visits the US

1   Cindy Wooden, "2006 Vatican budget closes with surplus; Peter's Pence up $42 million" *Catholic News Service* July 6, 2007 http://www.catholicnews.com/data/stories/cns/0703867.htm

2   John L. Allen, Jr., "Discovering America," *Boston College Magazine* Winter 2005http://

bcm.bc.edu/issues/winter_2005/ft_vatican.html

3   Cindy Wooden, "Despite papal transition, Vatican shows $12 million surplus for 2005" Catholic News Service July 12, 2006 http://www.catholicnews.com/data/stories/cns/0603949.htm

4   "A Talk with the Vatican's Moneyman" *BusinessWeek Online* April 15, 2002 http://www.businessweek.com/magazine/content/02_15/b3778006.htm

5   Wooden, supra note 1.

6   John Thavis, "2007 promises a world of busyness for Pope Benedict" *Catholic News Service* December 22, 2006 http://www.catholicnews.com/data/stories/cns/0607324.htm

7   *CWNews.com* April 27, 2007 http://www.cwnews.com/news/viewstory.cfm?recnum=50777

8   Michael Paulson, "O'Malley invites pope to Boston next year" *Boston Globe* June 3, 2007 http://www.boston.com/news/local/articles/2007/06/03/omalley_invites_pope_to_boston_next_year/

9   Andrea Kirk Assaf, "Bush and Benedict: First Meeting" *Inside the Vatican* June 10, 2007 http://www.insidethevatican.com/newsflash/2007/newsflash-jun10-07.htm

10   "Pope Benedict's 2008 US visit may include Boston, DC and New York" *Catholic News Agency* September 17, 2007 http://www.catholicnewsagency.com/new.php?n=10398

11   John L. Allen Jr., "USCCB Day One: It's official: Pope to visit United States April 15-20" *National Catholic Reporter* November 12, 2007

12   Richard Owen, "Vatican PR ensures rebranded Pope Benedict XVI will triumph in US" *Times Online* March 22, 2008 http://www.timesonline.co.uk/tol/comment/faith/article3599479.ece

13   Rev. Andrew J. Weaver Ph.D, "Neocon Catholics target mainline Protestants" *Media Transparency* August 11, 2006 http://www.mediatransparency.org/storyprinter-friendly.php?storyID=142

14   John L. Allen Jr. "Interview with Ambassador Glendon" *National Catholic Reporter* May 2, 2008 http://ncronline.org/mainpage/specialdocuments/interview_glendon.pdf

15   Richard Owen, "Pope calls for continuous prayer to rid priesthood of paedophilia" *Times Online* January 7, 2008 http://www.timesonline.co.uk/tol/comment/faith/article3142511.ece

16   Richard Owen, "That Martin Luther? He wasn't so bad, says Pope" *Times Online* March 6, 2008 http://www.timesonline.co.uk/tol/comment/faith/article3492299.ece

17   Ibid

18   Richard Owen, "Pope to pray for redemption of Islamic terrorists during US tour" *Times Online* April 14, 2008 http://www.timesonline.co.uk/tol/comment/faith/article3740311.ece

19   Richard Owen, "Vatican proclaims its 'respect and esteem' for Jews before Pope tours US" *Times Online* April 8, 2008 http://www.timesonline.co.uk/tol/comment/faith/article3683461.ece

20   Chaz Muth, "Costs of papal visit to U.S. hard to pin down but total millions" *Catholic News Service* April 29, 2008 http://www.catholicnews.com/data/stories/cns/0802375.htm

21   Neela Banerjee, "Pope T-Shirt, Anyone? Turning to Big Donors, and Souvenirs, for a Costly Visit" *New York Times* April 15, 2008 http://www.nytimes.com/2008/04/15/us/nationalspecial2/15money.html?_r=1&ref=nationalspecial2&oref=slogin

22   Alessandra Stanley, "Long Looks at the Pope, but a Glimpse of the Man" *New York Times* April 17, 2008 http://www.nytimes.com/2008/04/17/us/nationalspecial2/17popewatch.html?ref=nationalspecial2

23   John Thavis, "Pope brings Vatican with him when he leaves Vatican City for U.S." *Catholic News Service* April 3, 2008 http://www.catholicnews.com/data/stories/cns/0801801.htm

24   Alessandra Stanley, "Long Looks at the Pope, but a Glimpse of the Man" *New York Times* April 17, 2008 http://www.nytimes.com/2008/04/17/us/nationalspecial2/17popewatch.html?ref=nationalspecial2

25   Franco Nuschese, "A Lunch Made With Devotion" *Washington Post* April 23,

2008 http://www.washingtonpost.com/wp-dyn/content/article/2008/04/22/AR2008042202900_pf.html

26   Ralph Z. Hallow, "But where is the pope?" *Washington Times* April 16, 2008 http://video1.washingtontimes.com/fishwrap/2008/04/but_where_is_the_pope.html

27   "5 Supreme Court justices on White House guest list" *Associated Press* April 16, 2008 http://www.breitbart.com/article.php?id=D90321N00&show_article=1

28   Carol Zimmerman, "For pope's birthday, bishops give $870,000 gift to support charitable works" *Catholic News Service* April 17, 2008 http://www.americancatholic.org/News/PopeUS/April20/PapalTrip042008-3.asp

29   Cindy Wooden, "Brooklyn students greet Pope Benedict as he arrives in New York." *Catholic News Service* April 18, 2008 http://www.catholicnews.com/data/stories/cns/0802120.htm

30   John Hooper and Rory Carroll, "Pope faces German revolt as anger grows in Latin America" *The Guardian* May 25, 2007 http://www.guardian.co.uk/pope/story/0,,2087937,00.html

31   Rocco Palmo, "Father-President, UN Edition" *Whispers-in-the-Loggia* June 5, 2008 http://whispersintheloggia.blogspot.com/

32   Paul Vitello, "In Another Historic Act, Pope Benedict Visits a Manhattan Synagogue" *New York Times* April 19, 2008 http://www.nytimes.com/2008/04/19/us/nationalspecial2/19synagogue.html?ref=nationalspecial2

33   Rabbi James Rudin, "Symbolism, Yes. Substance? Not Yet" *New York Times* April 20, 2008 http://thepope.blogs.nytimes.com/2008/04/20/symbolism-yes-substance-still-waiting/index.html?ref=nationalspecial2

34   John L. Allen Jr. "The story behind the pope's meeting with sex abuse victims; Cardinal O'Malley interview" *National Catholic Reporter* April 25, 2008 http://ncrcafe.org/node/1763

35   Daniel Wakin and Julia Preston, "Pope Speaks Up for Immigrants, Touching a Nerve" *New York Times* April 20, 2008 http://www.nytimes.com/2008/04/20/us/20catholics.html?pagewanted=1&ref=nationalspecial2

36   "During U.S. Papal Visit, Media Focused on the Shepherd and His Flock" *The Pew Forum on Religion & Public Life* May 6, 2008 http://pewforum.org/docs/?DocID=302

37   Ibid

38   http://www.kofc.org/un/cmf/resources/Communications/documents/catholics_reflect.pdf

39   Interview with Carrie Gress, "Michael Novak on Pope's US Visit (Part 1)" *Zenit.org* April 22, 2008 http://www.zenit.org/article-22382?l=english

40   Sheryl Henderson Blunt, "Q&A: Richard Mouw " *Christianity Today* June 2008 - posted May 8, 2008 : http://www.christia nitytoday. com/ct/2008/ june/1.17. html

41   Francis X. Rocca, "For Bush and Benedict, a personal and political bond" *Religion News Service* June 5, 2008 http://www.pewforum .org/news/ display.php? NewsID=15766

42   Ray McGovern, "What About the War, Benedict?" *Consortiumnews.com* April 21, 2008 http://www.consortiumnews.com/2008/042108a.html

43   Colman McCarthy, "Pope's visit should have had different focus" *Belleville News-Democrat* April 23, 2008 http://www.bnd.com/285/story/318855.html andJohn Dominic Crossan, "Pope Looked Outward, but Not Inward" *Washington Post* April 27, 2008 http://newsweek. washingtonpost. com/onfaith/ john_dominic_ crossan/2008/ 0 4/is_the_roman_ catholic_ hierarch. html and Editorial Group "Benedict evolves as a pastor but still misses the mark on several fronts" *New Catholic Times*, April 25, 2008 http://www.newcatholictimes.com/index.php?module=articles&func=display&ptid=1&aid=184 and Peter Steinfels, "Pope Benedict and the Lasting Impact of His U.S. Trip" *New York Times* April 26, 2008 http://www.nytimes. com/2008/ 04/26/us/ nationalspecial2 /26beliefs. html?_r=1&ref=us&oref=slogin

44   Angela Bonavoglia, "Benedict in America: The Man Show" *Huffington Post* April 22, 2008http://www.huffingtonpost.com/angela-bonavoglia/benedict-in-america-the-m_b_98002.html

45   John L. Allen Jr., "What abortion is to American Catholics, the death penalty is for Italians" *National Catholic Reporter* April 25, 2008 http://ncronline3.org/

drupal/?q=node/764

46   Interview in *Our Sunday Visitor*, quoted by Rocco Palmo, "The Sense of Liberation" *Whispers in the Loggia* May 28, 2008 http://whispersintheloggia.blogspot.com/2008/05/sense-of-liberation.html

47   Ibid

48   Laurie Goodstein and Sheryl Gay Stolberg, "Pope Praises U.S., but Warns of Secular Challenges" *New York Times* April 17, 2008 http://www.nytimes.com/2008/04/17/us/nationalspecial2/17pope.html?pagewanted=1&ref=nationalspecial2

49   Don Lattin, "Levada Takes Heat over Abuse Inquiry" *San Francisco Chronicle* November 12, 2004 BishopAccountability.org http://www.bishop-accountability.org/news3/2004_11_12_Lattin_LevadaTakes_John_Heaney_ETC_1.htm

50   Leon J. Podles "Pope Rewards Bishop Who Transferred Abuser" *DIALOGUE A Discussion on Faith and Culture* December 29th, 2007

51   David O'Reilly, "Report 'Slanted,' Rigali Says" *Philadelphia Inquirer* September 23, 2005 http://www.philly.com/mld/inquirer/news/front/12717577.htm

52   "Pope praises disgraced Polish archbishop" *The Tablet* July 2, 2009 http://www.thetablet.co.uk/latest-news.php

53   "Bishop Burke moves to Vatican position" *SNAP Press Release* June 29, 2008

54   John L. Allen Jr. "More on Burke's move to Vatican Court" *National Catholic Reporter* July 3, 2008 http://ncrcafe.org/node/1959

Chapter 17: The 2008 Presidential Campaign

1   http://www.antiwar.com/casualties/

2   http://www.iraqbodycount.org/

3   Kim Gamel, "AP IMPACT: Secret tally has 87,215 Iraqis dead" *Associated Press*, April 23, 2009 http://news.yahoo.com/s/ap/20090423/ap_on_re_mi_ea/ml_iraq_death_tol

4   Jim Michaels, "Military retools detainee releases" *USA TODAY*, May 28, 2008 http://www.usatoday.com/news/military/2008-05-19-detainees-military_N.htm and https://no.amnesty.org/web2.nsf/pages/2621FC04BAA58291C125707C003C2613

5   Cenk Uygur, "What if Khalid Sheikh Mohammed Had Died" *Huffington Post* April 23, 2009 http://www.huffingtonpost.com/cenk-uygur/what-if-khalid-sheikh-moh_b_190385.html

6   Dafna Linzer, "Dozens of Prisoners Held by CIA Still Missing, Fates Unknown" *ProPublica* April 22, 2009 http://www.propublica.org/article/dozens-of-prisoners-held-by-cia-still-missing-fates-unknown-422

7   Greg Mitchell, "U.S. Soldier Killed Herself -- After Refusing to Take Part in Torture" *Huffington Post* April 23, 2009 http://www.huffingtonpost.com/greg-mitchell/us-soldier-killed-herself_b_190517.html

8   "Border Crossing Deaths have Doubled Since 1995" http://www.gao.gov/htext/d06770.html

9   Arloc Sherman, "Income Gaps Hit Record Levels In 2006, New Data Show" Center on Budget and Policy Priorities, April 17, 2009 http://www.cbpp.org/cms/index.cfm?fa=view&id=2789

10   Tom Costello, "100 days later, nation waits for FDA overhaul" *NBC News* April 25, 2009 http://www.msnbc.msn.com/id/30388073/

11   http://www.cpb.org

12   http://www.nrlc.org/ABORTION/facts/abortionstats.html

13   http:// www.guttmacher.org/pubs/fb_induced_abortion.html

14   Peter J. Boyer, "Party Faithful" *The New Yorker* September 8, 2008 http://www.newyorker.com/reporting/2008/09/08/080908fa_fact_boyer?currentPage=all

15   Kyle "'Pompous, Self-Serving Son of a Bitch'" Endorses McCain" *Right Wing Watch* September 16, 2008 http://www.rightwingwatch.org/content/%E2%80%9Cpompous-self-serving-son-bitch%E2%80%9D-endorses-mccain

16   Mike Allen, "Counsel to GOP Senator Wrote Memo On Schiavo - Martinez Aide Who Cited Upside For Party Resigns" *Washington Post* April 7, 2005 http://www.washingtonpost.com/wp-dyn/articles/A32554-2005Apr6.html

17   http://www.johnmccain.com/informing/news/PressReleases/4e3a4cc1-466c-4d4b-

b0b3-ea54d673228a.htm

18   Sam Stein, "McCain's Catholic Committee Full of Controversial Figures" *The Huffington Post* May 5, 2008 http://www.huffingtonpost.com/2008/05/05/mccains-catholic-committe_n_100277.html

19   Michelle Boorstein, "Catholic Activists Ask McCain to Boot Faith Adviser" *Washington Post Blog* July 16, 2008 http://blog.washingtonpost.com/the-trail/2008/07/16/catholic_activists_ask_mccain.html

20   Bill Berkowitz, "Neocon Catholic leaders nurtured by GOP and Conservative Philanthropy on their heels" *Media Transparency* September 23, 2007 http://www.mediatransparency.org/story.php?storyID=212

21   Bill Moyers Journal, "Christians United for Israel (CUFI)" *PBS* March 7, 2008 http://www.pbs.org/moyers/journal/03072008/profile.html

22   Boyer, supra note 14.

23   Boyer, supra note 14.

24   Boyer, supra note 14.

25   Elizabeth Holmes, "McCain Backer John Hagee Apologizes to Catholics" *Wall Street Journal Blog* May 13, 2008 http://blogs.wsj.com/washwire/2008/05/13/mccain-backer-john-hagee-apologizes-to-catholics/?mod=WSJBlog

26   Boyer, supra note 14.

27   Chris Korzen, "Catholics United Questions Partisanship of National Catholic Prayer Breakfast" *Catholics United for the Common Good* http://www.catholic s-united.org/?q=node/ 84

28   Francis X. Rocca, "President to meet with Pope Benedict during European trip in June" *Religion News Service* http://www.pewforum .org/news/ display.php? NewsID=15766

29   Philip Pullella and Jeremy Pelofsky, "Bush, pope take break in calm of Vatican Gardens" *Reuters* June 13, 2008 http://news.yahoo.com/s/nm/20080613/ts_nm/bush_europe_dc

30   "Demonstrators greet Bush in Rome" June 11, 2008 http://www.radionet herlands.nl/news/internat ional/5826892/ Demonstrators- greet-Bush- in-Rome

31   Malcome Moore, "George W Bush meets Pope amid claims he might convert to Catholicism" *The Telegraph* June 13. 2008 http://www.telegrap h.co.uk/news/worldnews/ northamerica/ usa/2122733/ George-W- Bush-meets- Pope-amid-claims-he- might-convert- to-Catholicism. html

32   Boyer, supra note 14.

33   Ray McGovern, "What About the War, Benedict?" *The Consortium News* April 21, 2008 http://www.consortiumnews.com/2008/042108a.html

34   Rev. Andrew J. Weaver, Ph.D., "Neocon Catholics target mainline Protestants" *Media Transparency* August 11, 2006 http://www.mediatransparency.org/storyprinterfriendly.php?storyID=142

35   Ibid

36   Michael Humphrey, "'Faithful Citizenship' in an election year" *National Catholic Reporter* June 27, 2008 http://ncronline3.org/drupal/?q=node/1269

37   Rocco Palmo, "Naumann to Obama: Scrap Sebelius" *Whispers in the Loggia* August 15, 2008http://whispersintheloggia.blogspot.com/

38   Mike Hendricks "Hendricks: Kansas bishops say a vote for pro-choice Dems is a vote for 'evil'" *KansasCity.com* August 11, 2008 http://primebuzz.kcstar.com/?q=node/13672

39   "Catholics who support abortion should not receive Communion, says Archbishop Burke" *Catholic News Agency* August 20, 2008 http://www.catholicnewsagency.com/new.php?n=13562

40   Cindy Wooten, "U.S. archbishop at Vatican says Democrats becoming 'party of death'" *Catholic News Service* September 29, 2008 http://www.catholicnews.com/data/stories/cns/0804933.htm

41   "Denver Prelate Addresses Obama's Catholic Fans, Says Voters Need to Be Ready to Meet Abortion Victims in Next Life" May 20, 2008 *Zenit.org* http://www.zenit.org/article-22637?l=english

42   Margaret O'Brien Steinfels, "Sebelius and Kmiec" *Commonweal Magazine Blog* May 16, 2008 http://www.commonwe almagazine. org/blog/ ?p=2000

43 *Reuters* May 7, 2008 http://www.msnbc.msn.com/id/24506486

44 Anthony M. Stevens-Arroyo, "Catholics Have New Reasons to Rethink Abortion Politics" *On Faith* August 26, 2008 http://newsweek.washingtonpost.com/onfaith/catholicamerica/2008/08/the_end_of_the_abortion_issue.html

45 Peter Steinfels, "For Ex-G.O.P. Official, Obama Is Candidate of Catholic Values" *New York Times* August 29, 2008 http://www.nytimes.com/2008/08/30/us/30beliefs.html?_r=1&em&oref=slogin

46 Ibid

47 Eric Gorski, "Biden's Catholic faith offers risks, rewards" *Associated Press* August 24, 2008 http://news.yahoo.com/s/ap/20080824/ap_on_el_pr/cnv_biden_catholic

48 "Biden Pick Assailed On Abortion Grounds" *On the Hill* August 23, 2008http://onthehillblog.blogspot.com/2008/08/biden-pick-assailed-on-abortion-grounds.html

49 John-Henry Westen, "Biden's Bishop Will not Permit Him, Even if Elected VP, to Speak at Catholic Schools" *LifeSiteNews.com* August 26, 2008 http://www.lifesite-news.com/ldn/2008/aug/08082606.html

50 Gorski, supra note 47.

51 Rocco Palmo, "Prelates v. Pelosi: As DNC Opens, Speaker Taken to Task" *Whispers in the Loggia* August 25, 2008 http://whispersintheloggia.blogspot.com/ and "Bishops say Pelosi misrepresented abortion teaching in TV interview" *Catholic News Service* August 26, 2008 http://www.catholicnews.com/data/stories/cns/0804350.htm and "Bishop: Pelosi "Created Confusion" on Abortion - Says Church's Stance Remains Unchanged" *Zenit.org* August 28, 2008 http://www.zenit.org/article-23489?l=english and Rachel Zoll, "Pelosi gets unwanted lesson in Catholic theology" *Associated Press* August 28, 2008 http://ap.google.com/article/ALeqM5gAMUhth44LfK24KzhSn8tB-bGYhaAD92R51LG0

52 Rocco Palmo, "Pelosi on... Pelosi: The Speaker Responds " *Whispers in the Loggia* August 26, 2008 http://whispersintheloggia.blogspot.com/

53 http://av.madisondi ocese.org/ madisonspp/ audio/?f= BishopMorlino/ Homily,%20 09- 07-2008,% 20Bishop% 20Robert% 20Morlino. mp3

54 "Denver Bishops Say Biden Is Wrong, Too" *Zenit.org* September 8, 2008 : http://www.zenit.org/article-23574?l=english

55 Amy Sullivan, "Does Biden Have a Catholic Problem?" *TIME* September 13, 2008. http://www.time.com/time/politics/article/0,8599,1840965,00.html

56 Rocco Palmo, "On the Agenda" *Whispers in the Loggia* September 10, 2008 http://whispersintheloggia.blogspot.com/

57 Rocco Palmo "Bishops on Biden" *Whispers in the Loggia* September 9, 2008 http://whispersintheloggia.blogspot.com/

58 Rocco Palmo, "Munus Docendi, Election Desk" *Whispers in the Loggia* September 12, 2008 http://whispersintheloggia.blogspot.com/

59 Thomas C. Fox, "Catholic Democrat group hits K of C attack on Biden" *National Catholic Reporter* September 25, 2008 http://ncronline3.org/drupal/?q=node/1963

60 Carol Marin, "Cardinal all but endorses McCain and Palin" *Chicago Sun-Times* September 10, 2008 http://www.suntimes.com/news/marin/1154298,CST-EDT-carol10.article

61 Robert Moore, "Archbishop: Clergy should not endorse, contribute in partisan races" *Coloradoan* June 30, 2008 http://www.colorado an.com/apps/ pbcs.dll/ article?AID= 2008806290346

62 Jim Galloway, "Biden and the abortion issue comes to Georgia Catholics" *The Atlanta Journal-Constitution* September 18, 2008 http://www.ajc.com/metro/content/shared-blogs/ajc/politicalinsider/entries/2008/09/18/biden_and_the_abortion_issue_c.html

63 Valerie Richardson, "Archbishop grabs spotlight from Dems" *Washington Times* August 28, 2008 http://washingtontimes.com/news/2008/aug/28/archbishop-grabs-spotlight-from-democrats/

64 "Democratic Party courts Catholics, other faith-based voters" *Catholic News Service* August 29, 2008 http://www.catholicnews.com/data/briefs/cns/20080829.htm#head1

65 NCR Staff (Tom Roberts, John L. Allen Jr. and Mary Barron contributed), "Catholics boost values talk at convention" *National Catholic Reporter* September 5, 2008 http://ncronline3.org/drupal/?q=node/1711

66   David Finnigan, "McCain to make full-throttle push for Catholic vote" *Religion News Service* September 3, 2008 http://ncronline3.org/drupal/?q=node/1754 and Michael Humphrey, "At GOP Convention, two Catholics, two causes, two paths" *National Catholic Reporter* September 2, 2008 http://ncronline3.org/drupal/?q=node/1748

67   Peter Mucha, "McCain's in town, mum on schedule" *Philadelphia Inquirer* September 2, 2008 http://www.philly.com/philly/hp/news_update/20080902_McCains_in_town__mum_on_schedule.html

68   David D. Kirkpatrick, "Abortion Issue Again Dividing Catholic Votes" *New York Times* September 16, 2008 http://www.nytimes.com/2008/09/17/us/politics/17catholics.html?th=&adxnnl=1&emc=th&adxnnlx=1221649822-jZs/4f21hcXIabEFNdOF+A

69   Rocco Palmo, "At the Crossroads" *Whispers in the Loggia* September 1, 2008 http://whispersintheloggia.blogspot.com/

70   Rocco Palmo, "From Scranton, 'Moral Force'" *Whispers in the Loggia* September 26, 2008 http://whispersintheloggia.blogspot.com/

71   Laura Legere, "Groups criticize bishop's letter on abortion issue" *standardspeaker.com* October 2, 2008 http://www.standardspeaker.com/articles/2008/10/02/news/hz_standspeak.20081002.a.pg1.hz02_ttcatholic_s1.1986172_top4.txt

72   "Republicans rally fellow Catholics to support McCain-Palin" *Catholic News Service* September 5, 2008 tickethttp://www.catholicnews.com/data/briefs/cns/20080905.htm#head5

73   Palmo, supra 58.

74   David D. Kirkpatrick, "A Fight Among Catholics Over Which Party Best Reflects Church Teachings" *New York Times* October 4, 2008 http://www.nytimes.com/2008/10/05/us/politics/05catholic.html?_r=1&oref=slogin

75   "GOP platform decries abortion, calls for human life amendment" *Catholic News Service* September 4, 2008 http://www.catholicnews.com/data/briefs/cns/20080904.htm

76   "Alaskans to receive state payouts topping $3,200" *Associated Press* September 5, 2008 http://www.bostonherald.com/news/national/west/view.bg?articleid=1117272

77   David Talbot, "Mean girl" *Salon.com* September 23, 2008http://www.salon.com/news/feature/2008/09/23/palin/html

78   Daniel Kurtzman, "Sarah Palin, by the Numbers" *The Huffington Post* September 18, 2008 http://www.huffingtonpost.com/daniel-kurtzman/sarah-palin-by-the-number_b_127355.html

79   Steve Waldman, "Palin's Religion: What's Scary, What's Not?" *Beliefnet.com* September 7, 2008posted by Steve Waldman @ http://blog.beliefnet.com/stevenwaldman/2008/09/palins-religion-whats-scary-wh.html

80   David Talbot, "The pastor who clashed with Palin" *Salon.com* September 15, 2008 http://www.salon.com/news/feature/2008/09/15/bess/index.html

81   Ruth, "The 'Lions In the Pews'" *Talk2Action.org* September 24, 2008 http://www.talk2action.org/story/2008/9/24/82239/9750

82   Julia Palermo, "Sarah Palin and the Deborah Anointing by J. Lee Grady" September 12, 2008 http://juliapalermo.wordpress.com/2008/09/12/sarah-palin-and-the-deborah-anointing-by-j-lee-grady/

83   Esther Kaplan, "A Palin Pastor Primer" *Talk2action.com* September 9, 2008 http://www.talk2action.org/story/2008/9/9/103326/3656/Front_Page/A_Palin_Pastor_Primer and Randi Kaye, "Pastor: GOP may be downplaying Palin's religious beliefs" September 8, 2008 http://www.cnn.com/2008/POLITICS/09/08/palin.pastor/index.html and Steve Weissman, "Sarah Palin: A Gidget for God's Truth" *t r u t h o u t* September 9, 2008 http://www.truthout.org/article/sarah-palin-a-gidget-gods-truth

84   Bruce Wilson, "Sarah Palin's Demon Haunted Churches - The Complete Edition" *talk2action.org* September 8, 2008 http://www.talk2action.org/story/2008/9/8/114332/7479/Front_Page/Sarah_Palin_s_Demon_Haunted_Churches_The_Complete_Edition

85   Mar Celo, "Palin Per Diem: Sarah Palin Billed State Nights Spent At Home" *News.Spreadit.org* September 9, 2008 http://news.spreadit.org/palin-per-diemsarah-palin-billed-state-nights-spent-at-home/

86   Wilson, supra 84.

87   Wilson, supra 84.

88   Wilson, supra 84.

89   Sarah Posner, "Sarah Palin, faith-based mayor" *Salon.com* September 18, 2008http://www.salon.com/news/feature/2008/09/18/palin_iacc/

90   Sam Stein, "Rick Davis's Hugh Hewitt Fantasy World: McCain Is The Victim" *Huffington Post* September 11, 2008 http://www.huffingtonpost.com/2008/09/11/rick-davis-fantasy-world_n_125747.html

91   John Dickerson, "Palin's Campaign vs. McCain's" *Slate* October 20, 2008 http://www.slate.com/id/2202658/?GT1=38001

92   "Catholics unite for California marriage vote; Knights give $1 million" *Catholic News Service* August 25, 2008 http://www.catholicnews.com/data/briefs/cns/20080825.htm#head2

93   Howard Fischer, "2 bishops urge OK of ballot ban on gay marriages" *Capitol Media Services* September 5, 2008 http://www.azstarnet.com/sn/metro/256161.php

94   "Florida Supreme Court strikes down vote on faith-based programs" *Catholic News Service* September 5, 2008 http://www.catholicnews.com/data/briefs/cns/20080905.htm#head5

95   "New book, report assess status of abortion at state level" *Catholic News Service* October 1, 2008 http://www.catholicnews.com/data/briefs/cns/20081001.htm#head13

96   Seth Colter Wallis, "Obama: Anti-Abortion Activists Lying About Me" *The Huffington Post* August 17, 2008 http://www.huffingtonpost.com/2008/08/17/obama-anti-abortion-activ_n_119410.html and Seth Colter Wallis, "Obama 'Infanticide' Smear Gains Traction: Campaign Force to Rebut" *The Huffington Post* August 20, 2008 http://www.huffingtonpost.com/2008/08/20/obama-infanticide-smear-g_n_120138.html

97   Bill Berkowitz, "Right-Wing Magnate Takes Up Anti-Abortion Banner" *Inter Press Service* October 8, 2008 http://www.truthout.org/100908WA

98   Gerald Warner, "Joe Biden loses Barack Obama the Catholic vote" *Telegraph Blogs* September 19, 2008 http://blogs.telegraph.co.uk/gerald_warner/blog/2008/09/19/joe_biden_loses_barack_obama_the_catholic_vote

99   Nicholas P. Cafardi, "I'm Catholic, staunchly anti-abortion, and support Obama" *Religion News Service* September 30, 2008 http://ncronline3.org/drupal/?q=node/2058

100   Chaz Muth, "Cafardi resigns as Franciscan University trustee" *Catholic News Service* October 8, 2008 http://ncronline3.org/drupal/?q=node/2105

101   http://www.rightwingwatch.org/content/alliance-defense-fund

102   Peter Slevin, "Ban on Political Endorsements by Pastors Targeted" *Washington Post* September 8, 2008 http://www.washingtonpost.com/wp-dyn/content/article/2008/09/07/AR2008090702460.html

103   Ibid

104   Rocco Palmo, "Faithful Citizenship, K-Far Edition" *Whispers in the Loggia* October 10, 2008http://whispersintheloggia.blogspot.com/ and John Allen Jr., "Wuerl: 'Conceptually possible' not to support Roe v Wade ban" *National Catholic Reporter,* October 11, 2008 http://ncronline3.org/drupal?g=node2120

105   IRS Should Investigate N.J. Catholic Diocese For Campaign Intervention, Says Americans United" October 22, 2008 http://www.au.org/site/News2?JServSessionldr001=qlzmzmnth2.app5b&abbr=pr&page=NewsArticle&id=10100&security=1002&news_iv_ctrl=1241

106   Randall A. Terry, "Bishop Gracida Releases Ad, Catholic Protests Planned" *Catholic Online* October 24, 2008 http://www.catholic.org/politics/story.php?id=30221

107   "Religious Right Leader Randall Terry Censured By New York Church" *Americans United* April 2000 http://www.au.org/media/church-and-state/archives/2000/04/pampe.html

108   http://en.wikipedia.org/wiki/Randall_Terry

109   Ibid

110   "Terry gets 'Clinton' to endorse opponent" *WorldNetDaily.com* August 12, 2006http://worldnetdaily.com/news/article.asp?ARTICLE_ID=51499

111   Randy Sly, "Pro-Life Workers Arrested at St. Petersburg, FL Cathedral" *Catholic Online* January 26, 2008 http://www.catholic.org/national/national_story.php?id=26597

112   Randall Terry, "Breaking News: Catholic Bishop Rene Henry Gracida confirms that a Catholic cannot vote for pro-abortion politicians 'in good conscience'" *Catholic-Citizens.org* October 17, 2008 http://www.catholiccitizens.org/news/contentview.asp?c=48385

113   Michael Sean Winters, "Why they didn't listen" *The Tablet* November 15, 2008 http://www.thetable t.co.uk/article/ 12271

114   E. J Dionne, Jr. "A Catholic shift to Obama?" October 21, 2008 http://www.paxchristiusa.org/news_Events_more.asp?id=1483 and Thomas C. Fox, "Memphis Bishop calls upon Catholics to avoid 'one issue' votes" *National Catholic Reporter* October 21, 2008 http://www.paxchristiusa.org/news_Events_more.asp?id=1484

115   Steven Waldman, "How Obama Lured Millions of Religious Voters" *The Wall Street Journal* November 5, 2008 http://pewforum.org/news/display.php?NewsID=16835

116   Ibid

117   Jane Lampman, "New Christian group airs ads – for Obama" *The Christian Science Monitor* August 21, 2008 http://features.csmonitor.com/politics/2008/08/21/new-christian-group-airs-ads-%E2%80%93-for-obama/

118   *Reuters* May 7, 2008 http://www.msnbc.msn.com/id/24506486

119   Bill Berkowitz, "Neocon Catholic leaders nurtured by GOP and Conservative Philanthropy on their heels" *Media Transparency* September 23, 2007 http://www.mediatransparency.org/story.php?storyID=212

120   http://pewforum.org/docs/?DocID=334

121   Jeff Diamant, "Catholic shift gives Democrats big boost" *Star-Ledger* November 9, 2006 http://www.nj.com/printer/printer.ssf?/base/news-9/116305437017070.xml&coll=1

122   David D. Kirkpatrick, "Abortion Issue Again Dividing Catholic Votes" *New York Times* September 16, 2008 http://www.nytimes.com/2008/09/17/us/politics/17catholics.html?th=&adxnnl=1&emc=th&adxnnlx=1221649822-jZs/4f21hcXIabEFNdOF+A

123   Scott Swenson, "Pro-Choice Catholic Biden Fits with New Poll of Catholic Voters" *The Huffington Post* August 23, 2008   http://www.huffingtonpost.com/scott-swenson/pro-choice-catholic-biden_b_120811.html

124   "Presidential Race Draws Even" *The Pew Research Center for the People & the Press* August 13, 2008 http://people-press.org/report/443/presidential-race-draws-even

125   Eric Gorski, "The Conservatives Grow Wary of Mixing Church, Politics" *Associated Press* August 21, 2008 http://www.washingtonpost.com/wp-dyn/content/article/2008/08/21/AR2008082102845.html?hpid=sec-religion

126   Steven Waldman, "The Crucial Catholic Vote: Does It Exist?" *Wall Street Journal Blog*, August 25, 2008 http://blogs.wsj.com/politicalperceptions/2008/08/25/the-crucial-catholic-vote-does-it-exist/?mod=googlenews_wsj

127   http://religions.pewforum.org/portraits

Chapter 18: Epilogue

1   Paul Krugman, "Yes, we can" *New York Times* July 2, 2009 http://krugman.blogs.nytimes.com/2009/07/02/yes-we-can/

2   Jesse Drucker, "Americans See Their Income Share Grow" *The Wall Street Journal* July 23, 2008

3   David Schweickart quoted by http://www.lcurve.org/

4   Gardiner Harris, "Infant Deaths Drop in U.S., but Rate Is Still High" *New York Times* October 15, 2008   http://www.nytimes.com/2008/10/16/health/16infant.html?th&emc=thandStephen Ohlemache, "US Slipping in Life Expectancy Rankings" *Associated Press* August 12, 2007 http://www.washingtonpost.com/wp-dyn/content/article/2007/08/12/AR2007081200113.html

5   Al Traugott, "The Beast Awakens" *Michigan Today - Spring 1998 " Letters"* http://www.umich.edu/~newsinfo/MT/98/Spr98/mtltrs98.html

6   Robert Parry "Reverand Moon's Anti-Obama Agit-Prop" *Consortium News* January 23, 2008 http://www.truthout.org/docs_2006/012307F.shtml

7   Ibid

8   "First Obama attack book in the works" *Politico* June 23, 2008 http://news.yahoo.com/s/politico/20080623/pl_politico/11263

9   Eric Kleefeld, "Whoops! Top Republican Admits That GOP Is Running 'Ministry Of Truth' Against Obama" *TPM Election Central* August 26, 2008 http://tpmelectioncentral.talkingpointsmemo.com/2008/08/whoops_top_republican_admits_t.php

10   http://www.usccb.org/comm/archives/2009/09-058.shtml

11   Cathleen Kaveny, "The Right to Refuse" *Commonweal* May 8, 2009 / Volume CXXXVI, Number 9 http://www.commonwe almagazine. org/article. php3?id_article=2532

12   http://www.usccb.org/comm/archives/2009/09-100.shtml

13   "List of Bishops Opposing the Notre Dame Invitation and Award to President Obama" *LifeSiteNews* May 6, 2009 http://www.lifesitenews.com/ldn/2009/may/09050607.html

14   http://www.archden.org/index.cfm/ID/2081

15   "Kansas City Bishop to pro-lifers: 'We are at war!'" *National Catholic Reporter* April 28, 2009 http://ncronline.org/news/faith-parish/kansas-city-bishop-pro-lifers-we-are-war.

16   Melinda Henneberger, "Wuerl: Why I Won't Deny Pelosi Communion" *Politics Daily* May 6, 2009 http://www.politicsdaily.com/2009/05/06/archbishop-wuerl-why-i-won-t-deny-pelosi-communion/

17   John L. Allen Jr., "Former papal theologian praises Obama's 'realism,' even on abortion" *National Catholic Reporter* July 03, 2009 http://ncronline.org/blogs/ncr-today/former-papal-theologian-praises-obamas-realism-even-abortion

18   Cindy Wooden, "Vatican reports deficit for 2007, partly due to poor stock market" *Catholic News Service* July 10, 2008 http://www.catholicnews.com/data/stories/cns/0803583.htm

19   "More Americans Question Religion's Role in Politics" August 21, 2008 http://pewforum.org/docs/?DocID=334

20   Southern Baptist membership, baptisms decline" *Associated Press* April 24, 2008 http://www.ajc.com/wireless/content/news/stories/2008/04/24/southernbaptists_0424.html

21   Eric Gorski, "Younger evangelicals split over Palin choice as VP" *Associated Press* September 14, 2008 http://news.yahoo.com/s/ap/20080914/ap_on_el_pr/rel_palin_young_evangelicals

22   "New poll finds growing 'religion gap' between old, young Americans" *Catholic News Service* July 1, 2009 http://www.catholicnews.com/data/briefs/cns/20090701.htm#head2

23   http://cara.georgetown.edu/bulletin/index.htm

24   Andrew Nelson, "Catholics Embrace Jesus' Message, Not Practices" *Georgia Bulletin* February 21, 2008 http://www.georgiabulletin.org/local/2008/02/21/young/.

25   Ibid

26   John Schneider, "Lansing Catholic Diocese to unveil reorganization Monday" *LSJ.com* September 12, 2008 http://www.lansingstatejournal.com/apps/pbcs.dll/article?AID=/20080912/NEWS01/809120384

27   Andrew M. Greeley, "Signs of Life: A Sociologist Looks Ahead" *Commonweal* August 15, 2008 / Volume CXXXV, Number 14 http://www.commonwe almagazine. org/article. php?id_article= 2287

28   Thomas Merton, *The Hidden Ground of Love* (New York: Farrar Straus Giroux) 1985 230

29   "Young Catholics not turning to sanctity of life and marriage as voting issues, poll finds" *Catholic News Agency* October 8, 2008 http://www.catholicnewsagency.com/new.php?n=14008

30   Janet Maslin, "Thanks to Today's Global Youth, a Rosy Tomorrow?" *The New York Times* August 10, 2008 http://www.nytimes.com/2008/08/11/books/11masl.html?_r=1&oref=slogin

31   Robert P. Jones and Daniel Cox, "Dispatches from the Beltway: God-Gap Flip-Flop" *Religion Dispatches* October 15, 2008 http://www.religion dispatches. org/archive/dispatchesfrom/ 604/dispatches_ from_the_ beltway%3A_ god-gap_flip- flop

32   John Allen, Jr. "Coverage of World Youth Day: Picking up where John Paul II left off" *National Catholic Reporter* August 18, 2005 http://www.nationalcatholicreporter. org/word/wyd081805.htm

33   Justin Philpot, "The Kids are Religious Right: Punk Rock and the New Pro-Life Youth" *Religion Dispatches* October 15, 2008 http://www.religion dispatches. org/archive/ election08/ 517/the_kids_ are_religious_ right%3A_ punk_rock_ and_the_new_ pro-life_ youth/?page= entire

34   Sean Salai, SJ, "Busted Review: Quitting Church—Why the Faithful are Fleeing and What to Do about It. by Julia Duin" *Busted Halo* October 28th, 2008 http:// www.bustedhalo.com/features/busted-review-quitting-church-why-the-faithful-are- fleeing-and-what-to-do-about-it-by-julia-duin/

INDEX